STEPS TO WRITING WELL

JEAN WYRICK

Colorado State University

STEPS TO WRITING WELL

A Concise Guide to Composition

Fifth Edition

HARCOURT BRACE JOVANOVICH COLLEGE PUBLISHERS

Fort Worth New York Philadelphia Orlando Austin San Antonio
Montreal Toronto London Sydney Tokyo

This book is dedicated to DAVID
and to SARAH, KATE, and AUSTIN

Publisher	Ted Buchholz
Acquisitions Editor	Michael Rosenberg
Developmental Editor	Camille Adkins
Project Editor	Katherine Vardy Lincoln
Production Manager	Debra A. Jenkin
Art and Design Supervisor	Garry Harman
Photo/Permissions Editor	Van Strength
Compositor	Publications Development Company of Texas

Library of Congress Cataloging-in-Publication Number: 92–073421

ISBN: 0-03-076694-X

Literary Credits are listed in the back of the book.

Copyright © 1993, 1990, 1987, 1984, 1979 by Holt, Rinehart and Winston, Inc.

Address for Editorial Correspondence: Harcourt Brace Jovanovich, College Publishers, 301 Commerce Street, Suite 3700, Fort Worth, Texas 76102

Address for Orders:
Harcourt Brace Jovanovich, Publishers, 6277 Sea Harbor Drive, Orlando, FL 32887 / Tel: 1-800-782-4479, or 1-800-443-0001 (in Florida)

Printed in the United States of America

2 3 4 5 6 7 8 9 0 1   039   9 8 7 6 5 4 3 2 1

TO THE TEACHER ···········

The fifth edition of *Steps to Writing Well* has been written and revised for teachers of composition who have had trouble finding a textbook that is accessible to their students. Too many books on today's market, these teachers rightfully complain, are still unnecessarily complex, dry, or massive for the majority of students. Written simply in an informal, straightforward style and addressed to the student, this textbook offers a clear step-by-step guide to writing a variety of 500-to-800-word essays. The combination of concise, practical advice, a number of student and professional samples, and a brief handbook should provide more than enough helpful information for students enrolled in a one-semester or one-quarter course without intimidating them with more material than they can possibly master.

Although many parts of the book have been revised or expanded for this edition, its organization remains essentially the same. Part One offers advice on "The Basics of the Short Essay"; Part Two discusses "Modes and Strategies"; and Part Three presents "A Concise Handbook." This textbook still begins with the essay "To the Student," which not only argues that students can learn to write better with practice and dedication but also gives them a number of practical reasons why they *should* learn to write better.

Part One, containing seven chapters, moves students through the process of writing the short essay. Chapter 1, on prewriting, stresses finding the proper attitude ("the desire to communicate") and presents helpful suggestions for selecting a subject. Two new prewriting techniques have been added to this chapter, which now offers students ten methods for finding a significant purpose and focus for their essays. In addition, a section on using the journal explains more than a dozen ways that students may improve their skills by writing a variety of nonthreatening—and even enjoyable—assignments. The section on audience should also help student writers identify their particular readers and communicate more effectively with them. After finding a topic and identifying their audience, students are then ready for Chapter 2, devoted almost entirely to a discussion of the thesis statement. This chapter first explains the role of the "working thesis" in early drafts and then clearly outlines what a good thesis is and isn't by presenting a host of examples to illustrate the advice. Also included in this chapter is an explanation of the "essay map," an organizational tool that can help students outline their essays and plan their body paragraphs.

Chapter 3 discusses in detail the requirements of good body paragraphs: topic sentences, unity, order and coherence, adequate development, use of specific detail, and logical sequence. Over forty paragraphs illustrate both strengths and weaknesses of student writing. These paragraphs are not complex literary or professional excerpts but rather well-designed, precise examples of the principles under examination, written on subjects students can understand and appreciate. This chapter twice provides the opportunity for students to see how a topic may progress from a working thesis statement to an informal essay outline, which in turn helps produce well-developed paragraphs in the body of an essay. To complete the overview of the short essay, Chapter 4 explains, through a number of samples, how to write good introductions, conclusions, and titles.

Chapter 5, "Drafting and Revising: Creative Thinking, Critical Thinking," has been thoroughly revised for this edition. Because too many students still think of revision as merely proofreading their essays rather than as an essential, recursive activity, this chapter is devoted to explaining the revision process and to emphasizing the need for revision in all good writing. These pages offer a system for revising drafts in stages, while cautioning novice writers against trying to revise too many parts of their essays at once. An important new section on critical thinking is designed to help students analyze and evaluate their ideas and those of others. This section stresses the role of critical thinking skills in the selection of evidence for all writing assignments. Chapter 5 contains a new section that offers advice for participants in "peer workshops" (instructors may also find useful advice on organizing effective peer workshops in the revised Instructor's Manual for this edition). Also included in this chapter is a student essay, annotated to show how a writer (or a workshop partner) might use the questions suggested in the discussion of the revision process. This chapter ends with a list of suggestions for beating writer's block.

Chapter 6, on effective sentences, emphasizes the importance of clarity, conciseness, and vividness, with nearly one hundred and fifty sample sentences illustrating the chapter's advice. Chapter 7, on word choice presents practical suggestions for selecting accurate, appropriate words that are specific, memorable, and persuasive. This chapter also contains sections on avoiding sexist language and "bureaucratese."

Each chapter in Part One contains new samples and exercises. As in previous editions, the "Practicing What You've Learned" exercises follow each major section in each chapter so that both teacher and students may quickly discover if particular material needs additional attention. Moreover, by conquering small steps in the writing process, one at a time, students should feel more confident and should learn more rapidly. Assignments, which also follow each major section in these chapters, suggest class activities and frequently emphasize "peer teaching," a useful method that asks students to prepare appropriate exercises for classmates and then to evaluate the results. Such assignments, operating under the premise that "you don't truly learn a subject until you teach it," provide engaging classroom activity for all the students and also remove from the teacher some of the burden of creating exercises.

Throughout the chapters in Part One, activities called "Applying What You've Learned to *Your* Writing" follow the exercises and assignments. Each of these activities encourages students to "follow through" by incorporating into a current draft the skill they have just read about and practiced. By following a three-step procedure—reading the advice in the text, practicing the advice through the exercises, and then applying the advice directly to their own prose—students should improve their writing processes. In addition, each of the chapters in Part One concludes with a summary, designed to help students review the important points in the material under study.

Part Two concentrates on the four rhetorical modes: exposition, argumentation, description, and narration. Chapter 8 on exposition is divided into separate discussions of the expository strategies: example, process, comparison/contrast, definition, division and classification, and causal analysis. Each discussion in Chapter 8 and each of the chapters on argument, description, and narration follow a similar format by offering the students (a) a clear definition of the mode (or strategy), explained with familiar examples; (b) practical advice on developing each essay; (c) warnings against common problems; (d) suggested essay topics on subjects that appeal to students' interests and capabilities; (e) a topic proposal sheet; (f) a sample student essay with marginal notes; (g) a professional essay followed by questions on content, structure, and style, and a vocabulary list; (h) a revision worksheet to guide student writers through their rough drafts; and (i) a progress report. The advice on developing the essay and the section on common problems are both explained in easy-to-understand language accompanied by numerous examples. The ten student essays should encourage student writers by showing them that others in their situation can indeed compose organized, thoughtful essays. The student essays that appear here are not perfect, however; consequently, teachers may use them in class to generate suggestions for still more revision. The ten professional essays were also selected to spur class discussion and to illustrate the rhetorical principles presented in this text. The five professional essays most popular with users of the fourth edition were retained in this edition; five new essays replace previous readings.

Two important additions to this part of the text bear noting. Because the selection of subject matter can be critical to an essay's success, a Topic Proposal form has been added to each of the nine discussions of essays in Part Two. The form is designed to encourage students to think through their choice of topic, rather than wait until the last minute to select a subject that neither appeals to them nor is appropriate for the particular assignment. (Instructors may find it helpful to collect these forms, or to discuss them in class, to ensure that students have understood the nature of an assignment.) Another important addition to Part Two is a series of questions called "Reviewing Your Progress," which also follows each essay discussion. These questions ask students to evaluate their progress as writers by analyzing the strengths and problems in the essay they have just completed. By becoming aware of their own effective writing skills, students should gain the confidence to tackle the challenges of new writing tasks.

Chapter 12, "Writing a Paper Using Research," includes a discussion of both the MLA and APA styles of documentation and samples of the most frequently used entries. As before, this chapter shows students how to use the library, take notes, and incorporate source material into their essays. Examples are provided to help students understand the difference between summary and paraphrase and between plagiarism in its various forms and proper documentation. A "problem-solving" student essay that uses research material to support its points concludes the chapter.

Part Three contains a concise handbook with nontechnical explanations and easy-to-understand examples showing how to correct the most common errors in grammar, punctuation, and mechanics. This edition also includes nine sets of exercises covering the grammar and punctuation rules. Instead of following each and every rule with five or ten simplistic sentences containing the error in question, this test offers a series of exercises systematically placed so that the students may practice applying several rules at one sitting, just as they must do when they write their own prose. A brief section on spelling hints may offer some limited relief to students who suffer from the malady of being poor spellers.

Once again, readers of this edition may note an occasional attempt at humor. The lighthearted tone of some samples and exercises is the result of the author's firm belief that while learning to write is serious business, solemn composition classrooms are not always the most beneficial environments for anxious beginning writers. The author takes full responsibility (and all of the blame) for the bad jokes and even worse puns.

Finally, an updated Instructor's Manual, with suggestions for teaching and answers to exercises and essay questions, is available from Harcourt, Brace, Jovanovich Publishers; 7555 Caldwell Avenue; Chicago, IL 60648.

Although a fifth edition of this textbook has allowed its author to make a number of changes and additions, the book's purpose remains as stated in the original preface: "While there are many methods of teaching composition, *Steps to Writing Well* tries to help inexperienced writers by offering a clearly defined sequential approach to writing the short essay. By presenting simple, practical advice directly to the students, this text is intended to make the demanding jobs of teaching and learning the basic principles of composition easier and more enjoyable for everyone."

ACKNOWLEDGMENTS

I would like to thank English Acquisitions Editor Michael Rosenberg for his continuing support, encouragement, and sound judgment on this project. I appreciated the helpful advice of Stacy Schoolfield, the former Developmental Editor with whom I began this edition, and the excellent guidance of Katherine V. Lincoln, the Senior Project Editor. I am deeply indebted to Developmental Editor Camille Adkins, who improved this project in numerous ways, always working with great care, skill, and patience. Thanks also go to Van Strength for obtaining the many permission rights for this edition, to Charles Naylor, for his meticulous care in the proofing of final pages, and to Kimberly Miller for her outstanding work on the Instructor's Manual. I am also grateful to the Colorado State University students who allowed me to reprint their writing and to Sharon Strauss, at the College of Charleston, for permission to reprint her prize-winning student essay "Treeclimbing."

In addition, I would like to thank a number of colleagues across the country who offered many useful suggestions for this edition: Deborah Barberovase Horry, Georgetown Technical College; Ellen Bourland, George C. Wallace, State Community College; Edith Burford, University of Texas-Pan American; Cary Ser, Miami Dade Community College; Terry Scott, Laramie County Community College; and Richard White, Edison Community College.

And, as always, love and gratitude to my husband David Hall and our children, Sarah, Kate, and Austin, for their patience and encouragement during the preparation of this new edition.

TO THE STUDENT ···········

FINDING THE RIGHT ATTITUDE

If you agree with one or more of the following statements, we have some serious myth-killing to do before you begin this book:

1. I'm no good in English—never have been, never will be.

2. Only people with natural talent for writing can succeed in composition class.

3. My composition teacher is a picky, comma-hunting old fogey/radical, who will insist I write just like him or her.

4. I write for myself, not for anyone else, so I don't need this class or this book.

5. Composition classes are designed to put my creativity in a straitjacket.

The notion that good writers are born, not made, is a widespread myth that may make you feel defeated before you start. But the simple truth is that good writers *are* made—simply because *effective writing is a skill that can be learned.* Despite any feelings of insecurity you may have about composition, you should realize that you already know many of the basic rules of good writing; after all, you've been writing since you were six years old. What you need now is some practical advice on composition, some coaching to sharpen your skills, and a strong dose of determination to practice those skills until you can consistently produce the results you want. Talent, as the French writer Flaubert once said, is nothing more than long patience.

Think about learning to write well as you might consider your tennis game. No one is born a tennis star. You first learn the basic rules and movements and then go out on the court to practice. And practice. No one's tennis will improve if he or she stays off the court; similarly, you must write regularly and receive feedback to improve your composition skills. Try to see your teacher not as Dr. Frankenstein determined to reproduce his or her style of writing in you, but rather as your coach, your loyal trainer who wants you to do the very best you can. Like any good coach, your teacher will point out your strengths and weaknesses; she or he will often send you to this text for practical suggestions for improvement. And while there are no quick, magic solutions for learning to write well, the most important point to remember is this: with this text, your own common sense, and determination, *you can improve your writing.*

WHY WRITE?

"OK," you say, "so I can improve if I try—but why should I bother? Why should I write well? I'm not going to be a professional writer."

In the first place, writing helps us explore our own thoughts and feelings. Writing forces us to articulate our ideas, to discover what we really think about an issue. For example, let's suppose you're faced with a difficult decision and that the arguments pro and con are jumbled in your head. You begin to write down all the pertinent facts and feelings, and suddenly, you begin to see that you do, indeed, have stronger arguments for one side of the question than the other. Once you "see" what you are thinking, you may then scrutinize your opinions for any logical flaws or weaknesses and revise your argument accordingly. In other words, writing lays out our ideas for examination, analysis, and thoughtful reaction. Thus when we write, we (and the world at large) see who we are, and what we stand for, much more clearly. Moreover, writing can provide a record of our thoughts that we may study and evaluate in a way that conversation cannot. In short, writing well enables us to see and know ourselves—our feelings, ideas, and opinions—better.

On a more practical level, we need to write effectively to communicate with others. While some of our writing may be done solely for ourselves, the majority of it is created for others to share. In this world, it is almost impossible to claim that we write only for ourselves. We are constantly asked to put our feelings, ideas, and knowledge in writing for others to read. In four years of college, no matter what your major, you will be repeatedly required to write essays, tests, reports, and exercises (not to mention letters home). Later, you may need to write formal letters of application for jobs or graduate training. And on a job you may have to write numerous kinds of reports, proposals, analyses, and requisitions. To be successful in any field, you must make your correspondence with business associates and co-workers clearly understood; remember that enormous amounts of time, energy, and profit have been lost because of a single unclear office memo.

There's still a third—more cynical—reason for studying writing techniques. Once you begin to improve your ability to use language, you will become more aware of the ways others write and speak. Through today's mass media, we are continually bombarded with words from politicians, advertisers, scientists, preachers, and teachers. We need to understand and evaluate what we are hearing, not only for our benefit but also for self-protection. Language is frequently manipulated to manipulate us. For example, years ago some government officials on trial preferred us to see Watergate as an "intelligence information gathering mission" rather than as simple breaking and entering. CIA members have long referred to the "neutralization" of enemies, and, more recently, Pentagon officials noted "collateral damage" rather than civilian deaths when our "physics packages" (bombs) fell on "soft" (human) targets during the 1991 Gulf War. (One year not so long ago, the National Council of Teachers of English gave their Doublespeak Award to the U.S. officers who, after accidentally shooting down a plane of civilians, reported that the plane didn't crash—rather, it had "uncontrolled contact with the ground.") Some members of Congress have seen no recessions, just "meaningful downturns in aggregate output," so they have treated themselves to a "pay equalization concept," rather than a raise. Advertisers frequently try to sell us "authentic art reproductions" that are, of course, fakes all the same; the television networks treat us to "encore presentations" that are the same old summer reruns. And "fenestration engineers" are still window cleaners; "environmental superintendents" are still janitors; "drain surgeons" are still plumbers.

By becoming better writers ourselves, we can learn to recognize and reject the irresponsible, cloudy, or dishonest language of others before we become victims of their exploitation.

A GOOD PLACE TO START

If improving writing skills is not only possible but important, it is also something else: hard work. H. L. Mencken, American critic and writer, once remarked that "for every difficult and complex problem, there is an obvious solution that is simple, easy and wrong." No composition textbook can promise easy formulas guaranteed to improve your writing overnight. Nor is writing always fun for everyone. But this text can make the learning process easier, less painful, and more enjoyable than you might anticipate. Written in plain, straightforward language addressed to you, the student, this book will suggest a variety of practical ways for you to organize and write clear, concise prose. Because each of your writing tasks will be different, this textbook cannot provide a single, simple blueprint that will apply in all instances. Later chapters, however, will discuss some of the most common methods of organizing essays, such as development by example, definition, classification, causal analysis, comparison/contrast, and argument. As you become more familiar with, and begin to master, these patterns of writing, you will find yourself increasingly able to assess, organize, and explain the thoughts you have about the people, events, and situations in your own life. And while it may be true that in learning to write well there is no free ride, this book, along with your own willingness to work and improve, can start you down the road with a good sense of direction.

J.W.

CONTENTS ·····················

To the Teacher   *v*
To the Student   *xi*

PART ONE   THE BASICS OF THE SHORT ESSAY

1 Prewriting **3**

Getting Started (Or Soup-Can Labels Can
Be Fascinating) *3*
Selecting a Subject *4*
Finding Your Essay's Purpose and Focus *6*
Pump-Primer Techniques *7*
After You've Found Your Focus *19*
   Practicing What You've Learned 19
Discovering Your Audience *20*
How to Identify Your Readers *20*
   Practicing What You've Learned 24
Keeping a Journal (Talking to Yourself *Does* Help) *27*
Uses of the Journal *27*
Chapter 1 Summary *30*

2 The Thesis Statement **31**

What Is a Thesis? What Does a "Working
Thesis" Do? *32*
Can a "Working Thesis" Change? *32*
Guidelines for Writing a Good Thesis *33*
Avoiding Common Errors in Thesis Statements *37*
   Practicing What You've Learned 39
   Assignment 41

Using the Essay Map *41*
   Practicing What You've Learned *43*
   Assignment *44*
Chapter 2 Summary *46*

3   The Body Paragraphs **47**

Planning the Body of Your Essay *47*
Composing the Body Paragraphs *50*
The Topic Sentence *51*
   Practicing What You've Learned *56*
   Assignment *59*
   *Applying What You've Learned to
   Your Writing* *60*
Paragraph Development *60*
Paragraph Length *65*
   Practicing What You've Learned *65*
   Assignment *66*
   *Applying What You've Learned to
   Your Writing* *66*
Paragraph Unity *67*
   Practicing What You've Learned *69*
   *Applying What You've Learned to
   Your Writing* *71*
Paragraph Coherence *71*
   Practicing What You've Learned *78*
Paragraph Sequence *82*
Transitions between Paragraphs *83*
   *Applying What You've Learned to
   Your Writing* *84*
Chapter 3 Summary *85*

4   Beginnings and Endings **87**

How to Write a Good Lead-In *87*
Avoiding Errors in Lead-Ins *91*
   Practicing What You've Learned *92*
How to Write a Good Concluding Paragraph *92*

Avoiding Errors in Conclusions *94*
   Practicing What You've Learned *95*
How to Write a Good Title *95*
   Assignment *96*
   Applying What You've Learned to Your *Writing* *96*
Chapter 4 Summary *97*

5   Drafting and Revising: Creative Thinking,
    Critical Thinking **99**

What Is Revision? *100*
When Does Revision Occur? *100*
Myths about Revision *100*
Can I Learn to Improve My Revision Skills? *102*
Preparing to Draft and Revise *102*
A Revision Process for Your Drafts *104*
What Is Critical Thinking? *107*
Thinking Critically as a Writer *107*
A Final Checklist for Your Essay *113*
Benefiting from Revision Workshops *114*
   Practicing What You've Learned *117*
   Assignment *120*
Some Last Advice: How to Play with Your
Mental Blocks *120*
Chapter 5 Summary *122*

6   Effective Sentences **123**

Developing a Clear Style *124*
Developing a Concise Style *130*
   Practicing What You've Learned *135*
   Assignment *137*
Developing a Lively Style *138*
   Practicing What You've Learned *142*
   Assignment *143*
Developing an Emphatic Style *143*
   Practicing What You've Learned *147*
   Assignment *149*

Applying What You've Learned to Your
Writing **150**
Chapter 6 Summary **151**

7 Word Logic **153**

Selecting the Correct Words **154**
    Practicing What You've Learned **160**
Selecting the Best Words **161**
    Practicing What You've Learned **172**
    Assignment **174**
    Applying What You've Learned to Your
    Writing **175**

Chapter 7 Summary **176**

The Basics of the Short Essay: Part One Summary . . **176**

PART TWO MODES AND STRATEGIES

8 Exposition **179**

The Strategies of Exposition **179**

Strategy One: Development by Example **180**
    Essay Topics **185**
    A Topic Proposal for Your Essay **186**
    Sample Student Essay **187**
    *Professional Essay: "So What's So Bad about
    Being So-So?"* **189**
        The drive for perfection is preventing too many people
        from enjoying sports and hobbies, says author Lisa
        Wilson Strick (who proudly plays the piano badly but
        with great pleasure).
    A Revision Worksheet **192**
    Reviewing Your Progress **193**

Strategy Two: Development by Process Analysis **193**
    Essay Topics **196**
    A Topic Proposal for Your Essay **197**
    Sample Student Essay **198**

Professional Essay: "To Bid the World Farewell" **201**

> By describing the embalming process in vivid, step-by-step detail, social critic and author Jessica Mitford questions the value—and necessity—of the entire procedure.

A Revision Worksheet **208**

Reviewing Your Progress **208**

Strategy Three: Development by Comparison and Contrast **209**

Essay Topics **213**

A Topic Proposal for Your Essay **214**

Sample Student Essay **214**

Professional Essay: "Grant and Lee: A Study in Contrasts" **217**

> Noted historian Bruce Catton compares and contrasts the two great generals of the Civil War, concluding that their roles at Appomatox made possible "a peace of reconciliation."

A Revision Worksheet **221**

Reviewing Your Progress **221**

Strategy Four: Development by Definition **222**

Essay Topics **226**

A Topic Proposal for Your Essay **227**

Sample Student Essay **228**

Professional Essay: "The Androgynous Male" **230**

> Columnist Noel Perrin defines a new class of men and argues that they may have more freedom than those who imitate the he-man, all-American-who-loves-football male stereotype.

A Revision Worksheet **234**

Reviewing Your Progress **235**

Strategy Five: Development by Division and Classification **235**

Essay Topics **238**

A Topic Proposal for Your Essay **239**

Sample Student Essay **240**

Professional Essay: "The Plot Against People" **242**

> According to well-known columnist Russell Baker, all inanimate objects may be classified into three categories: those that don't work, those that get lost, and those that break down.

A Revision Worksheet **245**

Reviewing Your Progress **245**

Strategy Six: Development by Causal Analysis **246**

Essay Topics **249**

A Topic Proposal for Your Essay **250**

Sample Student Essay **251**

Professional Essay: "Scaring the Public to Death" **253**

> Journalist Frank Trippett discusses the effects of increased bicycle use in this country, including a growing number of reckless riders who antagonize both motorists and pedestrians in a new—and often dangerous—battle for the road.

A Revision Worksheet **256**

Reviewing Your Progress **257**

9   Argumentation **259**

Developing Your Essay **260**

Common Logical Fallacies **269**

Practicing What You've Learned **272**

Assignment **273**

Essay Topics **273**

A Topic Proposal for Your Essay **275**

Sample Student Essay **275**

Professional Essay: "Motorcycle Helmet Laws Protect Everyone" and "Motorcycle Helmet Laws Mock Freedom" **278**

> Motorcycle helmet laws protect everyone, not just the cyclists themselves, claims an editorial in *USA Today,* which cites soaring medical costs and insurance rates. But attorney Paul Lax disagrees, arguing that helmet laws are not only ineffective but are also a dangerous infringement on our civil rights.

Pro/Con Advertising: "I'm the NRA" and "A $29 Handgun Shattered My Family's Life" **280**

Two Advertisements in a Series: Nuclear Energy Means Cleaner Air **283**

A Revision Worksheet **283**

Reviewing Your Progress **286**

10   Description   287

How to Write Effective Description   *287*
  Essay Topics   *293*
  A Topic Proposal for Your Essay   *293*
  Sample Student Essay   *294*
  Professional Essay: "The Discus Thrower"   *297*
    Surgeon Richard Selzer describes the last hours of a
    terminally-ill patient—a man who is vigorously following
    the poet Dylan Thomas's advice: "Do not go gentle into
    that good night."
  A Revision Worksheet   *301*
  Reviewing Your Progess   *301*

11   Narration   303

How to Write Effective Narration   *304*
  Essay Topics   *306*
  A Topic Proposal for Your Essay   *307*
  Sample Student Essay   *308*
  Professional Essay: "Graduation"   *310*
    Multi-talented writer and performer Maya Angelou
    remembers—with both pain and pride—her
    graduation ceremony marred by the disturbing
    words of a racist guest speaker.
  A Revision Worksheet   *320*
  Reviewing Your Progress   *321*

12   Writing a Paper Using Research   323

Searching for Your Topic   *324*
Beginning Your Library Research   *324*
Taking Notes   *326*
Distinguishing Paraphrase from Summary   *328*
Choosing Your Sources   *329*
Incorporating Your Source Material   *331*
Avoiding Plagiarism   *333*
  Practicing What You've Learned   *336*
  Assignment   *337*

Choosing the Documentation Style for
Your Essay *337*
    Sample Entries: MLA Style *337*
    Sample Entries: APA Style *344*
    Sample Student Paper Using MLA Style *348*

PART THREE A CONCISE HANDBOOK

13 Major Errors in Grammar **355**

Errors with Verbs *355*
    Practicing What You've Learned *359*
Errors with Nouns *360*
Errors with Pronouns *361*
    Practicing What You've Learned *364*
Errors with Adverbs and Adjectives *365*
Errors in Modifying Phrases *366*
    Practicing What You've Learned *367*
Errors in Sentences *368*
    Practicing What You've Learned *371*

14 A Concise Guide to Punctuation **373**

The Period *374*
The Question Mark *374*
The Exclamation Point *374*
The Comma *374*
    Practicing What You've Learned *379*
The Semicolon *380*
The Colon *380*
    Practicing What You've Learned *381*
The Apostrophe *382*
Quotation Marks *383*
    Practicing What You've Learned *385*
Parentheses *386*
Brackets *387*
The Dash *387*
The Hyphen *388*

Italics *389*
The Ellipsis Mark *390*
    Practicing What You've Learned 391

15   A Concise Guide to Mechanics **393**

Capitalization *393*
Abbreviations *395*
Numbers *395*
    Practicing What You've Learned 396
Spelling *397*

    Index *400*

PART ONE

THE BASICS OF THE SHORT ESSAY

he first section of this text is designed to move you through the writing process as you compose a short essay, the kind you are most likely to encounter in composition class and in other college courses. Chapters 1 and 2, on prewriting and the thesis statement, will help you find a topic, purpose, and focus for your essay. Chapter 3, on paragraphs, will show you how to plan, organize, and develop your ideas; Chapter 4 will help you complete your essay. Chapter 5 will offer suggestions for revising your writing, and Chapters 6 and 7 will present additional advice on selecting your words and composing your sentences.

PREWRITING

GETTING STARTED (OR SOUP-CAN LABELS CAN BE FASCINATING)

For many writers, getting started is the hardest part. You may have noticed that when it is time to begin a writing assignment, you suddenly develop an enormous desire to defrost your refrigerator, water your plants, or sharpen your pencils for the fifth time. If this situation sounds familiar, you may find it reassuring to know that many professionals undergo these same strange compulsions before they begin writing. Jean Kerr, author of *Please Don't Eat the Daisies,* admits that she often finds herself in the kitchen reading soup-can labels—or anything—in order to prolong the moments before taking pen in hand. John C. Calhoun, vice-president under Andrew Jackson, insisted he had to plow his fields before he could write, and Joseph Conrad, author of *Lord Jim* and other novels, is said to have cried on occasion from the sheer dread of sitting down to compose his stories.

To spare you as much hand-wringing as possible, this chapter presents some practical suggestions on how to begin writing your short essay. Although all writers must find the methods that work best for them, you may find some of the following ideas helpful.

But no matter how you actually begin putting words on paper, it is absolutely essential to maintain two basic ideas concerning your writing task. Before you write a single sentence, you should always remind yourself that

1. You have some valuable ideas to tell your reader, and

2. More than anything, you want to communicate those ideas to your reader.

These reminders may seem obvious to you, but without a solid commitment to your own opinions as well as to your reader, your prose will be lifeless and boring. If *you* don't care about your subject, you can't very well expect anyone else to. Have confidence that your ideas are worthwhile and that your reader genuinely wants, or needs, to know what you think.

Most important, however, you must have a strong desire to tell others exactly what you are thinking. The single most serious mistake inexperienced writers make is writing for themselves only. The very act of composing an essay demonstrates that you have ideas about your subject; the point is to communicate your opinions to others clearly and persuasively. Whether you wish to inform your readers, change their minds, or stir them to action, you cannot accomplish your purpose by writing so that only you understand what you mean. Remember that the burden of communicating your thoughts falls on *you*, not the reader, who is under no obligation at all to struggle through confused, unclear prose; paragraphs that begin and end for no apparent reason; sentences that come one after another with no more logic than lemmings following one another into the sea. Therefore, before you begin writing, commit yourself to becoming more sensitive to the feelings of your reader. Ask yourself as you revise your writing, "Am I making myself clear to others, or am I merely jotting down a conversation with myself?" Other chapters in this book will give you concrete advice on ways to make your writing clearer, but for now, at the jumping-off point in the writing process, the goal is to become *determined to communicate with your readers.*

SELECTING A SUBJECT

Once you have decided that communicating with others is your primary goal, you are ready to select the subject of your essay. Here are some suggestions on how to begin:

Start early. Writing teachers since the earth's crust cooled have been pushing this advice, and for good reason. It's not because teachers are egoists competing for the dubious honor of having the most time-consuming course; it is because few writers, even experienced ones, can do a good job when rushed. You need time to mull over ideas, organize your thoughts, revise and polish your prose. Rule of thumb: always give yourself twice as much time as you think you'll need to avoid the 2:00-A.M.-why-did-I-come-to-college panic.

Select something in which you currently have a strong interest. If the essay subject is left to you, think of something fun, fascinating, or frightening you've done or seen lately, perhaps something you've already told a friend about. The subject might be the pleasure of a new hobby, the challenge of a recent book or movie, or even the harassment of registration—anything in which you are personally involved. If you aren't enthusiastic enough about your subject to want to spread the word, pick something else. Bored writers write boring essays.

Don't feel you have nothing from which to choose your subject. Your days are full of activities, people, joys, and irritations. Essays do not have to be written on lofty intellectual or poetic subjects—in fact, some of the world's best essays have been written on such subjects as china teacups, roast pig, and chimney sweeps. Think: what have you been talking or thinking about lately? What have you been doing that you're excited about? Or what about your past? Reflect a few moments on some of your most vivid memories—special people, vacations, holidays, childhood hideaways, your first job or first date—all of which are possibilities.

If a search of your immediate or past personal experience doesn't turn up anything inspiring, you might try looking in the campus newspaper for stories that arouse your strong feelings; don't skip the "Letters to the Editor" column. What are the current topics of controversy on your campus? How do you feel about open admissions? Dorm hours and restrictions? Compulsory class attendance? Consider the material you are studying in your classes—information on spies during the Civil War might lead to a thought-provoking essay comparing nineteenth-century espionage to the modern methods of the CIA or FBI. Finally, your local newspaper or national news magazine might suggest essay topics to you on local, national, or international affairs that affect your life.

In other words, when you're stuck for an essay topic, take a closer look at your environment: your own life—past, present, and future; your hometown; your college town; your state; your country; and your world. You'll probably discover more than enough subjects to satisfy the assignments in your writing class.

Narrow a large subject. Once you've selected a general subject to write on, you may find that it is too broad for effective treatment in a short essay; therefore, you may need to narrow it somewhat. Suppose, for instance, you like to work with plants and have decided to make them the subject of your essay. The subject of "plants," however, is far too large and unwieldy for a short essay, perhaps even for a short book. Consequently, you must make your subject less general. "Houseplants" is more specific, but, again, there's too much to say. "Minimum-care houseplants" is better, but you still need to pare this large, complex subject further so that you may treat it in depth in your short essay. After all, there are many houseplants that require little attention. After several more tries, you might arrive at more specific, manageable topics such as "houseplants that thrive in dark areas" or "the easy-care Devil's Ivy."

Then again, let's assume you are interested in sports. A 500- to 800-word essay on "sports" would obviously be superficial since the subject covers so much ground. Instead, you might divide the subject into categories such as "sports heroes," "my years on the high school tennis team," "women in gymnastics," "my love of jogging," and so forth. Perhaps several of your categories would make good short essays, but after looking at your list, you might decide that your real interest at this time is jogging and that it will be the topic of your essay.

FINDING YOUR ESSAY'S PURPOSE AND FOCUS

Even after you've narrowed your large subject to a more manageable topic, you still must find a specific *purpose* for your essay. Why are you writing about this topic? Do your readers need to be informed, persuaded, entertained? What do you want your writing to accomplish?

In addition to knowing your purpose, you must also find a clear *focus* or direction for your essay. You cannot, for example, inform your readers about every aspect of jogging. Instead, you must decide on a particular part of the sport and then determine the main point you want to make. If it helps, think of a camera: you see a sweeping landscape you'd like to photograph but you know you can't get it all into one picture, so you pick out a particularly interesting part of the scene. Focus in an essay works in the same way; you zoom in, so to speak, on a particular part of your topic and make that the focus of your paper.

Sometimes part of your problem may be solved by your assignment; your teacher may choose the focus of your essay for you by asking for certain specific information or by prescribing the method of development you should use (compare jogging to aerobics, explain the process of jogging properly, analyze the effects of daily jogging, and so forth). But if the purpose and focus of your essay are decisions you must make, you should always allow your interest and knowledge to guide you. Often a direction or focus for your essay will surface as you narrow your subject, but don't become frustrated if you have to discard several ideas before you hit the one that's right. For instance, you might first consider writing on how to select running shoes and then realize that you know too little about the shoe market, or you might find that there's just too little of importance to say about jogging paths to make an interesting 500-word essay.

Let's suppose for a moment that you have thought of a subject that interests you—but now you're stuck. Deciding on something to write about this subject suddenly looks as easy as nailing Jell-O to your kitchen wall. What should you say? What would be the purpose of your essay? What would be interesting for you to write about and for readers to hear about?

At this point you may profit from trying more than one prewriting exercise, designed to help you generate some ideas about your topic. The exercises described next are, in a sense, "pump primers" that will get your creative juices flowing again. Because all writers compose differently, not all of these exercises will work for you—in fact, some of them may lead you nowhere. Nevertheless, try all of them at least once or twice; you may be surprised to discover that some pump-primer techniques work better with some subjects than with others.

PUMP-PRIMER TECHNIQUES

1. Listing

Try jotting down all the ideas that pop into your head about your topic. Free-associate; don't hold back anything. Try to brainstorm for at least ten minutes.

A quick list on jogging might look like this:

fun	races
healthy	both sexes
relieves tension	any age group
no expensive equipment	running with friend or spouse
shoes	too much competition
poor shoes won't last	great expectations
shin splints	good for lungs
fresh air	improves circulation
good for heart	firming
jogging paths vs. streets	no weight loss
hard surfaces	warm-ups before run
muscle cramps	cool-downs after
going too far	getting discouraged
going too fast	hitting the wall
sense of accomplishment	marathons

As you read over the list, look for connections between ideas or one large idea that encompasses several small ones. In this list you might first notice that many of the ideas focus on improving health (heart, lungs, circulation), but you discard that subject because a "jogging improves health" essay is too obvious; it's a topic that's been done too many times to say anything new. A closer look at your list, however, turns up a number of ideas that concern how *not* to jog or reasons why someone might get discouraged and quit a jogging program. You begin to think of friends who might have stuck with jogging as you have if only they'd warmed up properly beforehand, chosen the right places to run, paced themselves more realistically, and so on. You decide, therefore, to write an essay telling first-time joggers how to start a successful program, how to avoid a number of problems, from shoes to track surfaces, that might otherwise defeat their efforts before they've given the sport a chance.

Freewriting

Some people simply need to start writing to find a focus. Take out several sheets of blank paper, give yourself at least ten to fifteen minutes, and begin writing whatever comes to mind on your subject. Don't worry about spelling, punctuation, or even complete sentences. Don't change, correct, or delete anything. If you run out of things to say, write "I can't think of anything to say" until you can find a new thought. At the end of the time period you may discover that by continuously writing you will have written yourself into an interesting topic.

Here are examples of freewriting from students who were given ten minutes to write on the general topic of "nature."

STUDENT 1:

I'm really not the outdoorsy type. I'd rather be inside somewhere than out in Nature tromping through the bushes. I don't like bugs and snakes and stuff like that. Lots of my friends like to go hiking around or camping but I don't. Secretly, I think maybe one of the big reasons I really don't like being out in Nature is because I'm deathly afraid of bees. When I was a kid I was out in the woods and ran into a swarm of bees and got stung about a million times, well, it felt like a million times. I had to go to the hospital for a few days. Now every time I'm outside somewhere and something, anything, flies by me I'm terrified. Totally paranoid. Everyone kids me because I immediately cover my head. I keep hearing about killer bees heading this way, my worst nightmare come true. . . .

STUDENT 2:

We're not going to have any Nature left if people don't do something about the environment. Despite all the media attention to recycling, we're still trashing the planet left and right. People talk big about "saving the environment" but then do such stupid things all the time. Like smokers who flip their cigarette butts out their car windows. Do they think those filters are just going to disappear overnight? The parking lot by this building is full of butts this morning where someone dumped their car ashtray. This campus is full of pop cans, I can see at least three empties under desks in this classroom right now. . . .

These two students reacted quite differently to the same general subject. The first student responded personally, thinking about her own relationship to "nature" (defined as being out in the woods), whereas the second student obviously associated nature with environmental concerns. More freewriting might lead student 1 to a humorous essay on her bee phobia or even to an inquiry about those dreaded killer bees; student 2 might write an interesting paper suggesting ways college students could clean up their campus or easily recycle their aluminum cans.

Often freewriting will not be as coherent as these two samples; sometimes freewriting goes nowhere or in circles. But it's a technique worth trying. By allowing our minds to roam freely over a subject, without worrying about "correctness" or organization, we may remember or discover topics we want to write about or investigate, topics we feel strongly about and wish to introduce to others.

3. Looping*

Looping is a variation on freewriting that works amazingly well for many people, including those who are frustrated rather than helped by freewriting.

Let's assume you've been assigned that old standby "My Summer Vacation." Obviously you must find a focus, something specific and important to say. Again, take out several sheets of blank paper and begin to freewrite, as described previously. Write for at least ten minutes. At the end of this period read over what you've written and try to identify a central idea that has emerged. This idea may be an important thought that occurred to you in the middle or at the end of your writing, or perhaps it was the idea you liked best for whatever reason. It may be the idea that was pulling you onward when time ran out. In other words, look for the thought that stands out, that seems to indicate the direction of your thinking. Put this thought or idea into one sentence called the "center-of-gravity sentence." You have now completed loop 1.

To begin loop 2, use your center-of-gravity sentence as a jumping-off point for another ten minutes of freewriting. Stop, read what you've written, and complete loop 2 by composing another center-of-gravity sentence. Use this second sentence to start loop 3. You should write at least three loops and three center-of-gravity sentences. At the end of three loops, you may find that

---

* This technique is suggested by Peter Elbow in *Writing Without Teachers* (New York: Oxford University Press, 1975).

you have focused on a specific topic that might lead to a good essay. If you're not satisfied with your topic at this point, by all means try two or three more loops until your subject is sufficiently narrowed and focused.

Here's an example of one student's looping exercise:

SUMMER VACATION

Loop 1

I think summer vacations are very important aspects of living. They symbolize getting away from daily routines, discovering places and people that are different. When I think of vacations I think mostly of traveling somewhere too far to go, say, for a weekend. It is a chance to get away and relax and not think about most responsibilities. Just have a good time and enjoy yourself. Vacations can also be a time of gathering with family and friends.

Center-of-gravity sentence
Loop 2

Vacations are meant to be used for traveling.

Vacations are meant for traveling. Last summer my family and I drove to Yellowstone National Park. I didn't want to go at first. I thought looking at geysers would be dumb and boring. I was really obnoxious all the way up there and made lots of smart remarks about getting eaten by bears. Luckily, my parents ignored me and I'm glad they did, because Yellowstone turned out to be wonderful. It's not just Old Faithful—there's lots more to see and learn about, like these colorful boiling pools and boiling patches of mud. I got interested in the thermodynamics of the pools and how new ones are surfacing all the time, and how algae make the pools different colors.

Center-of-gravity sentence
Loop 3

Once I got interested in Yellowstone's amazing pools, my vacation turned out great.

Once I got interested in the pools, I had a good time, mainly because I felt I was seeing something really unusual. I knew I'd never see anything like this again unless I went to Iceland or New Zealand (highly unlikely!). I felt like I was learning a lot, too. I liked the idea of learning a lot about the inside of the earth without having to go to class and study books. I really hated to leave—Mom and Dad kidded me on the way back about how much I'd griped about going on the trip in the first place. I felt pretty dumb. But I was really glad I'd given the Park a closer look instead of holding on to my view of it as a boring bunch of water fountains. I would have had a terrible time, but now I hope to go back

Center-of-gravity
sentence

someday. I think the experience made me more open-minded about trying new places.

My vacation this summer was special because I was willing to put aside my expectations of boredom and learn some new ideas about the strange environment at Yellowstone.

At the end of three loops, this student has moved from the general subject of "summer vacation" to the more focused idea that her willingness to learn about a new place played an important part in the enjoyment of her vacation. Although her last center-of-gravity sentence still contains some vague words ("special," "new ideas," "strange environment"), the thought stated here may eventually lead to an essay that will not only say something about this student's vacation but may also persuade the readers to reconsider their attitude toward taking trips to new places.

The Boomerang

Still another variation on freewriting is the technique called the boomerang, named appropriately because, like the Australian stick, it invites your mind to travel over a subject from opposite directions to produce new ideas.

Suppose, for example, members of your class have been asked to write about their major field of study, which in your case is Liberal Arts. Begin by writing a statement that comes into your mind about majoring in the Liberal Arts and then freewrite on that statement for five minutes. Then write a second statement that approaches the subject from an opposing point of view, and freewrite again for five minutes. Continue this pattern several times. Boomeranging, like looping, can help writers see their subject in a new way and consequently help them find an idea to write about.

Here's an abbreviated sample of boomeranging:

1. Majoring in the Liberal Arts is impractical in today's world.

[Freewrite for five minutes.]

2. Majoring in the Liberal Arts is practical in today's world.

[Freewrite for five minutes.]

3. Liberal Arts is a particularly enjoyable major for me.

[Freewrite for five minutes.]

4. Liberal Arts is not always an enjoyable major for me.

[Freewrite for five minutes.]

And so on.

By continuing to "throw the boomerang" across your subject, you may not only find your focus but also gain insight into other people's views of your topic, which can be especially valuable if your paper will address a controversial issue or one that you feel is often misunderstood.

5.   Clustering

Another excellent technique is clustering (sometimes called "mapping"). Place your general subject in a circle in the middle of a blank sheet of paper and begin to draw other lines and circles that radiate from the original subject. Cluster those ideas that seem to fall together. At the end of ten minutes see if a topic emerges from any of your groups of ideas.

Ten minutes of clustering on the subject of "A Memorable Holiday" might look like the drawing on page 14.

This student may wish to brainstorm further on the Christmas he spent in the hospital with a case of appendicitis or perhaps the Halloween he first experienced a house of horrors. By using clustering, he has recollected some important details about a number of holidays that may help him focus on an occasion he wants to describe in his paper.

6.   Cubing

Still another way to generate ideas is cubing. Imagine a six-sided cube that looks something like this:

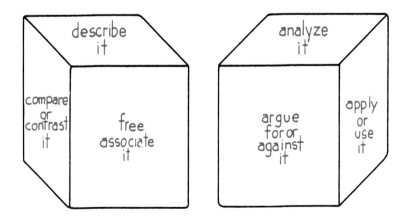

Mentally, roll your subject around the cube and freewrite the answers to the questions that follow. Write whatever comes to mind for ten or fifteen minutes; don't concern yourself with the "correctness" of what you write.

   a. *Describe it:*   What does your subject look like? What size, colors, textures does it have? Any special features worth noting?

b. *Compare or contrast it:*   What is your subject similar to? What is your subject different from? In what ways?

c. *Free-associate it:*   What does this subject remind you of? What does it call to mind? What memories does it conjure up?

d. *Analyze it:*   How does it work? How are the parts connected? What is its significance?

e. *Argue for or against it:*   What arguments can you make for or against your subject? What advantages or disadvantages does it have? What changes or improvements should be made?

f. *Apply it:*   What are the uses of your subject? What can you do with it?

A student who had recently volunteered at a homeless shelter wrote the following responses about her experience:

a. *Describe it:*   I and five other members of my campus organization volunteered three Saturdays to work at the shelter here in town. We mainly helped in the kitchen, preparing, serving, and cleaning up after meals. At the dinners we served about 70 homeless people, mostly men but also many families with small children and babies.

b. *Compare or contrast it:*   I had never done anything like this before so it's hard to compare or contrast it to anything. It was different though from what I expected. I hadn't really thought much about the people who would be there—or to be honest I think I thought they would be pretty weird or sad and I was kind of dreading going there after I volunteered. But the people were just regular normal people. And they were very, very polite to us.

c. *Free-associate it:*   Some of the people there reminded me of some of my relatives! John, the kitchen manager, said most of the people were just temporarily "down on their luck" and that reminded me of my aunt and uncle who came to stay with us for a while when I was in high school after my uncle lost his job.

d. *Analyze it:*   I feel like I got a lot out of my experience. I think I had some wrong ideas about "the homeless" and working there made me think more about them as real people not just a faceless group.

e. *Argue for or against it:*   I would encourage others to volunteer there. The work isn't hard and it isn't scary. It makes you appreciate what you've got and also makes you think about what you or your family might do if things went wrong for a while. It also makes you feel good to do something for people you don't even know.

f. *Apply it:*   I feel like I am more knowledgeable when I hear people talk about the poor or the homeless in this town, especially those people who criticize those who use the shelter.

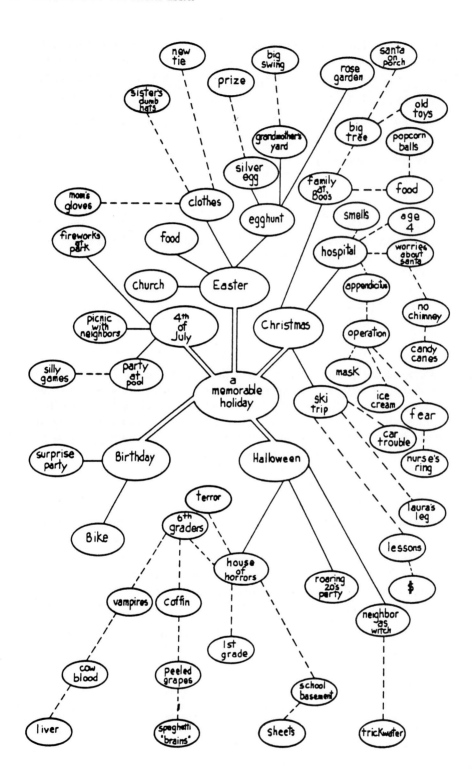

After you've written your responses, see if any one or more of them give you an idea for a paper. The student who wrote the preceding responses decided she wanted to write an article for her campus newspaper encouraging people to volunteer at the shelter not only to provide much-needed help but also to challenge their own preconceived notions about the homeless in her college town. Cubing helped her realize she had something valuable to say about her experience and gave her a purpose for writing.

7. Interviewing

Another way to find a direction for your paper is through interviewing. Ask a classmate or friend to discuss your subject with you. Let your thoughts range over your subject as your friend asks you questions that arise naturally in the conversation. Or your friend might try asking what are called "reporter's questions" as she or he "interviews" you on your subject:

Who?   When?
What?   Why?
Where?   How?

Listen to what you have to say about your subject. What were you most interested in talking about? What did your friend want to know? Why? By talking about your subject, you may find that you have talked your way into an interesting focus for your paper. If, after the interview, you are still stumped, question your friend: if he or she had to publish an essay based on the information from your interview, what would that essay focus on? Why?

8. The Cross-Examination

If a classmate isn't available for an interview, try interviewing, or cross-examining, yourself. Ask yourself questions about your general subject, just as a lawyer might if you were on the witness stand. Consider using the five categories described below, which are adapted from those suggested by Aristotle, centuries ago, to the orators of his day. Ask yourself as many questions in each category as you can think of, and then go on to the next category. Jot down brief notes to yourself as you answer.

Here are the five categories, plus six sample questions for each to illustrate the possibilities:

1. Definition
   a. How does the dictionary or encyclopedia define or explain this subject?
   b. How do most people define or explain it?
   c. How do I define or explain it?

    d. What do its parts look like?

    e. What is its history or origin?

    f. What are some examples of it?

2.   Comparison and Contrast

    a. What is it similar to?

    b. What does it differ from?

    c. What does it parallel?

    d. What is it opposite to?

    e. What is it better than?

    f. What is it worse than?

3.   Relationship

    a. What causes it?

    b. What are the effects of it?

    c. What larger group or category is it a part of?

    d. What larger group or category is it in opposition to?

    e. What are its values or goals?

    f. What contradictions does it contain?

4.   Circumstance

    a. Is it possible?

    b. Is it impossible?

    c. When has it happened before?

    d. What might prevent it from happening?

    e. Why might it happen again?

    f. Who has been or might be associated with it?

5.   Testimony

    a. What do people say about it?

    b. What has been written about it?

    c. What authorities exist on the subject?

    d. Are there any relevant statistics?

    e. What research has been done?

    f. Have I had any direct experience with it?

Some of the questions suggested here, or ones you think of, may not be relevant or useful to your subject. But some may lead you to ideas you wish to explore in more depth, either in a discovery draft or by using another prewriting technique described in this chapter, such as looping or mapping.

9. Sketching

Sometimes when you have found or been assigned a general subject, the words to explain or describe it just won't come. Although listing or freewriting or one of the other methods suggested here work well for some people, other writers find these techniques intimidating or unproductive. Some of these writers are visual learners—that is, they respond better to pictorial representations of material than they do to written descriptions or explanations. If, on occasion, you are stuck for words, try drawing or sketching or even cartooning the pictures in your mind.

You may be surprised at the details that you remember once you start sketching. For example, you might have been asked to write about a favorite place or a special person in your life or to compare or contrast two places you have lived or visited. See how many details you can conjure up by drawing the scenes or the people; then look at your details to see if some dominant impression or common theme has emerged. Your Aunt Sophie's insistence on wearing two pounds of costume jewelry might become the focus of a paragraph on her sparkling personality, or the many details you recalled about your grandfather's barn might lead you to a paper on the hardships of farm life. For some writers, a picture can be worth a thousand words—especially if that picture helps them begin putting those words on paper.

10. Dramatizing the Subject

Some writers find it helpful to visualize their subject as if it were a drama or play unfolding in their minds. Kenneth Burke, a thoughtful writer himself, suggests that writers might think about human action in dramatists' terms and then see what sorts of new insights arise as the "drama" unfolds. Burke's dramatists' terms might be adapted for our use and pictured this way:

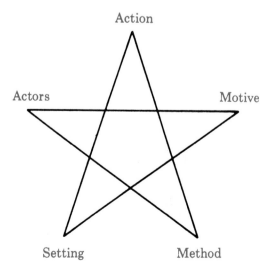

Just as you did in the cubing exercise, try mentally rolling your subject around the star on the preceding page and explore the possibilities that emerge. For example, suppose you want to write about your recent decision to return to college after a long period of working, but you don't know what you want to say about your decision. Start thinking about this decision as a drama and jot down brief answers to such questions as these:

Action: What happened?
What were the results?
What is going to happen?

Actors: Who was involved in the
action?
Who was affected by the
action?
Who caused the action?
Who was for it and who was
opposed?

Motive: What were the reasons behind
the action?
What forces motivated the
actors to perform as they did?

Method: How did the action occur?
By what means did the actors
accomplish the action?

Setting: What was the time and place of
the action?
What did the place look like?
What positive or negative
feelings are associated with
this time or place?

These are only a few of the dozens of questions you might ask yourself about your "drama." (If it helps, think of your "drama" as a murder mystery and answer the questions the police detective might ask: what happened here? to whom? who did it? why? with what? when? where? and so on.)

You may find that you have a great deal to write about the combination of actor and motive but very little to say in response to the questions on setting or method. That's fine—simply use the "dramatists' approach" to help you find a specific topic or idea you want to write about.

If at any point in this stage of the writing process, you are experiencing *Writer's Block,* you might turn to the suggestions for overcoming this common affliction, which appear on pages 120–122 in Chapter 5. You might also find it helpful to read the section on *Keeping a Journal,* pages 27–30 in this chapter, as writing in a relaxed mood on a regular basis may be the best long-term cure for your writing anxiety.

AFTER YOU'VE FOUND YOUR FOCUS

Once you think you've found the focus of your essay, you may be ready to compose a *working thesis statement,* an important part of your essay discussed in great detail in the next chapter. If you've used one of the prewriting exercises outlined in this chapter, by all means hang onto it. The details and observations you generated as you focused your topic may be useful to you as you begin to organize and develop your body paragraphs.

PRACTICING WHAT YOU'VE LEARNED

A. Some of the subjects listed below are too broad for a 500- to 800-word essay. Identify those topics that might be treated in short papers and those that still need to be narrowed.

1. The role of the modern university

2. My first (and last) experience with cross-country skiing

3. The characters of William Shakespeare

4. Nuclear accidents

5. Collecting baseball cards

6. Gun-control laws

7. Down with throwaway bottles

8. Computers

9. The best teacher I've ever had

10. Selecting the right bicycle

B. Select two of the large subjects that follow, and, through looping or listing details or another prewriting technique, find focused topics that would be appropriate for essays of 500 to 800 words.

1. music

2. cars

3. education

4. jobs

5. television commercials

6. politics

7. drugs

8. childhood

9. pollution

10. athletics

DISCOVERING YOUR AUDIENCE

Once you have a focused topic and perhaps some ideas about developing your essay, you need to stop a moment to consider your *audience.* Before you can decide what information needs to go in your essay and what should be omitted, you must know who will be reading your paper and why. Knowing your audience will also help you determine what *voice* you should use to achieve the proper tone in your essay.

Suppose, for example, you are attending a college organized on the quarter system, and you decide to write an essay arguing for a switch to the semester system. If your audience is composed of classmates, your essay will probably focus on the advantages to the student body, such as better opportunities for in-depth study in one's major, the ease of making better grades, and the benefits of longer mid-winter and summer vacations. However, if you are addressing the Board of Regents, you might emphasize the power of the semester system to attract more students, cut registration costs, and use professors more efficiently. If your audience is composed of townspeople who know little about either system, you will have to devote more time to explaining the logistics of each one and then discuss the semester plan's advantages to the local merchants, realtors, restauranteurs, and so on. *In other words, such factors as the age, education, profession, and interests of your audience can make a difference in determining which points of your argument to stress or omit, which ideas need additional explanation, and what kind of language to adopt.*

HOW TO IDENTIFY YOUR READERS

To help you analyze your audience before you begin writing your working thesis statement and rough drafts, here are some steps you may wish to follow:

1. First, see if your writing assignment specifies a particular audience (editors of a journal in your field or the Better Business Bureau of your town, for example) or a general audience of your peers (your classmates or readers of the local newspaper, for instance). Even if your assignment does not mention an intended audience, try to imagine one anyway. Imagining specific readers will help you stick to your goal of communicating with others. Forgetting that they have an audience of real people often causes writers to address themselves to their typing paper, a mistake that usually results in dull or unclear prose.

2. If a specific audience is designated, ask yourself some questions about their motivation or *reasons for reading* your essay.

- What do these readers want to learn?

- What do they hope to gain?

- Do they need your information to make a decision? Formulate a new plan? Design a new project?

- What action do you want them to take?

The answers to such questions will help you find both your essay's purpose and its content. If, for example, you're trying to persuade an employer to hire you for a particular job, you certainly would write your application in a way that stresses the skills and training the company is searching for. You may have a fine hobby or wonderful family, but if your prospective employer-reader doesn't need to hear about that particular part of your life, toss it out of this piece of writing.

3. Next, try to discover what *knowledge* your audience has of your subject.

- What, if anything, can you assume that your readers already know about your topic?

- What background information might they need to know to understand a current situation clearly?

- What facts, explanations, or examples will best present your ideas? How detailed should you be?

- What terms need to be defined? Equipment explained?

Questions like these should guide you as you collect and discard information for your paper. An essay written to your colleagues in electrical engineering, for instance, need not explain commonly used technical instruments; to do so might even insult your readers. But the same report read by your composition classmates would probably need more detailed explanation in order for you to make yourself understood. Always put yourself in your readers' place and then ask: what else do they need to know to understand this point completely?

4.   Once you have decided what information is necessary for your audience, dig a little deeper into your readers' identities. Pose some questions about their *attitudes* and emotional states.

- Are your readers already biased for or against your ideas in some way?
- Do they have positive or negative associations with your subject?
- Are they fearful or anxious, reluctant or bored?
- Do they have radically different expectations or interests?

It helps enormously to know the emotional attitudes of your readers toward your subject. Let's suppose you were arguing for the admission of a child with AIDS into a local school system, and your audience was the parent-teacher organization. Some of your readers might be frightened or even hostile; knowing this, you would wisely begin your argument with a disarming array of information showing that no cases of AIDS have developed from the casual contact of schoolchildren. In other words, the more you know about your audience's attitudes before you begin writing, the more convincing your prose, because you will make the best choices about both content and organization.

5.   Last, think of any *special qualities* that might set your audience apart from any other.

- Are they older or younger than your peers?
- Do they share similar educational experiences or training?
- Are they from a particular part of the world or country that might affect their perspective? Urban or rural?
- Are they in positions of authority?

Knowing special facts about your audience makes a difference, often in your choice of words and tone. You wouldn't, after all, use the same level of vocabulary addressing a group of fifth-graders as you would writing to the children's teacher or principal. Similarly, your tone and word choice probably wouldn't be as formal in a letter to a friend as in a letter to the telephone company protesting your most recent bill.

Without question, analyzing your specific audience is an important step to take before you begin to shape your rough drafts. And before you move on to writing a working thesis, here are a few tips to keep in mind about *all* audiences, no matter who your readers are or what their reasons for reading your writing.

1. Readers don't like to be bored. Grab your readers' attention and fight to keep it. Remember the last dull movie you squirmed—or slept—through? How much you resented wasting not only your money but your valuable time as well? How you turned it off mentally and drifted away to someplace more exciting? As you write and revise your drafts, keep imagining readers who are as intelligent—and busy—as you are. Put yourself in their place: would you find this piece of writing stimulating enough to keep reading?

2. Readers hate confusion and disorder. Can you recall a time when you tried to find your way to a party, only to discover that a friend's directions were so muddled you wound up hours later out of gas cursing in a cornfield? Or the afternoon you spent trying to follow a friend's notes for setting up a chemistry experiment, with explanations that twisted and turned as often as a wandering stray cat? Try to relive such moments of intense frustration as you struggle to make *your* writing clear and direct.

3. Readers want to think and learn (whether they realize it or not). Every time you write, you strike a bargain of sorts with your readers: in return for their time and attention, you promise to inform and interest them, to tell them something new or show them something familiar in a different light. You may enlighten them or amuse them or even try to frighten them—but they must feel, in the end, that they've gotten a fair trade. As you plan, write, and revise, ask yourself, "What are my readers learning?" If the honest answer is "nothing important," you may be writing only for yourself. (If you yourself are bored rereading your drafts, you're probably not writing for anybody at all.)

4. Readers want to see what you see, feel what you feel. Writing that is vague keeps your readers from fully sharing the information or experience you are trying to communicate. Clear, precise language—full of concrete details and specific examples—lets your readers know that you understand your subject and that you want them to understand it, too. Even a potentially dull topic such as tuning a car can become engaging to a reader if the right details are provided in the right places: your terror as blue sparks leap under your nose when the wrong wire is touched, the depressing sight of the screwdriver squirming from your greasy fingers and disappearing into the oil pan, the sudden shooting pain when the wrench slips and turns your knuckles to raw hamburger. Get your readers involved and interested—and they'll listen to what you have to say. (Details also persuade your reader that you're an authority on your subject; after all, no reader likes to waste time listening to someone whose tentative, vague prose style announces "I only sort-of know what I'm talking about here.")

5.   Readers are turned off by writers with pretentious, phony voices. Too often inexperienced writers feel they must sound especially scholarly, scientific, or sophisticated for their essays to be convincing. In fact, the contrary is true. When you assume a voice that is not yours, when you pretend to be someone you're not, you don't sound believable at all—you sound phony. Your readers want to hear what *you* have to say, and the best way to communicate with them is in a natural voice. You may also believe that to write a good essay it is necessary to use a host of unfamiliar, unpronounceable, polysyllabic words gleaned from the pages of your thesaurus. Again, the opposite is true. Our best writers agree with Mark Twain, who once said, "Never use a twenty-five-cent word when a ten-cent word will do." In other words, avoid pretension in your writing just as you do in everyday conversation. Select simple, direct words you know and use frequently; keep your voice natural, sincere, and reasonable. (For additional help choosing the appropriate words and the level of your diction, see Chapter 7.)

> ### *Don't Ever Forget Your Readers!*
> Thinking about them both before and as you write will help you choose your ideas, organize your information effectively, and select the best words.

▶ PRACTICING WHAT YOU'VE LEARNED

The article that follows appeared in newspapers across the country some time ago. Read about the new diet called "Breatharianism" and then write the assignments that follow the article.

THE ULTIMATE IN DIET CULTS: DON'T EAT ANYTHING AT ALL

1   Corte Madera, Calif.—Among those seeking enlightenment through diet cults, Wiley Brooks seemed to have the ultimate answer—not eating at all. He called himself a "Breatharian" and claimed to live on air, supplemented only by occasional fluids taken to counteract the toxins of urban environments.

Reprinted with permission. Pacific News Service/Bay Area Institute.

2   "Food is more addictive than heroin," the tall, gaunt black man told hundreds of people who paid $500 each to attend five-day "intensives," at which he would stand before them in a camel velour sweatsuit and talk for hours without moving, his fingers meditatively touching at their tips.

3   Brooks, 46, became a celebrity on the New Age touring circuit. ABC-TV featured him in October, 1980, as a weight lifter; he allegedly hoisted 1,100 pounds, about 10 times his own weight. He has also been interviewed on radio and in newspapers.

4   Those who went to his sessions during the past six months on the West Coast and in Hawaii were not just food faddists, but also physicians and other professionals who—though not necessarily ready to believe—thought this man could be onto something important. Some were convinced enough by what they saw to begin limiting their own diets, taking the first steps toward Breatharianism.

5   In his intensives, Brooks did not recommend that people stop eating altogether. Rather, he suggested they "clean their blood" by starting with the "yellow diet"—24 food items including grapefruit, papaya, corn products, eggs, chicken, fish, goat's milk, millet, salsa piquante (Mexican hot sauce) and certain flavors of the Häagen Dazs brand ice cream, including "rum raisin." These foods, he said, have a less toxic effect because, among other things, "their vibrational quality is yellow."

6   Last week, however, aspirants toward Breatharianism were shocked by reports that Brooks had been eating—and what's more, eating things that to health food purists are the worst kind of junk.

7   Word spread that during an intensive in Vancouver, Brooks was seen emerging from a 7-Eleven store with a bag of groceries. The next morning there were allegedly room service trays outside his hotel room, while inside, the trash basket held empty containers of chicken pot pie, chili and biscuits.

8   Kendra Wagner, regional Breatharian coordinator, said she herself had seen Brooks drinking a Coke. "When I asked him about it he said, 'That's how dirty the air is here,'" she explained. "We (the coordinators) sat down with Wiley after the training and said, 'We want you to tell us the truth.' He denied everything. We felt tricked and deceived."

9   As the rumors grew, some Breatharians confronted their leader at a lecture in San Francisco. Brooks denied the story and said that the true message of Breatharianism did not depend on whether he ate or not, anyway.

10   The message in his promotional material reads that "modern man is the degenerate descendant of the Breatharian," and that "living on air alone leads to perfect health and perfect happiness." Though followers had the impression Brooks has not eaten for 18 years, his leaflets merely declare that "he does not eat, and seldom drinks any fluid. He sleeps

less than seven hours a week and is healthier, more energetic and happier than he ever dreamed possible."

11   In a telephone interview, Brooks acknowledged that this assertion is not quite correct. "I'm sure I've taken some fruit, like an apple or an orange, but it's better in public to keep it simple." He again staunchly denied the 7-Eleven story.

12   Among those who have been on the yellow diet for months is Jime Collison, 24, who earlier tried "fruitarianism," fasting and other special regimens, and moved from Texas to the San Francisco Bay area just to be around the Breatharian movement. "Now I'm a basket case," he said. "My world revolved around Wiley's philosophy." He had thought Wiley "made the jump to where all of us health food fanatics were going," Collison said.

13   Other Brooks disciples, though disappointed, feel they nevertheless benefitted from their experience. Said a physician who has been on the yellow diet for four months: "I feel very good. I still don't know what the truth is, but I do know that Wiley is a good salesman. So I'll be patient, keep an open mind and continue to observe."

14   "Breatharianism is the understanding of what the body really needs, not whether Wiley eats or doesn't," said James Wahler, 35, who teaches a self-development technique called "rebirthing," in Marin County. "I'm realizing that the less I eat the better I feel." He also suggested that Brooks may have lied for people's own good, to get them to listen.

15   "Everyone has benefitted from what I'm saying," Brooks said. "There will be a food shortage and a lot of unhappy people when they realize that I was trying to save their lives."

Each of the assignments listed below is directed to a different audience, none of whom know much about Breatharianism. What information does each audience need to know? What kinds of details will be the most persuasive? What sort of organization will work best for each purpose and audience?

1. Write a brief radio advertisement for the five-day intensives. What appeals will persuade people to pay $500 each to attend a seminar to learn to eat air?

2. Assume you are a regional Breatharian coordinator. Write a letter to your City Council petitioning for a parade permit that will allow members of your organization to parade down your main street in support of this diet and its lifestyle. What do Council members need to know and understand before they vote for such a permit?

3. You are a former Breatharian who is now unhappy with the diet and its unfulfilled promises. Write a report for the Vice Squad calling for

an investigation into the organization. Convince the investigators that the organization is defrauding local citizens and should be stopped.

After writing these assignments, you might exchange them with those written by some of your classmates. Which ads, petitions, and reports are the most persuasive and why?

KEEPING A JOURNAL (TALKING TO YOURSELF *DOES* HELP)

Many professional writers carry small notebooks with them so they can jot down ideas and impressions for future use. Other people have kept daily logs or diaries for years to record their thoughts for their own enjoyment. In your composition class, you may find it useful to keep a journal that will help you with your writing process, especially in the early stages of prewriting. Journals can also help you to prepare for class discussions and to remember important course material.

You may have kept a journal in another class. There, it may have been called a daybook or learning log or some other name. Although the journal has a variety of uses, it frequently is assigned to encourage you to record your responses to the material read or discussed in class as well as your own thoughts and questions. Most often the journal is kept in a notebook of some kind (spiral is fine, although you may find a prong or ring notebook more convenient because it will allow you to add or remove pages where and when you wish). Even if a journal is not an assigned part of your composition class, it is still a useful notebook for you to keep.

Writers who have found journal writing effective advise trying to write a minimum of three entries a week, with each entry at least a half page. To keep your entries organized, you might start each entry on a new page and date each entry you write. You might also leave the backs of your pages blank so that you can return and respond to an entry at a later date if you wish.

Uses of the Journal

Here are some suggested uses for your journal as you begin and move through the writing process. You may want to experiment with a number of these suggestions to see which are the most productive for you.

1. Use the journal, especially in the first weeks of class, to confront your fears of writing, to conquer the blank page. Write anything you want to—thoughts, observations, notes to yourself, letters home, anything at all. Best your enemy by writing down that witty retort you thought of later and wished you had said. Write about your ideal job, vacation, car, or home. Write a self-portrait or make a list of all the subjects that you are (or would like to become) an "authority" on. The more you write, the easier writing becomes—

or at least, the easier it is to begin writing because, like a sword swallower, you know you have accomplished the act before and lived to tell about it.

2.   Improve your powers of observation. Record interesting snippets of conversations you overhear or catalog noises you hear in a ten-minute period in a crowded place, such as your student center, a bookstore, or a mall. Eat something with multiple layers (a piece of fruit such as an orange) and list all the tastes, textures, and smells you discover. Look around your room and write down a list of everything that is yellow. By becoming sensitive to the sights, sounds, smells, and textures around you, you may find that your powers of description and explanation will expand, enabling you to help your reader "see" what you're talking about in your next essay.

3.   Save your own brilliant ideas. Jot down those bright ideas that might turn into great essays. Or save those thoughts you have now for the essay you know is coming later in the semester so you won't forget them. Expand or elaborate on any ideas you have; you might be able to convert your early thoughts into a paragraph when it's time to start drafting.

4.   Save other people's brilliant ideas. Record interesting quotations, facts, and figures from other writers and thinkers. You may find some of this information useful in one of your later essays. It's also helpful to look at the ways other writers made their words emphatic, moving, and arresting so you can try some of their techniques in your own prose. (Important: Don't forget to note the source of any material you record, so if you do quote any of it in a paper later, you will be able to document it properly.)

5.   Be creative. Write a poem or song or story or joke. Parody the style of someone you've heard or read. Become an inanimate object and complain to the humans around you (for example, what would a soft-drink machine like to say to those folks constantly beating on its stomach?). Become a little green creature from Mars and convince a human to accompany you back to your planet as a specimen of Earthlings (or be the invited guest and explain to the creature why you are definitely not the person to go). The possibilities are endless, so go wild.

6.   Prepare for class. If you've been given a reading assignment (an essay or article or pages from a text, for instance), try a split-page entry. Draw a line down the middle of a page in your journal and on the left side of the page write a summary of what you've read or perhaps list the main points. Then on the right side of the same page, write your responses to the material. Your responses might be your personal reaction to the content (what struck you hardest? why?), or it might be your agreement or disagreement with a particular point or two. Or the material might call up some long-forgotten idea or memory. By thinking about your class material both analytically and personally, you almost certainly will remember it for class discussion. You might also find that a good idea for an essay will arise as you think about the reading assignments in different ways.

7. Record responses to class discussions. A journal is a good place to jot down your reactions to what your teacher and your peers are saying in class. You can ask yourself questions ("What did Megan mean when she said . . . ") or note any confusion ("I got mixed up when . . . ") or record your own reactions ("I disagree with Jason when he argued that . . . "). Again, some of your reactions might become the basis of a good essay.

8. Focus on a problem. You can restate the problem or explore the problem or solve the problem. Writing about a problem often encourages the mind to flow over the information in ways that allow discoveries to happen. Sometimes, too, we don't know exactly what the problem is or how we feel about it until we write about it (you can see the truth of this statement almost every week if you're a reader of advice columns such as "Dear Abby"—invariably someone will write a letter asking for help and end by saying, "Thanks for letting me write; I know now what I should do").

9. Practice audience awareness. Write letters to different companies, praising or panning their product; then write advertising copy for each product. Become the third critic on a popular movie-review program and show the other two commentators why your review of your favorite movie is superior to theirs. Thinking about a specific audience when you write will help you plan the content, organization, and tone of each writing assignment.

10. Describe your own writing process. It's helpful sometimes to record how you go about writing your essays. How do you get started? How much time do you spend getting started? Do you write an "idea" draft or work from an outline? How do you revise? Do you write multiple drafts? These and many other questions may give you a clue to any problems you may have as you write your next essay. If, for example, you see that you're having trouble again and again with conclusions, you can turn to Chapter 4 for some extra help. Sometimes it's hard to see that there's a pattern in our writing process until we've described it several times.

11. Write a progress report. List all the skills you've mastered as the course progresses. You'll be surprised at how much you have learned. Read the list over if you're ever feeling frustrated or discouraged, and take pride in your growth.

12. Become sensitive to language. Keep a record of jokes and puns that play on words. Record people's weird-but-funny uses of language (overheard at the dorm cafeteria: "She was so skinny she was emancipated" and "I'm tired of being the escape goat"). Rewrite some of today's bureaucratic jargon or retread a cliché. Come up with new images of your own. Playing with language in fun or even silly ways may make writing tasks seem less threatening.

13. Write your own textbook. Make notes on material that is important for you to remember. For instance, make your own grammar or punctuation handbook with only those rules you find yourself referring to often. Or keep a list of spelling rules that govern the words you misspell frequently. Writing out the rules in your own words and having a convenient place to refer to them may help you teach yourself quicker than studying any textbook (including this one).

These suggestions are some of the many uses you may find for your journal once you start writing in one on a regular basis. Obviously, not all of the suggestions here will be appropriate for you, but some might be, so you might consider using a set of divider tabs to separate the different functions of your journal (one section for class responses, one section for your own thoughts, one for your own handbook, and so on).

You may find, as some students have, that the journal is especially useful during the first weeks of your writing course when putting pen to paper is often hardest. Many students, however, continue to use the journal throughout the entire course, and others adapt their journals to record their thoughts and responses to their other college courses and experiences. Whether you continue using a journal beyond this course is up to you, but consider trying the journal for at least six weeks. You may find that it will improve your writing skills more than anything else you have tried before.

CHAPTER 1 SUMMARY

Here is a brief summary of what you should know about the prewriting stage of your writing process:

1. Before you begin writing anything, remember that you have valuable ideas to tell your readers.

2. Moreover, it's not enough that these valuable ideas are clear to you, the writer. Your single most important goal is to communicate those ideas clearly to your readers, who cannot know what's in your mind until you tell them.

3. Whenever possible, select a subject to write on that is of great interest to you, and always give yourself more time than you think you'll need to work on your essay.

4. Try a variety of prewriting techniques to help you find your essay's purpose and a narrowed, specific focus.

5. Review your audience's knowledge of and attitudes toward your topic before you begin your first draft; ask yourself questions such as "Who needs to know about this topic, and why?"

6. Consider keeping a journal to help you explore good ideas and possible topics for writing in your composition class.

2

THE THESIS STATEMENT

•
•
•

The famous American author Thomas Wolfe had a simple formula for beginning his writing: "Just put a sheet of paper in the typewriter and start bleeding." For some writers, the "bleeding" method works well. You may find that, indeed, you are one of those writers who must begin by freewriting or by writing an entire "discovery draft"* to find your purpose and focus—you must write yourself into your topic, so to speak. Other writers are more structured; they may prefer prewriting in lists, maps, or cubes. Sometimes writers begin certain projects by composing one way, whereas other kinds of writing tasks profit from another method. There is no right or wrong way to find a topic or to begin writing; simply try to find the methods that work best for you.

Let's assume at this point that you have identified a topic you wish to write about—perhaps you found it by working through one of the prewriting activities mentioned in Chapter 1 or by writing in your journal. Perhaps you had an important idea you have been wanting to write about for some time, or perhaps the assignment in your class suggested the topic to you. Suppose that through one of these avenues you have focused on a topic and you have

* If you do begin with a discovery draft, you may wish to turn at this point to the manuscript suggestions on pages 102–103 in Chapter 5.

given some thought to a possible audience for your paper. You may now find it helpful to formulate a *working thesis*.

WHAT IS A THESIS? WHAT DOES A "WORKING THESIS" DO?

The thesis statement declares the main point or controlling idea of your entire essay. Frequently located near the beginning of a short essay, the thesis answers the questions "What is the subject of this essay?"; "What is the writer's opinion on this subject?"; "What is the writer's purpose in this essay?" (for example; to explain something? to argue a position? to move people to action? to entertain?).

Consider a "working thesis" a statement of your main point in its trial or rough-draft form. Allow it to "work" for you as you move from prewriting through drafts and revision. Your working thesis may begin as a very simple sentence. For example, one of the freewriting exercises on nature in Chapter 1 (pages 8–9) might lead to a working thesis such as "Our college needs an on-campus recycling center." Such a working thesis states an opinion about the subject (the need for a center) and suggests what the essay will do (give arguments for building such a center). Similarly, the prewriting list on jogging (page 7) might lead to a working thesis such as "Before beginning a successful jogging program, novice runners must learn a series of warm-up and cool-down exercises." This statement not only tells the writer's opinion and purpose (the value of the exercises) but also indicates an audience (novice runners).

A working thesis statement can be your most valuable organizational tool. Once you have thought about your essay's main point and purpose, you can begin to draft your paper to accomplish your goals. *Everything in your essay should support your thesis.* Consequently, if you write your working thesis statement at the top of your first draft and refer to it often, your chances of drifting away from your purpose should be reduced.

CAN A "WORKING THESIS" CHANGE?

It's important for you to know at this point that there may be a difference between the working thesis that appears in your rough drafts and your final thesis. As you begin drafting, you may have one main idea in mind that surfaced from your prewriting activities. But as you write, you discover that what you really want to write about is different. Perhaps you discover that one particular part of your essay is really what you want to concentrate on (instead of covering three or four problems you have with your current job, for instance, you decide you want to explore in depth only the difficulties with your boss), or perhaps in the course of writing you find another approach to your subject more satisfying or persuasive (explaining how employees may avoid problems with a particular kind of difficult boss as opposed to describing various kinds of difficult bosses in your field).

Changing directions is not uncommon: *writing is an act of discovery.* Frequently we don't know exactly what we think or what we want to say until we write it. A working thesis appears in your early drafts to help you focus and organize your essay; don't feel it's carved in stone.

A warning comes with this advice, however. If you do write yourself into another essay—that is, if you discover that as you write you are finding a better topic or main point to make, consider this piece of writing a "discovery draft," extended prewriting that has helped you find your real focus. Occasionally, your direction changes so slightly that you can rework or expand your thesis to accommodate your new ideas. But more frequently you may find that it's necessary to begin another draft with your newly discovered working thesis as the controlling idea. When this is the case, don't be discouraged—this kind of "reseeing" or revision of your topic is a common practice among experienced writers (for more advice on revising as rethinking, see Chapter 5). Don't be tempted at this point to leave your original thesis in an essay that has clearly changed its point, purpose, or approach—in other words, don't try to pass off an old head on the body of a new statue! Remember that ultimately you want your thesis to guide your readers rather than confuse them by promising an essay they can't find as they read on.

GUIDELINES FOR WRITING A GOOD THESIS

To help you draft your thesis statement, here is some advice:

A good thesis states the writer's clearly defined opinion on some subject. You must tell your reader what you think. Don't dodge the issue; present your opinion specifically and precisely. For example, if you were asked to write a thesis statement expressing your position on the national law that designates twenty-one the legal minimum age to purchase or consume alcohol, the first three theses listed below would be confusing:

Poor Many people have different opinions on whether people under twenty-one should be able to drink alcohol, and I agree with some of them. [The writer's opinion on the issue is not clear to the reader.]

Poor The question of whether we need a national law governing the minimum age to drink alcohol is a controversial issue in many states. [This statement might introduce the thesis, but the writer has still avoided stating a clear opinion on the issue.]

Poor I want to give my opinion on the national law that sets twenty-one as the legal age to drink alcohol and the reasons I feel this way. [What is the writer's opinion? The reader still doesn't know.]

Better To reduce the number of highway fatalities, our country needs to enforce the national law that designates twenty-one as the legal minimum age to purchase and consume alcohol. [The writer clearly states an opinion that will be supported in the essay.]

Better   The legal minimum age for purchasing alcohol should be eighteen rather than twenty-one. [Again, the writer has asserted a clear position on the issue that will be argued in the essay.]

A good thesis asserts one main idea. Many essays drift into confusion because the writer is trying to explain or argue two different, large issues in one essay. You can't effectively ride two horses at once; pick one main idea and explain or argue it in convincing detail.

Poor   The proposed no-smoking ordinance in our town will violate a number of our citizens' civil rights, and no one has proved secondary smoke is dangerous anyway. [This thesis contains two main assertions—the ordinance's violation of rights and secondary smoke's lack of danger—that require two different kinds of supporting evidence.]

Better   The proposed no-smoking ordinance in our town will violate our civil rights. [This essay will show the various ways the ordinance will infringe on personal liberties.]

Better   The most recent U.S. Health Department studies claiming that secondary smoke is dangerous to nonsmokers are based on faulty research. [This essay will also focus on one issue: the validity of the studies on secondary smoke danger.]

Poor   High school athletes shouldn't have to maintain a certain grade-point average to participate in school sports, and the value of sports is often worth the lower academic average. [Again, this essay moves in two different directions.]

Better   High school athletes shouldn't have to maintain a certain grade-point average to participate in school sports. [This essay will focus on one issue: reasons why a particular average shouldn't be required.]

Better   For some students, participation in sports is often more valuable than achieving a high grade-point average. [This essay will focus on why the benefits of sports may sometimes outweigh those of academics.]

Incidentally, at this point you may recall from your high school days a rule about always expressing your thesis in one sentence. Writing teachers often insist on this rule to help you avoid the double-assertion problem discussed above. Although not all essays have one-sentence theses, many do, and it's a good habit to strive for in this early stage of your writing.

A good thesis has something worthwhile to say. Although it's true that almost any subject can be made interesting with the right treatment, some subjects are more predictable and therefore more boring than others. Before you write your thesis, think hard about your subject: does your position lend itself to trite, shallow, or overly obvious ideas? For example, most readers would find the following theses tiresome unless the writers had some original method of developing their essays:

Poor   Dogs have always been man's best friends. [This essay might be full of ho-hum clichés about dogs' faithfulness to their masters.]

Poor   Friendship is a wonderful thing. [Again, watch out for tired truisms that restate the obvious.]

Poor   Food in my dorm is horrible. [Although this essay might be enlivened by some vividly repulsive imagery, the subject itself is ancient.]

Frequently in composition classes you will be asked to write about yourself; after all, you are the world's authority on that subject, and you have many significant ideas and interests to talk about whose subject matter will naturally intrigue your readers. However, some topics that you may consider writing about won't necessarily appeal to other readers because the material is simply too personal or restricted to be of general interest. In these cases, it often helps to universalize the essay's thesis so your readers can also identify with or learn something about the general subject, while learning something about you at the same time:

Poor   The four children in my family have completely different personalities. [This statement may be true, but would anyone but the children's parents really be fascinated with this topic?]

Better   Birth order can influence children's personalities in startling ways. [The writer is wiser to offer this controversial statement, which is of more interest to readers than the preceding one because most readers have brothers and sisters of their own. The writer can then illustrate her claims with examples from her own family, and from other families, if she wishes.]

In other words, try to select a subject that will interest, amuse, challenge, persuade, or enlighten your readers. If your subject itself is commonplace, find a unique approach or an unusual, perhaps even controversial, point of view. If your subject is intensely personal, ask yourself if the topic alone will be sufficiently interesting to readers; if not, think about universalizing the thesis to include your audience. Remember that a good thesis should encourage readers to read on with enthusiasm rather than invite groans of "not this again" or shrugs of "so what."

A good thesis is limited to fit the assignment. Your thesis should show that you've narrowed your subject matter to an appropriate size for your essay. Don't allow your thesis to promise more of a discussion than you can adequately deliver in a short essay. You want an in-depth treatment of your subject, not a superficial one. Certainly you may take on important issues in your essays; don't feel you must limit your topics to local or personal sub-jects. But one simply cannot refight Vietnam or effectively defend U.S. foreign policy in Central America in five to eight paragraphs. Focus your essay on an important part of a broader subject that interests you. (For a review of ways to narrow and focus your subject, see pp. 6–18.)

Poor   Nuclear power should be banned as an energy source in this country. [Can the writer give the broad subject of nuclear power a fair treat-ment in three to five pages?]

Better   Because of its poor safety record during the past two years, the Collin County nuclear power plant should be closed. [This writer could probably argue this focused thesis in a short essay.]

Poor   The parking permit system at this university should be completely re-vised. [An essay calling for the revision of the parking permit system would involve discussion of permits for various kinds of students, fac-ulty, administrators, staff, visitors, delivery personnel, disabled per-sons, and so forth. Therefore, the thesis is probably too broad for a short essay.]

Better   Because of the complicated application process, the parking permit system at this university penalizes disabled students. [This thesis is focused on a particular problem and could be argued in a short paper.]

Poor   Black artists have contributed a lot to American culture. ["Black artists," "culture," and "a lot" cover more ground than can be dealt with in one short essay.]

Better   Scott Joplin was a major influence in the development of the uniquely American music called ragtime. [This thesis is more specifically de-fined.]

    A good thesis is clearly stated in specific terms. More than anything, a vague thesis reflects lack of clarity in the writer's mind and almost inevitably leads to an essay that talks around the subject but never makes a coherent point. Try to avoid words whose meanings are imprecise or those that depend largely on personal interpretation, such as "interesting," "good," and "bad."

Poor   The women's movement is good for our country. [What group does the writer refer to? How is it good? For whom?]

Better   The Colorado Women's Party is working to ensure the benefits of equal pay for equal work for both males and females in our state. [This tells who will benefit and how—clearly defining the thesis.]

Poor   Registration is a big hassle. [No clear idea is communicated here. How much trouble is a "hassle"?]

Better   Registration's alphabetical fee-paying system is inefficient. [The issue is specified.]

Poor   Living in an apartment for the first time can teach you many things about taking care of yourself. ["Things" and "taking care of yourself" are both too vague—what specific ideas does the writer want to discuss? And who is the "you" the writer has in mind?]

Better   By living in an apartment, freshmen can learn valuable lessons in financial planning and time management. [The thesis is now clearly defined and directed.]

A good thesis is clearly located, often in the first or second paragraph. Many students are hesitant to spell out a thesis at the beginning of an essay. To quote one student, "I feel as if I'm giving everything away." Although you may feel uncomfortable "giving away" the main point so soon, the alternative of waiting until the last page to present your thesis can seriously weaken your essay.

Without an assertion of what you are trying to prove, your reader does not know how to assess the supporting details your essay presents. For example, if your roommate comes home one afternoon and points out that the roof on your apartment leaks, the rent is too high, and the closet space is too small, you may agree but you may also be confused. Does your roommate want you to call the owner or is this merely a gripe session? How should you respond? On the other hand, if your roommate first announces that he or she wants to move to a new place, you can put the discussion of the roof, rent, and closets into its proper context and react accordingly. Similarly, you write an essay to have a specific effect on your readers. You won't have a chance of producing this effect unless the readers understand what you are trying to do.

Granted, some essays whose position is unmistakably obvious from the outset can get by with a strongly *implied thesis,* and it's true that some essays, often those written by professional writers, are organized to build dramatically to a climax. But if you are an inexperienced writer, the best choice at this point still may be to give a clear statement of your main idea. It is, after all, your responsibility to make your purpose clear, with as little expense of time and energy on the readers' part as possible. Readers should not be forced to puzzle out your essay's main point—it's your job to tell them.

Remember: an essay is not a detective story, so don't keep your readers in suspense until the last minute. Until you feel comfortable with more sophisticated patterns of organization, plan to put your clearly worded thesis statement near the beginning of your essay.

AVOIDING COMMON ERRORS IN THESIS STATEMENTS

Here are five mistakes to avoid when forming your thesis statements:

1. Don't make your thesis merely an announcement of your subject matter or a description of your intentions. State an attitude toward the subject.

Poor   The subject of this theme is my experience with a pet boa constrictor. [This is an announcement of the subject, not a thesis.]

Poor   I'm going to discuss boa constrictors as pets. [This represents a statement of intention but not a thesis.]

Better   Boa constrictors do not make healthy indoor pets. [The writer states an opinion that will be explained and defended in the essay.]

Better   My pet boa constrictor, Sir Pent, was a much better bodyguard than my dog, Fang. [The writer states an opinion that will be explained and illustrated in the essay.]

2. Don't clutter your thesis with expressions such as "in my opinion," "I believe," and "in this essay I'll argue that. . . ." These unnecessary phrases weaken your thesis statement because they often make you sound timid or uncertain. This is your essay; therefore, the opinions expressed are obviously yours. Be forceful: speak directly, with conviction.

Poor   My opinion is that the federal government should devote more money to solar energy research.

Poor   My thesis states that the federal government should devote more money to solar energy research.

Better   The federal government should devote more money to solar energy research.

Poor   In this essay I will present lots of reasons why horse racing should not be legalized in Texas.

Better   Horse racing should not be legalized in Texas.

3. Don't be unreasonable. Making irrational or oversimplified claims will not persuade your reader that you have a thorough understanding of the issue. Don't insult any reader; avoid irresponsible charges, name calling, and profanity.

Poor   Radical religious fanatics across the nation are trying to impose their right-wing views by censoring high school library books. [Words such as "radical," "fanatics," "right-wing," and "censoring" will antagonize many readers immediately.]

Better   Only local school board members—not religious leaders or parents—should decide which books high school libraries should order.

Poor   Too many corrupt books in our high school libraries selected by liberal or atheistic educators are undermining the morals of our youth. [Again, some readers will be offended.]

Better   To ensure that high school libraries contain books that reflect community standards, parents should have a voice in selecting new titles.

4. Don't merely state a fact. A thesis is an assertion of opinion that leads to discussion. Don't select an idea that is self-evident or dead-ended.

Poor   Child abuse is a terrible problem. [Yes, of course; who wouldn't agree that child abuse is terrible?]

Better   Child-abuse laws in this state are too lenient for repeat offenders. [This thesis will lead to a discussion in which supporting arguments and evidence will be presented.]

Poor   Advertisers often use sex in their ads to sell products. [True, but how could this essay be turned into something more than a list describing one ad after another?]

Better   A number of liquor advertisers, well known for using pictures of sexy models to sell their products, are now using special graphics to send subliminal sexual messages to their readers. [This claim is controversial and will require persuasive supporting evidence.]

Better   Although long criticized for their sexist portrayal of women in television commercials, the auto industry is just as often guilty of stereotyping men as brainless idiots unable to make a decision. [This thesis makes a point that may lead to an interesting discussion.]

5. Don't express your thesis in the form of a question unless the answer is already obvious to the reader.

Poor   Why should every college student be required to take two years of foreign language?

Better   Chemistry majors should be exempt from the foreign language requirement.

Remember:
Many times writers "discover" a better thesis near the end of their first draft. That's fine—consider that draft a prewriting or focusing exercise and begin another draft, using the newly discovered thesis as a starting point.

▶ PRACTICING WHAT YOU'VE LEARNED

A. Identify each of the following thesis statements as adequate or inadequate. If the thesis is weak or insufficient in some way, explain the problem.

1. I think *Dances with Wolves* is a really interesting movie that everyone would enjoy.

2. Which cars are designed better, the Japanese imports or those made in America?

3. Some people think that college entrance examinations are biased against women and minorities.

4. My essay will tell you how to apply for a college loan with the least amount of trouble.

5. During the fall term, final examinations should be given before the Winter break, not after the holidays as they are now.

6. Raising the cost of tuition will be a terrible burden on the students and won't do anything to help the quality of education at this school.

7. Bicycle riding is my favorite exercise because it's so good for me.

8. The passage of the newly proposed health-care bill for the elderly will lead to socialized medicine in this country.

9. Persons over seventy-five should be required to renew their driver's licenses every year.

10. Having a close friend you can talk to is very important.

B. Rewrite the sentences below so that each one is a clear thesis statement. Be prepared to explain why you changed the sentences as you did.

1. Applying for a job can be a negative experience.

2. Skiing is a lot of fun, but it can be expensive and dangerous.

3. There are many advantages and disadvantages to the county's new voting machines.

4. The deregulation of the telephone system has been one big headache.

5. In this paper I will debate the pros and cons of the controversial motorcycle helmet law.

6. We need to do something about the billboard clutter on the main highway into town.

7. The gun-control laws in this country need to be rewritten.

8. People who want to change our team's name from the Redskins to the Eagles should lighten up.

9. In my opinion, Santa Barbara is a fantastic vacation spot.

10. The Civil Rights Movement of the 1960s had a tremendous effect on this country.

▶ ASSIGNMENT

Narrow the subject and write one good thesis sentence for five of the following topics:

1. A political or social issue

2. College or high school

3. Family

4. A hobby or pastime

5. A recent book or movie

6. Vacations

7. An environmental issue

8. A current fad or fashion

9. A job or profession

10. A rule, law, or regulation

USING THE ESSAY MAP*

Many thesis sentences will benefit from the addition of an *essay map*, a brief statement in the introductory paragraph introducing the major points to be discussed in the essay. Consider the analogy of beginning a trip by checking your map to see where you are headed. Similarly, an essay map allows the readers to know in advance where you, the writer, will be taking them in the essay.

Let's suppose you have been assigned the task of praising or criticizing some aspect of your campus. You decide that your thesis will be "The campus bookstore is the worst place in town to buy textbooks." Although your thesis does take a stand ("worst place"), your reader will not know why the bookstore is so poor or what points you will cover in your argument. With

---

* I am indebted to Susan Wittig for this useful concept, introduced in *Steps to Structure: An Introduction to Composition and Rhetoric* (Cambridge, MA: Winthrop Publishers, 1975), pp. 125–126.

an essay map added, the reader will have a brief but specific idea where the essay is going and how it will be developed:

Essay map (underlined)

Thesis: The campus bookstore is the worst place in town to buy textbooks. The unreasonable prices, the lack of qualified employees, and the constant book shortages discourage all but the most loyal customers.

Thanks to the essay map, the reader knows that the essay will discuss the store's prices, employees, and book shortages.

Here's another example—this time let's assume you decided to praise your school's Study Skills Center:

Essay map (underlined)

Thesis: The Study Skills Center is an excellent place for freshmen to receive help with basic courses. The Center's numerous free services, well-trained tutors, and variety of supplementary learning materials can often mean the difference between academic success and failure for many students.

After reading the introductory paragraph, the reader knows the essay will discuss the Center's services, tutors, and supplementary learning aids. In other words, the thesis statement defines the main purpose of your essay, and the essay map indicates the route you will take to accomplish that purpose.

The essay map often follows the thesis, but it can also appear before it. It is, in fact, frequently part of the thesis statement itself, as illustrated in the following examples:

Thesis with underlined essay map

Unreasonable prices, unqualified employees, and constant shortages make the campus bookstore a terrible place to buy texts.

Thesis with underlined essay map

Because of its free services, well-trained tutors, and useful learning aids, the Study Skills Center is an excellent place for freshmen seeking academic help.

Thesis with underlined essay map

For those freshmen who need extra help with their basic courses, the Study Skills Center is one of the best resources because of its numerous free services, well-trained tutors, and variety of useful learning aids.

In addition to suggesting the main points of the essay, the map provides two other benefits. It will provide a set of guidelines for organizing your essay, and it will help keep you from wandering off into areas only vaguely related to your thesis. A clearly written thesis statement and essay map provide a skeletal outline for the sequence of paragraphs in your essay, frequently with one body paragraph devoted to each main point mentioned in your map. (Chapter 3, on paragraphs, will explain in more detail the relationships among the thesis, the map, and the body of your essay.) Note that the number of points in the essay map may vary, although three or four may be the number found most often in 500- to 800-word essays. (More than four main points in a short essay may result in underdeveloped paragraphs; see pp. 60–62 for additional information.)

Some important advice: although essay maps can be helpful to both writers and readers, they can also sound too mechanical, repetitive, or obvious. If you choose to use a map, always strive to blend it with your thesis as smoothly as possible.

Poor   The campus bookstore is a bad place to buy texts for three reasons. The reasons are high prices, unqualified employees, and book shortages.

Better   Unreasonable prices, unqualified employees, and book shortages combine to give the campus bookstore its well-deserved reputation as the worst place in town to buy texts.

If you feel your essay map is too obvious or mechanical, try using it only in your rough drafts to help you organize your essay. Once you're sure it isn't necessary to clarify your thesis or to guide your reader, you might consider dropping it from your final draft.

▶ PRACTICING WHAT YOU'VE LEARNED

A. Identify the thesis and the essay map in the following sentences by underlining the map.

1. *Citizen Kane* deserves to appear on a list of "Top Movies of All Times" because of its excellent ensemble acting, its fast-paced script, and its innovative editing.

2. Our state should double the existing fines for first-offense drunk drivers. Such a move would lower the number of accidents, cut the costs of insurance, and increase the state revenues for highway maintenance.

3. To guarantee sound construction, lower costs, and personalized design, more people should consider building their own log cabin home.

4. Apartment living is preferable to dorm living because it's cheaper, quieter, and more luxurious.

5. Not everyone can become an astronaut. To qualify, a person must have intelligence, determination, and training.

6. Through unscrupulous uses of propaganda and secret assassination squads, Hitler was able to take control of an economically depressed Germany.

7. Because it builds muscles, increases circulation, and burns harmful fatty tissue, weight lifting is a sport that benefits the entire body.

8. The new tax bill will not radically reform the loophole-riddled revenue system: deductions on secondary residences will remain, real estate tax shelters are untouched, and nonprofit health organizations will be taxed.

9. Avocados make excellent plants for children. They're inexpensive to buy, easy to root, quick to sprout, and fun to grow.

10. His spirit of protest and clever phrasing blended into unusual musical arrangements have made Bob Dylan a recording giant for over twenty years.

B. Review the thesis statements you wrote for the Assignment on page 41. Write an essay map for each thesis statement. You may place the map before or after the thesis, or you may make it part of the thesis itself. Identify which part is the thesis and which is the essay map by underlining the map.

ASSIGNMENT

Use one of the following quotations to help you think of a subject for an essay of your own. Don't merely repeat the quotation itself as your thesis statement but, rather, allow the quotation to lead you to your subject and a main point of your own creation that is appropriately narrowed and focused. Don't forget to designate an audience for your essay, a group of readers who need or want to hear what you have to say.

1. "Few things are harder to put up with than the annoyance of a good example"—Mark Twain, writer and humorist.

2. "It is amazing how complete is the delusion that beauty is goodness"—Leo Tolstoy, writer.

3. "Flattery is like a cigarette; it is all right if you don't inhale"—Adlai Stevenson, senator and statesman.

4. "Sports do not build character. They reveal it"—Heywood Hale Broun, sportscaster.

5. "It is never too late to give up your prejudices"—Henry Thoreau, writer and naturalist.

6. "When a thing is funny, search it carefully for a hidden truth"—George Bernard Shaw, writer.

7. "I am a great believer in luck, and I find the harder I work the more I have of it"—Stephen Leacock, economist and humorist.

8. "Noncooperation with evil is as much a moral obligation as is cooperation with good"—Martin Luther King, Jr., statesman and civil-rights activist.

9. "Though familiarity may not breed contempt, it takes the edge off admiration"—William Hazlitt, writer.

10. "In this world there are only two tragedies. One is not getting what one wants, and the other is getting it"—Oscar Wilde, writer.

11. "It is never too late to be what one might have been"—George Eliot, writer.

12. "Happiness is not something you experience; it's something you remember"—Oscar Levant, writer.

13. "People change and forget to tell each other"—Lillian Hellman, writer.

14. "Nobody can make you feel inferior without your consent"—Eleanor Roosevelt, stateswoman.

15. "When a person declares that he's going to college, he's announcing that he needs four more years of coddling before he can face the real world"—Al Capp, creator of the *Li'l Abner* cartoon.

16. "Family jokes are the bond that keeps most families alive"—Stella Benson, writer.

17. "Nobody ever went broke underestimating the intelligence of the American public"—H.L. Mencken, writer and critic.

18. "Even if you are on the right track, you will get run over if you just sit there"—Will Rogers, humorist and author.

CHAPTER 2 SUMMARY

Here's a brief review of what you need to know about the thesis statement:

1. A thesis statement declares the main point of your essay; it tells the reader what clearly defined opinion you hold.

2. Everything in your essay should support your thesis statement.

3. A good thesis statement asserts one main idea, narrowed to fit the assignment, and is stated in clear, specific terms.

4. A good thesis statement makes a reasonable claim about a topic that is of interest to its readers as well as to its writer.

5. A good thesis statement is often presented near the beginning of the essay, usually in the first or second paragraph, or is so strongly implied that readers cannot miss the writer's main point.

6. A "working" or trial thesis is an excellent organizing tool to use as you begin drafting because it can help you decide which ideas to include.

7. Because writing is an act of discovery, you may write yourself into a better thesis statement by the end of your first draft. Don't hesitate to begin a new draft with the new thesis statement.

8. Some writers may profit from using an essay map, a brief statement accompanying the thesis that introduces the supporting points discussed in the body of the essay.

3

THE BODY PARAGRAPHS

•
•
•

The middle or *body* of your essay is composed of paragraphs that support the thesis statement. By citing examples, explaining causes, offering reasons, or using other strategies in these paragraphs, you supply enough specific evidence to persuade your reader that the opinion expressed in your thesis is a sensible one. Each paragraph in the body usually presents and develops one main point in the discussion of your thesis. Generally, but not always, a new body paragraph signals another major point in the discussion.

PLANNING THE BODY OF YOUR ESSAY

Many writers like to have a plan before they begin drafting the body of their essay. To help you create a plan, first look at your thesis. If you used an essay map, as suggested in Chapter 2, you may find that the points mentioned there will provide the basis for the body paragraphs of your essay. For example, recall from Chapter 2 the thesis and essay map praising the Study Skills Center (p. 42): "Because of its free services, well-trained tutors, and useful learning aids, the Study Skills Center is an excellent place for freshmen seeking academic help." Your plan for developing the body of your essay might look like this:

Body paragraph one: discussion of free services
Body paragraph two: discussion of tutors
Body paragraph three: discussion of learning aids

At this point in your writing process you may wish to sketch in some of the supporting evidence you will include in each paragraph. You might find it helpful to go back to your prewriting activities (listing, looping, freewriting, mapping, cubing, and so on) to see what ideas surfaced then. Adding some examples and supporting details might make a scratch outline of the Study Skills paper appear like this:

I.   Free services

    A.   Mini-course on improving study skills

    B.   Tutoring < composition / math

    C.   Weekly seminars < stress management / test anxiety / building vocabulary

    D.   Testing for learning disabilities

II. Tutors

    A.   Top graduate students in their fields
    B.   Experienced teachers
    C.   Some bilingual
    D.   Have taken training course at Center

III. Learning aids

    A.   Supplementary texts
    B.   Workbooks
    C.   Audiovisual aids

Notice that this sketch is an *informal* or *scratch outline* rather than a *formal outline*—that is, it doesn't have strictly parallel parts nor is it expressed in complete sentences. Unless your teacher requests a formal sentence or topic outline, don't feel you must make one at this early stage. Just consider using the scratch outline to plot out a tentative plan that will help you start your first draft.

Here's an example of a scratch outline at work: let's suppose you have been asked to write about your most prized possession—and you've chosen your 1966 Mustang, a car you have restored. You already have some ideas but as yet they're scattered and too few to make an interesting, well-developed essay. You try a scratch outline, jotting down your ideas thus far:

I. Car is special because it was a gift from Dad

II. Fun to drive

III. Looks great—new paint job

IV. Engine in top condition

V. Custom features

VI. Car shows—fun to be part of

After looking at your scratch outline, you see that some of your categories overlap and could be part of the same discussion. For example, your thoughts about the engine are actually part of the discussion of "fun to drive" and "custom features" are what make the car look great. Moreover, the outline may help you discover new ideas—custom features could be divided into those on the interior as well as those on the exterior of the car. The revised scratch outline might look like this:

I. Gift from Dad

II. Fun to drive
   A. Engine
   B. Steering

III. Looks great
   A. New paint job
   B. Custom features
      1. exterior
      2. interior

IV. Car shows

You could continue playing with the scratch outline, even moving big chunks of it around; for example, you might decide that what really makes the car so special is that it was a graduation gift from your Dad and that is the note you want to end on. So you move "I. Gift from Dad" down to the last position in your outline.

The important point to remember about a scratch or working outline is that it is there to help you—not control you. The value of a scratch outline is its ability to help you plan, to help you see logical connections between your ideas, and to help you see obvious places to add new ideas and details. (The scratch outline is also handy to keep around in case you're interrupted for a long period while you're drafting; you can always check the outline to see where you were and where you were going when you stopped.) In other words, *don't be intimidated by the outline!*

Here's one more sample scratch outline, this time for the thesis and essay map on the campus bookstore, from Chapter 2:

> Thesis-map: Unreasonable prices, unqualified employees, and book shortages combine to give the Campus Bookstore its well-deserved reputation of the worst place in town to buy texts.

I.   Unreasonable prices

    A.   Too expensive compared to other stores
    B.   Sudden markups
    C.   Cheap buy-back policy

II.   Unqualified personnel

    A.   Clerks with little knowledge of prices or book orders
    B.   Untrained cashiers

III.   Book shortages

    A.   Too few books ordered
    B.   Wrong books ordered
    C.   Wrong edition ordered
    D.   Late orders

Of course, you may have more than three points to make in your essay. And, on occasion, you may need more than one paragraph to discuss a single point. For instance, you might discover that you need two paragraphs to explain fully the services at the Study Skills Center (for advice on splitting the discussion of a single point into two or more paragraphs, see p. 65). At this stage, you needn't bother trying to guess whether you'll need more than one paragraph per point; just use the outline to get going. Most writers don't know how much they have to say before they begin writing—and that's fine because writing itself is an act of discovery and learning.

When you are ready to begin drafting, read Chapter 5 for advice on composing and revising. Remember, too, that Chapter 5 contains suggestions for beating Writer's Block, should this condition arise while you are planning or drafting any part of your essay.

COMPOSING THE BODY PARAGRAPHS

There are many ways to organize and develop body paragraphs. Paragraphs developed by such common patterns as example, comparison, definition, and so forth will be discussed in specific chapters in Part Two; at this point, however, here are some comments about the general nature of all good body paragraphs that should help as you draft your essay.

> Most of the body paragraphs in your essay will profit from a focused *topic sentence*. In addition, body paragraphs should have adequate *development, unity, and coherence*.

THE TOPIC SENTENCE

Most body paragraphs present one main point in your discussion, expressed in a *topic sentence*. The topic sentence of a body paragraph has three important functions:

1. It supports the thesis by clearly stating a main point in the discussion.

2. It announces what the paragraph will be about.

3. It controls the subject matter of the paragraph. The entire discussion—the examples, details, and explanations—in a particular paragraph must directly relate to and support the topic sentence.

Think of a body paragraph (or a single paragraph) as a kind of mini-essay in itself. The topic sentence is, in a sense, a smaller thesis. It too asserts one main idea on a limited subject that the writer can explain or argue in the rest of the paragraph. Like the thesis, the topic sentence should be stated in as specific language as possible.

To see how a topic sentence works in a body paragraph, study this sample:

Essay thesis: The Study Skills Center is an excellent place for freshmen who need academic help.

Topic Sentence
1. The topic sentence supports the thesis by stating a main point (one reason why the Center provides excellent academic help).
2. The topic sentence announces the subject matter of the paragraph (a variety of free services that improve basic skills).

The Center offers students a variety of free services designed to improve basic skills. Freshmen who discover their study habits are poor, for instance, may enroll in a six-week mini-course in study skills that offers advice on such topics as how to read a text, take notes, and organize material for review. Students whose math or writing skills are below par can sign up for free tutoring sessions held five days a week throughout each semester. In addition, the Center presents weekly seminars on special topics such as stress management and overcoming test anxiety for those students who are finding college more of a

3. The topic sentence controls the subject matter (all the examples—the mini-course, the tutoring, the seminars, and the testing—support the claim of the topic sentence).

nerve-wracking experience than they expected; other students can attend evening seminars in such worthwhile endeavors as vocabulary building or spelling tips. Finally, the Center offers a series of tests to identify the presence of any learning disabilities, such as dyslexia, that might prevent a student from succeeding academically. With such a variety of free services, the Center could help almost any student.

Here's another example from the essay on the bookstore:

Essay thesis: The Campus Bookstore deserves its reputation as the worst place in town for students to buy their texts.

Topic Sentence
1. The topic sentence supports the thesis by stating a main point (one reason why the store is a bad place to buy texts).
2. The topic sentence announces the subject matter of the paragraph (unreasonable pricing policies).
3. The topic sentence controls the subject matter (all the examples—the high prices, the mark-ups, and the refund problems—support the claim of the topic sentence).

The Campus Bookstore's unreasonable pricing policies discourage potential customers. In the first place, the store's prices are, on the average, far higher than those of the other two bookstores that carry college texts. For instance, while the basic text required for Introduction to Biology costs $18.95 at both other stores, it's marked up to $21.98 at the campus store. Similarly, the required freshman math book is $16.95 at the campus store whereas it's $14.50 elsewhere. Moreover, the prices at the store don't remain constant during the book-buying period. One day a book might be $11.95 and the next day it's $13.95. The campus store management defends this policy by noting it reflects "shifting overhead costs," but it's bothersome for the students who are trying to plan their tight budgets. And if high, fluctuating prices aren't bad enough, the campus store's buy-back policy is terrible. The refund on returned books is 10 percent lower than that at the other stores, and the semester's refund period is but three days, often too brief a time for students to finish arranging their class schedules. Policies such as these often drive customers to the store's competitors.

Always be sure your topic sentences actually support the particular thesis of your essay. For example, the second topic sentence presented here doesn't belong in the essay promised by the thesis:

Thesis: Elk hunting should be permitted because it financially aids people in our state.

Topic Sentences

1. Fees for hunting licenses help pay for certain free, state-supported social services.

2. Hunting helps keep the elk population under control.

3. Elk hunting offers a means of obtaining free food for those people with low incomes.

Although topic sentence 2 is about elk and although it may be true, it doesn't support the thesis's emphasis on financial aid and therefore should be tossed out of this essay.

Here's another example:

> **Thesis:** In the past fifty years, movie stars have often tried to change the direction of America's politics.

Topic Sentences

1. During World War II stars sold liberty bonds to support the country's war effort.

2. Many stars refused to cooperate with the blacklisting of their colleagues in the 1950s.

3. Some stars were actively involved in protests against the Vietnam War.

4. More recently, stars have appeared in Congress criticizing the lack of legislative help for struggling farmers.

Topic sentences 2, 3, and 4 all show how stars have tried to effect a change. But topic sentence 1 says only that stars sold bonds to support, not *change,* the political direction of the nation. Although it does show stars involved in politics, it doesn't illustrate the claim of this particular thesis.

Sometimes a topic sentence needs only to be rewritten or slightly recast to fit:

> **Thesis:** The recent tuition hike will discourage students from attending our college.

Topic Sentences

1. Students already pay more here than at other in-state schools.

2. Out-of-state students would have to pay an additional "penalty" to attend.

3. Tuition funds should be used to give teachers raises.

As written, topic sentence 3 doesn't show why students won't want to attend the school. However, a rewritten topic sentence does support the thesis:

3. Because the tuition money will not be used for teachers' salaries, many top professors may take job offers elsewhere, and their best students may follow them there.

In other words, always check carefully to make sure that *all* your topic sentences clearly support your thesis's assertion.

Focusing Your Topic Sentence

A vague, fuzzy, or unfocused topic sentence most often leads to a paragraph that touches only on the surface of its subject or that wanders away from the writer's main idea. On the other hand, a topic sentence that is tightly focused and stated precisely will not only help the reader to understand the point of the paragraph but will also help you select, organize, and develop your supporting details.

Look, for example, at these unfocused topic sentences and their revisions:

Unfocused   Too many people treat animals badly in experiments. (What people? Badly how? What kinds of experiments?)

Focused   The cosmetic industry often harms animals in unnecessary experiments designed to test their products.

Unfocused   Grades are an unfair pain in the neck. (Again, the focus is too broad: all grades? Unfair how?)

Focused   Course grades based solely on one term paper don't accurately measure a student's knowledge of the subject.

Unfocused   Getting the right job is important and can lead to rewarding experiences. (Note both vague language and a double focus—"important" and "can lead to rewarding experiences.")

Focused   Getting the right job can lead to an improved sense of self-esteem.

Before you practice writing focused topic sentences, you may wish to review pages 33–39, the advice on composing good thesis statements, as the same rules generally apply.

Placing Your Topic Sentence

Although the topic sentence most frequently occurs as the first sentence in the body paragraph, it also often appears as the second or last sentence. A topic sentence that directly follows the first sentence of a paragraph usually does so because the first sentence provides an introductory statement or some kind of a "hook" to the preceding paragraph. A topic sentence frequently appears at the end of a paragraph that first presents particular details and then concludes with its central point. Here are two paragraphs in which the topic sentences do not appear first:

Introductory sentence

Topic sentence

Millions of Americans have watched the elaborate Rose Bowl Parade televised nationally each January from Pasadena, California. *Less well known, but growing in popularity, is Pasadena's Doo Dah Parade, an annual parody of the Rose Bowl spectacle, that specializes in wild-and-crazy participants.* Take this year's Doo Dah Precision Drill Team, for instance. Instead of marching in unison, the members cavorted down the avenue displaying—what else—a variety of precision electric drills. In heated competition with this group was the Synchronized Briefcase Drill Team, whose male and female members wore gray pinstripe suits and performed a series of tunes by tapping on their briefcases. Another crowd-pleasing entry was the Citizens for the Right to Bare Arms, whose members sang while carrying aloft unclothed mannequin arms. The zany procession, led this year as always by the All-Time Doo Dah Parade Band, attracted more than 150,000 fans and is already preparing for its next celebration.

In the previous paragraph, the first sentence serves as an introduction leading into the topic sentence; in the following paragraph, the writer places the topic sentence last to make a general comment about the importance of VCRs.

Topic sentence

Because of VCRs, we no longer have to miss a single joke on our favorite sitcom. Sporting events can be recorded in their entirety even though we may have to go to work or class after the fifth inning or second quarter. Even our dose of television violence does not have to be postponed forever just because a popular special is on another channel at the same time. Moreover, events of historical significance can be captured and replayed for future generations even if Aunt Tillie keeps us eating tacos until after the show begins. *In but a few years, VCRs have radically changed America's television viewing habits.*

As you can see, the position of topic sentences largely depends on what you are trying to do in your paragraph. And it's true that the purposes of some paragraphs are so obvious that no topic sentence is needed. However, if you are a beginning writer, you may want to practice putting your topic sentences first for a while to help you organize and unify your paragraphs.

Some paragraphs with a topic sentence near the beginning also contain a concluding sentence that makes a final general comment based on the supporting details. The last sentence below, for example, sums up and restates the main point of the paragraph.

Topic sentence

Of all nature's catastrophes, tornadoes cause the most bizarre destruction. Whirling out of the sky at speeds up to 300 miles per hour, tornadoes have been known to drive broom handles through brick walls and straws into tree trunks. In one extreme case, a Kansas farmer reported that his prize rooster had been sucked into a two-gallon distilled-water bottle. More commonly, tornadoes lift autos and deposit them in fields miles away or uproot trees and drop them on lawns in neighboring towns. One tornado knocked down every wall in a house but one—luck-

Concluding sentence

ily, the very wall shielding the terrified family. *Whenever a tornado touches the earth, spectacular headlines are sure to follow.*

◣ PRACTICING WHAT YOU'VE LEARNED

A. Point out the topic sentences in the following paragraphs; identify those paragraphs that also contain concluding sentences.

Denim is one of America's most widely used fabrics. It was first introduced during Columbus's voyage, when the sails of the Santa Maria were made of the strong cloth. During our pioneer days, denim was used for tents, covered wagons, and the now-famous blue jeans. Cowboys found denim an ideal fabric for protection against sagebrush, cactus, and saddle sores. World War II also gave denim a boost in popularity when sailors were issued jeans as part of their dress code. Today, denim continues to be in demand as more and more casual clothes are cut from the economical fabric. Because of its low cost and durability, manufacturers feel that denim will continue as one of America's most useful fabrics.

Adlai Stevenson, American statesman and twice an unsuccessful presidential candidate against Eisenhower, was well known for his intelligence and wit. Once on the campaign trail, after he had spoken eloquently and at length about several complex ideas, a woman in the audience was moved to stand and cheer, "That's great! Every thinking person in America will vote for you!" Stevenson immediately retorted, "That's not enough. I need a majority!" Frequently a reluctant candidate but never at a loss for words, Stevenson once reflected on the country's highest office: "Yes, in America any boy may become President. . . . I suppose it's just one of the risks he takes."

Cooking in a microwave oven has simplified my hectic life. Instead of having to wait the interminable ten minutes for my morning coffee, I can place my cup in the micro and have hot coffee in seconds. I no longer have to decide in the foggy morning what ingredients must be defrosted for the evening meal. I can now come home at 5 P.M., decide what I feel like eating, and have it defrosted in a matter of minutes. The shortened cooking time means I can have full-course meals that once took me hours to cook. The microwave also makes cleanup much easier because the dish I cook in is the dish I eat in. Microwaves may be expensive, but the time and effort they save is worth a million to those of us with too-busy lives.

You always think of the right answer five minutes after you hand in the test. You always hit the red light when you're already late for class. The one time you skip class is the day of the pop quiz. Back-to-back classes are always held in buildings at opposite ends of campus. The one course you need to graduate will not be offered your last semester. If any of these sound familiar, you've obviously been a victim of the "Murphy's Laws" that govern student life.

Want to win a sure bet? Then wager that your friends can't guess the most widely sold musical instrument in America today. Chances are they won't get the answer right—not even on the third try. In actuality, the most popular instrument in the country is neither the guitar nor the trumpet but the lowly kazoo. Last year alone, some three and one-half million kazoos were sold to music lovers of all ages. Part of the instrument's popularity arises from its availability, since kazoos are sold in variety stores and music centers nearly everywhere; another reason is its inexpensiveness—it ranges from the standard thirty-nine-cent model to the five-dollar gold-plated special. But perhaps the main reason for the kazoo's popularity is the ease with which it can be played by almost anyone—as can testify the members of the entire Swarthmore College marching band, who have now added a marching kazoo number to their repertoire. Louie Armstrong, move over!

It's a familiar scenario: Dad won't stop the car to ask directions, despite the fact that he's been hopelessly lost for over forty-five minutes. Mom keeps nagging Dad to slow down and finally blows up because your little sister suddenly remembers she's left her favorite doll, the one she can't sleep without, at the rest stop you left over an hour ago. Your legs are sweat-glued to the vinyl seats, you need desperately to go to the bathroom, and your big brother has just kindly acknowledged that he will relieve you of your front teeth if you allow any part of your body to extend over the imaginary line he has drawn down the back seat. The wonderful institution known as the "family vacation" has begun.

B. Rewrite these topic sentences so that they are clear and focused rather than fuzzy or too broad.

1. My personality has changed a lot in the last year.

2. His blind date turned out to be really great.

3. The movie's special effects were incredible.

4. The Memorial Day celebration was more fun than ever before.

5. The evening with her parents was an unforgettable experience.

C. Add topic sentences to the following paragraphs:

Famous inventor Thomas Edison, for instance, did so poorly in his first years of school that his teachers warned his parents that he'd never be a success at anything. Similarly, Henry Ford, the father of the auto industry, had trouble in school with both reading and writing. But perhaps the best example is Albert Einstein, whose parents and teachers suspected that he was retarded because he responded to questions so slowly and in a stuttering voice. Einstein's high school record was poor in everything but math, and he failed his college entrance exams the first time. Even out of school the man had trouble holding a job—until he announced the theory of relativity.

A 1950s felt skirt with Elvis's picture on it, for example, now sells for $150, and Elvis scarves go for as much as $200. Elvis handkerchiefs, originally 50 cents or less, fetch $150 on today's market as do wallets imprinted with the singer's face. Posters from the Rock King's movies can sell for $50, and cards from the chewing gum series can run $30 apiece. Perhaps one of the most expensive collectors' items is the Emene Elvis guitar that can cost a fan from $500 to $700, regardless of musical condition.

When successful playwright Jean Kerr once checked into a hospital, the receptionist asked her occupation and was told, "Writer." The receptionist said, "I'll just put down 'housewife.'" Similarly, when a British official asked W. H. Auden, the late award-winning poet and essayist, what he did for a living, Auden replied, "I'm a writer." The official jotted down "no occupation."

Cumberland College, for example, set the record back in 1916 for the biggest loss in college ball, having allowed Georgia Tech to run up 63 points in the first quarter and ultimately succumbing to them with a final score of 222 to nothing. In pro ball, the Washington Redskins are the biggest losers, going down in defeat 73 to 0 to the Chicago Bears in 1940. The award for the longest losing streak, however, goes to Northwestern University's team, who by 1981 had managed to lose 29 consecutive games. During that year, morale was so low that one disgruntled fan passing a local highway sign that read "Interstate 94" couldn't resist adding "Northwestern 0."

D. Write a focused topic sentence for five of the following subjects:

1. job interviews
2. friends
3. food
4. money
5. selecting a major or occupation
6. clothes
7. music
8. dreams
9. housing
10. childhood

◤ ASSIGNMENT

Review the thesis statements with essay maps you wrote for the practice exercise on page 44. Choose two, and from each thesis create at least three topic sentences for possible body paragraphs.

◤ APPLYING WHAT YOU'VE LEARNED TO *YOUR* WRITING

If you currently have a working thesis statement you have written in response to an assignment in your composition class, try sketching out an outline or plan for the major ideas you wish to include. After you write a draft, underline the topic sentences in your body paragraphs. Do your topic sentences directly support your thesis? If you find that they do not clearly support your thesis, you must decide if you need to revise your draft's organization or whether you have, in fact, discovered a new, and possibly better, subject to write about. If the latter is true, you'll need to redraft your essay so that your readers will not be confused by a paper that announces one subject but discusses another. (See Chapter 5 for more information on revising your drafts.)

PARAGRAPH DEVELOPMENT

Possibly the most serious—and most common—weakness of all essays by novice writers is *the lack of effectively developed body paragraphs*. The information in each paragraph must adequately explain, exemplify, define, or in some other way *support* your topic sentence. Therefore, you must include *enough supporting information* or *evidence* in each paragraph to make your readers understand your topic sentence. Moreover, you must make the information in the paragraph clear and specific enough for the readers to accept your ideas.

The next paragraph is *underdeveloped*. Although the topic sentence promises a discussion of Jesse James as a Robin Hood figure, the paragraph does not provide enough specific supporting evidence (in this case, examples) to explain this unusual view of the gunfighter.

> Although he was an outlaw, Jesse James was considered a Robin Hood figure in my hometown in Missouri. He used to be generous to the poor, and he did many good deeds, not just robberies. In my hometown people still talk about how lots of the things James did weren't all bad.

Rewritten, the paragraph might read as follows:

> Although he was an outlaw, Jesse James was considered a Robin Hood figure in my hometown in Missouri. Jesse and his gang chose my hometown as a hiding place, and they set out immediately to make friends with the local people. Every Christmas for four years, the legend goes, he dumped bags of toys on the doorsteps of poor children. The parents knew the toys had been bought with money stolen from richer people, but they were

grateful anyway. On three occasions, Jesse gave groceries to the dozen neediest families—he seemed to know when times were toughest—and once he supposedly held up a stage to pay for an old man's operation. In my hometown, some people still sing the praises of Jesse James, the outlaw who wasn't all bad.

The topic sentence promises a discussion of James's generosity and delivers just that by citing specific examples of his gifts to children, the poor, and the sick. The paragraph is, therefore, better developed.

The following paragraph offers supporting reasons but no specific examples or details to support those reasons:

Living with my ex-roommate was unbearable. First, she thought everything she owned was the best. Secondly, she possessed numerous filthy habits. Finally, she constantly exhibited immature behavior.

The writer might provide more evidence this way:

Living with my ex-roommate was unbearable. First, she thought everything she owned, from clothes to cosmetics, was the best. If someone complimented my pants, she'd point out that her designer jeans looked better and would last longer because they were made of better material. If she borrowed my shampoo, she'd let me know that it didn't get her hair as clean and shiny as hers did. My hand cream wasn't as smooth; my suntan lotion wasn't as protective; not even my wire clothes hangers were as good as her padded ones! But despite her pickiness about products, she had numerous filthy habits. Her dirty dishes remained in the sink for ages before she got the incentive to wash them. Piles of the "best" brand of tissues were regularly discarded from her upper bunk and strewn about the floor. Her desk and closets overflowed with heaps of dirty clothes, books, cosmetics, and whatever else she owned, and she rarely brushed her teeth (when she did brush, she left oozes of toothpaste on the sink). Finally, she constantly acted immaturely by throwing tantrums when things didn't go her way. A poor grade on an exam or paper, for example, meant books, shoes, or any other small object within her reach would hit the wall flying. Living with such a person taught me some valuable lessons about how not to win friends or keep roommates.

By adding more supporting evidence—specific examples and details—to this paragraph, the writer has a better chance of convincing the reader of the roommate's real character.

Where does evidence come from? Where do writers find their supporting information? Evidence comes from many sources. Personal experiences, memories, observations, hypothetical examples, reasoned arguments, facts, statistics, testimony from authorities, many kinds of studies and research— all these and more can help you make your points clear and persuasive. In the paragraph on Jesse James, for example, the writer relied on stories and memories from his hometown. The paragraph on the obnoxious roommate was supported by examples gained through the writer's personal observation. The kind of supporting evidence you choose for your paragraphs depends on your purpose and your audience; as the writer, you must decide what will work best to make your readers understand and accept each important point in your discussion. (For advice on ways to think critically about evidence, see Chapter 5; for more information on incorporating research material into your essays, see Chapter 12.)

Having a well-developed paragraph is more than a matter of additional material or expanding length, however. The information in each paragraph must effectively explain or support your topic sentence. *Vague generalities or repetitious ideas are not convincing.* Look, for example, at the following paragraph, in which the writer offers only generalities:

> We ought to get rid of telephones in cars. Some people who have them think they're a really good idea but a lot of us don't agree. A car phone can cause too many dangerous accidents to happen, and even if there's no terrible accident, people using them have been known to do some really stupid things in traffic. Drivers using car phones are constantly causing problems for other drivers; pedestrians are in big trouble from these people too. I think car phones are getting to be a really dangerous nuisance and we ought to do something about them soon.

This paragraph is weak because it is composed of repetitious general statements stated in vague, unclear language. None of its general statements are supported with specific evidence. Why are car phones not a "good" idea? How do they cause accidents? What "stupid things" happened because of them? What are the "problems" and "trouble" the writer refers to? What exactly does "do something about them" mean? The writer obviously had some ideas in mind, but these ideas are not clear to the reader because they are not adequately developed with specific evidence and language. By adding supporting examples and details, the writer might revise the paragraph this way:

Although car telephones may be a time-saving convenience for busy executives or commuters, they are too distracting for use by drivers of moving vehicles, whose lack of full attention poses a serious threat to other drivers and to pedestrians. The simple acts of dialing or answering a telephone, for example, may take a driver's eyes away from traffic signals or other cars. Moreover, involvement in a complex or emotional conversation could slow down a driver's response time just when fast action is needed to avoid an accident. Last week I drove behind a man using his car phone. As he drove and talked, I could see him gesturing wildly, obviously agitated with the other caller. His speed repeatedly slowed and then picked up, slowed and increased, and his car drifted more than once, on a street frequently crossed by schoolchildren. Because the man was clearly not in full, conscious control of his driving, he was dangerous. My experience is not isolated; a recent study by the Foundation for Traffic Safety has discovered that car phones are far more distracting to drivers than listening to the radio or talking to a rider. With additional studies in progress, voters should soon be able to demand legislation to restrict use of car telephones to passengers or to drivers when the vehicles are not in motion.

The reader now has a better idea why the writer feels car phones are distracting and, consequently, dangerous. By using two hypothetical examples (looking away, slowed response time), one personal experience (observing the agitated man), and one reference to research (the safety study), the writer offers the reader three kinds of supporting evidence for the paragraph's claim.

After examining the two paragraphs below, decide which explains its point more effectively.

1

Competing in an Ironman triathlon is one of the most demanding feats known to amateur athletes. First, they have to swim many miles and that takes a lot of endurance. Then they ride a bicycle a long way, which is also hard on their bodies. Last, they run a marathon, which can be difficult in itself but is especially hard after the first two events. Competing in the triathlon is really tough on the participants.

2

Competing in an Ironman triathlon is one of the most demanding feats known to amateur athletes. During the first stage of the triathlon, the competitors must swim 2.4 miles in the open ocean. They have to battle the constantly choppy ocean, the strong currents, and the frequent swells. The wind is often an adversary, and stinging jellyfish are a constant threat. Once they have completed the ocean swim, the triathletes must ride 112 miles on a bicycle. In addition to the strength needed to pedal that far, the bicyclists must use a variety of hand grips to assure the continued circulation in their fingers and hands as well as to ease the strain on the neck and shoulder muscles. Moreover, the concentration necessary to steady the bicycle as well as the attention to the inclines on the course and the consequent shifting of gears causes mental fatigue for the athletes. After completing these two grueling segments, the triathletes must then run 26.2 miles, the length of a regular marathon. Dehydration is a constant concern as is the prospect of cramping. Even the pain and swelling of a friction blister can be enough to eliminate a contestant at this late stage of the event. Finally, disorientation and fatigue can set in and distort the athlete's judgment. Competing in an Ironman triathlon takes incredible physical and mental endurance.

The first paragraph contains, for the most part, repetitious generalities; it repeats the same idea (the triathlon is hard work) and gives few specific details to illustrate the point presented in the topic sentence. The second paragraph, however, does offer many specific examples and details—the exact mileage figures, the currents, jellyfish, inclines, grips, blisters, and so forth—that help the reader understand why the event is so demanding.

Joseph Conrad, the famous British novelist, once remarked that a writer's purpose was to use "the power of the written word to make you hear, to make you feel . . . before all, to make you *see.* That—and no more, and it is everything." By using specific details instead of vague, general statements, you can write an interesting, convincing essay. Ask yourself as you revise your paragraphs, "Have I provided enough information, presented enough clear, precise details to make my readers *see* what I want them to?" In other words, a well-developed paragraph effectively makes its point with *an appropriate amount of specific supporting evidence.* (Remember that a handwritten paragraph in your rough draft will look much shorter when it is typed. Therefore, if you can't think of much to say about a particular idea, you should gather more information or consider dropping it as a major point in your essay.)

PARAGRAPH LENGTH

"How long is a good paragraph?" is a question novice writers often ask. Like a teacher's lecture or a preacher's sermon, paragraphs should be long enough to accomplish their purpose and short enough to be interesting. In truth, there is no set length, no prescribed number of lines or sentences, for any of your paragraphs. In a body paragraph, your topic sentence presents the main point, and the rest of the paragraph must give enough supporting evidence to convince the reader. While too much unnecessary or repetitious detail is boring, too little discussion will leave the reader uninformed, unconvinced, or confused.

Although paragraph length varies, beginning writers should avoid the one- or two-sentence paragraphs frequently seen in newspapers or magazine articles. (Journalists have their own rules to follow; paragraphs are shorter in newspapers, for one reason, because large masses of print in narrow columns are hard to read quickly.) Essay writers do occasionally use the one-sentence paragraph, most often to produce some special effect, when the statement is especially dramatic or significant and needs to call attention to itself or when an emphatic transition is needed. For now, however, you should concentrate on writing well-developed body paragraphs.

One more note on paragraph length: sometimes you may discover that a particular point in your essay is so complex that your paragraph is growing far too long—well over a typed page, for instance. If this problem occurs, look for a logical place to divide your information and start a new paragraph. For example, you might see a convenient dividing point between a series of actions you're describing or a break in the chronology of a narrative or between explanations of arguments or examples. Just make sure you begin your next paragraph with some sort of transition phrase or key words to let the reader know you are still discussing the same point as before ("Still another problem caused by the computer's faulty memory circuit is . . .").

◢ PRACTICING WHAT YOU'VE LEARNED

Analyze the following paragraphs. Explain how you might improve the development of each one.

1. Professor Wilson is the best teacher I've ever had. His lectures are interesting, and he's very concerned about his students. He makes the class challenging but not too hard. On tests he doesn't expect more than one can give. I think he's a great teacher.

2. Newspaper advice columns are pretty silly. The problems are generally stupid or unrealistic, and the advice is out of touch with today's world. Too often the columnist just uses the letter to make a smart remark about some pet peeve. The columns could be put to some good uses, but no one tries very hard.

3. Driving tests do not adequately examine a person's driving ability. Usually the person being tested does not have to drive very far. The test does not require the skills that are used in everyday driving situations. Supervisors of driving tests tend to be very lenient.

4. Old-age homes are sad places. They are usually located in ugly old houses unfit for anyone. The people there are lonely and bored. What's more, they're often treated badly by the people who run the homes. It's a shame something better can't be done for the elderly.

5. There is a big difference between acquaintances and friends. Acquaintances are just people you know slightly, but friends give you some important qualities. For example, they can help you gain self-esteem and confidence just by being close to you. By sharing intimate things, they also help you feel happy about being alive.

ASSIGNMENT

A. Select two of the paragraphs from above and rewrite them, adding enough specific details to make well-developed paragraphs.

B. Write a paragraph composed of generalities and vague statements. Exchange this paragraph with a classmate's, and turn each other's faulty paragraph into a clearly developed one.

C. Find at least two well-developed paragraphs in an essay or book; explain why you think the two paragraphs are successfully developed.

APPLYING WHAT YOU'VE LEARNED TO *YOUR* WRITING

If you are currently drafting an essay, look closely at your body paragraphs. Find the topic sentence in each paragraph and circle the key words that most clearly communicate the main idea of the paragraph. Then ask yourself if the information in each paragraph effectively supports, explains, or illustrates the main idea of the paragraph's topic sentence. Is there enough information? If you're not sure, try numbering your supporting details. Are there too few to be persuasive? Does the paragraph present clear, specific supporting material or does it contain too many vague generalities to be convincing? Where could you add more details to help the reader understand your ideas better and to make each paragraph more interesting? (For more help revising your paragraphs, see Chapter 5.)

PARAGRAPH UNITY

Every sentence in a body paragraph should directly relate to the main idea presented by the topic sentence. A paragraph must stick to its announced subject; it must not drift away into another discussion. In other words, a good paragraph has *unity*.

Examine the unified paragraph below; note that the topic sentence clearly states the paragraph's main point and that each sentence thereafter supports the topic sentence.

> [1]Frank Lloyd Wright, America's leading architect of the first half of the twentieth century, believed that his houses should blend naturally with their building sites. [2]Consequently, he designed several "prairie houses," whose long, low lines echoed the flat earth plan. [3]Built of brick, stone, and natural wood, the houses shared a similar texture with their backgrounds; [4]large windows were often used to blend the interior and exterior of the homes. [5]Wright also punctuated the lines and spaces of the houses with greenery in planters to further make the buildings look like part of nature.

The first sentence states the main idea, that Wright thought houses should blend with their location; the other sentences support this assertion:

Topic sentence: Wright's houses blend with their natural locations

2. long, low lines echo flat prairie

3. brick, stone, wood provide same texture as location

4. windows blend inside with outside

5. greenery in planters imitates the natural surroundings

Now look at the next paragraph, in which the writer strays from his original purpose:

> [1]Cigarette smoke is unhealthy even for people who don't have the nicotine habit themselves. [2]Secondhand smoke can cause asthmatics and sufferers of sinusitis

serious problems; [3]doctors regularly advise heart patients to avoid confined smoky areas because coronary attacks might be triggered by the lack of clean air. [4]Moreover, having the smell of smoke in one's hair and clothes is a real nuisance. [5]Even if a person is without any health problems, exhaled smoke doubles the amount of carbon monoxide in the air, a condition that may cause lung problems in the future.

Sentence 4 refers to smoke as a nuisance and therefore does not belong in a paragraph that discusses smoking as a health hazard to nonsmokers.

Sometimes a large portion of a paragraph will drift into another topic. In the paragraph below, did the writer wish to focus on her messiness or on the beneficial effects of her engagement?

I have always been a very messy person. As a child, I was a pack rat, saving every little piece of insignificant paper that I thought might be important when I grew up. As a teenager, my pockets bulged with remnants of basketball games, candy bars, gum wrappers, and other important articles from my high school education. As a college student, I became a boxer—not a fighter, but the kind who cannot throw anything away and therefore it winds up in a box in my closet. But my engagement has changed everything. I'm really pleased with the new stage of my life, and I owe it all to my fiancé. My overall outlook on life has changed because of his influences on me. I'm neater, much more cheerful, and I'm even getting places on time like I never did before. It's truly amazing what love can do.

Note shift from the topic of messiness

This writer may wish to discuss the changes her fiancé has inspired and then use her former messiness, tardiness, and other bad habits as examples illustrating those changes; however, as presented here, the paragraph is not unified around a central idea. On the contrary, it first seems to promise a discussion of her messiness but then wanders into comments on "what love can do."

Also beware a tendency to end your paragraph with a new idea. A new point calls for an entirely new paragraph. For example, the paragraph below focuses on the *origins* of Muzak; the last sentence, on Muzak's *effects* on workers, should be omitted or moved to a following paragraph on Muzak's uses in the workplace.

Muzak, the ever-present sound of music that pervades elevators, office buildings, and reception rooms, was created over fifty years ago by George Owen Squier, an army general. A graduate of West Point, Squier was also an inventor and scientist. During World War I he headed the Signal Corps where he began experimenting with the notion of transmitting simultaneous messages over power lines. When he retired from the army in 1922, he founded Wired Radio, Inc., and later in 1934 the first Muzak medley was heard in Cleveland, Ohio, for home-owners willing to pay the great sum of $1.50 a month. That year he struck upon the now-famous name, which combined the idea of music with the brand name of the country's most popular camera, Kodak. *Today, experiments show that workers get more done when they listen to Muzak.*

Breaks unity

In general, think of paragraph unity in terms of the diagram below:

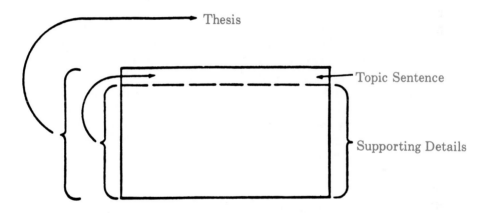

The sentences in the paragraph support the paragraph's topic sentence; the paragraph, in turn, supports the thesis statement.

PRACTICING WHAT YOU'VE LEARNED

In each of the following examples, delete or rewrite any information that interferes with the unity of the paragraph:

In the Great Depression of the 1930s, American painters suffered severely because few people had the money to spend on the luxury of owning art. To keep our artists from starving, the government ultimately set up the Federal Art Project, which paid then little-known painters such as Jackson Pollock, Arshile Gorky, and Willem de Kooning to paint murals in post offices, train stations, schools, housing projects, and other public places. During this period, songwriters were also affected by the depression, and they produced such memorable songs as "Buddy, Can You Spare a Dime?" The government-sponsored murals, usually depicting familiar American scenes and historical events, gave our young artists an opportunity to develop their skills and new techniques; in return, our country obtained thousands of elaborate works of art in over one thousand American cities. Sadly, many of these art works were destroyed in later years, as public buildings were torn down or remodeled.

After complaining in vain about the quality of food in the campus restaurant, University of Colorado students are having their revenge after all. The student body recently voted to rename the grill after Alferd Packer, the only American ever convicted of cannibalism. Packer was a Utah prospector trapped with an expedition of explorers in the southwest Colorado mountains during the winter of 1874; the sole survivor of the trip, he was later tried by a jury and sentenced to hang for dining on at least five of his companions. Colorado students are now holding an annual "Alferd Packer Day" and have installed a mural relating the prospector's story on the main wall of the restaurant. Some local wits have also suggested a new motto for the bar and grill: "Serving our fellow man since 1874." Another well-known incident of cannibalism in the West occurred in the winter of 1846, when the Donner party, a wagon train of eighty-seven California-bound immigrants, became trapped by ice and snow in the mountains south of the Great Salt Lake.

Inventors of food products often name their new creations after real people. In 1896 Leo Hirschfield hand-rolled a chewy candy and named it after his daughter Tootsie. In 1920 Otto Schnering gave the world the Baby Ruth candy bar, named after the daughter of former President Grover Cleveland. To publicize his new product, Schnering once dropped the candy tied to tiny parachutes from an airplane flying over Pittsburgh. And one of our most popular soft drinks was named by a young suitor who sought to please his sweetheart's physician father, none other than old Dr. Pepper. Despite the honor, the girl's father never approved of the match and the young man, Wade Morrison, married someone else.

States out West have often led the way in recognizing women's roles in politics. Wyoming, for example, was the first state to give women the right to vote and hold office, back in 1869 while the state was still a territory. Wyoming was also the first state to elect a woman as governor,

Nellie Tayloe Ross, in 1924. Montana elected Jeanette Rankin as the nation's first congresswoman. U.S. Representative from Colorado, Patricia Schroeder, claims to be the first person to take the congressional oath of office while clutching a handbag full of diapers. Ms. Schroeder later received the National Motherhood Award.

Living in a college dorm is a good way to meet people. There are activities every weekend such as dances and parties where one can get acquainted with all kinds of students. Even just sitting by someone in the cafeteria during a meal can start a friendship. Making new friends from foreign countries can teach students more about international relations. A girl on my dorm floor, for example, is from Peru, and I've learned a lot about the customs and culture in her country. She's also helping me with my study of Spanish.

◤ APPLYING WHAT YOU'VE LEARNED TO *YOUR* WRITING

If you have written a draft of an essay, underline the topic sentence in each body paragraph and circle the key words. For example, if in an essay on America's growing health consciousness, one of your topic sentences reads "In an effort to improve their health, Americans have increased the number of vitamins they consume," you might circle "Americans," "increased," and "vitamins." Then look closely at your paragraph. All the information in that paragraph should support the idea expressed in your topic sentence; nothing should detract from the idea of showing that Americans have increased their vitamins. Now study the paragraphs in your draft, one by one. Cross out any sentences or material that interferes with the ideas in your topic sentences. If one of your paragraphs begins to drift away from its topic-sentence idea, you will need to rethink the purpose of that paragraph and rewrite so that the reader will understand what the paragraph is about. (For additional help revising your drafts, turn to Chapter 5.)

PARAGRAPH COHERENCE

In addition to unity, *coherence* is essential to a good paragraph. Coherence means that all the sentences and ideas in your paragraph flow together to make a clear, logical point about your topic. Your paragraph should not be a confusing collection of ideas set down in random order. The readers should be able to follow what you have written and see easily and quickly how each sentence grows out of, or is related to, the preceding sentence. To achieve coherence, you should have a smooth connection or transition between the sentences in your paragraphs.

There are five important means of achieving coherence in your paragraphs:

1. A natural or easily recognized order
2. Transition words and phrases
3. Repetition of key words
4. Substitution of pronouns for key nouns
5. Parallelism

These transition devices are similar to the couplings between railroad cars; they enable the controlling engine to pull the train of thought along as a unit.

A Recognizable Ordering of Information

Without consciously thinking about the process, you may often organize paragraphs in easily recognized patterns that give the reader a sense of logical movement and order. Discussed below are four common patterns of ordering sentences in a paragraph:

The Order of Time

Some paragraphs are composed of details arranged in chronological order. You might, for example, explain the process of changing an oil filter on your car by beginning with the first step, draining the old oil, and concluding with the last step, installing the new filter. Here is a paragraph on black holes in which the writer chronologically orders her details:

> A black hole in space, from all indications, is the result of the death of a star. Scientists speculate that stars were first formed from the gases floating in the universe at the beginning of time. In the first stage in the life of a star, the hot gas is drawn by the force of gravity into a burning sphere. In the middle stage—our own sun being a middle-aged star—the burning continues at a regular rate, giving off enormous amounts of heat and light. As it grows old, however, the star eventually explodes to become what is called a nova, a superstar. But gravity soon takes over again, and the exploded star falls back in on itself with such force that all the matter in the star is compacted into a mass no larger than a few miles in diameter. At this point, no heavenly body can be seen in that area of the sky, as the tremendous pull of gravity lets nothing escape, not even light. A black hole has thus been formed.

The Order of Space

When your subject is a physical object, you should select some orderly means of describing it: from left to right, top to bottom, inside to outside, and so forth. For example, you might describe a sculpture as you walk around it from front to back. Below is a paragraph describing a goalie in which the writer has ordered the details of his description in a feet-to-head pattern.

> Hockey goalies must take ample time prior to a game to be sure their protective equipment is properly fitted. They start by lacing on their steel toe skates that include extra-thick tongue pads and arch guards. Then, the outside leg pads are strapped on top of an inner set of shin and knee protectors. These are clumsy and wide but absorb the bulk of the shots the goalies will deflect during a game. Loose-fitting hockey pants come next. These must allow for ample flexibility and protection of the hips. The leather gloves used both for catching and deflecting pucks are also large and flexible. They protect the wrist area as well as the hands. The upper arms, shoulders, and chest are guarded by a single unit body pad that resembles the armor knights wore generations ago; however, the pad is made of a lightweight synthetic. The throat protector is attached to the goalie's mask, a wirecage or molded piece of fiberglass. Finally, the hockey helmet holds the face mask in place while assuring total head protection.

Deductive Order

A paragraph ordered deductively moves from a generalization to particular details that explain or support the general statement. Perhaps the most common pattern of all paragraphs, the deductive paragraph begins with its topic sentence and proceeds to its supporting details, as illustrated in the following example:

> If 111 ninth-graders in Honolulu are typical of today's teenagers, spelling and social science teachers may be in for trouble. In a recent experiment, not one of the students tested could write the Pledge of Allegiance correctly. In addition, the results showed that the students apparently had little understanding of the pledge's meaning. For example, several students described the United States as a "nation under guard" instead of "under God,"

and the phrase "to the Republic for which it stands" appeared in several responses as "of the richest stand" or "for Richard stand." Many students changed the word "indivisible" to the phrase "in the visible," and over nine percent of the students, all of whom are Americans from varying racial and ethnic backgrounds, misspelled the word "America."

Inductive Order

An inductive paragraph begins with an examination of particular details and then concludes with a larger point or generalization about those details. Such a paragraph often ends with its topic sentence, as does the following paragraph on Little League baseball:

At almost every Little League baseball game, one or another adult creates a minor scene by yelling obscenely at an umpire or a coach. Similarly, it is fairly common to see such adults arguing loudly with one another in the stands over whose child should have caught a missed ball. Perhaps the most astounding spectacle of all, however, is an irate father or mother yanking a child off the field after a bad play for a humiliating lecture in front of the whole team. Sadly, Little League baseball today often seems intended more for childish parents than for the children who actually play it.

Transition Words and Phrases

Some paragraphs may need transition words to help you move smoothly from one thought to the next so that your ideas do not appear choppy or jerky.

Here is a list of common transition words and phrases and their uses:

giving examples	for example, for instance, specifically, in particular, namely, another
comparison	similarly, not only . . . but also, in comparison
contrast	although, but, while, in contrast, however, though, on the other hand

sequence	first . . . second . . . third, and finally, moreover, also, in addition, next, then, after, furthermore
results	therefore, thus, consequently, as a result

Notice the difference the use of transition words makes in the paragraphs below:

> Working in the neighborhood grocery store as a checker was one of the worst jobs I've ever had. In the first place, I had to wear an ugly, scratchy uniform cut at least three inches too short. My schedule of working hours was another inconvenience; because my hours were changed each week, it was impossible to make plans in advance, and getting a day off was out of the question. In addition, the lack of working space bothered me. Except for a half-hour lunch break, I was restricted to three square feet of room behind the counter and consequently felt as if I were no more than a cog in the cash register.

The same paragraph rewritten without transition words sounds choppy and childish:

> Working in the neighborhood grocery store as a checker was one of the worst jobs I've ever had. I had to wear an ugly, scratchy uniform. It was cut at least three inches too short. My schedule of working hours was inconvenient. My hours changed each week. It was impossible to make plans in advance. Getting a day off was out of the question. The lack of working space bothered me. Except for a half-hour break, I was restricted to three square feet of room behind the counter. I felt like a cog in the cash register.

Although transition words and phrases are useful in bridging the gaps between your ideas, don't overuse them. Not every sentence needs a transition phrase, so use one only when the relationship between your thoughts needs clarification. It's also a mistake to place the transition word in the same position in your sentence each time. Look at the paragraph on the following page.

It's a shame that every high school student isn't required to take a course in first aid. *For example,* you might need to treat a friend or relative for drowning during a family picnic. Or, *for instance,* someone might break a bone or receive a snakebite on a camping trip. *Also,* you should always know what to do for a common cut or burn. *Moreover,* it's important to realize when someone is in shock. *However,* very few people take the time to learn the simple rules of first aid. *Thus,* many injured or sick people suffer more than they should. *Therefore,* everyone should take a first aid course in school or at the Red Cross Center.

As you can see, a series of sentences each beginning with a transition word quickly becomes repetitious and boring. To hold your reader's attention, use transition words only when necessary to avoid choppiness, and vary their placement in your sentences.

Repetition of Key Words

Important words or phrases (and their synonyms) may be repeated throughout a paragraph to connect the thoughts into a coherent statement:

One of the most common, and yet most puzzling, phobias is the *fear* of *snakes.* It's only natural, of course, to be afraid of a poisonous *snake,* but many people are just as frightened of the harmless varieties. For such people, a tiny green grass *snake* is as terrifying as a cobra. Some researchers say this unreasonable *fear* of any and all *snakes* is a legacy left to us by our tree-dwelling ancestors, for whom these *reptiles* were a real and constant danger. Others maintain that the *fear* is a result of our associating the *snake* with the notion of evil, as in the Garden of Eden. Whatever the reason, the fact remains that for many otherwise normal people, the mere sight of a *snake* slithering through the countryside is enough to keep them city dwellers forever.

The repeated words "fear" and "snake" and the synonym "reptile" help tie one sentence to another so that the reader may follow the ideas easily.

Pronouns Substituted for Key Nouns

A pronoun is a word that stands for a noun. In your paragraph you may use a key noun in one sentence and then use a pronoun in its place in the following sentences. The pronoun "it" often replaces "shark" in the description below:

> [1]The great white shark is perhaps the best equipped of all the ocean's predators. [2]*It* can grow up to twenty-one feet and weigh three tons, with two-inch teeth that can replace themselves within twenty-four hours when damaged. [3]The shark's sense of smell is so acute *it* can detect one ounce of fish blood in a million ounces of water. [4]In addition, *it* can sense vibrations from six hundred feet away.

Sentences 2, 3, and 4 are tied to the topic sentence by the use of the pronoun "it."

Parallelism

Parallelism in a paragraph means using the same grammatical structure in several sentences to establish coherence. The repeated use of similar phrasing helps tie the ideas and sentences together. Next, for example, is a paragraph predominantly unified by its use of grammatically parallel sentences:

> The weather of Texas offers something for everyone. If you are the kind who likes to see snow drifting onto mountain peaks, a visit to the Big Bend area will satisfy your eye. If, on the other hand, you demand a bright sun to bake your skin a golden brown, stop in the southern part of the state. And for hardier souls, who ask from nature a show of force, the skies of the Panhandle regularly release ferocious springtime tornadoes. Finally, if you are the fickle type, by all means come to central Texas, where the sun at any time may shine unashamed throughout the most torrential rainstorm.

The parallel structures of sentences 2, 3, and 5 ("if you" + verb) keep the paragraph flowing smoothly from one idea to the next.

Using a Variety of Transition Devices

Most writers use a combination of transition devices in their paragraphs. In the following example, three kinds of transition devices are circled. See if you can identify each one.

Transitions are the glue that holds a paragraph together. These devices lead the reader from sentence to sentence, smoothing over the gaps between by indicating the relationship between the sentences. If this glue is missing, the paragraph will almost inevitably sound choppy or childish, even if every sentence in it responds to a single topic commitment. However, transitions are not substitutes for topic unity: like most glue, they are most effective when joining similar objects, or, in this case, similar ideas. For example, in a paragraph describing a chicken egg, no transition could bridge the gap created by the inclusion of a sentence concerned with naval losses in the Civil War. In other words, transitions can call attention to the topic relationships between sentences, but they cannot create those relationships.

transition words	repetition of pronouns	repetition of key words

PRACTICING WHAT YOU'VE LEARNED

A. Identify each of the following paragraphs as ordered by time, space, or parallelism:

My apartment is so small that it will no longer hold all my possessions. Every day when I come in the door, I am shocked by the clutter. The wall to my immediate left is completely obscured by art and movie posters that have become so numerous they often overlap, hiding even each other. Along the adjoining wall is my sound system: CDs and tapes are stacked several feet high on two long, low tables. The big couch that runs across the back of the room is always piled so high with school-books and magazines that a guest usually ends up sitting on the floor. To my right is a large sliding glass door that opens onto a balcony—or at least it used to, before it was permanently blocked by my tennis gear, golf clubs, and ten-speed bike. Even the tiny closet next to the front door is bursting with clothes, both clean and dirty. I think the time has come for me to move.

Once-common acts of greeting may be finding renewed popularity after three centuries. According to one historian, kissing was at the height of its popularity as a greeting in seventeenth-century England, when ladies and gentlemen of the court often saluted each other in this affectionate manner. Then the country was visited by a strange plague, whose cause was unknown. Because no one knew how the plague was spread, people tried to avoid physical contact with others as much as possible. Both kissing and the handshake went out of fash-ion and were replaced by the bow and curtsy, so people could greet others without having to touch them. The bow and curtsy remained in vogue for over a hundred years, until the handshake—for men only—returned to popularity in the nineteenth century. Today, both men and women may shake hands upon meeting others, and kissing as a greet-ing is making a comeback—especially among the jet-setters and Holly-wood stars.

Students have diverse ways of preparing for final exams. Some stay up the night before, trying to cram into their brains what they avoided all term. Others pace themselves, spending a little time each night going over the notes they took in class that day. Still others cross their fingers and hope they absorbed enough from lectures. A dishonest few pray that their fellow students will give them the answers. In the end, though, everyone hopes the tests are easy.

B. Circle and identify the transition devices in the following paragraphs:

Each year I follow a system when preparing firewood to use in my stove. First, I hike about a mile from my house with my bow saw in hand. I then select three good size oak trees and mark them with orange ties. Next, I saw through the base of each tree about two feet from the ground. After I fell the trees, not only do I trim away the branches, but I also sort the scrap from the usable limbs. I find cutting the trees into manageable length logs is too much for one day; however, I roll them off the ground so they will not begin to rot. The next day I cut the trees into eight-foot lengths, which allows me to handle them more easily. Once they are cut, I roll them along the fire lane to the edge of the road where I stack them neatly but not too high. The next day I borrow my uncle's van, drive to the pile of logs, and load as many logs as I can, thus reducing the number of trips. When I finally have all the logs in my backyard, I begin sawing them into eighteen-inch lengths. I create large piles that consequently have to be split and finally stacked. The logs will age and dry until winter when I will make daily trips to the woodpile.

Fans of professional baseball and football argue continually over which is America's favorite spectator sport. Though the figures on attendance for each vary with every new season, certain arguments remain the same, spelling out both the enduring appeals of each game and something about the people who love to watch. Football, for instance, is a quicker, more physical sport, and football fans enjoy the emotional involvement they feel while watching. Baseball, on the other hand, seems more mental, like chess, and attracts those fans who prefer a quieter, more complicated game. In addition, professional football teams usually play no more than fourteen games a year, providing fans with a whole week between games to work themselves up to a pitch of excitement and expectation. Baseball teams, however, play almost every day for six months, so that the typical baseball fan is not so crushed by missing a game, knowing there will be many other chances to attend. Finally, football fans seem to love the half-time pageantry, the marching bands, and the pretty cheerleaders, whereas baseball fans are more content to concentrate on the game's finer details and spend the breaks between innings filling out their own private scorecards.

C. These paragraphs lack common transition devices. Fill in each blank with the appropriate transition word or key word.

1

Scientists continue to debate the cause of the dinosaurs' disappearance. One group claims the _____ vanished after a comet smashed into the Earth; dust and smoke _____ blocked the sun for a long time. _____ of no direct sunlight, the Earth underwent a lengthy "winter," far too cold for the huge _____ to survive. A University of California paleontologist, _____, disputes this claim. He argues that _____ we generally think of _____ living in swampy land, fossils found in Alaska show that _____ could live in cold climates _____ warm ones. _____ group claims that the _____ became extinct following an intense period of global volcanic activity. _____ to killing the _____ themselves, these scientists _____ believe the volcanic activity killed much of the plant life that the _____ ate and, _____, many of the great _____ who survived the volcanic eruptions starved to death. Still _____ groups of _____ claim the _____ were destroyed by acid rain, _____ by a passing "death star," _____ even by visitors from outer space.

2

A recent study by the National Center for Health Statistics has revealed some fascinating information for those of us interested in living longer lives. The _____ shows, for _____, that people live longest in Hawaii, where the average _____ is 77.02 years. _____, in Washington, DC, the expected span is the lowest: only 69.2 years. _____ to Hawaii, states that boast long expectancies include Minnesota, Iowa, and Utah, _____ residents of Louisiana, South Carolina, Mississippi are on the lower end of the scale. _____, according to the _____ research, women can expect to live almost seven years longer than men. Congratulations to those Hawaiian women who will see us well into the twenty-first century!

D. The sentences in each of the following exercises are out of order. By noting the various transition devices, you should be able to arrange each group of sentences into a coherent paragraph.

Paragraph 1: How to Purchase a New Car

- If you're happy with the car's performance, find out about available financing arrangements.
- Later, at home, study your notes carefully to help you decide which car fits your needs.

- After you have discussed various loans and interest rates, you can negotiate the final price with the salesperson.

- A visit to the showroom also allows you to test-drive the car.

- Once you have agreed on the car's price, feel confident you have made a well-chosen purchase.

- Next, a visit to a nearby showroom should help you select the color, options, and style of the car of your choice.

- First, take a trip to the library to read the current auto magazines.

- As you read, take notes on models and prices.

Paragraph 2: Henry VIII and the Problems of Succession

- After Jane, Henry took three more wives, but all these marriages were childless.
- Jane did produce a son, Edward VI, but he died at age fifteen.

- The problem of succession was therefore an important issue during the reign of Henry VIII.

- Still hoping for a son, Henry beheaded Anne and married Jane Seymour.

- Thus, despite his six marriages, Henry failed in his attempts to secure the succession.

- In sixteenth-century England it was considered essential for a son to assume the throne.

- Henry's first wife, Catherine of Aragon, had only one child, the Princess Mary.

- But Anne also produced a daughter, the future Queen Elizabeth I.

- Consequently, he divorced Catherine and married Anne Boleyn.

PARAGRAPH SEQUENCE

The order in which you present your paragraphs is another decision you must make. In some essays, the subject matter itself will suggest its own order.* For instance, in an essay designed to instruct a beginning jogger, you might want to discuss the necessary equipment—good jogging shoes, loose-fitting clothing, and sweatband—before moving to a discussion of where to jog and how to

---

* For more information on easily recognized patterns of order, see pages 72–74.

jog. Other essays, however, may not suggest a natural order, in which case you yourself must decide which order will most effectively reach and hold the attention of your audience. Frequently, writers withhold their strongest point until last. (Lawyers often use this technique; they first present the jury with the weakest arguments, then pull out the most damning evidence—the "smoking pistol." Thus the jury members retire with the strongest argument freshest in their minds.) Sometimes, however, you'll find it necessary to present one particular point first so that the other points make good sense. Study your own major points and decide which order will be the most logical, successful way of persuading your reader to accept your thesis.

TRANSITIONS BETWEEN PARAGRAPHS

As you already know, each paragraph usually signals a new major point in your discussion. These paragraphs should not appear as isolated blocks of thought but rather as parts of a unified, step-by-step progression. To avoid a choppy essay, link each paragraph to the one before it with *transition devices.* Just as the sentences in your paragraphs are connected, so are the paragraphs themselves; therefore, you can use the same transition devices suggested on pages 74–78.

The first sentence of most body paragraphs frequently contains the transition device. To illustrate this point, here are some topic sentences lifted from the body paragraphs of a student essay criticizing a popular sports car, renamed the 'Gator to protect the guilty and to prevent lawsuits. The transition devices are italicized.

Thesis: The *'Gator* is one of the worst cars on the market.

- When you buy a *'Gator,* you buy physical inconvenience. [repetition of key word from thesis]

- *Another* reason the *'Gator* is a bad buy is the cost of insurance. [transition word, key word]

- You might overlook the *inconvenient* size and exorbitant *insurance* rates if the 'Gator were a strong, reliable car, *but* this automobile constantly needs repair. [key words from preceding paragraphs, transition word]

- When you decide to sell this *car*, you face *still another* unpleasant surprise: the extremely low resale value. [key word, transition phrase]

- *But* perhaps the most serious drawback is the *'Gator's* safety record. [transition word, key word]

Sometimes, instead of using transition words or repetition of key words or their synonyms, you can use an *idea* hook. The last idea of one paragraph may lead you smoothly into your next paragraph. Instead of re-peating a key word from the previous discussion, find a phrase that refers to the entire idea just expressed. If, for example, the previous paragraph discussed the highly complimentary advertising campaign for the 'Gator, the next paragraph might begin, "This view of the 'Gator as an economy car is ridiculous to anyone who's pumped a week's salary into this gas guzzler." The phrase "this view" connects the idea of the first paragraph with the one that follows. Idea hooks also work well with transition words: "This view, however, is ridiculous. . . ."

If you do use transition words, don't allow them to make your essay sound mechanical. For example, a long series of paragraphs beginning "first . . . second . . . third . . ." quickly becomes boring. Vary the type and position of your transition devices so that your essay has a subtle but logical movement from point to point.

◤ APPLYING WHAT YOU'VE LEARNED TO *YOUR* WRITING

If you are currently working on a draft of an essay, check each body para-graph for coherence, the smooth connection of ideas and sentences in a logi-cal, easy-to-follow order. You might try placing brackets around key words, pronouns, and transition words that carry the reader's attention from thought to thought and from sentence to sentence. Decide whether you have enough ordering devices, placed in appropriate places, or whether you need to add (or delete) others. (For additional help revising your drafts, turn to Chapter 5.)

CHAPTER 3 SUMMARY

Here is a brief restatement of what you should know about the paragraphs in the body of your essay:

1. Each body paragraph usually contains one major point in the discussion promised by the thesis statement.

2. Each major point is presented in the topic sentence of a paragraph.

3. Each paragraph should be adequately developed with clear supporting detail.

4. Every sentence in the paragraph should support the topic sentence.

5. There should be an orderly, logical flow from sentence to sentence and from thought to thought.

6. The sequence of your essay's paragraphs should be logical and effective.

7. There should be a smooth flow from paragraph to paragraph.

8. The body paragraphs should successfully persuade your reader that the opinion expressed in your thesis is valid.

4

BEGINNINGS AND ENDINGS

•
•
•

As you work on your rough drafts, you might think of your essay as a coherent, unified whole composed of three main parts: the introduction (lead-in, thesis, and essay map), the body (paragraphs with supporting evidence), and the conclusion (final address to the reader). These three parts should flow smoothly into one another, presenting the reader with an organized, logical discussion. The following pages will suggest ways to begin, end, and also name your essay effectively.

HOW TO WRITE A GOOD LEAD-IN

The first few sentences of your essay are particularly important; first impressions, as you know, are often lasting ones. The beginning of your essay, then, must catch the readers' attention and make them want to keep reading. Recall the way you read a magazine: if you are like most people, you probably skim the magazine, reading a paragraph or two of each article that looks promising. If the first few paragraphs hold your interest, you read on. When you write your own introductory paragraph, assume that you have only a few sentences to attract your reader. Consequently, you must pay particular attention to making those first lines especially interesting and well written.

In some essays, your thesis statement alone may be controversial or striking enough to capture the readers. At other times, however, you will want to use the introductory device called a *lead-in.** The lead-in (1) catches the readers' attention; (2) announces the subject matter and tone of your essay (humorous, satiric, serious, etc.); and (3) sets up, or leads into, the presentation of your thesis and essay map.

Here are some suggestions and examples of lead-ins:

1. A paradoxical or intriguing statement

> "Eat two chocolate bars and call me in the morning," says the psychiatrist to his patient. Such advice sounds like a sugar fanatic's dream, but recent studies have indeed confirmed that chocolate positively affects depression and anxiety.

2. An arresting statistic or shocking statement

> One of every seven women living in Smith County will be raped this year, according to a recent report prepared by the Country Rape Information and Counseling Services.

3. A question

> It is three times the number of people who belong to the Southern Baptist Convention, nine times the number who serve in the U.S. armed forces, and more than twice the number who voted for Barry Goldwater for President in 1964. What is it? It's the number of people in the United States who admit to having smoked marijuana: a massive 62 million.

---

*   Do note that for some writing assignments, such as certain kinds of technical reports, attention-grabbing lead-ins are not appropriate. Frequently, these reports are directed toward particular professional audiences and have their own designated format; they often begin, for example, with a statement of the problem under study or with a review of pertinent information or research.

4. A quotation or literary allusion

"I think onstage nudity is disgusting, shameful, and damaging to all things American," says actress Shelley Winters. "But if I were twenty-two with a great body, it would be artistic, tasteful, patriotic, and a progressive religious experience."

5. A relevant story, joke, or anecdote

Writer and witty critic Dorothy Parker was once assigned a remote, out-of-the-way office. According to the story, she became lonely, so desperate for company, that she ultimately painted "Gentlemen" on the door. Although this university is large, no one on this campus needs to feel as isolated as Parker obviously did: our excellent Student Activity Office has numerous clubs, programs, and volunteer groups to involve students of all interests.

6. A description, often used for emotional appeal

With one eye blackened, one arm in a cast, and third-degree burns on both her legs, the pretty, blond two-year-old seeks corners of rooms, refuses to speak, and shakes violently at the sound of loud noises. Tammy is not the victim of a war or a natural disaster; rather, she is the helpless victim of her parents, one of the thousands of children who suffer daily from America's hidden crime, child abuse.

7. A factual statement or a summary who-what-where-when-and-why lead-in

Texas's first execution of a woman in twenty-two years is scheduled for September 17 at the Huntsville Unit of the state's Department of Correction, despite the protests of various human rights groups around the country.

8. An analogy or comparison

The Romans kept geese on their Capitol Hill to cackle alarm in the event of attack by night. Modern Americans, despite their technology, have hardly improved on that old system of protection. According to the latest Safety Council report, almost any door with standard locks can be opened easily with a common plastic credit card.

9. A contrast

I used to search for toast in the supermarket. I used to think "blackened"—as in blackened Cajun shrimp—referred to the way I cooked anything in a skillet. "Poached" could only have legal ramifications. But all that has changed! Attending a class in basic cooking this summer has transformed the way I purchase, prepare, and even talk about food.

10. A personal experience

I realized times were changing for women when I overheard my six-year-old nephew speaking to my sister, a prominent New York lawyer. As we left her elaborate, luxurious office one evening, Tommy looked up at his mother and queried, "Mommy, can little boys grow up to be lawyers, too?"

11. A catalog of relevant examples

A two-hundred-pound teenager quit school because no desk would hold her. A three-hundred-pound chef who could no longer stand on his feet was fired. A three-hundred-fifty-pound truck driver broke furniture in his friends' houses. All these people are now living healthier, happier, and thinner lives, thanks to the remarkable intestinal bypass surgery first developed in 1967.

12. Statement of a problem or a popular misconception

Some people believe that poetry is written only by aging beatniks or solemn, mournful men and women with suicidal tendencies. The Poetry in the Schools Program is working hard to correct that erroneous point of view.

Thinking of a good lead-in is often difficult when you sit down to begin your essay. Many writers, in fact, skip the lead-in until the first draft is written.

They compose their working thesis first and then write the body of the essay, saving the lead-in and conclusion for last. As you write the middle of your essay, you may discover an especially interesting piece of information you might want to save to use as your lead-in.

AVOIDING ERRORS IN LEAD-INS

In addition to the previous suggestions, here is some advice to help you avoid common lead-in errors:

Make sure your lead-in introduces your thesis. A frequent weakness in introductory paragraphs is an interesting lead-in but no smooth or clear transition to the thesis statement. To avoid a gap or awkward jump in thought in your introductory paragraph, you may need to add a connecting sentence or phrase between your lead-in and thesis. Study the paragraph below, which uses a comparison as its lead-in. The italicized transition sentence takes the reader from a general comment on all disabled Americans to information about those in Smallville, smoothly preparing the reader for the thesis that follows.

Lead-in

Transition sentence

Thesis

> In the 1950s black Americans demanded and won the right to sit anywhere they pleased on public buses. Today, another large group of Americans—the disabled confined to wheelchairs—is fighting for the simple right to board those same buses. *Here in Smallville, as well as in other cities, the lack of proper boarding facilities often denies disabled citizens basic transportation to jobs, grocery stores, and medical centers.* In order to give persons confined to wheelchairs the same opportunities as those given to other residents, the Smallville City Council should vote the funds necessary to convert the public transportation system so that it may be used by disabled citizens.

Keep your lead-in brief. Long lead-ins in short essays often give the appearance of a tail wagging the dog. Use a brief, attention-catching hook to set up your thesis; don't make your introduction the biggest part of your essay.

Don't begin with an apology or complaint. Statements such as "It's difficult to find much information on this topic . . ." and "This controversy is hard to understand, but . . ." do nothing to entice your reader.

Don't assume your audience already knows your subject matter. Identify the pertinent facts even though you know your teacher knows the assignment. ("The biggest problem with the new requirement. . . ." What requirement?) If you are writing about a particular piece of literature, identify the title of the work and its author, using the writer's full name in the first reference.

Stay clear of overused lead-ins. If composition teachers had a nickel for every essay that began with a dry dictionary definition, they could all retire to Bermuda. Leave *Webster's* alone and find a livelier way to begin. Asking a question as your lead-in is becoming overused, too, so use it only when it is obviously the best choice for your opener.

PRACTICING WHAT YOU'VE LEARNED

Find three good lead-ins from essays, magazine articles, or newspaper feature stories. Identify the kinds of lead-ins you found, and tell why you think each effectively catches the reader's attention and sets up the thesis.

HOW TO WRITE A GOOD CONCLUDING PARAGRAPH

Like a good story, a good essay should not stop in the middle. It should have a satisfying conclusion, one that gives the reader a sense of completion on the subject. Don't allow your essay to drop off or fade out at the end—instead, use the concluding paragraph to emphasize the validity and importance of your thinking. Remember that the concluding paragraph is your last chance to convince the reader. (As one cynical but realistic student pointed out, the conclusion is the last part of your essay the teacher reads before putting a grade on your paper.) Therefore, make your conclusion count.

Some people feel that writing an essay shares a characteristic with a romantic fling—both activities are frequently easier to begin than they are to end. If you find, as many writers do, that you often struggle long while searching for an exit with the proper emphasis and grace, here are some suggestions, by no means exhaustive, that might spark some good ideas for your conclusions:

1. A restatement of both the thesis and the essay's major points (for long essays only)

> As much as we may dislike the notion, it's time to reinstate the military draft. With the armed services' failure to meet its recruitment goals, the rising costs of defense, and the racism and sexism inherent in our volunteer system, we have no other choice if we wish a protected future.

2. An evaluation of the importance of the essay's subject

> These amazing, controversial photographs of the comet will continue to be the subject of debate because,

according to some scientists, they yield the most important clues yet revealed about the origins of our universe.

3. A statement of the essay's broader implications

Because these studies of feline leukemia may someday play a crucial role in the discovery of a cure for AIDS in human beings, the experiments, as expensive as they are, must continue.

4. A call to action

The fate of the World War II hero Raoul Wallenberg is still unknown. Although Congress has awarded him honorary citizenship, such a tribute is not enough. We must write our congressional representatives today to voice our demand that they investigate his disappearance or produce proof of his death. No hero deserves less.

5. A warning based on the essay's thesis

Understanding the politics that led up to Hiroshima is essential for all Americans—indeed, for all the world's peoples. Without such knowledge, the frightful possibility exists that somewhere, sometime, someone may drop the bomb again.

6. A witticism that emphasizes or sums up the point of the essay

No one said dieting was easy. But for some of us who have surrendered, the cliché "half a loaf is better than none" has taken on new meaning!

7. A quotation, story, or joke that emphasizes or sums up the point of the essay

Bette Davis's role on and off the screen as the catty, wisecracking woman of steel helped make her an enduring star. After all, no audience, past or present, could ever resist a dame who drags on a cigarette and then mutters about a passing starlet, "There goes a good time that was had by all."

8. An image or description that lends finality to the essay

> As the last of the Big Screen's giant ants are inciner-
> ated by the army scientist, one can almost hear the movie
> audiences of the 1950s breathing a collective sigh of relief,
> secure in the knowledge that once again the threat of nu-
> clear radiation had been vanquished by the efforts of the
> U.S. military.

(For another brief image that captures the essence of an essay, see also the "open house" scene that concludes "To Bid the World Farewell," p. 206.)

9. A rhetorical question that makes the readers think about the essay's main point

> No one wants to see hostages put in danger. But
> what nation can afford to let terrorists know they can get
> away with murder?

10. A forecast based on the essay's thesis

> Soap operas will continue to be popular not only
> because they distract us from our daily chores but also
> because they present life as we want it to be: fast-paced,
> glamorous, and full of exciting characters.

AVOIDING ERRORS IN CONCLUSIONS

Try to omit the following common errors in your concluding paragraphs:

Avoid a mechanical ending. One of the most frequent weaknesses in student essays is the conclusion that merely restates the thesis, word for word. A
short essay of 500–750 words rarely requires a flat, point-by-point conclusion—
in fact, such an ending often insults the readers' intelligence by implying that
their attention spans are extremely short. Only after reading long essays do
most readers need a precise recap of the writer's main ideas. Instead of recopying your thesis and essay map, try finding an original, emphatic way to conclude your essay—or as a well-known newspaper columnist described it, a
good ending should snap with grace and authority, like the close of an expensive sports car door.

Don't introduce new points. Treat the major points of your essay in
separate body paragraphs rather than in your exit.

Don't tack on a conclusion. There should be a smooth flow from your last body paragraph into your concluding statements.

Don't change your stance. Sometimes writers who have been critical of something throughout their essays will soften their stance or offer apologies in their last paragraph. For instance, someone complaining about the poor quality of a particular college course might abruptly conclude with statements that declare the class wasn't so bad after all, maybe she should have worked harder, or maybe she really did learn something after all. Such reneging may seem polite, but in actuality it undercuts the thesis and confuses the reader who has taken the writer's criticisms seriously. Instead of contradicting themselves, writers should stand their ground, forget about puffy clichés or "niceties," and find an emphatic way to conclude that is consistent with their thesis.

Avoid trite expressions. Don't begin your conclusions by declaring, "in conclusion," "in summary," or "as you can see, this essay proves my thesis that. . . ." End your essay so that the reader clearly senses completion; don't merely announce that you're finished.

▶ PRACTICING WHAT YOU'VE LEARNED

Find three good concluding paragraphs. Identify each kind of conclusion and tell why you think it is an effective ending for the essay or article.

HOW TO WRITE A GOOD TITLE

As in the case of lead-ins, your title may be written at any time, but many writers prefer to finish their essays before naming them. A good title is similar to a good newspaper headline in that it attracts the readers' interest and makes them want to investigate the essay. Like the lead-in, the title also helps announce the tone of the essay. An informal or humorous essay, for instance, might have a catchy, funny title. Some titles show the writer's wit and love of wordplay; a survey of recent magazines revealed these titles: "Bittersweet News about Saccharin," "Coffee: New Grounds for Concern," and "The Scoop on the Best Ice Cream."

On the other hand, a serious, informative essay should have a more formal title that suggests its content as clearly and specifically as possible. Let's suppose, for example, that you are doing research on the meaning of color in dreams, and you run across an essay listed in the library's *Readers' Guide* titled merely "Dreams." You don't know whether you should read it. To avoid such confusion in your own essay and to encourage readers' interest, always use a specific title: "Animal Imagery in Dreams," "Dream Research in Dogs," and so forth. Moreover, if your subject matter is controversial, let the reader know which side you're on (e.g., "The Advantages of Solar Power"). Never substitute a mere label, such as "Football Games" or "Euthanasia," for a meaningful title. And never, never label your essays "Theme One" or "comparison and contrast essay." In all your writing, including the title, use your creativity to attract the readers' attention and to invite their interest in your ideas.

If you're unsure about how to present your title, here are two basic rules:

1. Your own title should *not* be underlined or put in quotation marks. It should be written at the top of page one of your essay or on an appropriate cover sheet with no special marks of punctuation.

2. Only the first word and the important words of your title should be capitalized. Generally, do not capitalize words such as "an," "and," "a," or "the," or prepositions, unless they appear as the first word of the title.

ASSIGNMENT

Select any three of the student or professional essays in this text; give the first one a new title; the second, an interesting lead-in; the third, a different conclusion. Why are your choices as effective or even better than those of the original writers?

APPLYING WHAT YOU'VE LEARNED TO *YOUR* WRITING

Look at the draft of the essay you are currently working on and ask yourself these questions:

• Does the opening of my essay make my reader want to continue reading? Does the lead-in smoothly set up my thesis or do I need to add some sort of transition to help move the reader to my main idea? Is the lead-in appropriate in terms of the tone and length of my essay?

• Does the conclusion of my essay offer an emphatic ending, one that is consistent with my essay's purpose? Have I avoided a mechanical, trite, or tacked-on closing paragraph? Have I refrained from adding a new point in my conclusion that belongs in the body of my essay or in another essay?

• Does my title interest my reader? Is its content and tone appropriate for this particular essay?

If you have answered "no" to any of the above questions, you should continue revising your essay. (For more help revising your prose, turn to Chapter 5.)

CHAPTER 4 SUMMARY

Here is a brief restatement of what you should remember about writing introductions, conclusions, and titles:

1. Many essays will profit from a lead-in, the first sentences of the introductory paragraph that attract the reader's attention and smoothly set up the thesis statement.

2. Essays should end convincingly, without being repetitious or trite, with thoughts that emphasize the writer's main purpose.

3. Titles should invite the reader's interest by indicating the general nature of the essay's content and its tone.

5

DRAFTING AND REVISING: CREATIVE THINKING, CRITICAL THINKING

There is no good writing, only rewriting—James Thurber

When I say writing, O, believe me, it is rewriting that I have chiefly in mind—Robert Louis Stevenson

The absolute necessity of revision cannot be overemphasized. All good writers rethink, rearrange, and rewrite large portions of their prose. The French novelist Colette, for instance, wrote everything over and over. In fact, she often spent an entire morning working on a single page. Hemingway, to cite another example, rewrote the ending to *A Farewell to Arms* thirty-nine times "to get the words right." While no one expects you to make thirty-nine drafts of each essay, the point is clear: *Writing well means revising*. All good writers revise their prose.

WHAT IS REVISION?

Revision is a *thinking process* that occurs any time you are working on a writing project. It means looking at your writing with a "fresh eye"—that is, reseeing your writing in ways that will enable you to make more effective choices throughout your essay. Revision often entails rethinking what you have written and asking yourself questions about its effectiveness; it involves discovery as well as change. As you write, new ideas surface, prompting you to revise what you have planned or have just written. Or perhaps these new ideas will cause changes in earlier parts of your essay. In some cases, your new ideas will encourage you to begin an entirely new draft with a different focus or approach. Revision means making important decisions about the best ways to focus, organize, develop, clarify, and emphasize your ideas.

WHEN DOES REVISION OCCUR?

Revision, as noted above, occurs throughout your writing process. Early on, you are revising as you sort through ideas to write about, and you almost certainly revise as you define your purpose and audience and sharpen your thesis. Some revising may be done in your head, and some may be on paper as you plan, sketch, or "discovery-write" your ideas. Later, during drafting, revision becomes more individualized and complex. Many writers find themselves sweeping back and forth over their papers, writing for a bit and then rereading what they wrote, making changes, and then moving ahead. Some writers like to revise "lumps," or pieces of writing, perhaps reviewing one major idea or paragraph at a time. Frequently, writers discover that a better idea is occurring almost at the very moment they are putting another thought on paper. And virtually all writers revise after "reseeing" a draft in its entirety.

Revision, then, occurs before drafting, during drafting, between parts of drafts, and at the ends of drafts. You can revise a word, a sentence, a paragraph, or an entire essay. If you are like most writers, you sometimes revise almost automatically as you write (crossing out one word or line and quickly replacing it with another as you move on, for example), and at other times you revise very deliberately (concentrating on a conclusion you know is weak, for example). Revision is "rethinking," and that activity can happen anytime, in many ways, in any part of your writing.

MYTHS ABOUT REVISION

If revision is rethinking, what is it not? Three misconceptions about revision are addressed here.

1. Revision is not autopsy.

Revision is not an isolated stage of writing that occurs *only* after your last draft is written or right before your paper is to be handed in. Revising is not merely a postmortem procedure, to be performed only after your creative juices have ceased to flow. Good writing, as Thurber noted, *is* revision, and revision occurs throughout the writing process.

2. Revision is not limited to editing or proofreading.

Too many writers mistakenly equate revision with editing and proofreading. *Editing* means revising for "surface errors"—mistakes in spelling, grammar, punctuation, sentence sense, and word choice. Certainly, good writers comb their papers for such errors, and they edit their prose extensively for clarity, conciseness, and emphasis, too. *Proofreading* to search out and destroy errors and typos that distort meaning or distract the reader is also important. Without question, both editing and proofreading are essential to a polished paper. But revision is not *limited* to such activities. It includes them but also encompasses those larger, global changes writers may make in purpose, focus, organization, and development. Writers who revise effectively not only change words and catch mechanical errors but also typically add, delete, rearrange, and rewrite large chunks of prose. In other words, revision is not cosmetic surgery on a body that may need major resuscitation.

3. Revision is not punishment or busywork.

At one time or another, most of us have found ourselves guilty of racing too quickly through a particular job and then moving on. And perhaps just as often we have found ourselves redoing such jobs because the results were so disappointing. Some people may regard revising in a similar light—as the repeat performance of a job done poorly the first time. But that attitude isn't productive. Revising isn't punishment for failing to produce a perfect first draft. Rarely, if ever, does anyone—even our most admired professional writers—produce the results they want without revising.* Remember that revising is not a tacked-on stage nor is it merely a quick touch-up; it's an integral part of the entire writing process itself. It's an ongoing opportunity to discover, remember, reshape, and refine your ideas.

If you've ever created something you now treasure—a piece of jewelry, furniture, painting, or music—recall the time you put into it. You probably thought about it from several angles, experimented with it, crafted it, worked it through expected and unexpected problems, and smoothed out its minor glitches, all to achieve the results you wanted. Similarly, with each revision you

---

* All of us have heard stories about famous essays or poems composed at one quick sitting. Bursts of creativity do happen. But it's also highly likely that authors of such pieces revise extensively in their heads before they write. They rattle ideas around in their brains for such a prolonged period that the actual writing does in fact flow easily or may even seem "dictated" by an inner voice. This sort of lengthy internal "cooking" may work well at various times for you too.

make, your paper becomes clearer, truer, more satisfying to you and to your readers. With practice, you will produce writing you are proud of—and you will discover that revising has become not only an essential but also a natural part of your writing process.

CAN I LEARN TO IMPROVE MY REVISION SKILLS?

Because revision is such a multifaceted and individual activity, no textbook can guide you through all the rethinking you may do as you move through each sentence of every writing project. But certainly you can learn to improve your ability to think creatively and critically about your prose. To sharpen your thinking and revision skills, this chapter will suggest a step-by-step method of self-questioning designed to help you achieve your writing goals.

PREPARING TO DRAFT AND REVISE

Before you begin drafting (either a "discovery" draft or a draft from your working thesis), remember this important piece of advice: No part of your draft is sacred or permanent. No matter what you write at this point, you can always change it. Drafting is discovering and recollecting as well as recording ideas from your earlier plans. Take the pressure off yourself: No one expects blue-ribbon prose in early drafts. (If you can't seem to get going or if you do become stuck along the way, try turning to pp. 120–122 of this chapter for suggestions to help you confront your writer's block.)

At this point, too, you might consider the actual format of your drafts. Because you will be making many changes in your writing, you may find revising less cumbersome and time-consuming if you prepare your manuscripts as described below.

If you are handwriting your drafts:

1. Always write on one side of your paper only, in case you want to cut and tape together portions of drafts or you want to experiment with interchanging parts of a particular draft. (If you have written on both sides, you may have to recopy the parts of your essay you want to save; your time is better spent creating and revising.)

2. Leave big margins on *both* sides of each page of your drafts so you can add information later or jot down new ideas as they occur. (Some writers also skip lines for this reason. If you choose to write every other line, however, do remember that you may not be getting a true picture of your paragraph development or essay length. A handwritten double-spaced body paragraph, for example, may appear skimpy in your typed final copy.)

3. Devise a system of symbols (circles, stars, checks, asterisks, etc.) that will remind you of changes you want to make later. For example, if you're in hot pursuit of a great idea but can't think of the exact word you want, put down a word that's close, circle it, and go on so that your thinking is not derailed. Similarly, a check in the margin might mean "return to this tangled sentence." A question mark might mean fuzzy idea, and a star, a great idea that needs expanding. A system of signals can save you from agonizing over every inch of your essay while you are still trying to discover and clarify your ideas.

4. If your ideas are flowing well but you realize you need more supporting evidence for some of your points, consider leaving some blank spots to fill in later. For example, let's say you are writing about the role of television in our presidential elections; your ideas are good but in a particular body paragraph you decide some statistics on commercial frequency would be most convincing. Or perhaps you need to cite an example of a particular kind of advertisement but you just can't think of a good one at that moment. Leave a spot for the piece of evidence with a key word or two to remind you of what's needed, and keep writing. Later, when you come back to that spot, you can add the appropriate support; if you can't find or think of the right supporting evidence to insert, you may decide to delete that point.

5. If you do decide to delete something—a sentence or an entire passage—mark a single "X" or line through it lightly. Don't scratch it out or destroy it completely; you may realize later you want to reinsert the material there or move it to another, better place.

6. At some point do try to work from a typed copy. Frankly, the more compact spacing of typed prose allows you to see better the relationship of the parts in your essay, making it easier for you to organize and develop your ideas. It is also far more likely that you will catch spelling and other mechanical errors if they are printed.

7. Always keep your drafts. Never burn your bridges—or your manuscripts! Sometimes essays change directions, and writers find they can return to prewriting or earlier drafts to recover ideas, once rejected, that now work well. Drafts also may contain ideas that didn't work in one paper but that look like great starts for another assignment. Tracking revisions from draft to draft can give writers a sense of accomplishment and insight into their composing processes. And drafts can be good insurance in case final copies of papers are lost or accidentally destroyed.

A Special Note for Writers with Word Processors

If you have access to a computer and any of the many word-processing programs available today, you have probably already discovered how helpful this technology can be to writers in all stages of the writing process. You can, for example, store your prewriting activities, journal entries, notes, or good ideas in various files until you need to recall certain information, and you can easily produce extra copies of your drafts or finished essays without having to search out a copy machine and correct change. Spell-checkers or dictionaries may identify many of your surface errors and typos.

But the most important use of the computer to a writer may be what it can do as you draft and revise your prose. At your command, a word-processing program enables you to add, delete, or change words easily; it allows you to move words, sentences, and even paragraphs or larger pieces of your essay. On any computer, for example, you can play "what if" by dropping the cursor below what you have written and try to phrase your idea in another way. Then you can delete the less effective passage. With some programs, you can even compare drafts side by side or with special "windows" that help you to see your choices more clearly. In other words, computers can help us as writers do the kind of deep-structure revision that is necessary to produce our best, most effective prose—the kind of major changes that, in the past, we may have been hesitant to make because of the time involved in recopying or retyping major portions of our drafts.

Whether the program you are using at home or at school is a series of simple commands or an elaborate instructional system that can ask questions or provide a sophisticated analysis of your writing, make a point of getting to know how to use the computer in the most effective ways. Study the manual that accompanies your word-processing program (or one of the many self-help manuals now on the market), and don't be afraid to ask your instructor or computer-lab monitor for assistance. The more you practice using your programs to help you organize, develop, and revise your prose, the better your writing will be. (Remember, to avoid the "agony of delete," always "save" what you have written every ten minutes or so, and do print out a copy of each major draft or set of revisions in case your system crashes or you accidentally hit the wrong keys.)

A REVISION PROCESS FOR YOUR DRAFTS

Let's assume at this point that you have completed a draft, using the first four chapters of this book as a guide. You feel you've chosen an interesting topic and presented some good ideas. Perhaps the ideas came quickly or perhaps you had to coax them. However your thoughts came, they're now on paper—you have a draft with meaning and general order, although it's probably much rougher in some spots than in others. Now it's time to "resee" this draft in a comprehensive way.

But wait. If possible, put a night's sleep or at least a few hours between this draft and the advice that appears on the next few pages. All writers become tired when they work on any project for too long at one sitting, and then they lose a sense of perspective. When you've looked at a piece of prose again and again, you may begin to read what's written in your head instead of what's on the page—that is, you may begin to "fill in" for yourself, reading into your prose what you meant to say rather than what your reader will actually see. Always try to start your writing process early enough to give yourself a few breaks from the action. You'll find that you will be better able to evaluate the strengths and weaknesses of your prose when you are fresh.

When you do return to your draft, *don't try to look at all the parts of your paper, from ideas to organization to mechanics, at the same time.* Trying to re-see everything at once is rarely possible and will only overload and frustrate you. It may cause you to overlook some important part of your paper that needs your full attention. Overload can also block your creative ideas. Therefore, instead of trying to revise an entire draft in one swoop, break your revising process into a series of smaller, more manageable steps. Here is a suggested process:

I.	rethink	purpose, thesis, and audience
II.	rethink	ideas and evidence
III.	rethink	organization
IV.	rethink	clarity and style
V.	edit	grammar, punctuation, and spelling
VI.	proofread	entire essay

IMPORTANT: Please note that these steps are not necessarily distinct, nor must you always follow this suggested order. You certainly might, for instance, add details to a paragraph when you decide to move or reorder it. Or you might replace a vague word with a specific one after thinking about your audience and their needs. After strengthening a particular point, you might decide to offer it last, and therefore you rearrange the order of your paragraphs. In other words, the steps offered above are not part of a forced march—they are here simply to remind you to rethink and improve any part of your essay that needs work.

Now let's look at each of the steps in the revision process suggested above in more detail.

I.   Revising for Purpose, Thesis, and Audience

To be effective, writers need a clear sense of purpose and audience. Their essays must present (or clearly imply) a main idea or thesis designed to fulfill that purpose and to inform their audience. As you reread your draft, ask yourself the following questions:

Have I fulfilled the objectives of my assignment? (For example, if you were asked to analyze the causes of a problem, did you merely describe or summarize it instead?)

Did I follow directions carefully? (If you were given a three-part assignment, did you treat all parts as requested?)

Do I understand the purpose of my essay? Am I trying to inform, persuade, or amuse my readers? Spur them to action? Convince them to change their minds? Give them a new idea? Am I myself clear about my exact intent—what I want to do or say—in this essay?

Does my essay reflect my clearly understood purpose by offering an appropriately narrowed and focused thesis? (After reading through your essay once, could a reader easily state its purpose and main point?)

Do I have a clear picture of my audience—their character, knowledge, and expectations?

Have I addressed both my purpose and my readers' needs by selecting an appropriate strategy of development for my essay? (For example, would it be better to write an essay developed with examples illustrating the community's need for a new hospital or should you present a more formal argument that also rebuffs objections to the project? Should you narrate the story of your accident or analyze its effects on your family?)

If you feel that your draft needs work in any of these areas, make changes. You might find it helpful to review Chapters 1 and 2 of this text to guide you as you revise.

II.   Revising for Ideas and Evidence

If you're satisfied that your purpose and thesis are clear to your readers, begin to look closely at the development of your essay's ideas.

You want your readers to accept your thesis. To achieve this goal, you must offer body paragraphs whose major points clearly support that main idea. As you examine the body of your essay, you might ask yourself questions such as these:

Is there a logical connection between each of the major points presented in the body of my essay and my thesis? That is, does each major point in my essay further my readers' understanding, and thus their acceptance, of my thesis's general claim?

Did I write myself into a new or slightly different position as I drafted my essay? If so, do I need to begin another draft with a new working thesis?

Have I included all the major points necessary to the readers' understanding of my subject or have I omitted pertinent ones? (On the other hand, have I included major ideas that aren't relevant or that actually belong in a different essay?)

Are my major points located and stated clearly in specific language so readers can easily see what position I am taking in each part of my discussion?

If you are happy with your choice and presentation of the major ideas in the body of your essay, it's time to look closely at the evidence you are offering to support your major ideas (which, in turn, support the claim of your thesis). To choose the best supporting evidence for their major points, effective writers use *critical thinking skills*.

WHAT IS CRITICAL THINKING?

Critical thinking means the ability to analyze and evaluate our own ideas and those of others. Because we are constantly bombarded today with all kinds of information and differing points of view, we need skills to examine ideas carefully before we accept or reject them.

Here's a common situation in which critical thinking comes into play: two of your friends are arguing over the use of fetal tissue in medical research. Each friend has many points to offer; each is presenting statistics, examples of actual case studies, the words of experts, and hypothetical situations that might arise. Many of the statistics and experts on one side of the argument seem to contradict directly the figures and authorities on the other side. Which side do you take? Why? Are there other points of view to consider? How can you know what to think?

Every day we are faced with just such decisions. We must be able to judge intelligently the merits of what we hear and read before we can feel confident about what we think of a particular issue. We must practice studying our beliefs and those held by others to analyze the reasons for maintaining those views. To think critically about ideas doesn't mean being constantly hostile or negative; it simply means that we need to examine opinions closely and carefully before we accept them.

THINKING CRITICALLY AS A WRITER

As a writer, you will be thinking critically in two important ways. First, you will need to think critically about any information you may be collecting to use as evidence in your essay. You may, for example, need to be a critical reader as you consider information from books or journals. You almost certainly will need to be a critical listener as you hear other people talk about their experiences and beliefs.

As you draft and revise your essay, you must become a critical thinker in a second way: you must become your own toughest reader-critic. To convince your readers that your essay has merit, you must stand back and try to assess objectively what you have written. Are your ideas clear not only to you but to your readers as well? Will readers find your opinions well developed, logical, and supported? In other words, to revise more effectively, try role-playing one of your own most thoughtful critical readers, someone who will be closely examining the ideas and evidence in your essay before agreeing with its position.

Here are six suggestions to help you think critically as you draft and revise:

1. Learn to distinguish fact from opinion.

A *fact* is an accepted truth whose verification is not affected by its source. No matter who presents it, a fact remains true. We accept some statements as facts because we can test them personally (fire is hot) or because they have been verified frequently by others (penguins live in Antarctica). We accept as fact, for example, that President John Kennedy was killed in Dallas, Texas, on November 22, 1963. However, the identity of the assassin remains, for many people, a matter of *opinion*. That is, depending on the speaker, Kennedy's killer(s) could be Lee Harvey Oswald, a CIA assassin, a foreign agent, a disgruntled politician, a member of organized crime, or someone else. As you think about your evidence, be careful that you don't present your opinions as facts accepted by everyone. Opinions are debatable, and therefore you must always support them before your readers will be convinced.

2. Support your opinions with evidence.

To support your opinions, you must offer evidence of one or more kinds. You have a variety of options to choose from. You might support one idea by using personal experiences. Or you might describe the experiences of friends or family. In another place you might decide to offer detailed examples or to cite statistics or to quote an expert on your subject. You can also use hypothetical examples, researched material, vivid descriptions, reasoned arguments, revealing comparisons, case studies, or testimony of relevant participants, just to name a few other strategies. Consider your purpose and your audience, review the possibilities, and choose the most effective kind of support. The more convincing the support, the more likely your readers are to accept your opinions as true. (If you need to review some sample paragraphs developed by various types of evidence, turn to pp. 60–65 of Chapter 3.)

3. Evaluate the strength of your evidence.

As you choose your evidence, you should consider its value for the particular point it will support. Scrutinize the nature and source of your evidence carefully. If you are using examples, do they clearly illustrate your claim? Does this example or another one (or both?) provide the best illustration of your particular point? Is description alone enough support here? Are your statistics or researched material from a reliable, current source? Was information from your research collected in a careful, professional way? Are your experts unbiased authorities from the field under discussion? Where did your experts obtain their information? (For example, are you claiming that crystals possess magical healing powers because you heard a woman on a radio talk show say so and she sounded reasonable to you? How much do you know about this woman's expertise?) Asking yourself the kinds of questions posed here (and others suggested throughout Part Two of this text) will help you develop a critical eye for choosing the best evidence to support your opinions.

4. Use enough specific supporting evidence.

Readers need to see strong, relevant supporting evidence throughout your essay. You must be sure, therefore, that you have enough clearly stated evidence for each of your major points. If you present, for instance, too few ex-amples or only a vague reference to an event that supports one of your ideas, a reader may remain unconvinced or may even be confused. As you revise, ask yourself questions such as these: "Do I need to provide additional information here?" "Do I need more details to develop the supporting evidence already present?" "Is any of my evidence concealed by vague or fuzzy language?" If you feel additional supporting evidence or details are needed, take another look at any prewriting you did—or use one of the "pump-primer" techniques described in Chapter 1 now to discover some new creative thoughts. For some topics, you may need to do more research or interviewing to find the information you need. (Writers occasionally need to prune ideas too, especially if they're repetitious or off the topic. But, in general, most early drafts are thin and will profit from more, rather than less, specific supporting evidence.)

5. Watch for biases and strong emotions that may undermine evidence.

As you think critically about evidence you are using, monitor any biases and emotional attitudes that may distort information you wish to incorporate in your essay. If you are using personal experiences, for example, have you calmed down enough from your anger over your landlord's actions to write about the clash in a rational, persuasive way? In an essay criticizing a particular product, are you so familiar with the frustrating item that you are making ambiguous claims? (If you write, "The new instructions for use are more confusing than ever," have you shown that they were confusing in the first place? Or why they are more so now?) Be sensitive to any racial, ethnic, cultural, religious, or gen-der-based assumptions you or your sources may have. Opinions based on gener-alizations and stereotypes ("Japanese cars are better because Orientals are more efficient workers than Americans"; "Women should stay home because they are better with children than men") are not convincing to thinking readers.

6. Check your evidence for logical fallacies.

Thinking critically about your drafts should help you support your ideas with reasonable, logical explanations and arguments. Logical fallacies are common errors in reasoning that good writers try to avoid. Those fallacies found most often today are explained on pages 269–272 of this text; review-ing them will enable you to identify problems in logic that might appear in the writing of others or in your own drafts.

Critical thinking is not, of course, limited to the six suggestions offered here. But by practicing this advice, you will begin to develop and sharpen analytical skills that should improve any writing project.

III. Revising for Organization

In reality, you have probably already made several changes in the order and organization of ideas in your draft. As noted before, it's likely that when you thought about your essay's meaning—its major points and their supporting evidence—you also thought about the arrangement of those ideas. As you take another look at your draft's organization, use these questions as a guide:

Am I satisfied with the organizational strategy I selected for my purpose? (For example, as you wrote did you decide that an essay primarily developed by comparison and contrast would achieve your purpose better than a narrative approach?)

Are my major points ordered in a logical, easy-to-follow pattern? Would readers understand my thinking better if certain paragraphs or major ideas were rearranged? Added? Divided? Omitted?

Are my major points presented in topic sentences that state each important idea clearly and specifically? (If any of your topic sentences are implied rather than stated, are you absolutely, 100 percent sure that your ideas cannot be overlooked or even slightly misunderstood by your readers?)

Is there a smooth flow between my major ideas? Between paragraphs? Within paragraphs? Have I used enough transition devices to guide the reader along?

Are any parts of my essay out of proportion? Too long or too short to do their job effectively?

Do my title and lead-in draw readers into the essay and toward my thesis?

Does my conclusion end my discussion thoughtfully? Perhaps emphatically or memorably?

Don't be afraid to restructure your drafts. Most good writers rearrange and recast large portions of their prose. Reviewing Chapters 3 and 4 may help you address questions on organization, beginnings, or endings.

IV.   Revising for Clarity and Style

As you've revised for purpose, ideas, and organization, you have also taken steps to clarify your prose. Making a special point now of focusing on sentences and word choice will ensure your readers' complete understanding of your thinking. Read through your draft, asking these kinds of questions:

Is each of my sentences as clear and precise as it could be for readers who do not know what I know? Are there sentences that contain misplaced words or convoluted phrases that might cause confusion?

Are there any sentences that are unnecessarily wordy? Is there deadwood that could be eliminated? (Remember that concise prose is more effective than wordy, "fat" prose because readers can find and follow key ideas and terms easier. Nearly every writer has a wordiness problem that chokes communication, so now is the season to prune.)

Do any sentences run on for too long to be fully understood? Can any repetitive or choppy sentences be combined to achieve clarity and a pleasing variation of sentence style? (To help you decide if you need to combine sentences, you might try this experiment. Select a body paragraph and count the number of words it contains. Then count the number of sentences; divide the number of words by the number of sentences to discover the average number of words per sentence. If your score is less than 15–18, you may need to combine *some* sentences. Good prose offers a variety of sentence lengths and patterns.)

Are all my words and their connotations accurate and appropriate?

Can I clarify and energize my prose by adding "showing" details and by replacing bland, vague words with vivid, specific ones? By using active verbs rather than passive ones?

Can I eliminate any pretentious or unnecessary jargon or language that's inappropriate for my audience? Replace clichés and trite expressions with fresh, original phrases?

Is my voice authentic, or am I trying to sound like someone else? Is my tone reasonable, honest, and consistent?

The issues raised by these questions—and many others—are discussed in detail in Chapters 6 and 7, on effective sentences and words, which offer more advice on clarifying language and improving style.

V. Editing for Errors

Writers who are proud of the choices they've made in content, organization, and style are, to use a baseball metaphor, rounding third base and heading for home. But there's more to be done. Shift from a baseball metaphor to car maintenance for a moment. All good essays are not only fine-tuned but also waxed and polished—they are edited and proofread repeatedly for errors until they shine. To help you polish your prose by correcting errors in punctuation, grammar, spelling, and diction, here are some hints for effective editing:

Read aloud. In addition to repeatedly reading your draft silently, reading your draft aloud is a good technique because it allows your ears to hear ungrammatical "clunks" or unintended gaps in sense or sound you may otherwise miss.

Know your enemies. Learn to identify your particularly troublesome areas in punctuation and grammar and then read through your draft for one of these problems at a time: once for fragments, once for comma splices, once for run-ons, and so on. (If you try to look for too many errors at each reading, you'll probably miss quite a few.)

Read backwards. Try reading your draft one sentence at a time starting at the *end* of your essay and working toward the beginning. Don't read each sentence word-for-word backwards—just read the essay one sentence at a time from back to front. When writers try to edit (or proofread) starting at the beginning of their essays, they tend to begin thinking about the content they're reading rather than concentrating on the task of editing for errors. By reading one sentence at a time from the back, you will find that the sentences will still make sense but that you are less likely to wander away from the job at hand.

Learn some tricks. There are special techniques for treating some punctuation and grammar problems. If you have trouble, for example, knowing when to use commas before words like "and" or "but," turn to the FANBOYS hint on page 375. If fragments plague your writing, try the "it is true that" test explained on page 368. Consider designating a special part of your journal or class notebook to record in your own words these tricks and other useful pieces of advice so that you can refer to them easily and often.

Eliminate common irritants. Review your draft for those diction and mechanical errors many readers find especially annoying because they often reflect sheer carelessness. For example, look at these frequently confused words: *it's/its, you/you're, there/their/they're, who's/whose* (other often-confused words are listed on page 154). Some readers are ready for a national march to protest the public's abandonment of the apostrophe, the Amelia Earhart of punctuation. (Apostrophes do change meaning: "The teacher called the students names." Was the instructor being rude or just taking roll?) It's a grammatical jungle out there, so be sensitive to your weary readers.

Use your tools. Keep your dictionary handy to check the spelling, usage, and meanings of words in doubt. A thesaurus can also be useful if you can restrain any tendencies you have for growing overly exotic prose. If you are using a word processor with a spell-checker, by all means run it after your last revisions are completed. Do remember, however, that computers only flag words whose spelling they don't recognize; they will not alert you to omitted or confused words (*affect/effect*), nor will they signal when you've typed in a wrong, but correctly spelled, word (*here* for *her*).

Use Part Three of this text to help resolve any questions you may have about grammar, mechanics, and spelling. Advice on untangling sentences and clarifying word choice in Chapters 6 and 7 may be useful too.

VI. Proofreading

Proofread your final draft several times, putting as much time between the last two readings as possible. Fresh eyes catch more typographical or careless errors. Remember that typing errors—even the simple transposing of letters—can change the meaning of an entire thought and occasionally bring unintended humor to your prose (imagine, for example, the surprise of restaurant owners whose new lease instructed them to "Please sing the terms of the agreement as stated above." Was the contract presented a cappella or with music? Or consider the ramifications of the newspaper ad that offered "Great dames for sale").

Make sure, too, that your paper looks professional before you turn it in. You wouldn't, after all, expect to be taken seriously if you went to an executive job interview dressed in cutoffs. Turning in a paper with a coffee stain or ink blot on it has about the same effect as spinach in your teeth—it distracts folks from hearing what you have to say. If your final draft has typos or small blemishes, use correction fluid to conceal them; if you've patched so frequently that your paper resembles the medicine-dotted face of a kindergartner with chicken pox, photocopy your pages for a fresh look.

Check to be sure you've formatted your paper exactly as your assignment requested. Some instructors ask for a title page; others want folders containing all your drafts and prewriting. Most readers appreciate papers with pages that are numbered, ordered correctly, clipped or stapled, with clean edges (not sheets violently ripped from a spiral notebook still dribbling the remains of angry buttonholes down one side nor computer paper with printer edges still attached). Putting your name on each page will identify your work if papers from a particular class are accidentally mixed up.

As it's often been said, essays are never really done—only due. Take a last reading using the checklist below, make some notes on your progress as a writer and thinker, and congratulate yourself on your fine efforts and accomplishment.

A FINAL CHECKLIST FOR YOUR ESSAY

If you have written an effective essay, you should be able to answer "yes" to the following questions:

1. Do I feel I have something important to say to my reader?

2. Am I sincerely committed to communicating with my reader and not just with myself?

3. Have I considered my audience's needs? (See Chapter 1.)

4. Do my title and lead-in attract the reader's attention and help set up my thesis? (See Chapter 4.)

5. Does my thesis statement assert one clearly focused idea? (See Chapter 2.)

6. Does my thesis and/or essay map give the reader an indication of what points the essay will cover? (See Chapter 2.)

7. Do my body paragraphs contain the necessary main points in the essay's discussion, and are those points expressed in clearly stated or implied topic sentences? (See Chapter 3.)

8. Is each major point in my essay well developed with enough detailed supporting evidence? (See Chapter 3.)

9. Does each body paragraph have unity and coherence? (See Chapter 3.)

10. Are all the paragraphs in my essay smoothly linked in a logical order? (See Chapter 3.)

11. Does my concluding paragraph provide a suitable ending for the essay? (See Chapter 4.)

12. Are all my sentences clear, concise, and coherent? (See Chapter 6.)

13. Are my words accurate, necessary, and meaningful? (See Chapter 7.)

14. Have I edited and proofread for errors in grammar, punctuation, spelling, or typing? (See Part Three.)

And most important:

15. Has my essay been effectively revised so that I am proud of this piece of writing?

BENEFITING FROM REVISION WORKSHOPS

Many writing courses today include revision workshops in which students comment helpfully on one another's drafts. This sort of revision activity may also be called peer editing, classroom critique, or reader review. Peer workshops may be arranged in a variety of ways, though frequently students will work in pairs or in small groups of three to five. Sometimes writers will simply talk about their papers or read them aloud; at other times students will be asked to write suggestions on one another's drafts. Sometimes instructors will give student-reviewers a list of questions to answer; at other times, the writers themselves will voice their concerns directly to their reviewers. Structured in many effective ways, peer workshops can be extremely valuable to writers, who will invariably profit from seeing their drafts from a reader's point of view.

Students taking part in revision workshops for the first time often have questions about the reviewing process. Some student-reviewers may feel uneasy about their role, wondering, "What if I can't think of any suggestions for the writer? How can I tell someone that the paper's really terrible? What if I sense something's wrong but I'm not sure what it is—or how to fix it?" Writers, too, may feel apprehensive or even occasionally defensive about receiving criticism of their papers. Because these concerns are genuine and widespread, here is some advice to help you get the most out of your participation in revision workshops, in the role of writer or reviewer.

When you are the writer:

1. **Develop a constructive attitude.** Admittedly, receiving criticism—especially on a creation that has required hard work—can sometimes be diffi-

cult, particularly if your self-image has become mixed up with your drafts. Try to realize that your reviewer is not criticizing *you* personally but rather is trying to help you by offering fresh insights. All drafts can be improved, and no writer need feel embarrassed about seeking or receiving advice. (Take comfort in the words of writer Somerset Maugham: "Only the mediocre person is always at his best.") See the workshop as a nonthreatening opportunity to reconsider your prose and improve your audience awareness.

2. Come prepared. If your workshop structure permits, tell your reviewer what sort of help you need at this point in your drafting or revising process. Ask for suggestions to fix a particularly troublesome area or ask for feedback on a choice you've made but are feeling unsure of. Don't hesitate to ask your reviewer for assistance with any part of your essay.

3. Evaluate suggestions carefully. Writing isn't math: most of the time there are no absolutely right or wrong answers—just better or worse rhetorical choices. That is, there are many ways to communicate an idea to a set of readers. You, as the writer, must decide on an effective way, the way that best serves your purpose and your readers' needs. Sometimes your reviewer will suggest a change that is brilliant or one so obviously right you will wonder why in the world you didn't think of it yourself. At other times you may weigh your reviewer's suggestion and decide that your original choice is just as good or perhaps even better. Be open to suggestions, but learn to trust thyself as well.

4. Find the good in bad advice. Occasionally you may have a reviewer who seems to miss a crucial point or misunderstands your purpose entirely, whose suggestions for revising your paper seem uniformly unproductive for one reason or another. You certainly shouldn't take bad advice—but do think about the issues it raises. Although it's helpful to receive a dynamite suggestion you can incorporate immediately, the real value of a revision workshop is its ability to encourage you to rethink your prose. Readers' responses (yes, even the bizarre ones) challenge writers to take still another look at their rhetorical choices and ask themselves, "Is this clear after all? Does this example really work here? Did something in my essay throw this reader off the track?" Revision workshops offer you benefits, even if you ultimately decide to reject many of your reviewer's suggestions.

When you are the reviewer:

1. Develop a constructive attitude. Sometimes it's hard to give honest criticism—most of us are uncomfortable when we think we might hurt someone's feelings—but remember that the writer has resolved to develop a professional attitude too. The writer expects (and is sometimes desperately begging for) sincere feedback, so be honest as you offer your best advice.

2. Be clear and specific. Vague or flippant responses ("This is confusing"; "Huh?") don't help writers know what or how to revise. Try putting some of your comments into this format: your response to X, the reason for your response, a request for change, and, if possible, a specific suggestion for the change ("I'm confused when you say you enjoy some parts of breakfast because this seems to contradict your thesis claim of 'wretched dorm food.' Would it be clearer to modify your thesis to exclude breakfast or to revise this paragraph to include only discussion of the rubbery eggs?").

3. Address important issues. Unless you have workshop directions that request certain tasks, read through the draft entirely at least once and then comment on the larger issues first. Writers want to know if they are achieving their overall purpose, if their thesis is clear and convincing, if their major points and evidence make sense, and if their paper seems logical and or- dered. Editing tips are fine too, but because workshops encourage authors to rewrite large portions of their prose, attention to minor details may be less valuable early on than feedback on ideas, organization, and development. (Of course, an editing workshop later in the revision process may be exclusively focused on sentence and word problems. Workshops may be designed to ad- dress specific problems that writers face.)

4. Encourage the writer. Writers with confidence write and revise better than insecure or angry writers. Praise honestly wherever you can, as specifi- cally as you can. When weaknesses do appear, show the writer that you know she or he is capable of doing better work by linking the weakness to a strength elsewhere in the draft. ("Could you add more 'showing' details here so that your picture of the dentist is as vivid as your description of the nurse?") Substi- tute specific responses and suggestions for one-word labels such as "awk" (awkward) or "unclear." Even positive labels don't always help writers repeat effective techniques. ("Good!" enthusiastically inscribed in the margin by a well-developed paragraph feels nice but might cause the writer to wonder, "'Good' what? Good point? Good supporting evidence? Good detail? How can I do 'good' again if I don't know exactly what it is?")

5. Understand your role as critical reader. Sometimes it's easy for a reviewer to take ownership of someone else's paper. Keep the writer's pur- pose in mind as you respond; don't insist on revisions that produce an essay that's in *your* head. Be sensitive to your own voice and language as a re- viewer. Instead of making authoritative pronouncements that might offend, ask reader-based questions. ("Will all your readers know the meaning of this technical term?" "Would some readers profit from a brief history of this con- troversy?") If you're unsure about a possible error, request verification. ("Could you recheck this quotation? Its wording here is confusing me be- cause. . . . ") Practice offering criticism in language that acknowledges the writer's hard work and accentuates the positive nature of revision. ("Would citing last year's budget figures make your good argument against the fish market even stronger?")

Last, always look over your own draft in light of the insightful sug- gestions you are offering your classmates. You may feel at first that it is far simpler to analyze someone else's writing than your own. As you participate in revision workshops, however, you will find it increasingly easy to transfer those same critical reading skills to your own work. Becoming a good reader-reviewer for your composition colleagues can be an important part of your training as a first-rate writer.

▶ PRACTICING WHAT YOU'VE LEARNED

A. The draft of the student essay below has been annotated according to some—*but not all*—of the questions presented in this chapter's discussion of revision. As you read the draft and the writer's marginal comments, think of specific suggestions you might offer to help this writer improve her essay. What other changes, in addition to the ones mentioned here, would you encourage this writer to make? What strengths do you see in this draft?

Dorm Life

My title and lead-in are too bland to attract reader's attention.

Would my thesis be clearer if I said what I did find?

Dorm life is not at all what I had expected it to be. I had anticipated meeting friendly people, quiet hours for studying, eating decent food, and having wild parties on weekends. My dreams, I soon found out, were simply illusions, erroneous perceptions of reality.

My supporting examples could use more "showing" details so the readers can really see the unfriendliness.

My roommate, Kathy, and I live in Holland Hall on the third floor. The people on our dorm floor are about as unfriendly as they can possibly be. I wonder whether or not they're just shy and afraid or if they are simply snobs. Some girls, for example, ignore my roommate and me when we say "hello." Occasionally, they stare straight ahead and act like we aren't even there. Other girls respond, but it's as if they do it out of a sense of duty rather than being just friendly. The guys seem nice, but some are just as afraid or snobby as the girls.

I remember signing up for "quiet hours" when I put in my application for a dorm room last December. Unfortunately, I was assigned to a floor that doesn't have any quiet hours at all. I am a person who requires peace and quiet when studying or reading. The girls in all the rooms around us love to stay up until early in the morning and yell and turn up their music full blast. They turn music on at about eight o'clock at night and turn it off early in the morning. There is always at least one girl who has a tape playing at maximum volume. Now, I am very appreciative of music, but listening to "hard rock" until three in the

This ¶ has some specific details but it rambles and repeats ideas. Tighten organization.

morning isn't really my idea of what music is. The girls right across from us usually play Bonnie Raitt or Paul Simon and I enjoy them. On the other hand, though, the girls on either side of our room love to listen to Metallica or Nirvana into the wee hours of the morning. It is these girls who run up and down the hall, yell at each other, laugh obnoxiously, and try to attract attention. All this continuous racket makes it nearly impossible to study, read, or get any sleep. Kathy and I usually end up going to the library or student cafeteria to study. As far as sleep goes, it doesn't matter what time we go to bed, but rather it depends on how noisy it is, and how late the stereos are on. Sometimes the noise gets so loud and rambles on for so long that even when it stops, my ears are ringing and my stomach keeps churning. It is on nights like this that I never go to sleep. I wish the people here were a little more considerate of the people around them.

This ¶ doesn't support my thesis claim. I mean the dorm has no good parties or no floor parties? Re-think.

Parties, on weekends, are supposedly the most important part of dorm life. Parties provide the opportunity to meet others and have a good time. Holland Hall has had two parties that are even worth mentioning. One of them was a Fifties dance held in the courtyard approximately three weeks ago. Unfortunately, all the other dormitories, the fraternities, and the sororities heard about it, and by eight o'clock at night there were masses of people. It was so packed that it was hard to move around. The other party, much to my dismay, turned out to be a luau party. I do not really care for roast pig, and my stomach turned from the scent of it when I entered the room. Our floor never has parties. Everyone leaves their doors open, turns up the music, yells back and forth. I suppose that there will be more dorm parties once everyone becomes adjusted to this life and begins to socialize.

As stated, this topic sentence contradicts my thesis.

Some good examples — could use even more discriptive language?

Dorm food is what I anticipated it would be, terrible, and I was right, it is awful. Breakfast is probably the hardest meal to digest. The bacon and sausage are cold, slightly uncooked, and very greasy. Sometimes, it's as though I am eating pure grease. The eggs look and taste like nothing I ever had before. They look like plastic and they are never hot. I had eggs once and I vowed I would never have another one as long as I lived in Holland Hall. The most enjoyable part of breakfast is the orange juice. It's always cold and it seems to be fresh. No one can say dorm food is totally boring because the cooks break up the monotony of the same food by serving "mystery meat" at least once every two weeks. This puts a little excitement in the student's day because everyone cracks jokes and wonders just what's in this "mystery meat." I think a lot of students are afraid to ask, fearful of the answer, and simply make snide remarks and shovel it in.

Can I conclude emphatically without switching positions?

All in all, I believe dorm life isn't too great, even though there are some good times. Even though I complain about dorm food, the people, the parties, and everything else, I am glad I am here. I am happy because I have learned a lot about other people, responsibilities, consideration, and I've even learned a lot about myself.

B. Assume that the essay below is a draft written by one of your classmates who has asked you for help during a class workshop. Using your best critical thinking skills, offer some marginal comments and questions that will guide your friend through an effective revision process.

Maybe You Shouldn't Go Away to College

Going away to college is not for everyone. There are good reasons why a student might choose to live at home and attend a local school. Money, finding stability while changes are occurring, and accepting responsibility are three to consider.

Money is likely to be most important. Not only is tuition more expensive, but extra money is needed for room and board. Whether room and board is a dorm or an apartment, the expense is great.

Most students never stop to consider that the money that could be saved from room and board may be better spent in future years on graduate school, which is likely to be more important in their careers.

Going to school is a time of many changes anyway, without adding the pressure of a new city or even a new state. Finding stability will be hard enough, without going from home to a dorm. Starting college could be an emotional time for some, and the security of their home and family might make everything easier.

When students decide to go away to school, sometimes because their friends are going away, or maybe because the school is their parents' alma mater, something that all need to decide is whether or not they can accept the responsibility of a completely new way of life.

Everyone feels as if they are ready for total independence when they decide to go away to college, but is breaking away when they are just beginning to set their futures a good idea?

Going away to school may be the right road for some, but those who feel that they are not ready might start looking to a future that is just around the corner.

◢ ASSIGNMENT

Select a body paragraph from one of the preceding student essays and revise it, making any change in focus, organization, development, sentence construction, or word choice, you feel is necessary. Feel free to elaborate on, eliminate, or change the content to improve the paragraph's organization and development.

SOME LAST ADVICE: HOW TO PLAY WITH YOUR MENTAL BLOCKS

Every writer, sooner or later, suffers from some form of Writer's Block, the inability to think of or organize ideas. Symptoms may include sweaty palms, pencil chewing, and a pronounced tendency to sit in corners and weep. Although not every "cure" works for everyone, here are a few suggestions to help minimize your misery:

Try to give yourself as much time as possible to write your essay. Don't try to write the entire paper in one sitting. By doing so, you may place yourself under too much pressure. Writer's Block often accompanies the "up against the wall" feeling that strikes at 2:00 A.M. the morning your essay is due at 9:00. Rome wasn't constructed in a day, and neither are most good essays.

Since most of you have had more experience talking than writing, try verbalizing your ideas. Sometimes it's helpful to discuss your ideas with a friend or classmate. Their questions and comments (not to mention their sympathy for your temporary block) will often trigger the thoughts you need to begin writing again. Or you might want to talk into a tape recorder so you can hear what you want to say.

When an irresistible force meets an immovable object, something's going to give. Conquer the task: break the paper into manageable bits. Instead of drooping with despair over the thought of a ten-page research paper, think of it as a series of small parts (explanation of the problem, review of current research, possible solutions, or whatever). Then tackle one part at a time and reward yourself when that section's done.

Get the juices flowing and the pen moving. Try writing the easiest or shortest part of your essay first. A feeling of accomplishment may give you the boost of confidence you need to undertake the other, more difficult sections. If no part looks easy or inviting, try more prewriting exercises, like the ones described in Chapter 1, until you feel prepared to begin the essay itself.

Play "Let's Make a Deal" with yourself. Sometimes we just can't face the failure that we are predicting for ourselves. Strike a bargain with yourself: promise yourself that you are only going to work on your paper for fifteen minutes—absolutely, positively fifteen minutes, not a second more, no sir, no way. If in fifteen minutes, you're on to something good, ignore your promise to yourself and keep going. If you're not, then leave and come back for another fifteen-minute session later (if you started early enough, you can do this without increasing your anxiety).

Give yourself permission to write garbage. Take the pressure off yourself by agreeing in advance to tear up the first page or two of whatever you write. You can always change your mind if the trash turns out to be treasure; if it isn't, so what? You said you were going to tear it up anyway.

Imagine that your brain is a water faucet. If you're like most people, you've probably lived in a house or apartment that contained a faucet that needed to run a few minutes before the hot water started to come out. Think of your brain in the same way, and do some other, easier writing task to warm up. Write a letter, make a grocery list, copy notes, whatever, to get your brain running. When you turn to your paper, your thoughts may be hotter than you thought.

Remove the threat by addressing a friendly face. Sometimes we can't write because we are too worried about what someone else will think about us or maybe we can't write because we can't figure out who would want to read this stuff anyway? Instead of writing into a void or to an audience that seems threatening, try writing to a friend. Imagine what that friend's responses might be and try to elaborate or clarify wherever necessary. If it helps, write the first draft as a letter ("Dear Clyde, I want to tell you what happened to me last week . . ."), and then redraft your ideas as an essay when you've found your purpose and focus, making whatever changes in tone or development are necessary to fit your real audience.

If Writer's Block does hit, remember that it is a temporary bogdown, not a permanent one. Other writers have had it—and survived to write again. Try leaving your papers and taking a walk outdoors or at least into another room. Think about your readers—what should they know or feel at this point in your essay? As you walk, try to complete the sentence "What I am trying to say is. . . ." Keep repeating this phrase and your responses aloud until you find the answer you want.

Sometimes while you're blocked at one point, a bright idea for another part of your essay will pop into your head. If possible, skip the section that's got you stuck and start working on the new part. (At least jot down the new idea somewhere so it won't be lost when you need it later.)

Change partners and dance. If you're thoroughly overcome by the vast white wasteland on the desk before you, get up and do something else for a while. Exercise, balance your checkbook, or put on music and dance. (Mystery writer Agatha Christie claimed she did her best planning while washing the dishes.) Give your mind a break and refresh your spirit. When you come back to the paper, you may be surprised to discover that your subconscious writer has been working while the rest of you played.

Here's the single most important piece of advice to remember: relax. No one—not even the very best professional writer—produces perfect prose every time pen hits paper. If you're blocked, you may be trying too hard; if your expectations of your first draft are too high, you may not be able to write at all for fear of failure. You just might be holding yourself back by being a perfectionist at this point. You can always revise and polish your prose in another draft—the first important step is jotting down your ideas. Remember that once the first word or phrase appears on your blank page, a major battle has been won.

CHAPTER 5 SUMMARY

Here is a brief summary of what you should remember about revising your writing:

1. Revision is an activity that occurs in all stages of the writing process.
2. All good writers revise their prose extensively.
3. Revision is not merely editing or last-minute proofreading; it involves important decisions about the essay's ideas, organization, and development.
4. To revise effectively, novice writers might review their drafts in steps, to avoid the frustration that comes with trying to fix everything at once.
5. Critical thinking skills are vitally important today to all good readers and writers.
6. Most writers experience Writer's Block at some time but live through it to write again.

6

EFFECTIVE SENTENCES

•
•
•

An insurance agent was shocked to open his mail one morning and read the following note from one of his clients: "In accordance with your instructions, I have given birth to twins in the enclosed envelope." However, he may not have been more surprised than the congregation who read this announcement in their church bulletin: "There will be a discussion tomorrow on the problem of adultery in the minister's office." Or the patrons of a health club who learned that "guest passes will not be given to members until the manager has punched each of them first."

Certainly, there were no babies born in an envelope, nor was there adultery in the minister's office, and one doubts that the club manager was planning to assault the membership. But the implications (and the unintended humor) are nevertheless present—solely because of the faulty ways in which the sentences were constructed.

To improve your own writing, you must express your thoughts in clear, coherent sentences that produce precisely the reader response you want. Effective sentences are similar to the threads in a piece of knitting or weaving: each thread helps form the larger design; if any one thread becomes tangled or lost, the pattern becomes muddled. In an essay, the same is true: if any sentence is fuzzy or obscure, the reader may lose the point of your discussion and in some cases never bother to regain it. Therefore, to retain your reader, you must concentrate on writing informative, effective sentences that consistently clarify the purpose of your essay.

Many problems in sentence clarity involve errors in grammar, usage, and word choice; the most common of these errors are discussed in Chapter 7 and Part Three of this text. In this chapter, however, you'll find some general suggestions for writing clear, concise, engaging sentences. However, *don't try to apply all the rules to the first draft of your essay.* Revising sentences before your ideas are firmly in place may be a waste of effort if your essay's stance or structure changes. Concentrate first on your essay's content and general organization; then, in a later draft, rework your sentences so that each one is informative and clear. Your reader reads only the words on the page, not those in your mind—so it's up to you to make sure the sentences in your essay approximate the thoughts in your head as closely and vividly as possible.

> **Remember:**
> All good writers revise and polish their sentences.

DEVELOPING A CLEAR STYLE

When you are ready to revise the sentences in your rough draft for clarity, try to follow the next five rules.

Give Your Sentences Content

Fuzzy sentences are often the result of fuzzy thinking. When you examine your sentences, ask yourself, "Do I know what I'm talking about here? Or are my sentences vague or confusing because I'm really not sure what my point is or where it's going?" Look at this list of content-poor sentences taken from student essays; how could you reword and put more information into each one?

If you were to view a karate class, you would become familiar with all the aspects that make it up.

The meaning of the poem isn't very clear the first time you read it, but after several readings, the poet's meaning comes through.

One important factor that is the basis for determining a true friend is the ability that person has for being a real human being.

Listening is important because we all need to be able to sit and hear all that is said to us.

Don't pad your paragraphs with sentences that run in circles, leading nowhere; rethink your ideas and revise your writing so that every sentence—

like each brick in a wall—contributes to the construction of a solid discussion. In other words, commit yourself to a position and make each sentence contain information pertinent to your point; leave the job of padding to mattress manufacturers.

Sometimes, however, you may have a definite idea in mind but still continue to write "empty sentences"—statements that alone do not contain enough information to make a specific point in your discussion. Frequently, an empty sentence may be revised by combining it with the sentence that follows, as shown in the examples below. The empty, or overly general, sentences are underlined.

Poor   There are many kinds of beautiful tropical fish. The kind most popular with aquarium owners is the angelfish.

Better Of the many kinds of beautiful tropical fish, none is more popular with aquarium owners than the angelfish.

Poor   D. W. Griffith introduced many new cinematic techniques. Some of these techniques were contrast editing, close-ups, fade-outs, and freeze-frame shots.

Better D. W. Griffith made movie history by introducing such new cinematic techniques as contrast editing, close-ups, fade-outs, and the freeze-frame shot.

Poor   There is a national organization called The Couch Potatoes. The group's 8,000 members are devoted television watchers.

Better The Couch Potatoes is a national organization whose 8,000 members are devoted television watchers.

For more help on combining sentences, see pages 144–147.

Make Your Sentences Specific

In addition to containing an informative, complete thought, each of your sentences should give readers enough clear details for them to "see" the picture you are creating. Sentences full of vague words produce blurry, boring prose and drowsy readers. Remember your reaction the last time you asked a friend about a recent vacation? If the only response you received was something like, "Oh, it was great—a lot of fun," you probably yawned and proceeded quickly to a new topic. But if your friend had begun an exciting account of a wilderness rafting trip, with detailed stories about narrow escapes from freezing white water, treacherous rocks, and uncharted whirlpools, you'd probably have stopped and listened. The same principle works in your writing—clear, specific details are the only sure way to attract and hold the reader's interest. Therefore, make each sentence contribute something new and interesting to the overall discussion.

The examples below first show sentences far too vague to sustain anyone's attention. Rewritten, these sentences contain specific details that add clarity and interest:

Vague   She went home in a bad mood. [What kind of a bad mood? How did she act or look?]

Specific She stomped home, hands jammed in her pockets, angrily kicking rocks, dogs, small children, and anything else that crossed her path.

Vague   My neighbor bought a really nice old desk. [Why nice? How old? What kind of desk?]

Specific My neighbor bought a solid oak rolltop desk made in 1885 that contains a secret drawer triggered by a hidden spring.

Vague   He was an attractive man. [Attractive in what ways—his appearance, personality, or both? Again, do you "see" this man?]

Specific He had Paul Newman's eyes, Robert Redford's smile, Sylvester Stallone's body, and Howard Hughes's money.

Keep Your Sentences Simple

Because our society is becoming increasingly specialized and highly technical, we tend to equate complexity with excellence and simplicity with simplemindedness. This assumption is unfortunate because it often leads to a preference for unnecessarily complicated and even contorted writing. In a recent survey, for example, a student chose a sample of bureaucratic hogwash over several well-written paragraphs, explaining his choice by saying that it must have been better since he didn't understand it.

Our best writers have always worked hard to present their ideas simply and specifically so that their readers could easily understand them. Mark Twain, for instance, once praised a young author this way: "I notice that you use plain simple language, short words, and brief sentences. This is the way to write English. It is the modern way and the best way. Stick to it." And when a critic asked Hemingway to define his theory of writing, he replied, "[I] put down what I see and what I feel in the best and simplest way I can tell it."

In your own writing, therefore, work for a simple, direct style. Avoid sentences that are overpacked (too many ideas or too much information at once) as in the following example on racquetball:

John told Phil that to achieve more control over the ball, he should practice flicking or snapping his wrist, because this action is faster in the close shots and placing a shot requires only a slight change of the wrist's angle instead of an acute movement of the whole arm, which gives a player less reaction time.

To make the overpacked sentence easier to understand, try dividing the ideas into two or more sentences:

> John told Phil that to achieve more control over the ball, he should practice flicking or snapping his wrist, because this action is faster in the close shots. Placing a shot requires only a slight change of the wrist's angle instead of an acute movement of the whole arm, which gives a player less reaction time.

Don't ever run the risk of losing your reader in a sentence that says too much to comprehend in one bite. This confusing notice, for example, came from a well-known credit card company:

> The Minimum Payment Due each month shall be reduced by the amounts paid in excess of the Minimum Payment Due during the previous three months which have not already been so applied in determining the Minimum Payment Due in such earlier months, unless you have exceeded your line of credit or have paid the entire New Balance shown on your billing statement.

Or consider the confusion of soccer players whose coach warned them in this manner:

> It is also a dangerous feeling to consider that where we are in the league is of acceptable standard because standard is relevant to the standards we have set, which thereby may well indicate that we have not aspired to the standard which we set ourselves.

Try too for a straightforward construction; former-president Ronald Reagan's sentence below, for example, takes far too many twists and turns for anyone to understand it easily on the first reading:

> My goal is an America where something or anything that is done to or for anyone is done neither because of nor in spite of any difference between them, racially, religiously or ethnic-origin-wise.

If the sentences in your rough draft are contorted, try rephrasing your meaning in short sentences and then combining thoughts where most appropriate.

Pay Attention to Word Order

The correct word order is crucial for clarity. Always place a modifier near the word it modifies. The position of a modifier can completely change the meaning of your sentence; for example, each sentence presented here offers a different idea because of the placement of the modifier "only."

A. Eliza said she loved only me. [Eliza loves me and no one else.]

B. Only Eliza said she loves me. [No other person said she loves me.]

C. Eliza only said she loves me. [Eliza said she loves me, but said nothing other than that.]

D. Eliza said only she loves me. [Eliza says no one else loves me.]

To avoid confusion, therefore, place your modifiers close to the words or phrases they modify.

A modifier that seems to modify the wrong part of a sentence is called "misplaced." Not only can misplaced modifiers change or distort the meaning of your sentence, they can also provide unintentional humor as well, as illustrated by the following excerpt from the 1929 Marx Brothers' movie *Coconuts:*

Woman   There's a man waiting outside to see you with a black mustache.

Groucho   Tell him I've already got one.

Of course, the woman didn't mean to imply that the man outside was waiting with (that is, accompanied by) a mustache; she meant to say, "There's a man with a black mustache who is waiting outside. . . ."

A poster advertising a lecture on campus provided this opportunity for humor: "Professor Elizabeth Sewell will discuss the latest appearance of Halley's Comet in room 104." Under the announcement a local wit had scribbled, "Shall we reserve room 105 for the tail?" Or take the case of this startling headline: "Kicking Baby Considered Healthy."

Here are some other examples of misplaced modifiers:

Misplaced   The lost child was finally found wandering in a frozen farmer's field. [Did the writer mean to say that the farmer was that cold?]

Revised   The lost child was finally found wandering in a farmer's frozen field.

Misplaced   Dilapidated and almost an eyesore, Shirley bought the old house to restore it to its original beauty. [Did the writer mean that Shirley needed a beauty treatment?]

Revised   Shirley bought the old house, which was dilapidated and almost an eyesore, to restore it to its original beauty.

Misplaced   Because she is thoroughly housebroken, Sarah can take her dog almost anywhere she goes. [Did the writer mean that Sarah—or the dog—was housebroken?]

Revised   Because she is thoroughly housebroken, Sarah's dog can accompany her almost anywhere she goes.

Misplaced   Three family members were found bound and gagged by the grandmother. [Did the writer mean that the grandmother had tied up the family?]

Revised   The grandmother found the three family members who had been bound and gagged.

In each of the preceding examples the writer forgot to place the modifying phrase so that it modifies the correct subject. In most cases, a sentence with a misplaced modifier can be corrected easily by moving the word or phrase closer to the word that should be modified.

In some sentences, however, the object of the modifying phrase is missing entirely. Such a phrase is called a "dangling modifier." Most of these errors may be corrected by adding the missing subject. Here are some examples followed by their revisions:

Dangling   Waving farewell, the plane began to roll down the runway. [Did the writer mean the plane was waving farewell?]

Revised   Waving farewell, we watched as the plane began to roll down the runway.

Dangling   After taking hours to plant hundreds of strawberry plants, the gophers came back to the garden and ate every one of them. [Did the writer mean that the gophers had a good meal after putting in such hard work?]

Revised   After Ralph spent hours planting hundreds of strawberry plants, the gophers came back to the garden and ate every one of them.

Dangling   While telling a joke to my roommate, a cockroach walked across my soufflé. [Did the writer mean that the cockroach was telling the joke?]

Revised   While telling a joke to my roommate, I saw a cockroach walking across my soufflé.

Dangling   Having tucked the children into bed, the cat was put out for the night. [Did the writer mean that the cat tucked the children into bed?]

Revised   Having tucked the children into bed, Mother and Father put the cat out for the night.

Misplaced and dangling modifiers frequently occur when you think faster than you write; a careful reading of your rough drafts will help you weed out any confused or unintentionally humorous sentences. (For additional examples of misplaced and dangling modifiers, see pages 366–367 in Part Three.)

Avoid Mixed Constructions and Faulty Predication

Sometimes you may begin with a sentence pattern in mind and then shift, midsentence, to another pattern—a change that often results in a generally confusing sentence. In many of these cases, you will find that the subject of your sentence simply doesn't fit with the predicate. Look at the following examples and note their corrections:

Faulty   Financial aid is a growing problem for many college students. [Financial aid itself isn't a problem; rather, it's the lack of aid.]

Revised   College students are finding it harder to obtain financial aid.

Faulty   Pregnant cows are required to teach a portion of two courses in Animal Science, AS100 (Breeding of Livestock) and AS200 (Problems in Reproduction of Cattle). [Obviously, the cows will not be the instructors for the classes.]

Revised   The Animal Science Department needs to purchase pregnant cows for use in two courses, AS100 (Breeding of Livestock) and AS200 (Problems in Reproduction of Cattle).

Faulty   Love is when you start rehearsing dinner-date conversation before breakfast. [A thing is never a "when" or a "where"; rewrite all "is when" or "is where" constructions.]

Revised   You're in love if you start rehearsing dinner-date conversation before breakfast.

Many mixed constructions occur because the writer is in too much of a hurry; check your rough drafts carefully to see if you have included sentences in which you started one pattern and switched to another. (For more help on faulty predications and mixed constructions, see pages 370–371 in Part Three.)

DEVELOPING A CONCISE STYLE

Almost all writing suffers from wordiness—the tendency to use more words than necessary. When useless words weigh down your prose, the meaning is often lost, confused, or hidden. Flabby prose calls for a reducing plan: put those obese sentences on a diet by cutting out unnecessary words, just as you avoid fatty foods to keep yourself trim. Mushy prose is ponderous and boring; crisp, to-the-point writing, on the other hand, is both accessible and pleasing. Beware, however, a temptation to overdiet—you don't want your prose to become so thin or brief that your meaning disappears completely. Therefore, cut out only the *unessential* words and phrases.

Wordy prose is frequently the result of using one or more of the following: (1) deadwood constructions (2) redundancies (3) pretentious diction.

Avoid Deadwood Constructions

Always try to cut empty "deadwood" from your sentences. Having a clear, concise style does not mean limiting your writing to choppy, childish Dick-and-Jane sentences; it only means that all unnecessary words, phrases, and clauses should be deleted. Below are some sentences containing common deadwood constructions and ways they may be pruned:

Faulty   The *reason* their football team plays on artificial turf *is because* their coach doesn't want the players to graze during halftime. ["The reason . . . is because" is both wordy and ungrammatical. If you have a reason, you don't need a "reason because."]

Revised   Their football team plays on artificial turf because their coach doesn't want the players to graze during halftime.

Poor   The land settlement *was an example where* the Kiowas did not receive fair treatment.

Revised   The land settlement was unfair to the Kiowas.

Poor   Because *of the fact that* his surfboard business failed after only a month, my brother decided to leave Minnesota.

Revised   Because his surfboard business failed after only a month, my brother decided to leave Minnesota.

Other notorious deadwood construction include the following:

regardless of the fact that	(use "although")
due to the fact that	(use "because")
the reason is that	(omit)
as to whether or not to	(omit "as to" and "or not")
at this point in time	(use "now" or "today")
it is believed that	(use a specific subject and "believes")
concerning the matter of	(use "about")
by means of	(use "by")
these are the kinds of . . . that	(use "these" plus a specific subject)

Watch a tendency to tack on empty "fillers" that stretch one word into an awkward phrase:

Wordy   Each candidate should be evaluated *on an individual basis.*

Concise   Each candidate should be evaluated *individually.*

Wordy   Television does not portray violence *in a realistic fashion.*

Concise   Television does not portray violence *realistically*.

Wordy   The New York blackout produced a *crisis-type situation*.

Concise   The New York blackout produced a *crisis*.

To retain your reader's interest and improve the flow of your prose, trim all the fat from your sentences.

"There are," "It is." These introductory phrases are often space wasters. When possible, omit them or replace them with specific subjects, as shown in the following:

Wordy   *There are* thirty thousand students attending this university.

Revised   Thirty thousand students attend this university.

Wordy   *It is* true that the County Fair offers many fun contests, including the ever-popular map fold-off.

Revised   The County Fair offers many fun contests, including the ever-popular map fold-off.

"Who" and "which" clauses. Some "who" and "which" clauses are unnecessary and may be turned into modifiers placed before the noun:

Wordy   The getaway car, *which* was stolen, turned the corner.

Revised   The stolen getaway car turned the corner.

Wordy   The chef, *who was* depressed, ordered his noisy lobsters to simmer down.

Revised   The depressed chef ordered his noisy lobsters to simmer down.

When adjective clauses are necessary, the words "who" and "which" may sometimes be omitted:

Wordy   Ms. Quito, *who is* a local English teacher, was delighted to hear that she had won the annual lottery, *which is* sponsored by the Shirley Jackson Foundation.

Revised   Ms. Quito, a local English teacher, was delighted to hear that she had won the annual lottery, sponsored by the Shirley Jackson Foundation.

"To be." Most "to be's" are unnecessary and ought not to be. Delete them every time you can.

Wordy   She seems *to be* angry.

Revised   She seems angry.

Wordy   Herb's charisma-bypass operation proved *to be* successful.

Revised   Herb's charisma-bypass operation proved successful.

Wordy   The new mayor wanted his archenemy, the local movie critic, *to be* arrested.

Revised   The new mayor wanted his archenemy, the local movie critic, arrested.

"Of" and infinitive phrases. Many "of" and infinitive ("to" plus verb) phrases may be omitted or revised by using possessives, adjectives, and verbs, as shown below:

Wordy   At the *time of registration* students are required *to make* payment *of their library fees.*

Revised   At registration students must pay their library fees.

Wordy   The producer fired the mother *of the director of the movie.*

Revised   The producer fired the movie director's mother.

Including deadwood phrases makes your prose puffy; streamline your sentences to present a simple, direct style.

Avoid Redundancy

Many flabby sentences contain *redundancies* (words that repeat the same idea or whose meanings overlap). Consider the following examples:

In this day and time, people expect to live at least seventy years. ["Day" and "time" present a similar idea.]

He repeated the winning bingo number over again. ["Repeated" means "to say again," so there is no need for "over again."]

The group consensus was that the pizza crust tasted like cardboard. ["Consensus" means "general agreement," so it's unnecessary to add "group."]

Some other common redundancies include:

reverted ba~~ck~~	n~~ew~~ innovation
reflected ba~~ck~~	red ~~in~~ co~~l~~or
retreated ba~~ck~~	burned do~~wn~~ ~~up~~
fell do~~wn~~	pa~~ir~~ ~~of~~ twins/t~~wo~~ twins
climb ~~up~~	res~~ul~~ting effect (or just "result")
a tr~~ue~~ fact	fi~~n~~al outcome

Carefully Consider Your Passive Verbs

When the subject of the sentence performs the action, the verb is *active*; when the subject of the sentence is acted on, the verb is *passive*. You can sometimes recognize sentences with passive verbs because they often contain the word "by," telling who performed the action.

Passive The wedding date *was announced* by the young couple.

Active The young couple *announced* their wedding date.

Passive His letter of resignation *was accepted* by the Board of Trustees.

Active The Board of Trustees *accepted* his letter of resignation.

Passive The trivia contest *was won* by the ever-popular Boulder team, The Godzillas Must Be Crazy.

Active The ever-popular Boulder team, The Godzillas Must Be Crazy, *won* the trivia contest.

In addition to being wordy and weak, passive sentences often disguise the performer of the action in question. You might have heard a politician, for example, say something similar to this: "It was decided this year to give all congressmen an increase in salary." The question of *who* decided to raise salaries remains foggy—perhaps purposefully so. But in your own prose, you should strive for clarity and directness; therefore, use active verbs as often as you can except when you wish to stress the person or thing that receives the action, as shown in the following samples:

The baby was born September 30, 1980.

The elderly man was struck by a drunk driver.

Special note: Authorities in some professional and technical fields still prefer the passive construction because they wish to put emphasis on the experiment or process rather than on the people performing the action. If the passive voice is preferred in your field, you should abide by that convention when you are writing reports or papers for your professional colleagues.

Avoid Pretentiousness

Another enemy of clear, concise prose is *pretentiousness*. Pompous, inflated language surrounds us, and because it often sounds learned or official, we may be tempted to use it when we want to impress others with our writing. But as George Orwell, author of *1984,* noted, an inflated style is like "a cuttlefish squirting out ink." If you want your prose easily understood, write as clearly and plainly as possible.

To illustrate how confusing pretentious writing can be, here is a copy of a government memo announcing a blackout order, issued in 1942 during World War II:

Such preparations shall be made as will completely obscure all Federal buildings and non-Federal buildings occupied by the Federal government during an air raid for any period of time from visibility by reason of internal or external illumination.

President Franklin Roosevelt intervened and rewrote the order in plain English, clarifying its message and reducing the number of words by half:

Tell them that in buildings where they have to keep the work going to put something across the windows.

By translating the obscure original memo into easily understandable language, Roosevelt demonstrated that a natural prose style can get necessary information to the reader more quickly and efficiently than bureaucratic jargon. (For more advice on ridding your prose of jargon, see pages 164–168.)

In other—shorter—words, to attract and hold your readers' attention, to communicate clearly and quickly, make your sentences as informative, straightforward, specific, and concise as possible.

PRACTICING WHAT YOU'VE LEARNED

A. Some of the following sentences are vague, "empty," overpacked, or contorted. Rewrite each one so that it is clear and specific, combining or dividing sentences as necessary.

1. Roger was a pretty awesome guy who was really an important part of his company.

2. There's a new detective show on television. It stars Phil Noir and is set in the 1940s.

3. Sarah's room was always a huge disaster.

4. The book *Biofeedback: How to Stop It* is a good one because of all the ideas the writer put into it.

5. Some people think capital punishment should be allowed to exist because it acts as a deterrent to people about to commit crimes or who are even considering them, but other people hold the view that

they shouldn't have to pay for feeding and housing them for years after crimes are committed, so they should be executed instead.

6. My junk mail is incredible.

7. I've signed up for a course at my local college. The class is "Cultivating the Mold in Your Refrigerator for Fun and Profit."

8. Reading your horoscope is a fun way to get information about your life, but some people think it's too weird.

9. I'm not sure but I think that Lois is the author of *The Underachiever's Guide to Very Small Business Opportunities* or is she the writer of *Whine Your Way to Success* because I know she's written several books since she's having an autograph party at the campus bookstore either this afternoon or tomorrow.

10. I can't help but wonder whether or not he isn't unwelcome.

B. The sentences below contain misplaced words and phrases as well as other faulty constructions. Revise them so that each sentence is clear.

1. If you are accosted in the subway at night, you should learn to escape harm from the police.

2. Desperation is when you try to lose weight through Pyramid Power.

3. Almost dead for five years now, I miss my dog so much.

4. The father fed the apple pie to the twins he earlier had dropped in the trash compactor.

5. The reason I finally got my leg operated on over Thanksgiving break is because it had been hanging over my head for years.

6. We need to hire two three-year-old teachers for preschool kids who don't smoke.

7. The story of Rip Van Winkle is one of the dangers endured by those who oversleep.

8. We gave our waterbed to friends we didn't want anymore.

9. People who are allergic to chocolate and children under 6 should not be given the new vaccine.

10. At 7:00 A.M. Brenda starts preparing for another busy day as an executive in her luxurious bathroom.

C. The sentences below are filled with deadwood, redundancies, and passive constructions. Rewrite each one so that it is concise and direct.

1. In point of fact, the main reason he lost the editing job was primarily because of his careless and sloppy proofreading work.

2. It was revealed today that there are some professors in the Prehistoric History department who are incompetent.

3. My brother, who happens to be older than me, can't drive to work this week due to the fact that he was in a wreck in his car at 2:00 A.M. Saturday morning.

4. In this modern world of today, we often criticize or disapprove of advertising that is thought to be damaging to women by representing them in an unfair way.

5. When the prosecution tried to introduce the old antique gun, this was objected to by the attorney defending the two twin brothers.

6. What the poet is trying to get across to the reader in the fourth stanza is her feeling of disgust with the telephone company.

7. We very often felt that although we expressed our deepest concerns to our boss, she often just sat there and gave us the real impression that she was taking what we said in a very serious manner although, in our opinion, she did not really and truly care about our concerns.

8. It is a true fact that certainly bears repeating over and over again that learning word processing can help you perform in a more efficient way at work and also can save you lots of time too.

9. Personally, I believe that there are too many people who go to eat out in restaurants who always feel they must continually assert their superior natures by acting in a rude, nasty fashion to the people who are employed to wait on their tables.

10. In order to enhance my opportunities for advancement in the workplace at this point in time, I arrived at the decision to seek the hand of my employer's daughter in the state of matrimony.

ASSIGNMENT

Write a paragraph of at least five sentences as clearly and concisely as you can. Then rewrite this paragraph, filling it with as many vague words, redundancies, and deadwood constructions as possible. Exchange this rewritten paragraph for a similarly faulty one written by a classmate; give yourselves fifteen minutes to "translate" each other's sentences into effective prose. Compare the translations to the original paragraphs. Which version is clearer? Why?

DEVELOPING A LIVELY STYLE

Good writing demands clarity and conciseness—but that's not all. Good prose must also be lively, forceful, and interesting. It should excite, intrigue, and charm; each line should seduce the reader into the next. Consider, for example, one of the duller textbooks you've read lately. It probably was written clearly, but it may have failed to inform because of its insufferably bland tone; by the time you finished your assignment, most likely your brain was asleep.

You can prevent your readers from succumbing to a similar case of the blahs by developing a vigorous prose style that continually surprises and pleases them. As one writer has pointed out, all subjects—with the possible exceptions of sex and money—are dull until somebody makes them interesting. As you revise your rough drafts, remember: bored readers are not born but made. Therefore, here are some practical suggestions to help you transform ho-hum prose into lively sentences and paragraphs:

Use specific, descriptive verbs. Avoid bland verbs that must be supplemented by modifiers.

Bland   His fist *broke* the window *into many little pieces.*

Better   His fist *shattered* the window.

Bland   Dr. Love *asked* his congregation about donating money to his "love mission" *over and over again.*

Better   Dr. Love *hounded* his congregation into donating money to his "love mission."

Bland   The exhausted runner *walked* up the last hill *very slowly.*

Better   The exhausted runner *staggered* up the last hill.

To cut wordiness that weighs down your prose, try to use active verbs instead of nouns and colorless verbs such as "to be," "to have," "to get," "to do," and "to make":

Wordy   By sunrise the rebels had *made their way* to the capital city.

Better   By sunrise the rebels had *battled* to the capital city.

Wordy   At first the players and managers *had an argument* over the money, but finally they *came to an agreement that got* the contract dispute settled.

Better   At first the players and managers *argued* over the money, but finally they *settled* the contract dispute.

Wordy   The executives *made the decision* to *have* another meeting on Tuesday.

Better   The executives *decided* to *meet* again on Tuesday.

Use specific, precise modifiers that help the reader see, hear, or feel what you are describing. Adjectives such as "good," "bad," "many," "more," "great," "a lot," "important," and "interesting" are too vague to paint the reader a clear picture. Similarly, the adverbs "very," "really," "too," and "quite" are overused and add little to sentence clarity. The following are examples of weak sentences and their revisions:

Imprecise   The potion changed the scientist into a *really old* man.

Better   The potion changed the scientist into a *one hundred-year-old* man.

Imprecise   Marcia is a *very interesting* person.

Better   Marcia is *witty, intelligent,* and *talented.*

Imprecise   The vegetables tasted *funny.*

Better   The vegetables tasted *like lichen mixed with Krazy Glue.*

(For more advice on using specific, colorful words, see also pages 161–164 in Chapter 7.)

Emphasize people when possible. Try to focus on persons rather than abstractions whenever you can. Next to our fascinating selves, we most enjoy hearing about other people. Although all the sentences in the first paragraph following are correct, the second one, revised by a class of composition students at Brown University, is clearer and more personal because the jargon has been eliminated and the focus changed from the tuition rules to the students.

Original   Tuition regulations currently in effect provide that payment of the annual tuition entitles an undergraduate-degree candidate to full-time enrollment, which is defined as registration for three, four, or five courses per semester. This means that at no time may an undergraduate student's official registration for courses drop below three without a dean's permission for part-time status and that at no time may the official course registration exceed five. (Brown University Course Announcement)

Revised   If students pay their tuition, they may enroll in three, four, or five courses per semester. Fewer than three or more than five can be taken only with a dean's permission.

Here's a similar example with a bureaucratic focus rather than a personal one:

Original   The salary deflations will most seriously impact the secondary educational profession.

Revised   High school teachers will suffer the biggest salary reductions.

Obviously, the revised sentence is the more easily understood of the two because the reader knows exactly who will be affected by the pay cuts. In your own prose, wherever appropriate, try to replace vague abstractions such as "society," "culture," "administrative concerns," "programmatic expectations," and so forth, with the human beings you're thinking about. In other words, remember to talk *to* people *about* people.

Vary your sentence style. The only torture worse than listening to someone's nails scraping across a blackboard is being forced to read a paragraph full of identically constructed sentences. To illustrate this point, below are a few sentences composed in the all-too-common subject + predicate pattern:

> Soccer is the most popular sport in the world. Soccer exists in almost every country. Soccer players are sometimes more famous than movie stars. Soccer teams compete every few years for the World Soccer Cup. Soccer fans often riot if their team loses. Soccer fans even commit suicide. Soccer is the only game in the world that makes people so crazy.

Excruciatingly painful, yes? Each of us has a tendency to repeat a particular sentence pattern (though the choppy subject + predicate is by far the most popular); you can often detect your own by reading your prose aloud. To avoid overdosing your readers with the same pattern, vary the length, arrangement, and complexity of your sentences. Of course, this doesn't mean that you should contort your sentences merely for the sake of illustrating variety; just read your rough draft aloud, listening carefully to the rhythm of your prose so you can revise any monotonous passages or disharmonious sounds. (Try, also, to avoid the hiccup syndrome, in which you begin a sentence with the same words that end the preceding sentence: "The first president to install a telephone on his desk was Herbert *Hoover. Hoover* refused to use the telephone booth outside his office.")

Avoid overuse of any one kind of construction in the same sentence. Don't, for example, pile up too many negatives, "who" or "which" clauses, and prepositional or infinitive phrases in one sentence.

> He *couldn't* tell whether she *didn't* want him to go or *not.*

> I gave the money to my brother, *who* returned it to the bank president, *who* said the decision to prosecute was up to the sheriff, *who* was out of town.

> I went to the florist *for* my father *for* a dozen roses *for* his date.

Try also to avoid stockpiling nouns, one on top of another, so that your sentences are difficult to read. Although some nouns may be used as adjectives to modify other nouns ("book mark," "gasoline pump," "food processor"), too many nouns grouped together sound awkward and confuse readers. If you have run too many nouns together, try using prepositional phrases ("an income tax bill discussion" becomes "discussion of an income tax bill") or changing the order or vocabulary of the sentence:

Confusing   The legislators are currently considering the *liability insurance multiple-choice premium proposal.*

Clearer   The legislators are currently considering the *proposal* that suggests *multiple-choice premiums* for *liability insurance.*

Confusing   We're concerned about the low *female labor force participation figures* in our department.

Clearer   We're concerned about the low *number of women working* in our department.

Don't change your point of view between or within sentences. If, for example, you begin your essay discussing students as "they," don't switch midway—or midsentence—to "we" or "you."

Inconsistent   Students pay tuition, which should entitle *them* to some voice in the university's administration. Therefore, *we* deserve one student on the Board of Regents.

Consistent   Students pay tuition, which should entitle *them* to some voice in the university's administration. Therefore, *they* deserve one student on the Board of Regents.

Inconsistent   *I* like my photography class because *we* learn how to restore *our* old photos and how to take better color portraits of *your* family.

Consistent   *I* like my photography class because *I'm* learning how to restore *my* old photos and how to take better color portraits of *my* family.

Perhaps this is a good place to dispel the myth that the pronoun "I" should never be used in an essay; on the contrary, many of our best essays have been written in the first person. Some of your former teachers may have discouraged the use of "I" for these two reasons: (1) overuse of "I" makes your essay sound like the work of an egomaniac; (2) writing in the first person often results in too many empty phrases such as "I think that" and "I believe that." Nevertheless, if the situation demands a personal point of view, feel free—if you're comfortable doing so—to use the first person, but use it in moderation; make sure that every sentence doesn't begin with "I" plus a verb.

▶ PRACTICING WHAT YOU'VE LEARNED

A. Replace the underlined words below so that the sentences are clear and vivid. In addition, rephrase any awkward constructions or unnecessarily abstract words you find.

1. Judging from the <u>crazy</u> sound of the reactor, it isn't obvious to me that nuclear <u>power as</u> we know it today isn't a technology with a less than wonderful future.

2. The City Council felt <u>bad</u> because the revised tourist development activities grant fund <u>application</u> form letters were mailed without stamps.

3. To watch Jim Bob eat pork chops was <u>most interesting</u>.

4. For sale: <u>very nice</u> antique bureau suitable for ladies or gentlemen with <u>thick legs</u> and extra-large side handles.

5. The workshop on family relationships we're attending is <u>great</u> because you learn to control your parents through blackmail <u>and guilt</u>.

6. The new diet made me feel <u>awful</u>, and it <u>did many horrible things</u> to my body.

7. After reading "The Looter's Guide to Riot-Prone Cities," Eddie <u>asked to have</u> a transfer really soon.

8. The wild oats soup was <u>fantastic</u>, so we drank <u>a lot of it very fast</u>.

9. When Alfred hit the ball to the top of the fence of the park, his teammates got <u>pretty excited</u>.

10. My roommate is <u>sort of different</u>, but he's a <u>good</u> guy at heart.

B. Fill in the blanks with colorful words. Make the paragraph as interesting, exciting, or humorous as you can. Avoid clichés and insta-prose (those predictable phrases that first come to mind). Make your responses original and creative.

As midnight approached, Janet and Brad _____ toward the

_____ castle to escape the _____ storm. Their _____ car

had _____, _____, and finally _____ on the road nearby.

The night was _____, and Brad _____ at the shadows with

_____ and _____. As they _____ up the _____

steps to the _____ door, the _____ wind was filled with _____ and _____ sounds. Janet _____ on the door, and moments later, it opened to reveal the _____ scientist, clutching a _____. Brad and Janet _____ at each other and then _____ (complete this sentence and then end the paragraph and the story).

> ## ASSIGNMENT

Find a short piece of writing you think is too bland, boring, abstract, or confusing. (Possible sources: your college catalog, a business contract or letter, your student health insurance policy, or a textbook.) In a well-written paragraph of your own, identify the sample's major problems and offer some specific suggestions for improving the writing. (If time permits, read aloud several of the samples and vote to give one the Most Lifeless Prose Award.)

DEVELOPING AN EMPHATIC STYLE

Some words and phrases in your sentences are more important than others and, therefore, need more emphasis. Three ways to vary emphasis are by (1) word order, (2) coordination, and (3) subordination.

Word Order

The arrangement of words in a sentence can determine which ideas receive the most emphasis. To stress a word or phrase, place it at the end of the sentence or at the beginning of the sentence. Accordingly, a word or phrase receives least emphasis when buried in the middle of the sentence. Compare the examples below, in which the word "murder" receives varying degrees of emphasis:

Least emphatic Colonel Mustard knew *murder* was his only solution.

Emphatic *Murder* was Colonel Mustard's only solution.

Emphatic Colonel Mustard knew only one solution: *murder.*

Another use of word order to vary emphasis is *inversion,* taking a word out of its natural or usual position in a sentence and inserting it in an unexpected place.

Usual order Parents who give their children both roots and wings are *wise.*

Inverted order   *Wise* are the parents who give their children both roots and wings.

Not all your sentences will contain words that need special emphasis; good writing generally contains a mix of some sentences in natural order and others rearranged for special effects.

Coordination

When you have two closely related ideas and want to stress them equally, coordinate them.* In coordination, you join two sentences with a coordinating conjunction. To remember the coordinating conjunctions ("for," "and," "nor," "but," "or," "yet," "so"), think of the acronym FANBOYS; then always join two sentences with a comma and one of the FANBOYS. Here are two samples:

Choppy   The most popular girl's name today is Jennifer.
The most popular boy's name today is Michael.

Coordinated   The most popular girl's name today is Jennifer, *and* the most popular boy's name is Michael.

Choppy   Imelda brought home a pair of ruby slippers.
Ferdinand made her return them.

Coordinated   Imelda brought home a pair of ruby slippers, *but* Ferdinand made her return them.

You can use coordination to show a relationship between ideas and to add variety to your sentence structures. Be careful, however, to select the right words while linking ideas, unlike the sentence that appeared in a church newsletter: "The ladies of the church have discarded clothing of all kinds, and they have been inspected by the minister." In other words, writers often need to slow down and make sure that their thoughts are not joined in misleading or even unintentionally humorous ways: "For those of you who have children and don't know it, we have a nursery downstairs."

Sometimes when writers are in a hurry, they join ideas that are clearly related in their own minds, but whose relationship is confusing to the reader:

Confusing   My laboratory report isn't finished, and today my sister is leaving for a visit home.

Clear   I'm still working on my laboratory report, so I won't be able to catch a ride home with my sister who's leaving today.

---

* To remember that the term "coordination" refers to equally weighted ideas, think of other words with the prefix "co," such as "copilots," "coauthors," or "cooperation."

You should also avoid using coordinating conjunctions to string too many ideas together like linked sausages:

Poor   We went inside the famous cave and the guide turned off the lights and we saw the rocks that glowed.

Revised   After we went inside the famous cave, the guide turned off the lights so we could see the rocks that glowed.

Subordination

Some sentences contain one main statement and one or more less emphasized elements; the less important ideas are subordinate to, or are dependent on, the sentence's main idea.* Subordinating conjunctions introducing dependent clauses show a variety of relationships between the clauses and the main part of the sentence. Here are four examples of subordinating conjunctions and their uses:

1. To show time

Without subordination   Superman stopped changing his clothes. He realized the phone booth was made of glass.

With subordination   Superman stopped changing his clothes *when* he realized the phone booth was made of glass.

2. To show cause

Without subordination   The country-western singer failed to gain success in Nashville. She sadly returned to Snooker Hollow to work in the sequin mines.

With subordination   *Because* the country-western singer failed to gain success in Nashville, she sadly returned to Snooker Hollow to work in the sequin mines.

3. To show condition

Without subordination   Susan ought to study the art of tattooing. She will work with colorful people.

With subordination   *If* Susan studies the art of tattooing, she will work with colorful people.

---

* To remember that the term "subordination" refers to sentences containing dependent elements, think of words such as "a subordinate" (someone who works for someone else) or a post office "substation" (a branch of the post office less important than the main branch).

4. To show place

Without subordination	Bulldozers are smashing the old movie theater. That's the place I first saw Roy Rogers and Dale Evans ride into the sunset.
With subordination	Bulldozers are smashing the old movie theater *where* I first saw Roy Rogers and Dale Evans ride into the sunset.

Subordination is especially useful in ridding your prose of choppy Dick-and-Jane sentences and those "empty sentences" discussed on pages 124–125. Below are some examples of choppy, weak sentences and their revisions, which contain subordinate clauses:

Choppy Lew makes bagels on Tuesday. Lines in front of his store are a block long.

Revised When Lew makes bagels on Tuesday, lines in front of his store are a block long.

Choppy I have fond memories of Zilker Park. My husband and I met there.

Revised I have fond memories of Zilker Park because my husband and I met there.

A correctly subordinated sentence is one of the marks of a sophisticated writer because it presents adequate information in one smooth flow instead of in monotonous drips. Subordination, like coordination, also adds variety to your sentence construction.

Generally, when you subordinate one idea, you emphasize another, so to avoid the tail-wagging-the-dog problem, put your important idea in the main clause. Also, don't let your most important idea become buried under an avalanche of subordinate clauses, as in the sentence that follows:

When he was told by his boss, *who* had always treated him fairly, that he was being fired from a job *that* he had held for twenty years at a factory *where* he enjoyed working *because* the pay was good, Henry felt angry and frustrated.

Practice blending choppy sentences by studying the sentence-combining exercise below. In this exercise a description of a popular movie or book has been chopped into simple sentences and then combined into one complex sentence.

1. *Psycho* (1960)
Norman Bates manages a motel.
It is remote.

It is dangerous.
Norman has a mother.
She seems overly fond of knives.
He tries to protect his mom.

In a remote—and dangerous—motel, manager Norman Bates tries to protect his mother, who seems overly fond of knives.

2. *King Kong* (1933)
A showman goes to the jungle.
He captures an ape.
The ape is a giant.
The ape is taken to New York City.
He escapes.
He dies fighting for a girl.
He loves her.
She is beautiful.

A giant ape, captured in the jungle by a showman, is taken to New York City, where he escapes and dies fighting for the beautiful girl he loves.

3. *Casablanca* (1942)
Rick is an American.
He is cynical.
He owns a café.
He lives in Casablanca.
He meets an old flame.
She is married.
Her husband is a French resistance leader.
Rick helps the couple.
He regains self-respect.

When Rick, a cynical American café-owner in Casablanca, helps his old flame and her husband, a French resistance leader, he regains his self-respect.

Please note that the sentences in these exercises may be combined effectively in a number of ways. For instance, the description of *King Kong* might be rewritten this way: "After a showman captures him in the jungle, a giant ape escapes in New York City but dies in a fight for the love of a beautiful girl." How might you rewrite the other two sample sentences?

◤ PRACTICING WHAT YOU'VE LEARNED

A. Revise the sentences that follow so that the underlined words receive more emphasis.

1. A remark attributed to the one-time heavyweight boxing champion <u>Joe Louis</u> is "I don't really like money, but it quiets my nerves."

2. According to recent polls, <u>television</u> is where most Americans get their news.

3. Of all the world's problems, it is <u>hunger</u> that is most urgent.

4. I enjoyed visiting many foreign countries last year, with <u>Greece</u> being my favorite of all of them.

5. The annoying habit of <u>knuckle-cracking</u> is something I can't stand.

B. Combine the pairs of sentences below using coordination or subordination.

1. The earthquake shook the city. Louise was practicing primal-scream therapy at the time.

2. John failed his literature test. John incorrectly identified Harper Lee as the author of the south-of-the-border classic *Tequila Mockingbird.*

3. Dr. Acula recently opened a new office. He specializes in acupuncture in the neck.

4. The police had only a few clues. They suspected Jean and David had strangled each other in a desperate struggle over control of the thermostat.

5. Bubba's favorite movie is *Sorority Babes in the Slimeball Bowl-O-Rama* (1988). A film critic called it "a pinhead chiller."

6. We're going to the new Psychoanalysis Restaurant. Their menu includes banana split personality, repressed duck, shrimp basket case, and self-expresso.

7. Juanita lost some old friends when she won the lottery. She made lots of new ones.

8. Jim Bob quit drinking beer last month. Our aluminum recycling plant closed a week later.

9. The guru rejected his dentist's offer of novocaine. He could transcend dental medication.

10. The mail carrier quit because the mailbag was too heavy. He also quit because he could not remember all the zip codes.

C. Combine the following simple sentences into one complex sentence. See if you can guess the name of the books or movies described in the sentences. (Answers appear on page 151.)

1. A boy runs away from home.
   His companion is a runaway slave.
   He lives on a raft.
   The raft is on the Mississippi River.
   He has many adventures.
   The boy learns many lessons.
   Some lessons are about human kindness.
   Some lessons are about friendship.

2. A young man returns from prison.
   He returns to his family.
   His family lives in the Dust Bowl.
   The family decides to move.
   The family expects to find jobs in California.
   The family finds intolerance.
   They also find dishonest employers.

3. A scientist is obsessed.
   He wants to re-create life.
   He creates a monster.
   The monster rebels against the scientist.
   The monster kills his creator.
   The villagers revolt.
   The villagers storm the castle.

ASSIGNMENT

A. Make up your own sentence-combining exercise by finding or writing one-sentence descriptions of popular or recent movies, books, or television shows. Divide the complex sentences into simple sentences and exchange papers with a classmate. Give yourselves ten minutes to combine sentences and guess the titles.

B. The two paragraphs below are poorly written because of their choppy, wordy, and monotonous sentences. Rewrite each passage so that it is clear, lively, and emphatic.

1. There is a new invention on the market. It is called a "dieter's conscience." It is a small box to be installed in one's refrigerator. When the door of the refrigerator is opened by you, a tape recorder begins to start. A really loud voice yells, "You eating again? No wonder you're getting fat." Then the very loud voice says, "Close the door; it's getting warm." Then the voice laughs a lot in an insane and

crazy fashion. The idea is one that is designed to mock people into a habit of stopping eating.

2. In this modern world of today, man has come up with another new invention. This invention is called the "Talking Tombstone." It is made by the Gone-But-Not-Forgotten Company, which is located in Burbank, California. This company makes a tombstone that has a device in it that makes the tombstone appear to be talking aloud in a realistic fashion when people go close by it. The reason is that the device is really a recording machine that is turned on due to the simple fact of the heat of the bodies of the people who go by. The closer the people get, the louder the sound the tombstone makes. It is this device that individual persons who want to leave messages after death may utilize. A hypochondriac, to cite one example, might leave a recording of a message that says over and over again in a really loud voice, "See, I told you I was sick!" It may be assumed by one and all that this new invention will be a serious aspect of the whole death situation in the foreseeable future.

APPLYING WHAT YOU'VE LEARNED TO *YOUR* WRITING

If you have drafted a piece of writing and are satisfied with your essay's ideas and organization, begin revising your sentences for clarity, conciseness, and emphasis. As you move through your draft, think about your readers. Ask yourself, "Are any of my sentences too vague, overpacked, or contorted for my readers to understand? Can I clarify any of my ideas by using simpler, more specific language or by using less confusing sentence constructions?

If one of your sentences is confusing but, after many tries, you can't seem to untangle it, follow the sentence-combining exercise described on pages 146–147 of this chapter—but in reverse. Instead of combining ideas, break your thought into a series of simpler units. Think about what you want to say and put the person or thing of importance in the subject position at the beginning of the sentence. Then select a verb and a brief phrase to complete the sentence. You will most likely need several of these simpler constructions to communicate the complexity of your original thought. Once you have your thought broken into smaller, simpler units, carefully begin to combine some of them as you strive for clarity and sentence variety.

Remember that it's not enough for you, the writer, to understand what your sentences mean—your readers must be able to follow your ideas too. When in doubt, always revise your writing so that it is clear, concise, and inviting. (For more help, turn to Chapter 5, on Revision.)

CHAPTER 6 SUMMARY

Here is a brief summary of what you should remember about writing effective sentences:

1. All good writers revise and polish their sentences.

2. You can help clarify your ideas for your readers by writing sentences that are informative, straightforward, and precise.

3. You can communicate your ideas more easily to your readers if you cut out deadwood, redundancies, confusing passives, and pretentious language.

4. You can maintain your readers' interest in your ideas if you cultivate a style that is specific, varied, and emphatic.

Answers to sentence-combining exercise:

1. *Huckleberry Finn*
2. *The Grapes of Wrath*
3. *Frankenstein* (or almost any late-night horror movie)

7

WORD LOGIC

The English language contains over a half million words—quite a selection for you as a writer to choose from. But such a wide choice may make you feel like a starving person confronting a six-page, fancy French menu. Which choice is best? How do I choose? Is the choice so important?

Word choice can make an enormous difference in the quality of your writing for at least one obvious reason: if you substitute an incorrect or vague word for the right one, you take the risk of being totally misunderstood. Ages ago Confucius made the same point: "If language is incorrect, then what is said is not meant. If what is said is not meant, then what ought to be done remains undone." It isn't enough that you know what you mean; you must transfer your ideas onto paper in the proper words so that others understand your exact meaning.

To help you avoid possible paralysis from indecision over word choice, this chapter offers some practical suggestions on selecting words that are not only accurate and appropriate but also memorable and persuasive.

SELECTING THE CORRECT WORDS

Accuracy: Confused Words

Unless I get a bank loan soon, I will be forced to lead an *immortal* life.

Dobermans make good pets if you train them with enough *patients.*

He dreamed of eating *desert* after *desert.*

She had dieted for so long that she had become *emancipated.*

The young man was completely in *ah* of the actress's beauty.

Socrates died from an overdose of *wedlock.*

The preceding sentences share a common problem: each one contains an error in word choice. In each sentence, the *underlined* word is incorrect, causing the sentence to be nonsensical or silly. To avoid such problems in word choice, make sure you check words for *accuracy.* Use only those words whose precise meaning, usage, and spelling you know; look in your dictionary to double-check any words whose definitions (or spellings) are fuzzy to you. As Mark Twain noted, the difference between the right word and the wrong one is the difference between lightning and the lightning bug.

Here is a list of words that are often confused in writing. Use your dictionary to determine the meanings or usage of any word unfamiliar to you.

its/it's	lead/led	choose/chose
to/too/two	cite/sight/site	accept/except
there/their/they're	affect/effect	council/counsel
your/you're	good/well	where/wear
complement/compliment	who's/whose	lose/loose
stationary/stationery	lay/lie	precede/proceed
capitol/capital	than/then	illusion/allusion
principal/principle	insure/ensure	farther/further

Accuracy: Idiomatic Phrases

Occasionally you may have an essay returned to you with words marked "awkward diction" or "idiom." In English, as in all languages, we have word groupings that seem governed by no particular logic except the ever-popular "that's-the-way-we-say-it" rule. Many of these idiomatic expressions involve prepositions that beginning writers sometimes confuse or misuse. Below are some common idiomatic errors and their corrected forms:

regardless ~~to~~ of	different ~~than~~ ~~to~~ from	relate ~~with~~ to
insight ~~of~~ into	must ~~of~~ have known	capable ~~to~~ of
similar ~~with~~ to	superior ~~than~~ to	aptitude ~~toward~~ for
comply ~~to~~ with	~~to~~ in my opinion	prior ~~than~~ to
contrast ~~against~~ to	meet ~~to~~ her standards	should ~~of~~

To avoid idiomatic errors, consult your dictionary and read your essay aloud; often your ears will catch mistakes in usage that your eyes have overlooked.*

Levels of Language

In addition to choosing the correct word, you should also select words whose status is suited to your purpose. For convenience here, language has been classified into three categories or levels of usage: (1) colloquial, (2) informal, and (3) formal.

Colloquial language is the kind of speech you use most often in conversation with your friends, classmates, and family. It may not always be grammatically correct ("it's me"); it may include fragments of speech, contractions, some slang, words identified as nonstandard by the dictionary (such as "yuck" or "lousy"), and shortened or abbreviated words ("grad school," "photos," "TV"). Colloquial speech is everyday language, and although you may use it in some writing (personal letters, journals, memos, and so forth), you should think carefully about using colloquial language in most college essays or in professional letters, reports, or papers because such a choice implies a casual relationship between writer and reader.

Informal language is called for in most college and professional assignments. The tone is more formal than in colloquial writing or speech; no slang or nonstandard words are permissible. Informal writing consistently uses correct grammar; fragments are used for special effect or not at all. Authorities disagree on the use of contractions in informal writing: some say avoid them entirely; others say they're permissible; still others advocate using them only to avoid stilted phrases ("let's go," for example, is preferable to "let us go"). Most, if not all, of your essays in English classes will be written in informal language.

---

* You may not immediately recognize what's wrong with words your teacher has labeled "diction" or "idiom," as these marks often cover many sins. If you're uncertain about an error, don't hesitate to ask your teacher for clarification; after all, if you don't know what's wrong with your prose, you can't very well avoid making the same mistake again. To illustrate this point, here's a true story: A bright young woman was having trouble with prepositional phrases in her essays, and although her professor repeatedly marked her incorrect expressions with the marginal note "idiom," she never improved. Finally, one day near the end of the term, she approached her teacher in tears and wailed, "Professor Jones, I know I'm not a very good writer, but must you write 'idiot,' 'idiot,' 'idiot' all over my papers?" The moral of this story is simple: it's easy to misunderstand a correction or misread your teacher's writing. Since you can't improve until you know what's wrong, always ask when you're in doubt.

Formal language is found in important documents and in serious, often ceremonial, speeches. Characteristics include an elevated—but not pretentious—tone, no contractions, and correct grammar. Formal writing often uses inverted word order and balanced sentence structure. John F. Kennedy's 1960 Inaugural Address, for example, was written in a formal style ("Ask not what your country can do for you; ask what you can do for your country"). Most people rarely, if ever, need to write formally; if you are called on to do so, however, be careful to avoid formal diction that sounds pretentious, pompous, or phony.

Tone

Tone is a general word that describes writers' attitudes toward their subject matter and audience. There are as many different kinds of tones as there are emotions. Depending on how the writer feels, an essay's "voice" may sound light-hearted, indignant, or solemn, to name but a few of the possible choices. In addition to presenting a specific attitude, a good writer gains credibility by maintaining a tone that is generally reasonable, sincere, and authentic.

Although it is impossible to analyze all the various kinds of tones one finds in essays, it is nevertheless beneficial to discuss some of those that repeatedly give writers trouble. Here are some tones that should be used carefully or avoided altogether:

Invective

Invective is unrestrained anger, usually expressed in the form of violent accusation or denunciation. Let's suppose, for example, you hear a friend argue, "Anyone who votes for Joe Smith is a Fascist pig." If you are considering Smith, you are probably offended by your friend's abusive tone. Raging emotion, after all, does not sway the opinions of intelligent people; they need to hear the facts presented in a calm, clear discussion. Therefore, in your own writing, aim for a reasonable tone. You want your readers to think, "Now here is someone with a good understanding of the situation, who has evaluated it with an unbiased, analytical mind." Keeping a controlled tone doesn't mean you shouldn't feel strongly about your subject—on the contrary, you certainly should—but you should realize that a hysterical or outraged tone defeats your purpose by causing you to sound irrational and therefore untrustworthy. For this reason, you should probably avoid using profanity in your essays; the shock value of an obscenity may not be worth what you might lose in credibility (and besides, is anyone other than your Aunt Fanny really amazed by profanity these days?). The most effective way to get your point across is to persuade, not offend, your reader.

Sarcasm

In most of your writing you'll discover that a little sarcasm—bitter, derisive remarks—goes a long way. Like invective, too much sarcasm can damage the reasonable tone your essay should present. Instead of saying, "You can recognize the supporters of the new tax law by the points on the tops of their heads," give your readers some reasons why you believe the tax bill is flawed. Sarcasm can be effective, but realize that it often backfires by causing the writer to sound like a childish name-caller rather than a judicious commentator.

Irony

Irony is a figure of speech whereby the writer or speaker says the opposite of what is meant; for the irony to be successful, however, the audience must understand the writer's true intent. For example, if you have slopped to school in a rainstorm and your drenched teacher enters the classroom saying, "Ah, nothing like this beautiful sunny weather," you know that your teacher is being ironic. Perhaps one of the most famous cases of irony occurred in 1938, when Sigmund Freud, the famous Viennese psychiatrist, was arrested by the Nazis. After being harassed by the Gestapo, he was released on the condition that he sign a statement swearing he had been treated well by the secret police. Freud signed it, but he added a few words after his signature: "I can heartily recommend the Gestapo to anyone." Looking back, we easily recognize Freud's jab at his captors; the Gestapo, however, apparently overlooked the irony and let him go.

Although irony is often an effective device, it can also cause great confusion, especially when it is written rather than spoken. Unless your readers thoroughly understand your position in the first place, they may become confused by what appears to be a sudden contradiction. Irony that is too subtle, too private, or simply out of context merely complicates the issue. Therefore, you must make certain that your reader has no trouble realizing when your tongue is firmly embedded in your cheek. And unless you are assigned to write an ironic essay (in the same vein, for instance, as Swift's "A Modest Proposal"), don't overuse irony. Like any rhetorical device, its effectiveness is reduced with overkill.

Flippancy or Cuteness

If you sound too flip, hip, or bored in your essay ("People with IQs lower than their sunscreen number will object . . ."), your readers will not take you seriously and, consequently, will disregard whatever you have to say. Writers suffering from cuteness will also antagonize their readers. For example, let's assume you're assigned the topic "Which Person Has Done the Most to Arouse the Laboring Class in Twentieth-Century England?" and you begin your essay with a discussion of the man who invented the alarm clock. Although that joke might be funny in an appropriate situation, it's not likely to impress your reader, who's looking for serious commentary. How much cuteness is too much is often a matter of taste, but if you have any doubts about the quality of your humor, leave it out. Also, omit personal messages or comic asides to your reader (such as "Ha, ha, just kidding!" or "I knew you'd love this part"). Humor is often effective, but remember that the point of any essay is to persuade an audience to accept your thesis, not merely to entertain with freestanding jokes. In other words, if you use humor, make sure it is appropriate to your subject matter and that it works to help you make your point.

Sentimentality

Sentimentality is the excessive show of cheap emotions—"cheap" because they are not deeply felt but evoked by clichés and stock, tear-jerking situations. In the nineteenth century, for example, a typical melodrama played on the sentimentality of the audience by presenting a black-hatted, cold-hearted, mustache-twirling villain tying a golden-haired, pure-hearted "Little Nell" to the railroad tracks after driving her ancient, sickly mother out into a snowdrift. Today, politicians (among others) often appeal to our sentimentality by conjuring up vague images they feel will move us emotionally rather than rationally to take their side: "My friends," says Senator Stereotype, "this fine nation of ours was founded by men like myself, dedicated to the principles of family, flag, and freedom. Vote for me, and let's get back to those precious basics that make life in America so grand." Such gush is hardly convincing; good writers and speakers use evidence and logical reason to persuade their audience. For example, don't allow yourself to become too carried away with emotion, as did this student: "My dog, Cuddles, is the sweetest, cutest, most precious little puppy dog in the whole wide world, and she will always be my best friend because she is so sweet and adorable." In addition to sending the reader into sugar shock, this passage fails to present any specific reasons why anyone should appreciate Cuddles. In other words, be sincere in your writing, but don't lose so much control of your emotions that you become mushy or maudlin.

Preachiness

Even if you are so convinced of the rightness of your position that a burning bush couldn't change your mind, try not to sound smug about it. No one likes to be lectured by someone perched atop the mountain of morality. Instead of preaching, adopt a tone that says, "I believe my position is correct, and I am glad to have this opportunity to explain why." Then give your reasons and meet objections in a positive but not holier-than-thou manner.

Pomposity

The "voice" of your essay should sound as natural as possible; don't strain to sound scholarly, scientific, or sophisticated. If you write "My summer sojourn through the Western states of this grand country was immensely pleasurable" instead of "My vacation last summer in the Rockies was fun," you sound merely phony, not dignified and learned. Select only words you know and can use easily. Never write anything you wouldn't say in an ordinary conversation. (For more information on correcting pretentious writing, see pp. 134–135 and pp. 164–168.)

> To achieve the appropriate tone, be as sincere, forthright, and reasonable as you can. Let the tone of your essay establish a basis of mutual respect between you and your reader.

Connotation and Denotation

A word's *denotation* refers to its literal meaning, the meaning defined by the dictionary; a word's *connotation* refers to the emotional associations surrounding its meaning. For example, "home" and "residence" both may be defined as the place where one lives, but "home" carries connotations of warmth, security, and family that "residence" lacks. Similarly, "old" and "antique" have similar denotative meanings, but "antique" has the more positive connotation because it suggests something that also has value. Reporters and journalists do the same job, but the latter name somehow seems to indicate someone more sophisticated and professional. Because many words with similar denotative meanings do carry different connotations, good writers must be careful with their word choice. *Select only words whose connotations fit your purpose.* If, for example, you want to describe your grandmother in a positive way as someone who stands up for herself, you might refer to her as "assertive" or "feisty"; if you want to present her negatively, you might call her "aggressive" or "pushy."

In addition to selecting words with the appropriate connotations for your purpose, be careful to avoid offending your audience with particular connotations. For instance, if you were trying to persuade a group of politically conservative doctors to accept your stand on a national health-care program, you would not want to refer to your opposition as "right-wingers" or "reactionaries," extremist terms that have negative connotations. Remember, you want to inform and persuade your audience, not antagonize them.

You should also be alert to the use of words with emotionally charged connotations, especially in advertising and propaganda of various kinds. Car manufacturers, for example, have often used names of swift, bold, or graceful animals (Jaguar, Cougar, Impala) to sway prospective buyers; cosmetic manufacturers in recent years have taken advantage of the trend toward lighter makeup by associating words such as "nature," "natural," and "healthy glow" with their products. Diet-conscious Americans are now deluged with "light" and "organic" food products. Politicians, too, are heavy users of connotation; they often drop in emotionally positive, but virtually meaningless, words and phrases such as "defender of the American Way," "friend of the common man," and "visionary" to describe themselves, while tagging their opponents with such negative, emotionally charged labels as "radical," "elitist," and "permissive." Of course, intelligent readers, like intelligent voters and con-sumers, want more than emotion-laden words; they want facts and logical ar-gument. Therefore, as a good writer, you should use connotation as only one of many persuasive devices to enhance your presentation of evidence; never depend solely on an emotional appeal to convince your audience that your position—or thesis—is correct.

▶ PRACTICING WHAT YOU'VE LEARNED

A. Some of the underlined words below are used incorrectly; some are cor-rect. Substitute the accurate word wherever necessary.

1. The finances of the chicken ranch are in fowl shape because the hens are lying down on the job.

2. The professor, whose famous for his photogenic memory, graciously excepted a large amount of complements.

3. Its to bad you don't like they're new Popsicle sculpture since their giving it to you for Christmas.

4. Vacations of to weeks with to friends are always to short, and while you're to tired to return to work, your to broke not to.

5. Sara June felt she deserved an "A" in math, irregardless of her 59 average in the coarse.

6. "I am impressed by the continuity of his physical presence"— Howard Cosell.

7. Did the high school principal loose you're heavy medal tape and it's case too?

8. The new city counsel parade ordinance will effect everyone in the capitol city except members of the Lawn Chair Marching Band.

B. The sentences below contain words and phrases that interfere with the sincere, reasonable tone good writers try to create. Rewrite each sentence, replacing sarcasm, sentimentality, cuteness, invective, and pretentiousness with more appropriate language.

1. The last dying rays of day were quickly ebbing in the West as if to signal the feline to begin its lonely vigil.

2. Only a jerk would support the President's Mideast peace plan.

3. I was desirous of acquiring knowledge about members of our lower income brackets.

4. If the bill to legalize marijuana is passed, we can safely assume that the whole country will soon be going to pot (heh, heh!).

5. I just love to look at those little white mice with their itty-bitty red eyes.

C. In each group of words listed below, identify the words with the most pleasing and most negative connotations.

1. teacher/instructor/educator/professor/lecturer

2. slender/slim/skinny/thin/slight/anorexic

3. famous/notorious/well-known/infamous

4. wealthy/opulent/rich/affluent/privileged

5. dull/drab/quiet/boring/colorless

D. Replace the underlined words in the sentences below with words arousing more positive feelings:

1. The <u>stench</u> from Jean's kitchen meant dinner was ready and was about to be served.

2. My neighbor was a <u>fat spinster lady</u>.

3. The coach had <u>rigid</u> rules for all his players.

4. His <u>obsession</u> with his yard pleased the city's beautification committee.

5. The <u>slick</u> car salesman made a <u>pitch</u> to the <u>old geezer</u> who walked in the door.

6. Textbook writers admit to having a few <u>bizarre</u> habits.

7. Carol was a <u>mediocre</u> student.

8. His <u>odd</u> clothes made Mary think he was a <u>bum</u>.

9. The High Priest explained his tribe's <u>superstitions</u>.

10. Many of the board members were amazed to see how Algernon <u>dominated</u> the meeting.

SELECTING THE BEST WORDS

In addition to selecting the correct word and appropriate tone, good writers also choose words that firmly implant their ideas in the minds of their readers. The best prose not only makes cogent points but also states these points memorably. To help you select the best words to express your ideas, the following is a list of do's and don't's covering the most common diction (word choice) problems in students' writing today.

Do make your words as precise as possible. Always choose vigorous, active verbs and colorful, specific nouns and modifiers. "The big tree was hit by lightning," for example, is not as informative or interesting as "Lightning splintered the neighbors' thirty-foot oak." *Don't* use words whose meanings are unclear:

Vague Verbs

Unclear   She is *involved* in a lawsuit. [How?]

Clear   She is suing her dentist for filling the wrong tooth.

Unclear   Tom can *relate* to Jennifer. [What's the relationship?]

Clear   Tom understands Jennifer's financial problem.

Unclear   He won't *deal* with his ex-wife. [In what way?]

Clear   He refuses to speak to his ex-wife.

Unclear   Clyde *participated* in an off-Broadway play. [How?]

Clear   Clyde held the cue cards for the actors.

Vague Nouns

Unclear   The burglar took several valuable *things* from our house.* [What items?]

Clear   The burglar took a *color TV, a VCR,* and a *microwave oven* from our house.

Unclear   When I have my car serviced, there is always *trouble.* [What kind?]

Clear   When I have my car serviced, *the mechanics always find additional repairs* and *never have the car ready when it is promised.*

Unclear   When I have *problems,* I always call my friends for advice. [What problems?]

Clear   *If my girlfriend breaks up with me, my roof needs repairing,* or *my dog needs surgery,* I always call my friends for advice.

---

* One specific piece of advice: banish the word "thing" from your writing. In nine out of ten cases, it is a lazy substitute for some other word. Unless you mean "an inanimate object," replace "thing" with the specific word it stands for.

Unclear   I like to have *fun* while I'm on vacation. [What sort of activities?]

Clear   I like to *eat in fancy restaurants, fly stunt kites,* and *walk along the beach* when I'm on vacation.

Vague Modifiers

Unclear   His *terrible* explanation left me *very* confused. [Why "terrible"? How confused?]

Clear   His disorganized explanation left me too confused to begin the project.

Unclear   The boxer hit the punching bag *really* hard. [How hard?]

Clear   The boxer hit the punching bag so hard it split open.

Unclear   *Casablanca* is a *good* movie *with something for everyone.* [Why "good" and for everyone?]

Clear   *Casablanca* is a witty, sentimental movie that successfully combines an adventure story and a romance.

Do make your word choices as fresh and original as possible. Instead of saying, "My hometown is very quiet," you might say, "My hometown's definition of an orgy is a light burning after midnight." In other words, if you can make your readers admire and remember your prose, you have a better chance of persuading them to accept your ideas.

Conversely, to avoid ho-hum prose, *don't* fill your sentences with clichés and platitudes—overworked phrases that cause your writing to sound lifeless and trite. Although we use clichés in everyday conversation, good writers avoid them in writing because (1) they are often vague or imprecise (just how pretty is "pretty as a picture?"), (2) they are used so frequently that they rob your prose style of personality and uniqueness ("It was raining cats and dogs"—does that phrase help your reader "see" the particular rainstorm you're trying to describe?).

Novice writers often include trite expressions because they do not recognize them as clichés; therefore, below is a partial list (there are literally thousands more) of phrases to avoid. Instead of using a cliché, try substituting an original phrase to describe what you see or feel. Never try to disguise a cliché by putting it in quotation marks—a baboon in dark glasses and a wig is still a baboon.

crack of dawn	needle in a haystack
a crying shame	bed of roses
white as a sheet	soft as silk
depths of despair	hard as nails

dead of night	white as snow
shadow of a doubt	almighty dollar
hear a pin drop	naked truth
blessed event	after all is said and done
first and foremost	to make a long story short

It would be impossible, of course, to memorize all the clichés and trite expressions in our language, but do check your prose for recognizable, over-worked phrases so that your words will not be predictable and, consequently, dull. If you aren't sure if a phrase is a cliché—but you've heard it used fre-quently—your prose will probably be stronger if you substitute an original phrase for the suspected one.

Don't use trendy expressions or slang in your essays. Slang generally consists of commonly used words made up by special groups to communicate among themselves. Slang has many origins, from sports to space travel; for example, surfing gave us the expression "to wipe out" (to fail), the military lent "snafu" (from the first letters of "situation normal—all fouled up"), the astronauts provided "A-OK" (all systems working).

Although slang often gives our speech color and vigor, it is unaccept-able in most writing assignments for several reasons. First, slang is often part of a private language understood only by members of a particular profes-sional, social, or age group. Second, slang often presents a vague picture or one that changes meanings from person to person or from context to context. More than likely, each person has a unique definition for a particular slang expression, and although these definitions may overlap, they are not pre-cisely the same. Consequently, your reader could interpret your words in one way whereas you mean them in another, a dilemma that might result in total miscommunication. Too often beginning writers rely on vague, popular clichés ("The party was truly awesome") instead of thinking of specific words to express specific ideas. Moreover, slang becomes dated quickly, and almost nothing sounds worse than yesterday's "in" expressions. (In his movie *Annie Hall,* Woody Allen pointed out the silliness of some of our psychological slang; when he was told to "mellow out," he replied, "When I get mellow, I ripen and then I rot.")

Try to write so that your prose will be as fresh and pleasing ten years from now as today. Don't allow slang to give your writing a flippant tone that detracts from a serious discussion. Putting slang in quotation marks isn't the solution—omit the slang and use precise words instead.

Do select simple, direct words your readers can easily understand. Don't use pompous or pseudosophisticated language in place of plain speech. Wherever possible, avoid *jargon*—that is, words and phrases that are unnec-essarily technical, pretentious, or abstract.

Technical jargon—terms specific to one area of study or specialization—should be omitted or clearly defined in essays directed to a general audience because such language is often inaccessible to anyone outside the writer's particular field. By now most of us are familiar with bureaucratese, journalese, and psychobabble, in addition to gobbledygook from business, politics, advertising, and education. If, for example, you worry that "a self-actualized person such as yourself cannot transcend either your hostile environment or your passive-aggressive behavior to make a commitment to a viable lifestyle and meaningful interpersonal relationships," you are indulging in psychological or sociological jargon; if you "review existing mechanisms of consumer input, thruput, and output via the consumer communications channel module," you are speaking business jargon. Although most professions do have their own terms, you should limit your use of specialized language to writing aimed solely at your professional colleagues; always try to avoid technical jargon in prose directed at a general audience.

Today the term "jargon" also refers to prose containing an abundance of abstract, pretentious, multisyllable words. The use of this kind of jargon often betrays a writer's attempt to sound sophisticated and intellectual; actually, it only confuses meaning and delays communication. Here, for instance, is an excerpt of incomprehensible jargon from a college president who obviously prefers twenty-five-cent words to simple, straightforward nickel ones: "We will divert the force of this fiscal stress into leverage energy and pry important budgetary considerations and control out of our fiscal and administrative procedures." Or look at the thirty-eight-word definition of "exit" written by an Occupational Safety and Health Administration bureaucrat: "That portion of a means of egress which is separated from all spaces of the building or structure by construction or equipment as required in this subpart to provide a protected way of travel to the exit discharge." Such language is not only pretentious and confusing but almost comic in its wordiness.

Jargon is so pervasive these days that even some English teachers are succumbing to its use. A group of high school teachers, for instance, was asked to indicate a preference for one of the following sentences:

> His expression of ideas that are in disagreement with those of others will often result in his rejection by them and his isolation from the life around him.

> If he expresses ideas that others disagree with, he will often be rejected by them and isolated from the life around him.

Surprisingly, only nineteen percent chose the more direct second sentence. The others saw the wordy, pompous first statement as "mature" and "educated," revealing that some teachers themselves may be both the victims and perpetrators of doublespeak.

To avoid such verbal litter in your own writing, follow these rules:

1. Always select the plainest, most direct words you know.

Jargon   The editor wanted to halt the proliferation of the product because she discovered an error on the page that terminates the volume.

Revised   The editor wanted to stop publishing the book because she found an error on the last page.

2. Replace nominalizations (nouns that are made from verbs and adjectives, usually by adding endings such as *-tion, -ism, -ness,* or *-al*) with simpler verbs and nouns.

Jargon   The departmental head has come to the recognition that the utilization of verbose verbalization renders informational content inaccessible.

Revised   The head of the department recognizes that wordiness confuses meaning.

3. Avoid adding *-ize* or *-wise* to verbs and adverbs.

Jargon   *Weatherwise,* it looked like a good day to *finalize* her report on wind tunnels.

Revised   The day's clear weather would help her finish her report on wind tunnels.

4. Drop out meaningless tack-on words such as "factor," "aspect," and "situation."

Jargon   The convenience factor of the neighborhood grocery store is one aspect of its success.

Revised   The convenience of the neighborhood grocery store contributes to its success.

Remember that good writing is clear and direct, never wordy, cloudy, or ostentatious. (For more hints on developing a clear style, see pp. 124–135.)

Do call things by their proper names. Don't sugarcoat your terms by substituting euphemisms—words that sound nice or pretty applied to subjects some people find distasteful. For example, you've probably heard someone say, "she passed away" instead of "she died," or "he was under the influence of alcohol" instead of "he was drunk." Airline stewards instruct passengers "in the event of a 'water landing.'" "Senior Citizens" (or worse, the "chronologically advantaged") may receive special discounts. Often euphemisms are used to soften names of jobs: "sanitary engineer" for garbage collector, "field representative" for salesperson, "information processor" for typist, "vehicle appearance specialist" for car washer, and so forth.

Some euphemisms are dated and now seem plain silly: in Victorian times, for example, the word "leg" was considered unmentionable in polite company, so people spoke of "piano limbs" and asked for the "first joint" of a chicken. The phrases "white meat" and "dark meat" were euphemisms some people used to avoid asking for a piece of chicken breast or thigh.

Today, euphemisms still abound. Though our generation is perhaps more direct about sex and death, many current euphemisms gloss over unpleasant or unpopular business, military, and political practices. Some stockbrokers, for example, once referred to an October market crash as "a fourth-quarter equity retreat," and General Motors didn't really shut down one of its plants—the closing was merely a "volume-related production schedule adjustment." In a similar move, Chrysler didn't lay off 5,000 workers; it simply "initiated a career alternative enhancement program." Nuclear power plants no longer have dumps; they have "containment facilities" with radiation "migration" rather than leaks and "inventory discrepancies" rather than thefts of plutonium. Simple products are now complex technology: clocks are "analog temporal displacement monitors," toothbrushes are "home plaque removal instruments," sinks are part of the "hygienic hand-washing media," and pencils are "portable hand-held communications inscribers." Vinyl is now "vegetarian leather."

Euphemisms abound in governments and official agencies as those in charge try to hide or disguise the truth from the public. On the national level, a former budget director gave us "revenue enhancements" instead of new taxes, and a former Secretary of Health, Education, and Welfare once tried to camouflage cuts in social services by calling them "advance downward adjustments." Wiretaps have become "technical collection sources" used by "special investigators units" instead of burglars, and plain lying has become on one important occasion merely "plausible deniability."

In a large Southwestern city, people were possibly surprised to learn that there are no potholes in the streets—only "pavement deficiencies." In some jails, a difficult prisoner who once might have been sent to solitary confinement is now placed in the "meditation room" or the "adjustment center." In some hospitals, sick people do not die—they experience "negative patient care outcome"; if they died because of a doctor's mistake, they underwent a "diagnostic misadventure of a high magnitude." (Incidentally, those patients who survive no longer receive greeting cards; instead, they open "social expression products.")

Perhaps the military is the all-time winner of the "substitute-a-euphemism" contest. Over the years the military has used a variety of words such as "neutralization," "pacification," and "liberation" to mean the invasion and destruction of other countries and governments. During the Gulf War with Iraq, for example, bombs that fell on civilians were referred to as "incontinent ordnance," with the dead becoming "collateral damage." Earlier, to avoid publicizing a retreat, the military simply called for "backloading our augmentation personnel." On the less serious side, the Navy changes ocean waves into "climatic disturbances at the air-sea interface," and the Army, not to be outdone, transforms the lowly shovel into a "combat emplacement evacuator."

Although many euphemisms seem funny and harmless, too many of them are not because people—often those with power to shape public opinion—have intentionally designed them to obscure the reality of a particular situation or choice of action. Because euphemisms can be used unscrupulously to manipulate people, you should always avoid them in your own prose and be suspicious of them in the writing of others. As Aldous Huxley, author of *Brave New World,* noted, "An education for freedom is, among other things, an education in the proper uses of language."

In addition to weakening the credibility of one's ideas, euphemisms can make prose unnecessarily abstract, wordy, pretentious, or even silly. For a clear and natural prose style, use terms that are straightforward and simple. In other words, call a spade a spade, not "an implement for use in horticultural environments."

Avoid sexist language. Most people will agree that language helps shape thought. Consequently, writers should avoid using any language that promotes demeaning stereotypes. Sexist language, in particular, often subtly suggests that women are less rational, intelligent, or capable of handling certain tasks or jobs. To make your writing as accurate and unbiased as possible, here are some simple suggestions for ways to write nonsexist prose:

1. Try using plural nouns to eliminate the need for the singular pronouns "he" and "she":

Original   Today's *doctor* knows *he* must carry extra malpractice insurance.

Revision   Today's *doctors* know *they* must carry extra malpractice insurance.

2. Try substituting gender-neutral occupational titles for those ending in "man" or "woman":

Original   The *fireman* and the *saleslady* watched the *policeman* arrest the *mailman.*

Revision   The *firefighter* and the *sales clerk* watched the *police officer* arrest the *mail carrier.*

3. Don't contribute to stereotyping by assigning particular roles solely to men or women:

Original   *Mothers* concerned about the possibility of Reyes syndrome should avoid giving their sick children aspirin.

Revision   *Parents* concerned about the possibility of Reyes syndrome should avoid giving their sick children aspirin.

4. Try substituting words such as "people," "persons," "one," "voters," "workers," "students," and so on, for "man" or "woman":

Original Any *man* who wants to become a corporation executive before thirty should buy this book.

Revision *Anyone* who wants to become a corporation executive before thirty should buy this book.

5. Don't use inappropriate diminutives:

Original In the annual office picture, the photographer asked the men to stand behind the *girls.*

Revision In the annual office picture, the photographer asked the men to stand behind the *women.*

6. Consider avoiding words that use "man" to describe the actions or characteristics of a group ("man the barricades") or that refer to people in general.

Original Rebuilding the space shuttle will call for extra money and *manpower,* but such an endeavor will benefit *mankind* in the generations to come.

Revision Rebuilding the space shuttle will call for extra money and *employees,* but such an endeavor will benefit future *generations.*

7. Be consistent in your treatment of men's and women's names, marital status, professional titles, and physical appearances:

Original Neither Herman Melville, the inspired novelist, nor Miss Emily Dickinson, the spinster poetess of Amherst, gained fame or fortune in their lifetimes.

Revision Neither Herman Melville, the novelist, nor Emily Dickinson, the poet, gained fame or fortune in their lifetimes.

Revising your writing to eliminate certain kinds of gender-specific references does not mean turning clear phrases into awkward or confusing jumbles of "he/she told him/her that the car was his/hers." By following the suggestions above, you should be able to make your prose both clear and inoffensive to all members of your audience.

Do enliven your writing with figurative language, when appropriate. Figurative language produces pictures or images in a reader's mind, often by comparing something unfamiliar to something familiar. The two most common figurative devices are the simile and the metaphor. A *simile* is a comparison between two people, places, feelings, or things, using the word "like" or "as"; a more forceful comparison, omitting the word "like" or "as," is a *metaphor*. Below are two examples:

Simile   George eats his meals like a hog.

Metaphor   George is a hog at mealtime.

In both sentences George, whose eating habits are unfamiliar to the reader, is likened to a hog, whose sloppy manners are generally well known. By comparing George to a hog, the writer gives the reader a clear picture of George at the table. Figurative language not only can help you present your ideas in clear, concrete, economical ways but also can make your prose more memorable—especially if the image or picture you present is a fresh, arresting one. Below are some examples of striking images designed to catch the reader's attention and to clarify the writer's point:

- An hour away from him felt like a month in the country.

- The atmosphere of the meeting room was as tense as a World Series game tied up in the ninth inning.

- The woman's earrings were as big as butter plates.

- The angry accusation flew like a spear: once thrown, it could not be retrieved and it cut deeply.

- Out of the night came the convoy of big trucks, modern-day buffalo thundering single-file across the prairie, eyes on fire.

- Behind her broad polished desk, Matilda was a queen bee with a legion of office drones lined up at her door.

- The factory squatted on the bank of the river like a huge black toad.

Figurative language can spice up your prose, but like any spice, it can be misused, thus spoiling your soup. Therefore, don't overuse figurative language; not every point needs a metaphor or simile for clarity or emphasis. Too many images are confusing. Moreover, don't use stale images. (Clichés—discussed on pp. 163–164—are often tired metaphors or similes: snake in the grass, hot as fire, quiet as a mouse, etc.) If you can't catch your readers' attention with a fresh picture, don't bore them with a stale one.

And finally, don't mix images—this too often results in a confusing or unintentionally comic scene. For example, a former mayor of Denver once responded to a question about city fiscal requirements this way: "I think the proper approach is to go through this Garden of Gethsemane that we're in now, give birth to a budget that will come out of it, and then start putting our ducks in order with an appeal and the backup we would need to get something done at the state level." Or consider the defensive attorney who didn't particularly like his client's plea-bargaining deal but nevertheless announced, "Given the attitude of the normal jury on this type of crime, I feel we would be paddling up a stream behind the eight ball." Perhaps a newspaper columnist wins the prize for confusion with this triple-decker: "The Assemblymen also were miffed at their Senate counterparts because they have refused to bite the bullet that now seems to have grown to the size of a millstone to the Assemblymen whose necks are on the line."

Think of figurative language as you might regard a fine cologne on the person sitting next to you in a crowded theater: just enough is engaging; too much is overpowering.

Do vary your word choice so that your prose does not sound wordy, repetitious, or monotonous. Consider the following sentence:

According to child psychologists, depriving a child of artistic stimulation in the earliest stages of childhood can cause the child brain damage.

Reworded, the sentence below eliminates the tiresome, unnecessary repetition of the word "child":

According to child psychologists, depriving infants of artistic stimulation can cause brain damage.

By omitting or changing repeated words, you can add variety and crispness to your prose. Of course, don't ever change your words or sentence structure to achieve variety at the expense of clarity or precision; at all times your goal is making your prose clear to your readers.

Do remember that wordiness is a major problem for all writers, even the professionals. State your thoughts directly and specifically in as few words as necessary to communicate your meaning clearly. In addition to the advice given here on avoiding wordy or vague jargon, euphemisms, and clichés, you might review the sections on simplicity and conciseness in Chapter 6.

The most important key to effective word choice is revision.
As you write your first draft, don't fret about selecting the best words to communicate your ideas; in later drafts one of your main tasks will be replacing the inaccurate or imprecise words with better ones (Dorothy Parker, famous for her witty essays, once lamented, "I can't write five words but that I change seven"). All good writers rewrite, so revise your prose to make each word count.

PRACTICING WHAT YOU'VE LEARNED

A. Underline the vague nouns, verbs, and modifiers in the sentences that follow. Then rewrite each sentence so that it says something clear and specific.

1. The experiment had very bad results.

2. The speaker came up with some odd items.

3. The house was big, old, and ugly.

4. The man was a nice guy with a good personality.

5. I felt that the whole ordeal was quite an experience.

6. The machine we got was missing a few things.

7. The woman was really something special.

8. The classroom material wasn't interesting.

9. The child made a lot of very loud noises.

10. The cost of the unusual meal was amazing.

B. Rewrite the following sentences, eliminating all the clichés, sexist language, and euphemisms you find.

1. When my mother didn't return from the little girl's room, we decided she was as slow as molasses.

2. According to former-President Jimmy Carter, the aborted rescue of the hostages in Iran was an incomplete success.

3. On election day, all of us over the ripe old age of eighteen should exercise our most sacred democratic privilege.

4. After all is said and done, the range technicians and the agricultural producers will still be the new disadvantaged class.

5. Each officer in the Armed Forces realizes that someday he may be called on to use the peacekeepers to depopulate an emerging nation in a lethal intervention.

6. Although he once regarded her as sweet and innocent, he realized then and there that she was really a wolf in sheep's clothing.

7. Any good cook will be green with envy when she tastes her neighbor's apple pie.

8. The city councilman was stewing in his juices when he learned that his son had been arrested for fooling around with the funds for the fiscal underachievers' home.

9. After the policemen detained the rebels, some of the newspapermen who had been watching the incident experienced unlawful deprivation of life.

10. The automobile company sent a letter warning that "driving with a failed bearing could . . . adversely affect vehicle control" but also praising the new man-made custom upholstery.

C. Rewrite the following sentences, replacing the jargon, slang, and cloudy language with clear, precise words and phrases.

1. To maintain a state of high-level wellness, one should use a wooden interdental stimulator at least once a day and avoid spending time at fake-bake salons.

2. According to the military, one should not attempt a predawn ventical insertion without an aerodynamic personnel decelerator because it could lead to sudden deceleration trauma upon landing.

3. American Airlines' passengers can now arrive and depart planes on customer conveyance mobile lounges.

4. If you are in the armed services, you should avoid receiving a ballistically induced aperture in the subcutaneous environment that might lead to your being terminated with extreme prejudice.

5. The U.S. Embassy in Budapest warned its employees: "It must be assumed that available casual indigenous female companions work for or cooperate with the Hungarian government security establishment."

6. "I thought the evening would be totally awesome but my blind date turned out to be a double-bagger babe with an attitude so I split," said Wayne, who was somewhat of a geek himself.

7. The employee was outplaced for a lack of interpersonal skills and for failing to optimize productivity.

8. My institute of higher learning announced today that its academic evaluation program had been delayed and in all probability indefinitely postponed due to circumstances relating to financial insolvency.

9. All of us could relate to Mabel's essay on the significant educational factors involved in the revenue enhancement tax-base erosion control program.

10. "We were not micromanaging Grenada intelligencewise until about that time frame," said Admiral Wesley L. McDonald, when asked what was happening on the island just prior to the United States' 1983 rescue mission.

ASSIGNMENT

A. The recipe below pokes fun at bureaucractic jargon. See if you can translate the bureaucratese into clear, simple instructions. Then look at your writing to make certain that you are not guilty of using similar gobbledygook in your own prose.

Input to output, 35 minutes

For government employees and bureaucrats who have problems with standard recipes, here's one that should make the grade—a classic version of the chocolate-chip cookie translated for easy reading.

Total Lead Time: 35 minutes.

Inputs:
    1 cup packed brown sugar
    $1/2$ cup granulated sugar
    $1/2$ cup softened butter
    $1/2$ cup shortening
    2 eggs
    $1^{1}/2$ teaspoons vanilla
    $2^{1}/2$ cups all-purpose flour
    1 teaspoon baking soda
    $1/2$ teaspoon salt
    12-ounce package semi-sweet chocolate pieces
    1 cup chopped walnuts or pecans

Guidance:
    After procurement actions, decontainerize inputs. Perform measurement tasks on a case-by-case basis. In a mixing type bowl, impact heavily on brown sugar, granulated sugar, softened butter and shortening. Coordinate the interface of eggs and vanilla, avoiding an overrun scenario to the best of your skills and abilities.
    At this point in time, leverage flour, baking soda and salt into a bowl and aggregate. Equalize with prior mixture and develop intense and continuous liaison among inputs until well-coordinated. Associate key chocolate and nut subsystems and execute stirring operations.

Within this time frame, take action to prepare the heating environment for throughput by manually setting the oven baking unit by hand to a temperature of 375 degrees Fahrenheit (190 Celsius). Drop mixture in an ongoing fashion from a teaspoon implement onto an ungreased cookie sheet at intervals sufficient enough apart to permit total and permanent separation of throughputs to the maximum extent practicable under operating conditions.

Position cookie sheet in a bake situation and surveil for 8 to 10 minutes or until cooking action terminates. Initiate coordination of outputs within the cooling rack function. Containerize, wrap in red tape and disseminate to authorized staff personnel on a timely and expeditious basis.

Output:
Six dozen official government chocolate-chip cookie units.

© 1982, *The Washington Post*

B. Write two of the following paragraphs and then exchange them with those written by a classmate. Translate faulty prose into crisp, clear sentences.

- A paragraph of clichés and vague language arguing the value of having a particular major in college

- A paragraph of jargon and euphemisms by a politician explaining why he or she abused a congressional privilege.

- A paragraph of vague language and clichés persuading your banker to advance you funds to invest in a get-rich-quick scheme

- A paragraph of slang, clichés, and sexist language advising your friends on their approaching marriage

- A paragraph of jargon and vague language praising a product you've invented and are trying to market

▶ APPLYING WHAT YOU'VE LEARNED TO *YOUR* WRITING

If you have drafted a piece of writing and you are satisfied with the development and organization of your ideas, you may want to begin revising your word choice. First, read your draft for accuracy. Circle and then look up any words you suspect may have been used incorrectly. Then focus your attention on your draft's tone, on the "voice" that your words are creating. Have you selected the right words for your purpose and for your audience? Last, change any words that you feel are vague, bland, or confusing; substitute clear prose for jargon, slang, clichés, or euphemisms. Make each word count: allow your words to clarify, not muddy, your meaning.

CHAPTER 7 SUMMARY

Here is a brief restatement of what you should remember about word choice:

1. Consult a dictionary if you are in doubt about the meaning or usage of a particular word.
2. Choose words that are appropriate for your purpose and audience.
3. Choose words that are clear, specific, and fresh rather than vague, bland, or clichéd.
4. Avoid language that is sexist, trendy, or that tries to hide truth behind jargon or euphemisms.
5. Work for prose that is concise rather than wordy, precise rather than foggy.

THE BASICS OF THE SHORT ESSAY: PART ONE SUMMARY

Here are ten rules to keep in mind while you are writing the rough drafts of your essay:

1. Be confident that you have something important and interesting to say.
2. Identify your particular audience and become determined to communicate effectively with them.
3. Use prewriting techniques to help you focus on one main idea that will become the thesis of your essay.
4. Organize your essay's points logically, in a persuasive and coherent order.
5. Develop each of your ideas with enough evidence and specific details.
6. Cut out any irrelevant material that disrupts the smooth flow from idea to idea.
7. Compose sentences that are clear, concise, and informative.
8. Select accurate, vivid words.
9. Revise your prose.
10. Revise your prose.

PART TWO

MODES AND STRATEGIES

Communication may be divided into four types (or "modes" as they are often called): exposition, argumentation, description, and narration. Although each one will be explained in greater detail in this section of the text, the four modes may be defined briefly as follows:

Exposition
the writer intends to explain or inform

Argumentation
the writer intends to convince or persuade

Description
the writer intends to create in words a picture of a person, place, object, or feeling

Narration
the writer intends to tell a story or recount an event

Although we commonly refer to exposition, argumentation, description, and narration as the basic types of prose, in reality it is difficult to find any one mode in a pure form. In fact, almost all essays are combinations of two or more modes; it would be virtually impossible, for instance, to write a story—narration—without including description or to argue without also giving some information. Nevertheless, by determining a writer's *main* purpose, we can usually identify an essay or prose piece as primarily exposition, argumentation, description, or narration. In other words, an article may include a brief description of a new mousetrap, but if the writer's main intention is to explain how the trap works, then we may designate the essay as exposition. In most cases, the primary mode of any essay will be readily apparent to the reader.

In Part Two of this text, you will study each of the four modes in detail and learn some of the patterns of development, called *strategies,* that will enable you to write the kind of prose most frequently demanded in college and professional work. Mastering the most common prose patterns in their simplest forms now will help you successfully assess and organize any kind of complex writing assignment you may face in the future.

EXPOSITION

8

.
.
.

Exposition refers to prose whose primary purpose is giving information. Some familiar examples of expository writing include encyclopedias, dictionaries, news magazines, and textbooks. In addition, much of your own college work may be classified as exposition: book reports, political analyses, laboratory and business reports, and most essay exams, to cite only a few of the possibilities.

But while all expository writing does present information, a good expository essay is more than a collection of facts, figures, and details. First, each essay should contain a thesis statement announcing the writer's purpose and position. Then the essay should be organized so that the body paragraphs explain and support that thesis. In an expository essay the writer says, in effect, here are the facts *as I see them;* therefore, the writer's main purpose is not only to inform the readers but also to convince them that this essay explains the subject matter in the clearest, most truthful way.

THE STRATEGIES OF EXPOSITION

There are a variety of ways to organize an expository essay, depending on your purpose. The most common strategies, or patterns, of organization include development by *example, process analysis, comparison and contrast, definition, classification,* and *causal analysis.* However, an essay is rarely developed completely by a single strategy (an essay developed by comparison and contrast, for instance, may also contain examples; a classification essay may contain definitions, and so forth); therefore, as in the case of the four modes, we identify the kind of expository essay by its *primary* strategy of development. To help you understand every expository strategy thoroughly before going on to the next, each is presented here separately. Each discussion section follows a similar pattern, which includes explanation of the strategy, advice on developing your essay, a list of essay topics, a topic proposal sheet, a revision checklist, two sample essays (one written by a student and the other by a professional writer), and a progress report.

STRATEGY ONE: DEVELOPMENT BY EXAMPLE

Perhaps you've heard a friend complain lately about a roommate. "Tina is an inconsiderate boor, impossible to live with," she cries. Your natural response might be to question your friend's rather broad accusation: "What makes her so terrible? What does she do that's so bad?" Your friend might then respond with specific examples of Tina's insensitivity: she never washes her dishes, she ties up the telephone for hours, and she plays her radio until three every morning. By citing several examples, your friend clarifies and supports her general criticism of Tina, thus persuading you to accept her point of view.

Examples in an essay work precisely the same way as in the hypothetical story above: they *support, clarify, interest,* and *persuade.*

In your writing assignments, you might want to assert that dorm food is cruel and inhuman punishment, that recycling is a profitable hobby, or that the cost of housing is rising dramatically. But without some carefully chosen examples to show the truth of your statements, these remain unsupported generalities or mere opinions. Your task, then, is to provide enough specific examples to support your general statements, to make them both clear and convincing. Below is a statement offering the reader only hazy generalities:

> Our locally supported TV channel presents a variety of excellent educational shows. The shows are informative on lots of different subjects for both children and adults. The information they offer makes channel 19 well worth the public funds that support it.

Rewritten below, the same paragraph explains its point clearly through the use of specific examples:

> Our locally supported TV channel presents a variety of excellent educational shows. For example, young children can learn their alphabet and numbers from *Sesame Street;* imaginative older children can be encouraged to create by watching *Kids' Writes,* a show on which four hosts read and act out stories written and sent in by youngsters from eight to fourteen. Adults may enjoy learning about antiques and collectibles from a program called *The Collector;* each week the show features an in-depth look at buying, selling, trading, and displaying collectible items, from Depression glass to teddy bears to Shaker furniture. Those folks wishing to become handy around the home can use information on repairs from plumbing to wiring on *This Old House,* while the nonmusical can learn the difference between skat singing and arias on such programs as *Jazz!* and *Opera Today.* And

the money-minded can profit from the tips dropped by stockbrokers who appear on *Wall Street Week*. The information offered makes these and other educational shows on channel 19 well worth the public funds that support the station.

Although the preceding example is based on real shows, you may also use personal experiences, hypothetical situations, anecdotes, research material, facts, testimony, or any combination thereof, to explain or support the points in your essays.

In some cases you may find that a series of short examples fits your purpose, illustrating clearly the idea you are presenting to your reader:

> In the earlier years of Hollywood, actors aspiring to become movie stars often adopted new names that they believed sounded more attractive to the public. Frances Ethel Gumm, for instance, decided to change her name to Judy Garland long before she flew over any rainbows, and Alexander Archibald Leach became Cary Grant on his way from England to America. Alexandra Cymboliak and Merle Johnson, Jr., might not have set teenage hearts throbbing in the early 1960s, but Sandra Dee and Troy Donahue certainly did. And while some names were changed to achieve a smoother flow (Frederic Austerlitz to Fred Astaire, for example), some may have also been changed to ensure a good fit on movie theater marquees as well as a place in their audience's memory: the little Turner girl, Julia Jean Mildred Frances, for instance, became just Lana.

Or you may decide that two or three examples, explained in some detail, provide the best support for your topic rather than a series of short examples. In the paragraph that follows, the writer chose to develop two examples to illustrate her point about her unusual dog:

> Our family dog Sparky always let us know when he wasn't getting enough attention. For instance, if he thought we were away from home too much, he'd perform his record trick. While we were out, Sparky would push an album out of the record rack and then tap the album cover in just such a way that the record would roll out. Then he would chomp the record! We'd return to find our favorite LP (somehow, always our current favorite) chewed into tiny bits of black vinyl scattered about the room. Another popular Sparky trick was the cat-sit. If the family was peacefully settled on the porch, not playing with him, Sparky would grab the family cat by the ear and drag her over to the steps, whereupon he would sit on top of her until someone paid attention to him. He never hurt the cat; he simply sat on her as one would sit on a fine cushion, with her head poking out under his tail, and a silly grin on his face that said, "See, if you'd play with me, I wouldn't get into such mischief."

You may also find that in some cases, one long, detailed example (called an *extended example*) is more useful than several shorter ones. If you were writing a paragraph urging the traffic department to install a stop sign at a particularly dangerous corner, you probably should cite numerous examples of accidents there. On the other hand, if you were praising a certain kind of local architecture, you might select one representative house and discuss it in detail. In the paragraph below, for instance, the writer might have supported his main point by citing a number of cases in which lives had been saved by seat belts; he chose instead to offer one detailed example, in the form of a personal experience:

> Wearing seat belts can protect people from injury, even in serious accidents. I know because seat belts saved me and my Dad two years ago when we were driving to see my grandparents who live in California. Because of the distance, we had to travel late on a rainy, foggy Saturday night. My Dad was driving, but what he didn't know was that there was a car a short way behind us driven by a drunk who was following our car's tail lights in order to keep himself on the road. About midnight, my Dad decided to check the map to make sure we were headed in the right direction, so he signaled, pulled over to the shoulder, and began to come to a stop. Unfortunately for us, the drunk didn't see the signal and moved his car over to the shoulder thinking that the main road must have curved slightly since our car had gone that way. As Dad slowed our car, the other car plowed into us at a speed estimated later by the police as over eighty miles an hour. The car hit us like Babe Ruth's bat hitting a slow pitch; the force of the speeding car slammed us hard into the dashboard, but not through the windshield and out onto the rocky shoulder, because, lucky for us, we were wearing our seat belts. The highway patrolmen, who arrived quickly on the scene, testified later at the other driver's trial that without question my Dad and I would have been seriously injured, if not killed, had it not been for our seat belts restraining us in the front seat.

The story of the accident illustrates the writer's claim that seat belts can save lives; without such an example, the writer's statement would be only an unsupported generalization.

In addition to making general statements specific and thus more convincing, good examples can explain and clarify unfamiliar, abstract, or difficult concepts for the reader. For instance, Newton's law of gravity might be more easily understood once it is explained through the simple, familiar example of an apple falling from a tree.

Moreover, clear examples can add to your prose vivid details that hold the reader's attention while you explain your points. A general statement decrying animal abuse, for instance, may be more effective accompanied by several examples detailing the brutal treatment of one particular laboratory's research animals.

The use of good examples is not, however, limited only to essays primarily developed by example. In actuality, you will probably use examples in every essay you write. You couldn't, for instance, write an essay classifying kinds of popular movies without including examples to help identify your categories. Similarly, you couldn't write essays defining the characteristics of a good teacher or a comparison between two kinds of cars without ample use of specific examples. To illustrate the importance of examples in all patterns of essay development, here are two excerpts from student essays reprinted in other parts of this text. The first excerpt comes from an essay classifying the Native American eras at Mesa Verde National Park (pp. 240–242). In his discussion of a particular time period, the writer uses a dwelling called Balcony House as an example to illustrate his claims about the Native Americans' skills in building construction.

> The third period lasted until A.D. 1300 and saw the innovation of pueblos, or groups of dwellings, instead of single-family units. Nearly eight hundred dwellings show the large number of people who inhabited the complex, tunneled houses, shops, storage rooms, courtyards, and community centers whose masonry walls, often elaborately decorated, were three and four stories high. At the spacious Balcony House pueblo, for example, an adobe court lies beneath another vaulted roof; on three sides stand two-story houses with balconies that lead from one room to the next. In back of the court is a spring, and along the front side is a low wall that kept the children from falling down the seven-hundred-foot cliff to the canyon floor below. Balcony House also contains two *kivas,* circular subterranean ceremonial chambers that show the importance of fellowship and religion to the people of this era.

Another student uses a personal example to help her support a point in her essay that contrasts a local co-op to a big chain grocery store (pp. 214–217). By using her friend's experience as an example, the writer shows the reader how a co-op may assist local producers in the community:

> Direct selling offers two advantages for producers: they get a better price for their wares than by selling them through a middleman, and at the same time they establish an independent reputation for their business, which can be immensely valuable to their success later on. In Fort Collins, for example, Luna tofu (bean curd) stands out as an excellent illustration of this kind of mutual support. Several years ago my friend Carol Jones began making tofu in small batches to sell to the co-op as a way to earn a part-time income as well as to contribute to the co-op. Her enterprise has now grown so well that last year her husband quit his job to go into business with her full time. She currently sells to distributors and independent stores from here to Denver; even Lane Grocer, who earlier would not consider selling her tofu even on a trial basis, is now thinking about changing its policy.

Learning to support, explain, or clarify your assertions by clear, thoughtful examples will help you develop virtually every piece of writing you are assigned, both in school and on the job. Development by example is the most widely used of all the expository strategies and by far the most important.

Developing Your Essay

An essay developed by example is one of the easiest to organize. In most cases, your first paragraph will present your thesis; each body paragraph will contain a topic sentence and as many effectively arranged examples as necessary to explain or support each major point; your last paragraph will conclude your essay in some appropriate way. Although the general organization is fairly simple, you should double-check the examples in your rough draft by asking these questions:

Are all my examples relevant? Each specific example should support, clarify, or explain the general statement it illustrates; each example should provide readers with additional insight into the subject under discussion. Keep the purpose of your paragraphs in mind: don't wander off into an analysis of the causes of crime if you are only supposed to show examples of it in your neighborhood. Keep your audience in mind, too: which examples will provide the kinds of information that your particular readers need to understand your point?

Are my examples well chosen? To persuade your readers to accept your opinion, you should select those examples that are the strongest and most convincing. Let's say you were writing a research paper exposing a government agency's wastefulness. To illustrate your claim, you would pick out those cases that most obviously show gross or ridiculous expenditures rather than asking your readers to consider some unnecessary but minor expenses. And you would try to select cases that represent recent or current examples of wastefulness rather than discussing expenditures too dated to be persuasive. In other words, when you have a number of examples to choose from, evaluate them and then select the best ones to support your point.

Are there enough examples to make each point clear and persuasive? Put yourself in your reader's place: would you be convinced with three brief examples? Five? One extended example? Two? Use your own judgment, but be careful to support or explain your major points adequately. It's better to risk overexplaining than to leave your reader confused or unconvinced.

Problems to Avoid

The most common weakness in essays developed by example is a lack of specific detail. Too often novice writers present a sufficient number of relevant, well-chosen examples, but the illustrations themselves are too general, vague, or brief to be helpful. Examples should be clear, specific, and adequately detailed so that the reader receives the full persuasive impact of each one. For instance, in an essay claiming that college football has become too violent, don't merely say, "Too many players got hurt last year." Such a statement only hints; it lacks enough development to be fully effective. Go into more detail by giving actual examples of jammed fingers, wrenched backs, fractured legs, crushed kneecaps, and broken dreams. Present these examples in specific, vivid language; once your readers begin to "see" that field covered with blood and bruised bodies, you'll have less trouble convincing them that your point of view is accurate.

The second biggest problem in example essays is the lack of coherence. The reader should never sense an interruption in the flow of thought from one example to the next in paragraphs containing more than one example. Each body paragraph of this kind should be more than a topic sentence and a choppy list of examples. You should first arrange the examples in an order that best explains the major point presented by your topic sentence; then carefully check to make sure each example is smoothly connected in thought to the statements preceding and following it. You can avoid a listing effect by using transition devices where necessary to ensure easy movement from example to example and from point to point. A few common transition words often found in essays of example include "for instance," "for example," "to illustrate," "another," and "in addition." (For a list of other transition words and additional help on writing coherent paragraphs, review pp. 74–78.)

▶ ESSAY TOPICS

Use the statements below to lead you to your essay topic. Be sure to focus these suggestions as you shape your thesis.

1. Heroes today are merely media creations rather than truly admirable people.

2. First impressions are often the best/worst means of judging people.

3. Failure is a better teacher than success.

4. My fear of flying (or some other fear) prevents me from living a normal life.

5. The willingness to undertake adventure is a necessary part of a happy life.

6. Doing good deeds can backfire.

7. Complaining can produce unforeseen results.

8. Travel can be the best medicine.

9. Consumers are often at the mercy of unscrupulous companies.

10. Visits to the doctor/dentist/veterinarian often prove more traumatic than the illness.

11. Failure to keep my mouth shut (or some other bad habit) leads me into trouble.

12. Too much pressure to succeed cripples young people today.

13. Modern technology often produces more inconvenience than convenience.

14. Job hunting today is a difficult process.

15. Discrimination exists in this community.

16. Movies today are unnecessarily violent.

17. Many required courses are/are not relevant to a student's education.

18. High schools do/do not adequately prepare students for college.

19. The most popular political attitude among students today is "I'm apathetic, and I don't care."

20. One important event can change the course of a life.

A Topic Proposal for Your Essay

Selecting the right subject matter is important to every writer. To help you clarify your ideas and strengthen your commitment to your topic, here is a proposal sheet that asks you to describe some of your preliminary ideas about your subject before you begin drafting. Although as you draft your ideas may change (they will almost certainly become more refined), thinking through your choice of topic now may help you avoid several false starts.

1. In a few words, note the subject of your essay as you have narrowed and focused it for this assignment. Write a rough statement of your opinion or attitude toward this topic.

2. Why are you interested in this topic? Do you have a personal or professional connection to the subject? State at least one reason for your choice of topic.

3. Is this a significant topic of interest to others? Why? Who specifically might find it interesting, informative, or entertaining?

4. Describe in one or two sentences the primary effect you would like to have on your audience. After they read your essay, what do you want your audience to think, feel, or do? (In other words, what is your purpose in writing this essay?)

5. Writers use examples to explain and clarify their ideas. Briefly list two or three examples you might develop in your essay to support discussion of your chosen topic.

6. What difficulties, if any, might this topic present during your drafting? For example, do you know enough about this topic to illustrate it with specific rather than vague examples? Might the topic still be too broad or unfocused for this assignment? Revise your topic now or make notes for an appropriate plan of action to resolve any difficulties you foresee.

SAMPLE STUDENT ESSAY

Study the use of specific examples in the brief student essay that follows. If the writer were to expand this essay, where might he add more examples or details?

RIVER RAFTING TEACHES WORTHWHILE LESSONS

Introduction: A
description

Sun-warmed water slaps you in the face, the blazing sun beats down on your shoulders, and canyon walls speed by as you race down rolling waves of water. No experience can equal that of river rafting. In addition to being fun and exciting, rafting has many educational advantages as well, especially for those involved in school-sponsored rafting trips. River trips teach students how to prevent some of the environmental destruction that concerns the park officials, and, in addition, river trips teach students to work together in a way few other experiences can.

Thesis

Essay map

Topic sentence one:
Trip teaches respect
for environment

The most important lesson a rafting trip teaches students is respect for the environment. When students are exposed to the outdoors, they can better learn to appreciate its beauty and feel the need to preserve it. For example, I went on a rafting trip three summers ago with the biology department at my high school. Our trip lasted seven days down the Green River through the isolated Desolation Canyon in Utah. After the first day of rafting, I found myself surrounded by steep canyon walls and saw virtually no evidence of human life. The starkly beautiful, unspoiled atmosphere soon became a major influence on us during the trip. By the second day I saw classmates, whom I had previously seen fill an entire room with candy wrappers and empty soda cans, voluntarily inspecting our

Two brief examples
illustrating respect:
1. Cleaning up trash
2. Foregoing suds in river

campsite for trash. And when twenty-four high school students sacrifice washing their hair for the sake of a sudless and thus healthier river, some new, better attitudes about the environment have definitely been established.

In addition to the respect for nature a rafting trip encourages, it also teaches the importance of group cooperation. Since school-associated trips put students in command of the raft, the students find that in order to stay in control each member must be reliable, be able to do his or her own part, and be alert to the actions of others. These skills are quickly learned when students see the consequences of noncooperation. Usually this occurs the first day, when the left side of the raft paddles in one direction, and the right the other way, and half the crew ends up seasick from going in circles. An even better illustration is another experience I had on my river trip. Because an upcoming rapid was usually not too rough, our instructor said a few of us could jump out and swim in it. Instead of deciding as a group who should go, though, five eager swimmers bailed out. This left me, an angry instructor, and another student to steer the raft. As it turned out, the rapid was fairly rough, and we soon found ourselves heading straight for a huge hole (a hole is formed from swirling funnel-like currents and can pull a raft under). The combined effort of the three of us was not enough to get the raft completely clear of the hole, and the raft tipped up vertically on its side, spilling us into the river. Luckily, no one was hurt, and the raft did not topple over, but the near loss of our food rations for the next five days, not to mention the raft itself, was enough to make us all more willing to work as a group in the future.

Despite the obvious benefits rafting offers, the number of river permits issued to school groups continues to decline because of financial cutbacks. It is a shame that those in charge of these cutbacks do not realize that in addition to having fun and learning about themselves, students are learning valuable lessons through rafting trips—lessons that may help preserve the rivers for future rafters.

PROFESSIONAL ESSAY

So What's So Bad about Being So-So?

Lisa Wilson Strick

Lisa Wilson Strick is a freelance writer who publishes in a variety of women's magazines, frequently on the subjects of family and education. This essay first appeared in Woman's Day *in 1984.*

1   The other afternoon I was playing the piano when my seven-year-old walked in. He stopped and listened awhile, then said: "Gee, Mom, you don't play that thing very well, do you?"

2   No, I don't. I am a piano lesson dropout. The fine points of fingering totally escape me. I play everything at half-speed, with many errant notes. My performance would make any serious music student wince, but I don't care. I've enjoyed playing the piano badly for years.

3   I also enjoy singing badly and drawing badly. (I used to enjoy sewing badly, but I've been doing that so long that I finally got pretty good at it.) I'm not ashamed of my incompetence in these areas. I do one or two other things well and that should be enough for anybody. But it gets boring doing the same things over and over. Every now and then it's fun to try something new.

4   Unfortunately, doing things badly has gone out of style. It used to be a mark of class if a lady or a gentleman sang a little, painted a little, played the violin a little. You didn't have to be *good* at it; the point was to be fortunate enough to have the leisure time for such pursuits. But in today's competitive world we have to be "experts"—even in our hobbies. You can't tone up your body by pulling on your sneakers and slogging around the block a couple of times anymore. Why? Because you'll be laughed off the street by the "serious" runners—the ones who log twenty-plus miles a week in their headbands, sixty-dollar running suits and fancy shoes. The shoes are really a big deal. If you say you're thinking about taking up almost any sport, the first thing the aficionados will ask is what you plan to do about shoes. Leather or canvas? What type of soles? Which brand? This is not the time to mention that the gym shoes you wore in high school are still in pretty good shape. As far as sports enthusiasts are concerned, if you don't have the latest shoes you are hopelessly committed to mediocrity.

5   The runners aren't nearly so snobbish as the dance freaks, however. In case you didn't know, "going dancing" no longer means putting on a pretty dress and doing a few turns around the ballroom with your favorite man on Saturday night. "Dancing" means squeezing into tights and a leotard and leg warmers, then sweating through six hours of warm-ups and five hours of ballet and four hours of jazz classes. Every week. Never tell anyone that you "like to dance" unless this is the sort of activity you enjoy. (At least the costume isn't so costly, as dancers seem to be cultivating a riches-to-rags look lately.)

6   We used to do these things for fun or simply to relax. Now the competition you face in your hobbies is likely to be worse than anything you run into on the job. "Oh, you've taken up knitting," a friend recently said to me. "Let me show you the adorable cable-knit, popcorn-stitched cardigan with twelve tiny reindeer prancing across the yoke that I made for my daughter. I dyed the yarn myself." Now why did she have to go and do that? I was getting a kick out of watching my yellow stockinette muffler grow a couple of inches a week up till then. And all I wanted was something to keep my hands busy while I watched television anyway.

7   Have you noticed what this is doing to our children? "We don't want that dodo on our soccer team," I overheard a ten-year-old sneer the other day. "He doesn't know a goal kick from a head shot." As it happens, the boy was talking about my son, who did not—like some of his friends—start soccer instruction at age three (along with preschool diving, creative writing and Suzuki clarinet). I'm sorry, Son, I guess I blew it. In *my* day when we played softball on the corner lot, we expected to give a little instruction to the younger kids who didn't know how. It didn't matter if they were terrible; we weren't out to slaughter the other team. Sometimes we didn't even keep score. To us, sports were just a way of having a *good time.* Of course we didn't have some of the nifty things kids have today—such as matching uniforms and professional coaches. All we had was a bunch of kids of various ages who enjoyed each other's company.

8   I don't think kids have as much fun as they used to. Competition keeps getting in the way. The daughter of a neighbor is a nervous wreck worrying about getting into the *best* gymnastics school. "I was a late starter," she told me, "and I only get to practice five or six hours a week, so my technique may not be up to their standards." The child is nine. She doesn't want to *be* a gymnast when she grows up; she wants to be a nurse. I asked what she likes to do for fun in her free time. She seemed to think it was an odd question. "Well, I don't actually *have* a lot of free time," she said. "I mean homework and gymnastics and flute lessons kind of eat it all up. I have flute lessons three times a week now, so I have a good shot at getting into the all-state orchestra."

9   Ambition, drive and the desire to excel are all admirable within limits, but I don't know where the limits are anymore. I know a woman who

has always wanted to learn a foreign language. For years she has complained that she hasn't the time to study one. I've pointed out that an evening course in French or Italian would take only a couple of hours a week, but she keeps putting it off. I suspect that what she hasn't got the time for is to become completely fluent within the year—and that any lesser level of accomplishment would embarrass her. Instead she spends her evenings watching reruns on television and tidying up her closets— occupations at which no particular expertise is expected.

10   I know others who are avoiding activities they might enjoy because they lack the time or the energy to tackle them "seriously." It strikes me as so silly. We are talking about *recreation*. I have nothing against self-improvement. But when I hear a teenager muttering "practice makes perfect" as he grimly makes his four-hundred-and-twenty-seventh try at hooking the basketball into the net left-handed, I wonder if some of us aren't improving ourselves right into the loony bin.

11   I think it's time we put a stop to all this. For sanity's sake, each of us should vow to take up something new this week—and to make sure we never master it completely. Sing along with grand opera. Make peculiar-looking objects out of clay. I can tell you from experience that fallen soufflés still taste pretty good. The point is to enjoy being a beginner again; to rediscover the joy of creative fooling around. If you find it difficult, ask any two-year-old to teach you. Two-year-olds have a gift for tackling the impossible with zest; repeated failure hardly discourages them at all.

12   As for me, I'm getting a little out of shape so I'm looking into tennis. A lot of people I know enjoy it, and it doesn't look too hard. Given a couple of lessons I should be stumbling gracelessly around the court and playing badly in no time at all.

Questions on Content, Structure, and Style

1. Why does Strick begin her essay with the comment from her son and the list of activities she does badly?

2. What is Strick's thesis? Is it specifically stated or clearly implied?

3. What examples does Strick offer to illustrate her belief that we no longer take up hobbies for fun? Are there enough well-chosen examples to make her position clear?

4. What is the effect, according to Strick, of too much competition on kids? In what ways does she show this effect?

5. Does Strick use enough details in her examples to make them clear, vivid, and persuasive? Point out some of her details to support your answer.

6. What does Strick gain by using dialogue in some of her examples?

7. What solution to the problem does Strick offer? How does she clarify her suggestion?

8. Characterize the tone of Strick's essay. Is it appropriate for her purpose and for her intended audience? Why or why not?

9. Evaluate Strick's conclusion. Does it effectively wrap up the essay?

10. Do you agree or disagree with Strick? What examples could you offer to support your position?

Vocabulary[1]

errant (2)	excel (9)
incompetence (3)	fluent (9)
aficionados (4)	zest (11)
mediocrity (4)	

◣ A REVISION WORKSHEET

As you write your rough drafts, consult Chapter 5 for guidance through the revision process. In addition, here are a few questions to ask yourself as you revise your example essay:

1. Is the essay's thesis clear to the reader?

2. Do the topic sentences support the thesis?

3. Do the examples in each paragraph effectively illustrate the claim of the topic sentence?

4. Are there enough well-chosen examples to make each point clear and convincing?

5. Is each example developed in enough specific detail? Where could more details be added?

6. If a paragraph contains multiple examples, are they arranged in the most effective order, with a smooth transition from one to another?

7. If a paragraph contains an extended example, does the discussion flow logically and with coherence?

After you've revised your essay extensively, you might exchange rough drafts with a classmate and answer these questions for each other, making specific

---

[1] Numbers in parentheses following vocabulary terms refer to paragraphs in the essay.

suggestions for improvement wherever appropriate. (For advice on productive participation in classroom workshops, see pp. 114–117.)

Reviewing Your Progress

After you have completed your essay developed by examples, take a moment to measure your progress as a writer by responding to the following questions. Such analysis will help you recognize growth in your writing skills and may enable you to identify areas that are still problematic.

1. What is the best feature of your essay? Why?

2. After considering your essay's supporting examples, which one do you think most effectively explains or illustrates your ideas? Why?

3. What part of your essay gave you the most trouble? How did you overcome the problem?

4. If you had more time to work on this essay, what would receive additional attention? Why?

5. What did you learn about your topic from writing this essay? About yourself as a writer?

STRATEGY TWO: DEVELOPMENT BY PROCESS ANALYSIS

Process analysis identifies and explains what steps must be taken to complete an operation or procedure. There are two kinds of process analysis essays: directional and informative.

A *directional process* tells the reader how to do or make something; in simple words, it gives directions. You are more familiar with directional process than you might think; when you open a telephone book, for example, you see the pages in the front explaining how to make a long-distance call. When you tell friends how to find your house, you're asking them to follow a directional process. The most widely read books in American libraries fall into the how-to-do-it (or how-to-fix-it) category: how to wire a house, how to repair a car, how to play winning poker, how to become a millionaire overnight, and so forth. And almost every home contains at least one cookbook full of recipes providing step-by-step directions for preparing various dishes. (Even Part One of this text is, in detailed fashion, a directional process telling how to write a short essay, beginning with the selection of a topic and concluding with advice on revision.)

An *informative process* tells the reader how something is or was made or done or how something works. Informative process differs from directional process in that it is not designed primarily to tell people how to do it; instead, it describes the steps by which someone other than the reader does or makes something (or how something was made or done in the past). For example, an informative process essay might describe how a television show is produced, how scientists discovered polio vaccine, how you chose your major in college, how the Huns sacked Rome, or how an engine propels a jet. In other words, this type of essay gives information on processes that are not intended to be—or cannot be—duplicated by the individual reader.

Developing Your Essay

Of all the expository essays, students usually agree that the process paper is the easiest to organize, mainly because it is presented in simple, chronological steps. To prepare a well-written process essay, however, you should remember the following advice:

Select an appropriate subject. First, make sure you know your subject thoroughly; one fuzzy step could wreck your entire process. Second, choose a process that is simple and short enough to describe in detail. In a 500- to 800-word essay, for instance, it's better to describe how to build a ship in a bottle than how to construct a life-size replica of Noah's Ark. On the other hand, don't choose a process so simple-minded, mundane, or mechanical that it insults your readers' intelligence. (Some years ago at a major state university it was popular to assign a process essay on "How to Sharpen a Pencil"; with the assignment of such stirring, creative topics, it's a wonder that English department produced any majors at all that year.)

Describe any necessary equipment and define special terms. In some process essays, you will need to indicate what equipment, ingredients, or tools are required. Such information is often provided in a paragraph following the thesis, before the process itself is described; in other cases, the explanation of proper equipment is presented as the need arises in each step of the process. As the writer, you must decide which method is best for your subject. The same is true for any terms that need defining. Don't lose your reader by using terms only you, the specialist, can comprehend. Always remember that you're trying to tell people about a process they don't understand.

State your steps in a logical, chronological order. Obviously, if someone wanted to know it how to bake bread, you wouldn't begin with "Put the prepared dough in the oven." Start at the beginning and carefully follow through, step by step, until the process is completed. Don't omit any steps or directions, no matter how seemingly insignificant. Without complete instructions, for example, the would-be baker might end up with a gob of dough rather than a loaf of bread—simply because the directions didn't say to heat the oven to a certain temperature.

Explain each step clearly, sufficiently, and accurately. If you've ever tried to assemble a child's toy or a piece of furniture, you probably already know how frustrating—and infuriating—it is to work from vague, inadequate directions. Save your readers from tears and tantrums by describing each step in your process as clearly as possible. Use enough specific details to distinguish one step from another. As the readers finish each step, they should know how the subject matter is supposed to look, feel, smell, taste, or sound at that stage of the process. You might also explain why each step is necessary ("Cutting back the young avocado stem is necessary to prevent a spindly plant"; "Senator Snort then had to win over the chair of the Arms Committee to be sure his bill would go to the Senate floor for a vote."). In some cases, especially in directional processes, it's helpful to give warnings ("When you begin tightrope walking, the condition of your shoes is critical; be careful the soles are not slick.") or descriptions of errors and how to rectify them ("If you pass a white church, you've gone a block too far; turn right at the church and circle back on Candle Lane"; "If the sauce appears gray and thick, add one teaspoon more of cornstarch until the gravy is white and bubbly.").

Organize your steps effectively. If you have a few big steps in your process, you probably will devote a paragraph to each one. On the other hand, if you have several small steps, you should organize them into a few manageable units. For example, in the essay "How to Prepare Fresh Fish" the list of small steps on the left has been grouped into three larger units, each of which becomes a body paragraph:

1. scaling	I. Cleaning
2. beheading	A. scaling
3. gutting	B. beheading
4. washing	C. gutting
5. seasoning	II. Cooking
6 breading	A. washing
7. frying	B. seasoning
8. draining	C. breading
9. portioning	D. frying
10. garnishing	III. Serving
	A. draining
	B. portioning
	C. garnishing

In addition, don't forget to use enough transition devices between steps to avoid the effect of a mechanical list. Some frequently used linking words in process essays include the following:

next	first, second, third, etc.
then	at this point
now	following
to begin	when
finally	at last
before	afterward

Vary your transition words sufficiently so that your steps are not linked by a monotonous repetition of "and then" or "next."

Problems to Avoid

Don't forget to include a thesis. You already know, of course, that every essay needs a thesis, but the advice bears repeating here because for some reason some writers often omit the statement in their process essays. Your thesis might be (1) your reason for presenting this process—why you feel it's important or necessary for the readers to know it ("Because rescue squads often arrive too late, every adult should know how to administer CPR to accident victims") or (2) an assertion about the nature of the process itself ("Needlepoint is a simple, restful, fun hobby for both men and women"). Here are some other subjects and sample theses:

* Donating blood is not the painful process one might suspect.

* The raid on Pearl Harbor wasn't altogether unexpected.

* Returning to school as an older-than-average student isn't as difficult as it may look.

* Sponsoring a five-mile run can be a fun way for your club or student organization to raise money for local charities.

* Challenging a speeding ticket is a time-consuming, energy-draining, but financially rewarding endeavor.

* The series of public protests that led to the return of the traditional Coca-Cola was an unparalleled success in the history of American consumerism.

Presenting a thesis and referring to it appropriately gives your essay unity and coherence, as well as ensuring against a monotonous list of steps.

Pay special attention to your conclusion. Don't allow your essay to grind to an abrupt halt after the final step. You might conclude the essay by telling the significance of the completed process or by explaining other uses it may have. Or, if it is appropriate, finish your essay with an amusing story or emphatic comment. However you conclude, leave the reader with a feeling of satisfaction, with a sense of having completed an interesting procedure. (For more information on writing good conclusions, see pp. 92–95.)

► ## ESSAY TOPICS

Below are suggested topics for both directional and informative process essays. Some of the topics may be used in humorous essays, such as "How to Flunk a Test," "How to Remain a Bench Warmer," or "How to Say Nothing in Eight-Hundred Words."

1. how to stop smoking (or break some other habit)

2. how to acquire a skill

3. how to begin a collection or hobby

4. how to buy a computer, CD player, VCR, or other recreational product

5. how a popular product or fad originated or grew

6. how to meet the person of your dreams (or escape the nightmare when it's over)

7. how something in nature works or was formed

8. how a company makes or sells a product

9. how a piece of equipment or a machine works

10. how to cure a cold or other common ailment

11. how to lose/gain weight or develop physical fitness

12. how you arrived at a major decision or solved an important problem

13. how to select a car (new or used), house, apartment, roommate

14. how to vacation on five dollars a day

15. how a famous invention or discovery occurred

16. how to get rid of pests (human or otherwise)

17. how to succeed or fail in a job interview (or in some other important endeavor)

18. how to build or repair some small item

19. how to plan the perfect party, wedding, funeral, birthday, etc.

20. how a historical event occurred

A Topic Proposal for Your Essay

Selecting the right subject matter is important to every writer. To help you clarify your ideas and strengthen your commitment to your topic, here is a proposal sheet that asks you to describe some of your preliminary ideas about your subject before you begin drafting. Although as you draft your ideas may change (they will almost certainly become more refined), thinking through your choice of topic now may help you avoid several false starts.

1. What process will you explain in your essay?

2. Is it a directional or an informative process? Can you address the complexity of this process in a short essay?

3. Why did you select this topic? Are you personally or professionally interested in this process? Cite at least one reason for your choice.

4. Why do you think this topic would be of interest to others? Who might find it especially informative or enjoyable?

5. Describe in one or two sentences the ideal response from your readers. What would you like them to do or know after reading about your topic?

6. List at least three of the larger steps or stages in the process.

7. What difficulties might this topic present during your drafting? Will this topic require any additional research on your part?

SAMPLE STUDENT ESSAY

The essay below is a directional process telling readers how to run a successful garage sale. To make the instructions clear and enjoyable, the writer adopted a chronological order and used many specific examples, details, and warnings.

Catching Garage Sale Fever

Introduction: A series of questions to hook the reader

Ever need some easy money fast? To repay those incredible overdue library fines you ran up writing your last research paper? Or to raise money for that much-needed vacation to old Mexico you put on credit cards last Spring Break? Or maybe you feel you simply have to clear out some junk before the piles block the remaining sunlight from your windows? Whether the problem is cash flow or trash flow, you can solve it easily by holding what is fast becoming an all-American sport: the weekend garage sale. As a veteran of some half-dozen successful ventures, I can testify that

Thesis

garage sales are the easiest way to make quick money, with a minimum of physical labor and the maximum of fun.

Step one: Taking inventory

Most garage sale "experts" start getting ready at least two weeks before the sale by taking inventory. Look through your closets and junk drawers to see if you actually have enough items to make a sale worthwhile. If all you have is a mass of miscellaneous small items, think about waiting or joining a friend's sale, because you do need at least a couple of larger items (furniture is always a big seller) to draw customers initially. Also, consider whether the season is appropriate for your items: sun dresses and shorts, for example, sell better in the spring and summer; coats and boots in the fall. As you collect your items, don't underestimate the "saleability" of some of your junk—the hideous purple china bulldog Aunt Clara gave you for Christmas five years ago may be perfect for someone's Ugly Mutt Collection.

Step two: Deciding when and where

As you sort through your junk closets, begin thinking about the time and place of your sale. First, decide if you want a one- or two-day sale. If you opt for only one day, Saturdays are generally best because most people are free that day. Plan to start early—by 8 A.M. if possible—because the experienced buyers get up and get going so they can hit more sales that way. Unless you have nothing else to do that day, plan to end your sale by mid-afternoon; most people have run out of buying energy (or money) by 3 P.M. Deciding on the location of your sale depends, of course, on your housing situation, but you still might need to make some choices. For instance, do you want to put your items out in a driveway, a backyard, or actually in the garage (weather might affect this decision)? Or perhaps a side yard gets more passers-by? Wherever you decide, be sure that there are plenty of places for customers to park close by without blocking your neighbors' driveways.

Step three: Advertising the sale

Unless you live in a very small town or on a very busy street, you'll probably want to place an inexpensive ad in the "garage sale" column of your local newspaper that is scheduled to run a day or two before, and the day of, your sale. Your ad should tell the times and place of the sale (give brief directions or mention landmarks if the location is hard to find) as well as a brief list of some of your items. Few people will turn out for "household goods" alone; some popular items include bookcases, antiques, books, fans, jewelry, toys, baby equipment, and name-brand clothes. One other piece of advice about the ad copy: it should include the phrase "no early sales" un-

A warning

less you want to be awakened at 6:30 A.M., as I was one Saturday, by a bunch of semi-pro garage sale buyers milling restlessly around in your yard, looking like zombies out of a George Romero horror movie. In addition to your newspaper ad, you may also wish to put up posters in places frequented by lots of people; laundromats and grocery stores often have bulletin boards for such announcements. You can also put up signs on nearby well-traveled streets, but one warning: in some towns it's ille-

Another warning

gal to post anything on utility poles or traffic signs, so be sure to check your local ordinances first.

Step four: Pricing the merchandise

Tagging your items with their prices is the least fun, and it can take a day or a week depending on how many items you have and how much time each day you can devote to the project. You can buy sheets of little white stickers or use pieces of masking tape to stick on the prices, but if you want to save time, consider grouping some items and selling them all for the same price—all shirts, for example, are 50¢. Be realistic about your prices; the hand-crafted rug from Greece may have been expensive and important to you, but to others, it's a worn doormat. Some experts suggest pricing your articles at about one-fourth their original value, unless you have special reasons not to (an antique or popular collectors' item, for instance, may be more valuable now than when you bought it). Remember that you can always come down on your prices if someone is interested in a particular item.

Step five: Setting up your sale

A note on equipment

By the day before your sale you should have all your items clean and tagged. One of the beauties of a garage sale is that there's very little equipment to collect. You'll need tables, benches, or boards supported by bricks to display your goods; a rope tied from side to side of your garage can double as a clothes rack. Try to spread out your merchandise rather than dumping articles in deep boxes; customers don't want to feel like they're rummaging through a trash barrel. Most important, you'll need a chair and a table to hold some sort of money box, preferably one with a lock. The afternoon before the sale, take a trip to the bank if you need to, to make sure you have enough one-dollar bills and coins to make plenty of change. The evening before the sale, set up your items on your display benches in the garage or indoors near the site of your sale so that you can quickly set things out in the morning. Get a good night's sleep so you can get up to open on time: the early bird does get the sales in this business.

Step six: Running the sale

The sale itself is, of course, the real fun. Half the enjoyment is haggling with the customers, so be prepared to joke and visit with the shoppers. Watching the different kinds of people who show up is also a kick—you can get a cross section from college students on a tight budget to harried mothers toting four kids to real eccentrics in fancy cars who will argue about the price of a 75¢ item (if you're a creative writer, don't forget to take notes for your next novel). If the action slows in the afternoon, you can resort to a half-price or two-for-one sale by posting a large sign to that effect; many shoppers can't resist a sale at a sale!

Step seven: Closing up

By late afternoon you should be richer and junk-free, at least to some extent. If you do have items left after the half-price sale, decide whether you want to box them up for the next sale or drop them by a charitable organization such as Goodwill (some organizations will even pick up your donations; others have convenient drop boxes). After you've taken your articles inside, don't forget to take down any signs you've posted in the neighborhood; old, withered garage sale signs fluttering in the breeze are an eyesore. Last, sit down and count your profits, so you can go out in the evening to celebrate a successful business venture.

Conclusion: A summary of the benefits and a humorous warning

The money you make is, of course, the biggest incentive for having one or two sales a year. But the combination of money, clean closets, and memories of the characters you met can be irresistible. Garage sales can rapidly get in your blood; once you hold a successful one, you're tempted to have another as soon as the junk starts to mount up. And having sales somehow leads to attending them too, as it becomes fun to see what other folks are selling at bargain prices. So be forewarned: you too can be transformed into a garage sale junkie, traveling with a now-popular car bumper sticker that proudly proclaims to the world: "Caution! I brake for garage sales"!

PROFESSIONAL ESSAY

To Bid the World Farewell
Jessica Mitford

Jessica Mitford has written many articles and books, including Daughters and Rebels *(1960),* The Trial of Doctor Spock *(1969); and* Kind and Unusual Punishment *(1973), a critical study of the American penal system. This essay is an excerpt from her best-selling book* The American Way of Death *(1963).*

1   Embalming is indeed a most extraordinary procedure, and one must wonder at the docility of Americans who each year pay hundreds of millions of dollars for its perpetuation, blissfully ignorant of what it is all about, what is done, how it is done. Not one in ten thousand has any

idea of what actually takes place. Books on the subject are extremely hard to come by. They are not to be found in most libraries or book-shops.

2   In an era when huge television audiences watch surgical operations in the comfort of their living rooms, when, thanks to the animated cartoon, the geography of the digestive system has become familiar territory even to the nursery school set, and in a land where the satisfaction of curiosity about almost all matters is a national pastime, the secrecy surrounding embalming can, surely, hardly be attributed to the inherent gruesomeness of the subject. Custom in this regard has within this century suffered a complete reversal. In the early days of American embalming, when it was performed in the home of the deceased, it was almost mandatory for some relative to stay by the embalmer's side and witness the procedure. Today, family members who might wish to be in attendance would certainly be dissuaded by the funeral director. All others, except apprentices, are excluded by law from the preparation room.

3   A close look at what does actually take place may explain in large measure the undertaker's intractable reticence concerning a procedure that has become his major *raison d'être*. Is it possible he fears that public information about embalming might lead patrons to wonder if they really want this service? If the funeral men are loath to discuss the subject outside the trade, the reader may, understandably, be equally loath to go on reading at this point. For those who have the stomach for it, let us part the formaldehyde curtain. . . .

4   The body is first laid out in the undertaker's morgue—or rather, Mr. Jones is reposing in the preparation room—to be readied to bid the world farewell.

5   The preparation room in any of the better funeral establishments has the tiled and sterile look of a surgery, and indeed the embalmer-restorative artist who does his chores there is beginning to adopt the term "dermasurgeon" (appropriately corrupted by some mortician-writers as "demisurgeon") to describe his calling. His equipment, consisting of scalpels, scissors, augers, forceps, clamps, needles, pumps, tubes, bowls and basins, is crudely imitative of the surgeon's as is his technique, acquired in a nine- or twelve-month post-high-school course in an embalming school. He is supplied by an advanced chemical industry with a bewildering array of fluids, sprays, pastes, oils, powders, creams, to fix or soften tissue, shrink or distend it as needed, dry it here, restore the moisture there. There are cosmetics, waxes and paints to fill and cover features, even plaster of Paris to replace entire limbs. There are ingenious aids to prop and stabilize the cadaver: a Vari-Pose Head Rest, the Edwards Arm and Hand Positioner, the Repose Block (to support the shoulders during the embalming), and the Throop Foot Positioner, which resembles an old-fashioned stocks.

6   Mr. John H. Eckels, president of the Eckels College of Mortuary Science, thus describes the first part of the embalming procedure: "In the hands of a skilled practitioner, this work may be done in a comparatively short time and without mutiliating the body other than by slight incision—so slight that it scarcely would cause serious inconvenience if made upon a living person. It is necessary to remove the blood, and doing this not only helps in the disinfecting, but removes the principal cause of disfigurement due to discoloration."

7   Another textbook discusses the all-important time element: "The earlier this is done, the better, for every hour that elapses between death and embalming will add to the problems and complications encountered. . . ." Just how soon should one get going on the embalming? The author tells us, "On the basis of such scanty information made available to this profession through its rudimentary and haphazard system of technical research, we must conclude that the best results are to be obtained if the subject is embalmed before life is completely extinct— that is, before cellular death has occurred. In the average case, this would mean within an hour after somatic death." For those who feel that there is something a little rudimentary, not to say haphazard, about this advice, a comforting thought is offered by another writer. Speaking of fears entertained in early days of premature burial, he points out, "One of the effects of embalming by chemical injection, however, has been to dispel fears of live burial." How true; once the blood is removed, chances of live burial are indeed remote.

8   To return to Mr. Jones, the blood is drained out through the veins and replaced by embalming fluid pumped in through the arteries. As noted in *The Principles and Practices of Embalming,* "every operator has a favorite injection and drainage point—a fact which becomes a handicap only if he fails or refuses to forsake his favorites when conditions demand it." Typical favorites are the carotid artery, femoral artery, jugular vein, subclavian vein. There are various choices of embalming fluid. If Flextone is used, it will produce a "mild flexible rigidity. The skin retains a velvety softness, the tissues are rubbery and pliable. Ideal for women and children." It may be blended with B. and G. Products Company's Lyf-Lyk tint, which is guaranteed to reproduce "nature's own skin texture . . . the velvety appearance of living tissue." Suntone comes in three separate tints: Suntan; Special Cosmetic Tint, a pink shade "especially indicated for young female subjects"; and Regular Cosmetic Tint, moderately pink.

9   About three to six gallons of a dyed and perfumed solution of formaldehyde, glycerin, borax, phenol, alcohol and water is soon circulating through Mr. Jones, whose mouth has been sewn together with a "needle directed upward between the upper lip and gum and brought out through the left nostril," with the corners raised slightly "for a more

pleasant expression." If he should be bucktoothed, his teeth are cleaned with Bon Ami and coated with colorless nail polish. His eyes, meanwhile, are closed with flesh-tinted eye caps and eye cement.

10   The next step is to have at Mr. Jones with a thing called a trocar. This is a long, hollow needle attached to a tube. It is jabbed into the abdomen, poked around the entrails and chest cavity, the contents of which are pumped out and replaced with "cavity fluid." This done, and the hole in the abdomen sewn up, Mr. Jones' face is heavily creamed (to protect the skin from burns which may be caused by leakage of the chemicals), and he is covered with a sheet and left unmolested for a while. But not for long—there is more, much more, in store for him. He has been embalmed, but not yet restored, and the best time to start the restorative work is eight to ten hours after embalming, when the tissues have become firm and dry.

11   The object of all this attention to the corpse, it must be remembered, is to make it presentable for viewing in an attitude of healthy repose. "Our customs require the presentation of our dead in the semblance of normality . . . unmarred by the ravages of illness, disease or mutilation," says Mr. J. Sheridan Mayer in his *Restorative Art.* This is rather a large order since few people die in the full bloom of health, unravaged by illness and unmarked by some disfigurement. The funeral industry is equal to the challenge: "In some cases the gruesome appearance of a mutilated or disease-ridden subject may be quite discouraging. The task of restoration may seem impossible and shake the confidence of the embalmer. This is the time for intestinal fortitude and determination. Once the formative work is begun and affected tissues are cleaned or removed, all doubts of success vanish. It is surprising and gratifying to discover the results which may be obtained."

12   The embalmer, having allowed an appropriate interval to elapse, returns to the attack, but now he brings into play the skill and equipment of sculptor and cosmetician. Is a hand missing? Casting one in plaster of Paris is a simple matter. "For replacement purposes, only a cast of the back of the hand is necessary; this is within the ability of the average operator and is quite adequate." If a lip or two, a nose or an ear should be missing, the embalmer has at hand a variety of restorative waxes with which to model replacements. Pores and skin texture are simulated by stippling with a little brush, and over this cosmetics are laid on. Head off? Decapitation cases are rather routinely handled. Ragged edges are trimmed, and head joined to torso with a series of splints, wires and sutures. It is a good idea to have a little something at the neck—a scarf or high collar—when time for viewing comes. Swollen mouth? Cut out tissue as needed from inside the lips. If too much is removed, the surface contour can easily be restored by padding with cotton. Swollen necks and cheeks are reduced by removing tissue through vertical incisions

made down each side of the neck. "When the deceased is casketed, the pillow will hide the suture incisions . . . as an extra precaution against leakage, the suture may be painted with liquid sealer."

13   The opposite condition is more likely to present itself—that of emaciation. His hypodermic syringe now loaded with massage cream, the embalmer seeks out and fills the hollowed and sunken areas by injection. In this procedure the backs of the hands and fingers and the under-chin area should not be neglected.

14   Positioning the lips is a problem that recurrently challenges the ingenuity of the embalmer. Closed too tightly, they tend to give a stern, even disapproving expression. Ideally, embalmers feel, the lips should give the impression of being ever so slightly parted, the upper lip protruding slightly for a more youthful appearance. This takes some engineering, however, as the lips tend to drift apart. Lip drift can sometimes be remedied by pushing one or two straight pins through the inner margin of the lower lip and then inserting them between the two front teeth. If Mr. Jones happens to have no teeth, the pins can just as easily be anchored in his Armstrong Face Former and Denture Replacer. Another method to maintain lip closure is to dislocate the lower jaw, which is then held in its new position by a wire run through holes which have been drilled through the upper and lower jaws at the midline. As the French are fond of saying, *il faut souffrir pour être belle.*[1]

15   If Mr. Jones has died of jaundice, the embalming fluid will very likely turn him green. Does this deter the embalmer? Not if he has intestinal fortitude. Masking pastes and cosmetics are heavily laid on, burial garments and casket interiors are color-correlated with particular care, and Jones is displayed beneath rose-colored lights. Friends will say, "How *well* he looks." Death by carbon monoxide, on the other hand, can be rather a good thing from the embalmer's viewpoint: "One advantage is the fact that this type of discoloration is an exaggerated form of a natural pink coloration." This is nice because the healthy glow is already present and needs but little attention.

16   The patching and filling completed, Mr. Jones is now shaved, washed and dressed. Cream-based cosmetic, available in pink, flesh, suntan, brunette and blond, is applied to his hands and face, his hair is shampooed and combed (and, in the case of Mrs. Jones, set), his hands manicured. For the horny-handed son of toil special care must be taken; cream should be applied to remove ingrained grime, and the nails cleaned. "If he were not in the habit of having them manicured in life, trimming and shaping is advised for better appearance—never questioned by kin."

[1] "One must suffer in order to be beautiful."

17   Jones is now ready for casketing (this is the present participle of the verb "to casket"). In this operation his right shoulder should be depressed slightly "to turn the body a bit to the right and soften the appearance of lying flat on the back." Positioning the hands is a matter of importance, and special rubber positioning blocks may be used. The hands should be cupped slightly for a more lifelike, relaxed appearance. Proper placement of the body requires a delicate sense of balance. It should lie as high as possible in the casket, yet not so high that the lid, when lowered, will hit the nose. On the other hand, we are cautioned, placing the body too low "creates the impression that the body is in a box."

18   Jones is next wheeled into the appointed slumber room where a few last touches may be added—his favorite pipe placed in his hand or, if he was a great reader, a book propped into position. (In the case of little Master Jones a Teddy bear may be clutched.) Here he will hold open house for a few days, visiting hours 10 A.M. to 9 P.M.

Questions on Content, Structure, and Style

1. By studying the first three paragraphs, summarize both Mitford's reason for explaining the embalming process and her attitude toward undertakers who wish to keep their patrons uninformed about this procedure.

2. Identify this process as either directional or informative.

3. Does Mitford use enough specific details to help you visualize each step as it occurs? Point out examples of details that create vivid descriptions by appealing to your sense of sight, smell, or touch.

4. How does the technique of using the hypothetical "Mr. Jones" make the explanation of the process more effective? Why didn't Mitford simply refer to "the corpse" or "a body" throughout her essay?

5. What is Mitford's general attitude toward this procedure? The overall tone of the essay? Study Mitford's choice of words and then identify the tone in each of the following passages:

   "The next step is to have at Mr. Jones with a thing called a trocar." (10)[2]

   "The embalmer, having allowed an appropriate interval to elapse, returns to the attack. . . ." (12)

   "Friends will say, 'How *well* he looks.'" (15)

---

[2]Numbers in parentheses following questions and vocabulary words refer to paragraphs in the essay.

"On the other hand, we are cautioned, placing the body too low 'creates the impression that the body is in a box.'" (17)

"Here he will hold open house for a few days, visiting hours 10 A.M. to 9 P.M." (18)

What other words and passages reveal Mitford's attitude and tone?

6. Why does Mitford repeatedly quote various undertakers and textbooks on the embalming and restorative process ("'needle directed upward between the upper lip and gum and brought out through the left nostril'")? Why is the quotation in paragraph 7 that begins "'On the basis of such scanty information made available to this profession through its rudimentary and haphazard system of technical research'" particularly effective in emphasizing Mitford's attitude toward the funeral industry?

7. What does Mitford gain by quoting euphemisms used by the funeral business, such as "dermasurgeon," "Repose Block," and "slumber room"? What are the connotations of the words "poked," "jabbed," and "left unmolested" in paragraph 10? What effect is Mitford trying to produce with the series of questions (such as "Head off?") in paragraph 12?

8. Does this process flow smoothly from step to step? Identify several transition devices connecting the paragraphs.

9. Evaluate Mitford's last sentence. Does it successfully sum up the author's attitude and conclude the essay?

10. By supplying information about the embalming process, did Mitford change your attitude toward this procedure or toward the funeral industry? Should we subject our dead to this process? Are there advantages Mitford fails to mention? How would you prepare an essay to defend your position?

Vocabulary

docility (1)
perpetuation (1)
inherent (2)
mandatory (2)
intractable (3)
reticence (3)
raison d'être (3)
ingenious (5)
cadaver (5)

somatic (7)
rudimentary (7)
dispel (7)
pliable (8)
semblance (11)
ravages (11)
stippling (12)
emaciation (13)

◀ A REVISION WORKSHEET

As you write your rough drafts, consult Chapter 5 for guidance through the revision process. In addition, here are a few questions to ask yourself as you revise your process essay:

1. Is the essay's purpose clear to the reader?

2. Has the need for any special equipment been noted and explained adequately? Are all terms unfamiliar to the reader defined clearly?

3. Does the essay include all the steps (and warnings, if appropriate) necessary to understanding the process?

4. Is each step described in enough detail to make it understandable to all readers? Where could more detail be effectively added?

5. Are all the steps in the process presented in an easy-to-follow chronological order, with smooth transitions between steps or stages?

6. Are there any steps that should be combined in a paragraph describing a logical stage in the process?

7. Does the essay have a pleasing conclusion?

After you've revised your essay extensively, you might exchange rough drafts with a classmate and answer these questions for each other, making specific suggestions for improvement wherever appropriate. (For advice on productive participation in classroom workshops, see pp. 114–117.)

Reviewing Your Progress

After you have completed your process essay, take a moment to measure your progress as a writer by responding to the following questions. Such analysis will help you recognize growth in your writing skills and may enable you to identify areas that are still problematic.

1. Which part of your essay is most successful? Why?

2. Select two details that contribute significantly to the clarity of your explanation. Why are these details effective?

3. What part of your essay gave you the most trouble? How did you overcome the problem?

4. If you had more time to work on this essay, what would receive additional attention? Why?

5. What did you learn about your topic from writing this essay? About yourself as a writer?

STRATEGY THREE: DEVELOPMENT BY COMPARISON AND CONTRAST

Every day you exercise the mental process of comparison and contrast. When you get up in the morning, for instance, you may contrast two choices of clothing—a short-sleeved shirt versus a long-sleeved one—and then make your decision after hearing the weather forecast. Or you may contrast and choose between Sugar-Coated Plastic Pops and Organic Mullet Kernels for breakfast, between the health advantages of walking to campus and the speed afforded by your car or bicycle. Once on campus, preparing to register, you may first compare both professors and courses; similarly, you probably compare the school you attend now to others before you made your choice. In short, you frequently use the process of comparison and contrast to come to a decision or make a judgment about two or more objects, persons, ideas, or feelings.

When you write a comparison or contrast essay, your opinion about the two elements* in question becomes your thesis statement; the body of the paper then shows why you arrived at that opinion. For example, if your thesis states that Mom's Kum-On-Back Hamburger Haven is preferable to McPhony's Mystery Burger Stand, your body paragraphs might contrast the two restaurants in terms of food, service, and atmosphere, revealing the superiority of Mom's on all three counts.

Developing Your Essay

There are two principal patterns of organization for comparison or contrast essays. For most short papers you should choose one of the patterns and stick with it throughout the essay. Later, if you are assigned a longer essay, you may want to mix the patterns for variety as some professional writers do, but do so only if you can maintain clarity and logical organization.

Pattern One: Point by Point

This method of organization calls for body paragraphs that compare or contrast the two subjects first on point one, then on point two, then point three, and so on. Study the example outlined below:

Thesis: Mom's Hamburger Haven is a much better restaurant than McPhony's because of its superior food, service, and atmosphere.

---

* It is, of course, possible to compare or contrast more than two elements. But until you feel confident about the organizational patterns for this kind of essay, you should probably stay with the simpler format.

Point 1: Food

> A. Mom's
> B. McPhony's

Point 2: Service

> A. Mom's
> B. McPhony's

Point 3: Atmosphere

> A. Mom's
> B. McPhony's

Conclusion

If you select this pattern of organization, you must make a smooth transition from subject "A" to subject "B" in each discussion to avoid a choppy seesaw effect. Be consistent: present the same subject first in each discussion of a major point. In the essay outlined above, for instance, Mom's is always introduced before McPhony's.

Pattern Two: The Block

This method of organization presents body paragraphs in which the writer first discusses subject "A" on points one, two, three, etc., then discusses subject "B" on the same points. The model below illustrates this block pattern:

Thesis: Mom's Hamburger Haven is a better restaurant than McPhony's because of its superior food, service, and atmosphere.

> A. Mom's
>   1. Food
>   2. Service
>   3. Atmosphere
> B. McPhony's
>   1. Food
>   2. Service
>   3. Atmosphere

Conclusion

If you use the block pattern, you should discuss the three points—food, service, atmosphere—in the same order for each subject. In addition, you must include in your discussion of subject "B" specific references to the points you made earlier about subject "A" (see outline). In other words, because your statements about Mom's superior food may be several pages away by the time your comments on McPhony's food appear, the readers may not remember precisely what you said. Gently, unobtrusively, remind them with a specific reference to the earlier discussion. For instance, you might begin your paragraph on McPhony's service like this: "Unlike the friendly, attentive help at Mom's, service at McPhony's features grouchy persons who wait on you as if they consider your presence an intrusion on their privacy." The discussion of atmosphere might begin, "McPhony's atmosphere is as cold, sterile, and plastic as its decor, in contrast to the warm, homey feeling that pervades Mom's." Without such connecting phrases, what should be one unified essay will look more like two distinct mini-essays, forcing readers to do the job of comparing or contrasting for you.

Problems to Avoid

The single most serious error is the "so-what" thesis. Writers of comparison and contrast essays often wish to convince their readers that something—a restaurant, a movie, a product—is better (or worse) than something else: "Mom's Haven is a better place to eat than McPhony's." But not all comparison or contrast essays assert the absolute superiority or inferiority of their subjects. Sometimes writers simply want to point out the similarities or differences in two or more people, places, or objects, and that's fine, too—*as long as the writer avoids the "so-what" thesis problem.*

Too often novice writers will present thesis statements such as "My sister and I are very different" or "Having a blended family with two stepbrothers and stepsisters has advantages and disadvantages for me." To such theses, readers can only respond, "So what? Who cares?" There are many similarities and differences (or advantages and disadvantages) between countless numbers of things—but why should your readers care about those described in your essay? Comparing or contrasting for no apparent reason is a waste of the readers' valuable time; instead, find a purpose that will draw in your audience. You may indeed wish to write an essay contrasting the pros and cons of your blended family, but do it in a way that has a universal appeal or application. For instance, you might revise your thesis to say something like "Although a blended family often does experience petty jealousies and juvenile bickering, the benefits of having stepsiblings as live-in friends far outweigh the problems," and then use your family to show the advantages and disadvantages. In this way, your readers realize they will learn something about the blended family, a common phenomenon today, as well as learning some information about you and your particular family.

Another way to avoid the "so-what" problem is to direct your thesis to a particular audience. For instance, you might say that "Although Stella's Sweatateria and the Fitness Fanatics Gym are similar in their low student-membership prices and excellent instructors, Stella's is the place to go for those seeking a variety of exercise classes rather than hard-core bodybuilding machines." Or your thesis may wish to show a particular relationship between two subjects. Instead of writing "There are many similarities between the movie *Riot of the Killer Snails* and Mary Sheeley's novel *Salt on the Sidewalk,*" write "The many similarities in character and plot (the monster, the scientist, and vegetable garden scene) clearly suggest that the movie director was greatly influenced by—if not actually guilty of stealing—parts of Mary Sheeley's novel."

In other words, tell your readers your point and then use comparison or contrast to support that idea; don't just compare or contrast items in a vacuum. Ask yourself, "What is the significant point I want my readers to learn or understand from reading this comparison/contrast essay? Why do they need to know this?"

Describe your subjects clearly and distinctly. To comprehend a difference or a similarity between two things, the reader must first be able to "see" them as you do. Consequently, you should use as many vivid examples and details as possible to describe both your subjects. Beware a tendency to overelaborate on one subject and then grossly skimp on the other, an especially easy trap to fall into in an essay that asserts "X" is preferable to "Y." By giving each side a reasonable treatment, you will do a better job of convincing your reader that you know both sides and have made a valid judgment.

Avoid a choppy essay. Whether you organize your essay by the point-by-point pattern or the block pattern, you need to use enough transition devices to ensure a smooth flow from one subject to another and from one point to the next. Without transitions, your essay may assume the distracting movement of a Ping-Pong game, as you switch back and forth between discussions of your two subjects. Listed below are some appropriate words to link your points:

COMPARISON	CONTRAST
also	however
similarly	on the contrary
too	on the other hand
both	in contrast
like	although
not only . . . but also	unlike
have in common	though
share the same	instead of
in the same manner	but

(For a review of other transition devices, see pp. 74–78.)

▶ ESSAY TOPICS

Here are some topics that may be compared or contrasted. Remember to narrow your subject, formulate a thesis that presents a clear point, and follow one of the two organizational patterns discussed on pages 209–211.

1. An expectation and its reality

2. A first impression and a later point of view

3. Two views on a current controversial issue (campus, local, national, or international)

4. Two conflicting theories you are studying in another college course

5. A memory of a person or place and a more recent encounter with that person or place

6. Coverage of the same story by two newspapers or magazines (the *National Enquirer* and the *Dallas Morning News,* for example, or *Time* and *Newsweek*)

7. A hero today and yesterday

8. Two commercials for a similar product

9. Two pieces of technology you've owned or operated

10. A public or private myth and its reality

11. Two solutions to a problem in your professional field

12. One of today's popular entertainments and one from an earlier era (board or card games, for instance)

13. Two places you've lived or visited

14. Two politicians or public figures from today or from the past

15. Two books; a book and its movie; a movie and its sequel

16. Two jobs or employers (or your current job and the job of your dreams)

17. Two places that are special for you in different ways

18. An opinion you held before coming to college that has changed now that you are in college

19. Two sports or athletes or pieces of sports equipment

20. Your attitude toward a social custom or political belief and your parents' (or grandparents') attitude toward that belief or custom

A Topic Proposal for Your Essay

Selecting the right subject matter is important to every writer. To help you clarify your ideas and strengthen your commitment to your topic, here is a proposal sheet that asks you to describe some of your preliminary ideas about your subject before you begin drafting. Although as you draft your ideas may change (they will almost certainly become more refined), thinking through your choice of topic now may help you avoid several false starts.

1. What two subjects will your essay discuss? In what ways are these subjects similar? Different?

2. Do you plan to compare or contrast your two subjects?

3. Write one or two sentences describing your attitude toward these two subjects. Are you stating a preference for one or are you making some other significant point?

4. Why are you interested in these subjects? Are they part of your personal, academic, or professional life?

5. Why would other people find this topic interesting and important? Would a particular group of people be more affected by your topic than others?

6. What difficulties might this topic present during your drafting? Do you, for example, know enough about both subjects to offer a balanced picture?

SAMPLE STUDENT ESSAY

Note that this writer takes a definite stand—that local food co-ops are superior to chain stores—and then contrasts two local stores, Lane Grocer and the Fort Collins, Colorado, Co-op, to prove her thesis. She selected the point-by-point pattern to organize her essay, contrasting prices, atmosphere, and benefits to local producers. See if you can identify her transition devices as well as some of her uses of detail that make the essay more interesting and convincing.

Bringing Back the Joy of Market Day

Thesis

Now that the old family-run corner grocery is almost extinct, many people are banding together to form their own neighborhood stores as food cooperatives. Locally owned by their members, food co-ops such as the one

Essay map

here in Fort Collins are welcome alternatives to the impersonal chain-store markets such as Lane Grocer. In exchange for volunteering a few hours each month, co-op members share savings and a friendly experience while they shop; local producers gain loyal, local support from the members as well as better prices for their goods in return for providing the freshest, purest food possible.

Point one: Prices

Perhaps the most crucial distinction between the two kinds of stores is that while supermarkets are set up to generate profit for their corporations, co-ops are non-profit groups whose main purpose is to provide their members and the community with good, inexpensive food and basic household needs. At first glance, supermarkets such as Lane Grocer may appear to be cheaper because they offer so many specials, which they emphasize heavily through ads and in store promotions. These special deals, known as "loss-leaders" in the retail industry, are more than made up for by the extremely high markups on other products. For example, around Thanksgiving Lane Grocer might have a sale on flour and shortening and then set up the displays with utmost care so that as customers reach for the flour they will be drawn to colorful bottles of pie spices, fancy jars of mincemeat, or maybe an inviting bin of fresh-roasted holiday nuts, all of which may be marked up 100% or more—way above what is being lost on the flour and shortening.

Examples of Lane Grocer's prices contrasted to examples of co-op prices

The Fort Collins Co-op rarely bothers with such pricing gimmicks; instead, it tries to have a consistent markup—just enough to meet overhead expenses. The flour at the co-op may cost an extra few cents, but that same fancy spice bottle that costs over $1.00 from the supermarket display can be refilled at the co-op for less than 25¢. The nuts, considered by regular groceries as a seasonal "gourmet" item, are sold at the co-op for about two-thirds the price. Great savings like these are achieved by buying in bulk and having customers bag their own groceries. Recycled containers are used as much as possible, cutting down substantially on overhead. Buying in bulk may seem awkward at first, but the extra time spent bagging and weighing their own food results in welcome savings for co-op members.

Point two: Atmosphere

Once people have become accustomed to bringing their own containers and taking part in the work at the co-ops, they often find that it's actually more fun to shop

Description of Lane Grocer's atmosphere contrasted to description of the co-op's atmosphere

in the friendly, relaxed atmosphere of the co-ops. At Lane Grocer, for example, I often find shopping a battle of tangled metal carts wielded by bored customers who are frequently trying to manage one or more cranky children. The long aisles harshly lit by rows of cold fluorescent lights and the bland commercial music don't make the chore of shopping any easier either. On the other hand, the Fort Collins Co-op may not be as expertly planned, but at least the chaos is carried on in a friendly way. Parents especially appreciate that they can safely let their children loose while they shop because in the small, open-spaced co-op even toddlers don't become lost as they do in the aisles of towering supermarket shelves. Moreover, most members are willing to look after the children of other members if necessary. And while they shop, members can choose to listen to the FM radio or simply to enjoy each other's company in relative quiet.

Point three: Benefits to local producers

As well as benefiting member consumers, co-ops also help small local producers by providing a direct market for their goods. Large chain stores may require minimum wholesale quantities far beyond the capacity of an individual producer, and mass markets like Lane Grocer often feel they are "too big" to negotiate with small local producers. But because of their small, independent nature co-ops welcome the chance to buy direct from the grower or producer. Direct selling offers two advantages for producers: they get a better price for their wares than by selling them through a middleman, and at the same time they establish an independent reputation for their business, which can be immensely valuable to their success later on. In Fort Collins, for example, Luna tofu (bean curd) stands out as an excellent illustration of this kind of mutual support. Several years ago my friend Carol Jones began making tofu in small batches to sell to the co-op as a way to earn a part-time income as well as to contribute to the co-op. Her enterprise has now grown so well that last year her husband quit his job to go into business with her full time. She currently sells to distributors and independent stores from here to Denver; even Lane Grocer, who earlier would not consider selling her tofu even on a trial basis, is now thinking about changing its policy.

No benefits at Lane Grocer contrasted to two benefits at the co-op

Conclusion: Summarizing the advantages of co-ops over chain stores

Of course, not all co-ops are like the one here in Fort Collins, but that is one of their best features. Each one reflects the personalities of its members, unlike the supermarket chain stores that vary only slightly. Most important, though, while each has a distinctive character, co-ops share common goals of providing members with high-quality, low-cost food in a friendly, cooperative spirit.

Grant and Lee: A Study in Contrasts
Bruce Catton

Bruce Catton, an authority on the Civil War, won both the Pulitzer Prize for histori-cal work and the National Book Award in 1955. He wrote numerous books, includ-ing Mr. Lincoln's Army *(1951),* A Stillness at Appomattox *(1953),* Never Call Retreat *(1966), and* Gettysburg: The Final Fury *(1974). This essay is a chapter of* The American Story *(1956), a collection of essays by noted historians.*

1   When Ulysses S. Grant and Robert E. Lee met in the parlor of a modest house at Appomattox Court House, Virginia, on April 9, 1865, to work out the terms for the surrender of Lee's Army of Northern Virginia, a great chapter in American life came to a close, and a great new chap-ter began.

2   These men were bringing the Civil War to its virtual finish. To be sure, other armies had yet to surrender, and for a few days the fugitive Confederate government would struggle desperately and vainly, trying to find some way to go on living now that its chief support was gone. But in effect it was all over when Grant and Lee signed the papers. And the little room where they wrote out the terms was the scene of one of the poignant, dramatic contrasts in American history.

3   They were two strong men, these oddly different generals, and they represented the strengths of two conflicting currents that, through them, had come into final collision.

4   Back of Robert E. Lee was the notion that the old aristocratic con-cept might somehow survive and be dominant in American life.

5   Lee was tidewater Virginia, and in his background were family, cul-ture, and tradition . . . the age of chivalry transplanted to a New World which was making its own legends and its own myths. He embodied a way of life that had come down through the age of knighthood and the English country squire. America was a land that was beginning all over again, dedicated to nothing much more complicated than the rather hazy belief that all men had equal rights, and should have an equal chance in

the world. In such a land Lee stood for the feeling that it was somehow of advantage to human society to have a pronounced inequality in the social structure. There should be a leisure class, backed by ownership of land; in turn, society itself should be keyed to the land as the chief source of wealth and influence. It would bring forth (according to this ideal) a class of men with a strong sense of obligation to the community; men who lived not to gain advantage for themselves, but to meet the solemn obligations which had been laid on them by the very fact that they were privileged. From them the country would get its leadership; to them it could look for the higher values—of thought, of conduct, of personal deportment—to give it strength and virtue.

6   Lee embodied the noblest elements of this aristocratic ideal. Through him, the landed nobility justified itself. For four years, the Southern states had fought a desperate war to uphold the ideals for which Lee stood. In the end, it almost seemed as if the Confederacy fought for Lee; as if he himself was the Confederacy . . . the best thing that the way of life for which the Confederacy stood could ever have to offer. He had passed into legend before Appomattox. Thousands of tired, underfed, poorly clothed Confederate soldiers, long-since past the simple enthusiasm of the early days of the struggle, somehow considered Lee the symbol of everything for which they had been willing to die. But they could not quite put this feeling into words. If the Lost Cause, sanctified by so much heroism and so many deaths, had a living justification, its justification was General Lee.

7   Grant, the son of a tanner on the Western frontier, was everything Lee was not. He had come up the hard way, and embodied nothing in particular except the eternal toughness and sinewy fiber of the men who grew up beyond the mountains. He was one of a body of men who owed reverence and obeisance to no one, who were self-reliant to a fault, who cared hardly anything for the past but who had a sharp eye for the future.

8   These frontier men were the precise opposites of the tidewater aristocrats. Back of them, in the great surge that had taken people over the Alleghenies and into the opening Western country, there was a deep, implicit dissatisfaction with a past that had settled into grooves. They stood for democracy, not from any reasoned conclusion about the proper ordering of human society, but simply because they had grown up in the middle of democracy and knew how it worked. Their society might have privileges, but they would be privileges each man had won for himself. Forms and patterns meant nothing. No man was born to anything, except perhaps to a chance to show how far he could rise. Life was competition.

9   Yet along with this feeling had come a deep sense of belonging to a national community. The Westerner who developed a farm, opened a

shop, or set up in business as a trader could hope to prosper only as his own community prospered—and his community ran from the Atlantic to the Pacific and from Canada down to Mexico. If the land was settled, with towns and highways and accessible markets, he could better himself. He saw his fate in terms of the nation's own destiny. As its horizons expanded, so did his. He had, in other words, an acute dollars-and-cents stake in the continued growth and development of his country.

10 And that, perhaps, is where the contrast between Grant and Lee becomes most striking. The Virginia aristocrat, inevitably, saw himself in relation to his own region. He lived in a static society which could endure almost anything except change. Instinctively, his first loyalty would go to the locality in which that society existed. He would fight to the limit of endurance to defend it, because in defending it he was defending everything that gave his own life its deepest meaning.

11 The Westerner, on the other hand, would fight with an equal tenacity for the broader concept of society. He fought so because everything he lived by was tied to growth, expansion, and a constantly widening horizon. What he lived by would survive or fall with the nation itself. He could not possibly stand by unmoved in the face of an attempt to destroy the Union. He would combat it with everything he had, because he could only see it as an effort to cut the ground out from under his feet.

12 So Grant and Lee were in complete contrast, representing two diametrically opposed elements in American life. Grant was the modern man emerging; beyond him, ready to come on the stage, was the great age of steel and machinery, of crowded cities and a restless, burgeoning vitality. Lee might have ridden down from the old age of chivalry, lance in hand, silken banner fluttering over his head. Each man was the perfect champion of his cause, drawing both his strengths and his weaknesses from the people he led.

13 Yet it was not all contrast, after all. Different as they were—in background, in personality, in underlying aspiration—these two great soldiers had much in common. Under everything else, they were marvelous fighters. Furthermore, their fighting qualities were really very much alike.

14 Each man had, to begin with, the great virtue of utter tenacity and fidelity. Grant fought his way down the Mississippi Valley in spite of acute personal discouragement and profound military handicaps. Lee hung on in the trenches at Petersburg after hope itself had died. In each man there was an indomitable quality . . . the born fighter's refusal to give up as long as he can still remain on his feet and lift his two fists.

15 Daring and resourcefulness they had, too; the ability to think faster and move faster than the enemy. These were the qualities which gave Lee

the dazzling campaigns of Second Manassas and Chancellorsville and won Vicksburg for Grant.

16   Lastly, and perhaps greatest of all, there was the ability, at the end, to turn quickly from war to peace once the fighting was over. Out of the way these two men behaved at Appomattox came the possibility of a peace of reconciliation. It was a possibility not wholly realized, in the years to come, but which did, in the end, help the two sections to become one nation again . . . after a war whose bitterness might have seemed to make such a reunion wholly impossible. No part of either man's life became him more than the part he played in their brief meeting in the McLean house at Appomattox. Their behavior there put all succeeding generations of Americans in their debt. Two great Americans, Grant and Lee—very different, yet under everything very much alike. Their encounter at Appomattox was one of the great moments of American history.

Questions on Content, Style, and Structure

1. What is Catton's thesis?

2. According to Catton, how did Lee view society? Summarize the aristocratic ideal that Lee symbolized.

3. Who did Grant represent? How did they view the country's social structure?

4. After carefully studying paragraphs four through sixteen, describe the pattern of organization Catton uses to present his discussion.

5. What new means of development begins in paragraph thirteen?

6. How does Catton avoid the choppy seesaw effect as he compares and contrasts his subjects? Point out ways in which Catton makes a smooth transition from point to point.

7. Evaluate Catton's ability to write unified, coherent paragraphs with clearly stated topic sentences. Are his paragraphs adequately developed with enough specific detail? Cite evidence to support your answer.

8. What is the advantage or disadvantage of having only one sentence in paragraph three? In paragraph four?

9. What is Catton's opinion of these men? Select words and passages to support your answer. How does Catton's attitude affect the tone of this essay? Is his tone appropriate? Why or why not?

10. Instead of including a separate paragraph, Catton presents his concluding remarks in paragraph sixteen, in which he discusses his last major point about Grant and Lee. Many essays lacking concluding

paragraphs end too abruptly or merely trail off; how does Catton avoid these weaknesses?

Vocabulary

chivalry (5)   diametrically (12)
deportment (5)   burgeoning (12)
embodied (6)   indomitable (14)
tenacity (11)   reconciliation (16)

▶ A REVISION WORKSHEET

As you write your rough drafts, consult Chapter 5 for guidance through the revision process. In addition, here are a few questions to ask yourself as you revise your comparison/contrast essay:

1. Does the essay contain a thesis that makes a significant point instead of a "so-what" thesis?

2. Is the material organized into the best pattern for the subject matter?

3. If the essay is developed by the point-by-point pattern, are there enough transition words used to avoid the see-saw effect?

4. If the essay is developed by the block pattern, are there enough transition devices and references connecting the two subjects to avoid the split-essay problem?

5. Are the points of comparison/contrast presented in a logical, consistent order that the reader can follow easily?

6. Are both subjects given a reasonably balanced treatment?

7. Are both subjects developed in enough specific detail so that the reader clearly understands the comparison or contrast? Where might more detail be added?

After you've revised your essay extensively, you might exchange rough drafts with a classmate and answer these questions for each other, making specific suggestions for improvement wherever appropriate. (For advice on productive participation in classroom workshops, see pp. 114–117.)

Reviewing Your Progress

After you have completed this essay developed by comparison/contrast, take a moment to measure your progress as a writer by responding to the following questions. Such analysis will help you to recognize growth in your writing skills and may enable you to identify areas that are still problematic.

1. Which part of your essay do you like the best? Why?

2. Which point of comparison or contrast do you think is the most successful? Why is it effective?

3. What part of your essay gave you the most trouble? How did you overcome the problem?

4. If you had more time to work on this essay, what would receive additional attention? Why?

5. What did you learn about your topic from writing this essay? About yourself as a writer?

STRATEGY FOUR: DEVELOPMENT BY DEFINITION

Frequently in conversation we must stop to ask, "What do you mean by that?" because in some cases our failure to comprehend just one particular term may lead to total misunderstanding. Suppose, for example, in a discussion with a friend, you refer to a new law as a piece of "liberal legislation"; if you and your friend do not share the same definition of "liberal," your remark may be completely misinterpreted. Take another example: you tell your parents that you're tired of listening to rap music; if they don't know what rap is, they miss the point entirely. In other words, definition of terms or ideas is often essential to meaningful communication.

Sometimes a dictionary definition or a one- or two-sentence explanation is all a term needs (Hemingway, for example, once defined courage as "grace under pressure"). And sometimes a brief, humorous definition can cut right to the heart of the matter (comedian Robin Williams, for instance, once defined "cocaine" as "God's way of saying you're making too much money").*

Frequently, however, you will find it necessary to provide an *extended definition*—that is, a longer, more detailed explanation that thoroughly defines the subject. Essays of extended definitions are quite common; think, for instance, of the articles you've seen lately on "mercy killing" that try to define death or the arguments on abortion that define "life" in a variety of ways. Other recent essays have grappled with such complex concepts as free speech, palimony, animal rights, pornography, discrimination, and "reverse" discrimination.

---

* Even graffiti employs definition. One bathroom wall favorite: "Death is Nature's way of telling you to slow down." Another, obviously written by an English major: "A double negative is a no-no."

Many national debates have centered on controversial definitions. For example, the conviction of John Hinckley, who attempted to assassinate former-president Ronald Reagan, produced many articles and editorials debating "criminal insanity," and the murder of a popular television actress brought new attention to the need for "stalker laws" to protect people from frequently dangerous, uninvited attention. The testimony of law professor Anita Hill at the 1991 Supreme Court confirmation hearing of Clarence Thomas stirred debate over the meaning of "sexual harassment," and in 1992 the trial of Los Angeles police officers charged with the beating of Rodney King caused furor over the meaning of "excessive force" in the line of duty. Today we continue to discuss new and controversial terms that often need clarification before we can make intelligent choices or take appropriate action.

Why Do We Define?

Essays of extended definition are usually written for one or more of the following reasons:

1. to provide an interpretation of a vague, controversial, or misunderstood term (such as "pro-choice," "pornoviolence," or "euthanasia")

2. to explain an abstract term or concept (such as "heroic," "success," or "friendship")

3. to define a new or unusual term, often found in slang, dialect, or the jargon of a particular field of study or industry (such as "geek," "objective correlative," or "computer virus")

4. to offer an objective definition of an unfamiliar term for a particular audience ("electron microscope," "tie beam," or "soft contact lenses")

5. to entertain by presenting the interesting history, uses, effects, or examples of a common word or expression ("soul food," "mad-scientist movies," or "detective fiction")

Developing Your Essay

Here are four suggestions to help you prepare your essay of extended definition:

Know your purpose. Sometimes we need to define a term as clearly and objectively as possible. As a laboratory assistant, for instance, you might need to explain a technical measuring instrument to a group of new students. At other times, however, we may wish to persuade as well as inform our readers. People's interpretations of words, especially abstract or controversial terms, can, and often do, differ greatly depending on their point of view. After all, one person's "protest march" can be another person's street riot. Consequently, before you begin writing, decide on your purpose. If your readers need objective information only, make your definition as unbiased as you can; if your goal is to convince them that your point of view is the right or best one, you may adopt a variety of persuasive techniques as well as subjective language. For example, readers of a paper entitled "Doc in the Box" should quickly realize that they are not getting an objective treatment of the new twenty-four-hour emergency-care offices springing up around the country.

Give your readers a reason to read. One way to introduce your subject is to explain the previous use, misuse, or misunderstanding of the term; then present your new or different interpretation of the term or concept. An introduction and thesis defining a slang word, for instance, might state, "Despite the visions of cornbread dressing and cranberries it conjures up for most Americans, the word 'turkey' does not always refer to the Thanksgiving bird. Today, 'turkey' is also a common slang expression designed primarily to tease or even insult someone." Or take this introduction and thesis aimed at a word the writer feels is unclear to many readers: "When the credits roll at the end of a movie, much of the audience may be perplexed to see the job of 'best boy' listed. No, the 'best boy' doesn't stand up with the groom at a wedding of children—he (or she) is, in fact, the key electrician's first assistant, who helps arrange the lights for the movie's director of photography."

Keep your audience in mind to anticipate and avoid problems of clarity. Because you are trying to present a new or improved definition, you must strive above all for clarity. Ask yourself, "Who is my intended audience? What terms or parts of my definition are strange to them?" You don't help your audience, for example, by defining one campus slang expression in terms of other bits of unfamiliar slang. If, in other words, you defined "space cadet" as an "airhead," you're probably confusing your readers more than you are informing them. If your assignment doesn't specify a particular audience, you may find it useful to imagine one. You might pretend, for instance, that you're defining a campus or slang expression for your grandparents or that you're explaining an ambiguous term to a foreign visitor. After all, your definition is effective only if your explanation is clear not just to you but to those unfamiliar with the term or concept under discussion.

Use as many strategies as necessary to clarify your definition. Depending on your subject, you may use any number of the following methods in your essay to define your term:

1. state some examples

2. describe the parts

3. compare and contrast to similar terms

4. explain an operation or process

5. give some familiar synonyms

6. define by negation (i.e., tell what the term doesn't mean)

7. present the history

8. discuss causes or effects

To illustrate some of the methods suggested above, let's suppose you wanted to write an extended definition of modern country music. You might choose one or more of these methods:

- describe the parts: music, lyrics, and typical subject matter

- compare or contrast to other kinds of music, such as bluegrass and Western swing

- give some examples of famous country songs

- trace its historical development from traditional country music to its present state

In the paper on country music or in any definition essay, you should, of course, use only those methods that will best define your term. Never include methods purely for the sake of exhibiting a variety of techniques. You, the writer, must decide which method or methods work best, which should receive the most emphasis, and in which order the chosen methods of definition should appear.

Problems to Avoid

Here is a list of "don'ts" for the writer of extended definition essays:

Don't present an incomplete definition. An inadequate definition is often the result of choosing a subject too broad or complex for your essay. You probably can't, for instance, do a good job of defining "twentieth-century modern art" in all its varieties in a short essay; you might, however, acquaint your reader with some specific school of modern art, such as impressionism, cubism, expressionism, surrealism, or pop. Therefore, narrow your subject to a manageable size and then define it as thoroughly as possible.

Don't introduce your essay with a quotation from Webster's. In fact, try to avoid long, direct quotes from dictionaries or encyclopedias altogether. If you must include a lengthy standard definition of the term, put the dictionary's definition in your own words. Dictionary definitions are generally so dull and overused that they often drive composition teachers to seek more interesting jobs, such as measuring spaghetti in a pasta factory. Don't bore your audience to death; it's a terrible way to go.

Don't define vaguely or by using generalities. As always, use specific, vivid details to explain your subject. If, for example, you define a Shaker chair as "something with four legs," you have also described a dog, cat, horse, and cow, none of which is remotely akin to your subject. Consequently, you must select details that will make your subject distinct from any other. Including concrete examples is frequently useful in any essay but especially so when you are defining an abstract term such as "pride," "faith," or "prejudice." To make your definition both interesting and clear, always add as many precise details as possible. (For a review of using specific, colorful language, see pp. 125–126 and 161–164.)

Don't offer circular definitions. To identify a poet as "one who writes poetry" or the American dream as "the dream most Americans hold dear" is about as helpful as a doctor telling a patient, "Your illness is primarily a lack of good health." Explain your subject; don't just rename it.

ESSAY TOPICS

Below are several suggestions for terms whose meanings are often unclear. Narrow any topic that seems too broad for your assignment, and decide before writing whether your definition will be objective or subjective. (Student writers, by the way, often note that abstract concepts are harder to define than the more concrete subjects, so proceed at your own risk, and remember to use plenty of specific detail in your essay.)

1. any current slang, campus, or local expression
2. a term from your field of study
3. conceit or hypocrisy
4. success or failure
5. a good/bad teacher, clerk, coach, friend, parent, date, or spouse
6. heroism or cowardice
7. a term from environmental issues
8. any kind of music, painting, architecture, or dance
9. a feminist or a chauvinist pig/sow
10. any current fad or style

11. a rebel or conformist

12. iridology or channeling (or some other counterculture activity)

13. a good/bad restaurant, store, movie theater, nightspot, class

14. self-respect

15. prejudice or discrimination

16. a freshman or senior

17. a controversial political idea or movement

18. a term from a hobby

19. a medical term or illness

20. a term from a sport or popular entertainment

A Topic Proposal for Your Essay

Selecting the right subject matter is important to every writer. To help you clarify your ideas and strengthen your commitment to your topic, here is a proposal sheet that asks you to describe some of your preliminary ideas about your subject before you begin drafting. Although as you draft your ideas may change (they will almost certainly become more refined), thinking through your choice of topic now may help you avoid several false starts.

1. What subject will your essay define? Will you define this subject objectively or subjectively? Why?

2. Why are you interested in this topic? Do you have a personal or professional connection to the subject? State at least one reason for your choice of topic.

3. Is this a significant topic of interest to others? Why? Who specifically might find it interesting, informative, or entertaining?

4. Is your subject a controversial, ambiguous, or new term? What will readers gain by understanding this term as defined from your point of view?

5. Writers use a variety of techniques to define terms. At this point, list two techniques you think you might use to help readers understand your topic.

6. What difficulties, if any, can you foresee during the drafting of this essay? For example, do you need to do any additional reading or interviewing to collect information for your definition?

► SAMPLE STUDENT ESSAY

A student with an interest in running wrote the following essay defining "runner's high." Note that he uses several methods to define his subject, one that is difficult to explain to those who have not experienced it firsthand.

Blind Paces

Introduction: An example and a general definition of the term

After running the Mile-Hi ten kilometer race in my hometown, I spoke with several of the leading runners about their experiences in the race. While most of them agreed that the course, which passed through a beautifully wooded yet overly hilly country area, was difficult, they also agreed that it was one of the best races of their running careers. They could not, however, explain why it was such a wonderful race but could rather only mumble something about the tall trees, cool air, and sandy path. When pressed, most of them didn't even remember specific details about the course, except the start and finish, and ended their descriptions with a blank—but content—stare. This self-satisfied, yet almost indescribable, feeling is often the result of an experienced runner running, a feeling often called, because of its similarities to other euphoric experiences, "runner's high."

Definition by negation, contrast

Because this experience is seemingly impossible to define, perhaps a description of what runner's high is *not* might, by contrast, lead to a better understanding of what it is. I clearly remember—about five years ago—when I first took up running. My first day, I donned my tennis shorts, ragged t-shirt, and white discount-store tennis shoes somewhat ashamedly, knowing that they were symbolic of my novice status. I plodded around my block—just over 1/2 mile—in a little more than four minutes, feeling and regretting every painful step. My shins and thighs revolted at every jarring move, and my lungs wheezed uncontrollably, gasping for air, yet denied that basic necessity. Worst of all, I was conscious of every aspect of my existence—from the swinging of my arms to the slap of my feet on the road, and from the sweat dripping into my eyes and ears and mouth to the frantic inhaling and exhaling of my lungs. I kept my eyes carefully peeled on the horizon or the next turn in the road, judging how far away it was, how long it would take me to get there, and how much torture was left before I reached home. These first few runs were, of course, the worst—as far from any euphoria or "high" as possible. They did, however, slowly get easier as my body became accustomed to running.

After a few months, in fact, I felt serious enough about this new pursuit that I decided to invest in a pair of real running shoes and shorts. Admittedly, these changes added to the comfort of my endeavor, but it wasn't until two full years later that the biggest change occurred— and I experienced my first real "high." It was a fall day. The air was a cool sixty-five degrees, the sun was shining intently, the sky was a clear, crisp blue, and a few dead leaves were scattered across the browning lawn. I stepped out onto the road and headed north towards a nearby park for my routine six mile jog. The next thing I remember, however, was not my run through the park, but rather my return, some forty-two minutes and six miles later, to my house. I woke, as if out of a dream, just as I slowed to a walk, warming down from my run. The only memory I had of my run was a feeling of floating on air—as if my real self was somewhere above and detached from my body, looking down on my physical self as it went through

Effects of the "high"

its blind paces. At first, I felt scared—what if I had run out in front of a car? Would I have even known it? I felt as if I had been asleep or out of control, that my brain had, in some real sense, been turned off.

Now, after five years of running and hundreds of such mystical experiences, I realize that I had never lost control while in this euphoric state—and that my brain hadn't been turned off, or, at least, not completely. But what does happened is hard to prove. George Sheehan, in a column for *Runner's World,* suggests that "altered states," such as runner's high, result from the loss of con-

Possible causes of the
feeling: two authorities

scious control, from the temporary cessation of left-brain messages and the dominance of right-brain activity (the left hemisphere being the seat of reason and rationality; the right, of emotions and inherited archetypal feelings). Another explanation comes from Dr. Jerry Lynch, who argues, in his book *The Total Runner,* that the "high" results from the secretion of natural opiates, called beta endorphins, in the brain (213). My own explanation draws on both these medical explanations and is perhaps slightly

The writer's explanation

more mystical. It's just possible that indeed natural opiates do go to work and consequently our brains lose track of the ins and outs of everyday activities—of jobs and classes and responsibilities. And because of this relaxed, drugged state, we are able to reach down into something more fundamental, something that ties us not only to each other but to all creation, here and gone. We rejoin nature, rediscovering the thread that links us to the universe.

Conclusion: An incomplete understanding doesn't hamper enjoyment

My explanation is, of course, unscientific and therefore suspect. But I found myself, that day of the Mile-Hi Ten K run, eagerly trying to discuss my experience with the other runners: I wanted desperately to discover where I had been and what I had been doing during the race for which I received my first trophy. I didn't discover the answer from my fellow runners that day, but it didn't matter. I'm still running and still feeling the glow—whatever it is.

Works Cited

Lynch, Jerry. *The Total Runner: A Complete Mind-Body Guide to Optimal Performance.* Englewood Cliffs, NJ: Prentice Hall, 1987.

Sheehan, George. "Altered States." *Runner's World.* Aug. 1988: 14.

PROFESSIONAL ESSAY

The Androgynous Male
Noel Perrin

Noel Perrin teaches English at Dartmouth College and frequently writes for The New Yorker. *His insights into rural life, or "essays of a sometime farmer," have been collected in three books:* First Person Rural *(1978),* Second Person Rural *(1980), and* Third Person Rural *(1983). Recent publications include* A Reader's Delight *(1988) and* Dr. Bowler's Legacy *(1992). This essay was published in* The New York Times Magazine *in 1984.*

The summer I was 16, I took a train from New York to Steamboat Springs, Colo., where I was going to be assistant horse wrangler at a camp. The trip took three days, and since I was much too shy to talk to strangers, I had quite a lot of time for reading. I read all of "Gone With the Wind." I read all the interesting articles in a couple of magazines I had, and then I went back and read all the dull stuff. I also took all the quizzes, a thing of which magazines were even fuller then than now.

2   The one that held my undivided attention was called "How Masculine/Feminine Are You?" It consisted of a large number of inkblots. The reader was supposed to decide which of four objects each blot most resembled. The choices might be a cloud, a steam engine, a caterpillar and a sofa.

3   When I finished the test, I was shocked to find that I was barely masculine at all. On a scale of 1 to 10, I was about 1.2. Me, the horse wrangler? (And not just wrangler, either. That summer, I had to skin a couple of horses that died—the camp owner wanted the hides.)

4   The results of that test were so terrifying to me that for the first time in my life I did a piece of original analysis. Having unlimited time on the train, I looked at the "masculine" answers over and over, trying to find what it was that distinguished real men from people like me—and eventually I discovered two very simple patterns. It was "masculine" to think the blots looked like man-made objects, and "feminine" to think they looked like natural objects. It was masculine to think they looked like things capable of causing harm, and feminine to think of innocent things.

5   Even at 16, I had the sense to see that the compilers of the test were using rather limited criteria—maleness and femaleness are both more complicated than *that*—and I breathed a huge sigh of relief. I wasn't necessarily a wimp, after all.

6   That the test did reveal something other than the superficiality of its makers I realized only many years later. What it revealed was that there is a large class of men and women both, to which I belong, who are essentially androgynous. That doesn't mean we're gay, or low in the appropriate hormones, or uncomfortable performing the jobs traditionally assigned our sexes. (A few years after that summer, I was leading troops in combat and, unfashionable as it now is to admit this, having a very good time. War is exciting. What a pity the 20th century went and spoiled it with high-tech weapons.)

7   What it does mean to be spiritually androgynous is a kind of freedom. Men who are all-male, or he-man, or 100 percent red-blooded Americans, have a little biological set that causes them to be attracted to physical power, and probably also to dominance. Maybe even to watching football. I don't say this to criticize them. Completely masculine men are quite often wonderful people: good husbands, good (though sometimes overwhelming) fathers, good members of society. Furthermore, they are often so unself-consciously at ease in the world that other men seek to imitate them. They just aren't as free as us androgynes. They pretty nearly have to be what they are; we have a range of choices open.

8   The sad part is that many of us never discover that. Men who are not 100 percent red-blooded Americans—say, those who are only 75 percent red-blooded —often fail to notice their freedom. They are too busy trying to copy the he-men ever to realize that men, like women, come in a wide variety of acceptable types. Why this frantic imitation? My answer is mere speculation, but not casual. I have speculated on this for a long time.

9   Partly they're just envious of the he-man's unconscious ease. Mostly they're terrified of finding that there may be something wrong with them deep down, some weakness at the heart. To avoid discovering that, they spend their lives acting out the role that the he-man naturally lives. Sad.

10   One thing that men owe to the women's movement is that this kind of failure is less common than it used to be. In releasing themselves from the single ideal of the dependent woman, women have more or less incidentally released a lot of men from the single ideal of the dominant male. The one mistake the feminists have made, I think, is in supposing that *all* men need this release, or that the world would be a better place if all men achieved it. It would just be duller.

11   So far I have been pretty vague about just what the freedom of the androgynous man is. Obviously it varies with the case. In the case I know best, my own, I can be quite specific. It has freed me most as a parent. I am, among other things, a fairly good natural mother. I like the nurturing role. It makes me feel good to see a child eat—and it turns me to mush to see a 4-year-old holding a glass with both small hands, in order to drink. I even enjoyed sewing patches on the knees of my daughter Amy's Dr. Dentons when she was at the crawling stage. All that pleasure I would have lost if I had made myself stick to the notion of the paternal role that I started with.

12   Or take a smaller and rather ridiculous example. I feel free to kiss cats. Until recently it never occurred to me that I would want to, though my daughters have been doing it all their lives. But my elder daughter is now 22, and in London. Of course, I get to look after her cat while she is gone. He's a big, handsome farm cat named Petrushka, very unsentimental, though used from kittenhood to being kissed on the top of the head by Elizabeth. I've gotten very fond of him (he's the adventurous kind of cat who likes to climb hills with you), and one night I simply felt like kissing him on the top of the head, and did. Why did no one tell me sooner how silky cat fur is?

13   Then there's my relation to cars. I am completely unembarrassed by my inability to diagnose even minor problems in whatever object I happen to be driving, and don't have to make some insider's remark to mechanics to try to establish that I, too, am a "Man With His Machine."

14   The same ease extends to household maintenance. I do it, of course. Service people are expensive. But for the last decade my house

has functioned better than it used to because I've had the aid of a volume called "Home Repairs Any Woman Can Do," which is pitched just right for people at my technical level. As a youth, I'd as soon have touched such a book as I would have become a transvestite. Even though common sense says there is really nothing sexual whatsoever about fixing sinks.

15   Or take public emotion. All my life I have easily been moved by certain kinds of voices. The actress Siobhan McKenna's, to take a notable case. Give her an emotional scene in a play, and within 10 words my eyes are full of tears. In boyhood, my great dread was that someone might notice. I struggled manfully, you might say, to suppress this weakness. Now, of course, I don't see it as a weakness at all, but as a kind of fulfillment. I even suspect that the true he-men feel the same way, or one kind of them does, at least, and it's only the poor imitators who have to struggle to repress themselves.

16   Let me come back to the inkblots, with their assumption that masculine equates with machinery and science, and feminine with art and nature. I have no idea whether the right pronoun for God is He, She or It. But this I'm pretty sure of. If God could somehow be induced to take that test, God would not come out macho, and not feminismo, either, but right in the middle. Fellow androgynes, it's a nice thought.

Questions on Content, Structure, and Style

1. What method does Perrin use to introduce his essay? How does his lead-in set up his thesis?

2. What is Perrin defining in his essay? Is his definition subjective or objective?

3. Discuss some of the methods Perrin uses to define what it means to be "spiritually androgynous." Which methods are the most effective, and why?

4. How does Perrin view "he-men"? Why does he mention them in this essay?

5. According to Perrin, the women's movement has helped men in what ways? What mistake, says Perrin, have feminists made in their attitude toward men? Do you agree with Perrin?

6. In paragraph 11 Perrin admits that he has been "pretty vague"; he then goes on to develop his definition with what sort of support?

7. Throughout his essay, Perrin primarily uses himself as an example of someone who has benefited from the freedom of androgyny. Is this an effective decision? What other examples can you think of that Perrin might have introduced to offer support for his claims?

8. Characterize Perrin's "voice" in this essay. How is his tone achieved? Is it appropriate and effective? Why or why not?

9. How does Perrin conclude his essay? Does his last image effectively end the essay?

10. What would you suggest is the purpose of Perrin's essay? What effect did he want to have on his readers? Do you think he was successful? Why or why not?

Vocabulary

androgynous (title)   paternal (11)
superficiality (6)   transvestite (14)
feminists (10)   suppress (15)

► A REVISION WORKSHEET

As you write your rough drafts, consult Chapter 5 for guidance through the revision process. In addition, here are a few questions to ask yourself as you revise your extended definition essay:

1. Is the subject narrowed to manageable size, and is the purpose of the definition clear to the readers?

2. If the definition is objective, is the language as neutral as possible?

3. If the definition is subjective, is the point of view obvious to the readers?

4. Are all the words and parts of the definition itself clear to the essay's particular audience?

5. Are there enough explanatory methods (examples, descriptions, history, causes, effects, etc.) used to make the definition clear and convincing?

6. Have the various methods been organized and ordered in an effective way?

7. Does the essay contain enough specific details to make the definition clear and distinct rather than vague or circular? Where could additional details be added?

After you've revised your essay extensively, you might exchange rough drafts with a classmate and answer these questions for each other, making specific suggestions for improvement wherever appropriate. (For advice on productive participation in classroom workshops, see pp. 114–117.)

Reviewing Your Progress

After you have completed your essay developed by definition, take a moment to measure your progress as a writer by responding to the following questions. Such analysis will help you recognize growth in your writing skills and may enable you to identify areas that are still problematic.

1. What do you like best about your essay? Why?

2. After considering the various methods of definition you used in your essay, which one do you think offered the clearest or most persuasive explanation of your topic? Why was that particular technique effective in this essay?

3. What part of your essay gave you the most trouble? How did you overcome the problem?

4. If you had more time to work on this essay, what would receive additional attention? Why?

5. What did you learn about your topic from writing this essay? About yourself as a writer?

STRATEGY FIVE: DEVELOPMENT BY DIVISION AND CLASSIFICATION

To make large or complex subjects easier to comprehend, we frequently apply the principles of *division* or *classification*.

Division

Division is the act of separating something into its component parts so that it may be better understood or used by the reader. For example, consider a complex subject such as the national budget. Perhaps you have seen a picture on television or in the newspaper of the budget represented by a circle or a pie that has been divided into parts and labeled: a certain percentage or "slice" of the budget for military spending, a certain amount designated for social services, another for education, and so on. By studying the budget after it has been divided into its parts, taxpayers may have a better sense of how their money is being spent.

As a student, you see division in action in many of your college courses. A literature teacher, for instance, might approach a particular drama by dividing its plot into stages such as exposition, rising action, climax, falling action, and dénouement. Or your chemistry lab instructor may ask you to break down a substance into its components to learn how the parts interact to form the chemical. Even this textbook is divided into chapters to make it easier for you to use. When you think of *division,* then, think of dividing or separating one subject (often a large or complex or unfamiliar one) into its parts to help people understand it more easily.

Classification

While the principle of division calls for separating one thing into its parts, *classification* systematically groups a number of things into categories to make the information easier to grasp. Without some sort of imposed system of order, a body of information can be a jumble of facts and figures. For example, at some point you've probably turned to the classified ads in the newspaper; if the ads were not classified into categories such as "houses to rent," "cars for sale," and "help wanted," you would have to search through countless ads to find the service or item you needed.

Classification occurs everywhere around you. As a student, you may be classified as a freshman, sophomore, junior, or senior; you may also be classified by your major. If you vote, you may be categorized as a Democrat, Republican, Socialist, or something else; if you attend religious services, you may be classified as Baptist, Methodist, Catholic, Jewish, and so on. The books you buy may be grouped and shelved by the bookstore into "mysteries," "Westerns," "biographies," "adventure stories," and other categories; the movies you see have already been typed as "G," "PG," "PG-13," "R," "NC-17, or "X." Professionals classify almost every kind of knowledge: ornithologists classify birds; etymologists classify words by origins; botanists classify plants; zoologists classify animals. Remember that *classification* differs from division in that it sorts and organizes *many* things into appropriate groups, types, kinds, or categories. *Division* begins with *one* thing and separates it into its parts.

Developing Your Essay

A classification or division paper is generally easy to develop. Each part or category is identified and described in a major part of the body of the essay. Frequently, one body paragraph will be devoted to each category. Here are three additional hints for writing your essay:

Select one principle of classification or division and stick to it. If you are classifying students by major, for instance, don't suddenly switch to classification by college: French, economics, psychology, *arts and sciences,* math, and chemistry. A similar error occurs in this classification of dogs by breeds because it includes a physical characteristic: spaniels, terriers, *long-haired,* hounds, and retrievers. Decide on what basis of division you will classify or divide your subject and then be consistent throughout your essay.

Make the purpose of your division or classification clear to your audience. Don't just announce that "There are four kinds of 'X'" or that "'Z' has three important parts." Why does your particular audience need this information? Consider these sample thesis statements:

> By recognizing the three kinds of poisonous snakes in this area, campers and backpackers may be able to take the proper medical steps if they are bitten.

> Knowing the four types of spinning reels will enable novice fishermen to purchase the equipment best suited to their needs.

> Although karate has become a popular form of exercise as well as of self-defense, few people know what the six levels of achievement—or "belts" as they are called—actually stand for.

Organize your material for a particular purpose and then explain to your readers what that purpose is.

Account for all the parts in your division or classification. Don't, for instance, claim to classify all the evergreen trees native to your hometown and then leave out one or more species. For a short essay, narrow your ruling principle rather than omit categories. You couldn't, for instance, classify all the architectural styles in America in a short paper, but you could discuss the *major* styles on your campus. In the same manner, the enormous task of classifying all types of mental illness could be narrowed to the most common forms of childhood schizophrenia. However you narrow your topic, remember that in a formal classification, all the parts must be accounted for.

Like most rules, the one above has an exception. If your instructor permits, you can also write a satirical or humorous classification. In this sort of essay, you make up your own categories as well as your thesis. One writer, for example, recently wrote about the kinds of moviegoers who spoil the show for everyone else, such as "the babbling idiot," "the laughing hyena," and "the wandering dawdler." Another female student described blind dates to avoid, including "Mr. Neanderthal," "Timothy Timid," "Red, the Raging Rebel," and "Frat-Rat Freddie," among others. Still another student classified the various kinds of people who frequent the school library at two A.M. In this kind of informal essay, the thesis rule still holds true: though you start by making a humorous or satirical point about your subject, your classification must be more than mere silliness. Effective humor should ultimately make good sense, not nonsense.

Problems to Avoid

Avoid underdeveloped categories. A classification or division essay is not a mechanical list; each category should contain enough specific details to make it clearly recognizable and interesting. To present each category or part, you may draw on the methods of development you already know, such as example, comparison and contrast, and definition. Try to use the same techniques in each category so that no one category or part of your essay seems underdeveloped or unclear.

Avoid indistinct categories. Each category should be a separate unit; there should be no overlap among categories. For example, in a classification of shirts by fabric, the inclusion of flannel with silk, nylon, and cotton is an overlap because flannel is a kind of cotton. Similarly, in a classification of soft drinks by flavor, to include sugar-free with cola, root beer, orange, grape, and so on, is misleading because sugar-free drinks come in many different flavors. In other words, make each category unique.

Avoid too few or too many categories. A classification essay should have at least three categories, avoiding the either-or dichotomy. On the other hand, too many categories give a short essay the appearance of a list rather than a discussion. Whatever the number, don't forget to use transition devices for an easy movement from category to category.

ESSAY TOPICS

Narrow your subject by selecting an appropriate principle of division or classification. Some of the suggestions are intended for humorous essays.

1. friends or relatives
2. the advantages or disadvantages of a choice or product
3. heroes in a particular field
4. books or movies popular today
5. methods of advertising for a particular product, such as cigarettes or perfume
6. bad drivers (or other public annoyances)
7. specializations in your field of study
8. approaches to studying a subject
9. classmates, roommates, or dates
10. salesclerks/waiters/airline stewards/doctors/dentists, etc.
11. sports fans or amateur athletes
12. chronic moochers or borrowers

13. people who accost you on campus or in airports

14. ways of accomplishing a task (such as three ways to conduct an experiment, four ways to introduce a bill into Congress, etc.)

15. people who play video or board games (or some other kind of game)

16. kinds of tools or equipment for a particular task in your field of study

17. theories explaining "X" (the disappearance of the dinosaurs, for example)

18. diets or exercise programs

19. reasons people participate in some activity

20. vegetarians or Breatharians (or some other special-interest group)

A Topic Proposal for Your Essay

Selecting the right subject matter is important to every writer. To help you clarify your ideas and strengthen your commitment to your topic, here is a proposal sheet that asks you to describe some of your preliminary ideas about your subject before you begin drafting. Although as you draft your ideas may change (they will almost certainly become more refined), thinking through your choice of topic now may help you avoid several false starts.

1. What is the subject of your essay? Will you write an essay of classification or division?

2. What principle of classification or division will you employ? Why is this a useful or informative principle for your particular topic and readers?

3. Why are you interested in this topic? Do you have a personal or professional connection to the subject? State at least one reason for your choice of topic.

4. Is this a significant topic of interest to others? Why? Who specifically might find it interesting, informative, or entertaining?

5. List at least three categories you are considering for development in your essay.

6. What difficulties, if any, might arise from this topic during the drafting of your essay? For example, do you know enough about your topic to offer details that will make each of your categories clear and distinct to your readers?

■ SAMPLE STUDENT ESSAY

In the essay below, the student writer divided the Mesa Verde Indian Era into three time periods that correspond to changes in the people's domestic skills, crafts, and housing. Note the writer's use of description and examples to help the reader distinguish one time period from another.

The Indian Era at Mesa Verde

Introduction: Establishing a reason for knowing the classification

Principle of division of the Indian Era

Time period one: Early cliff life

Visiting Mesa Verde National Park is a trip back in time to two-and-a-half centuries before Columbus. The park, located in southwestern Colorado, is the setting of a silent stone city, ten ruins built into protective seven-hundred-foot cliffs that housed hundreds of people from the pre-Columbian era to the end of the thirteenth century. If you visit the park, you'll enjoy its architecture and history more if you know a little about the various people who lived there. The Indian Era may be divided into three time periods that show growing sophistication in such activities as crafts, hunting, trade, and housing: Basket Maker (A.D. 1–450), Modified Basket Maker (A.D. 450–750), and Pueblo (A.D. 750–1300).*

The earliest Mesa Verdeans, the Basket Makers, whose ancestors had been nomads, sought shelter from the dry plains in the cliff caves and became farmers. During growing seasons they climbed up toeholds cut in the cliffs and grew beans and squash on the green mesa above. Settling down also meant more time for crafts. They didn't make pottery yet but instead wove intricate baskets that held water. Instead of depending on raw meats and vegetables, they could now cook food in these baskets by dropping heated rocks into the water. Because the Basket Makers hadn't discovered the bow and arrow yet, they had to rely on the inaccurate spear, which meant little fresh meat and few animal skins. Consequently, they wore little clothing but liked bone, seed, and stone ornaments.

* Last summer I worked at Mesa Verde as a guide for the Parks Service; the information in this paper is based on the tour I gave three times a week to hundreds of visitors to the park. [Student writer's note]

Time period two: New
crafts, trade, and
housing

The second period, A.D. 450–750, saw the invention of pottery, the bow and arrow, and houses. Pottery was apparently learned from other tribes. From crude clay baked in the sun, the Mesa Verdeans advanced to clay mixed with straw and sand and baked in kilns. Paints were concocted from plants and minerals, and the tribe produced a variety of beautifully decorated mugs, bowls, jars, pitchers, and canteens. Such pots meant that water could be stored for longer periods, and perhaps a water supply encouraged more trade with neighboring tribes. These Mesa Verdeans also acquired the bow and arrow, a weapon that improved their hunting skills, and enlarged their wardrobes to include animal skins and feather blankets. Their individual living quarters, called pithouses, consisted of twenty-foot-wide holes in the ground with log, grasses, and earthen framework over them.

Time period three:
Expanded community
living and trade

The third period lasted until A.D. 1300 and saw the innovation of pueblos, or groups of dwellings, instead of single-family units. Nearly eight hundred dwellings show the large number of people who inhabited the complex tunneled houses, shops, storage rooms, courtyards, and community centers whose masonry walls, often elaborately decorated, were three and four stories high. At the spacious Balcony House pueblo, for example, an adobe court lies beneath another vaulted roof; on three sides stand two-story houses with balconies that lead from one room to the next. In back of the court is a spring, and along the front side is a low wall that kept the children from falling down the seven-hundred-foot cliff to the canyon floor below. Balcony House also contains two *kivas,* circular subterranean ceremonial chambers that show the importance of fellowship and religion to the people of this era. During this period the Mesa Verdeans were still farmers and potters, but cotton cloth and other nonnative products found at the ruins suggest a healthy trade with the south. But despite the trade goods, sophisticated pottery, and such innovations in clothing as the "disposable" juniper-bark diapers of babies, life was still simple; the Mesa Verdeans had no system of writing, no wheel, and no metal.

Conclusion: The
importance of Mesa
Verde's people

Near the end of the thirteenth century, the cliff dwellings became ghost towns. Archaeologists don't know for certain why the Mesa Verdeans left their elaborate homes, but they speculate that a drought that lasted some twenty years may have driven them south into New Mexico and Arizona, where strikingly similar crafts and tools have been found. Regardless of their reason for leaving, they left an amazing architectural and cultural legacy. Learning about the people who lived in Mesa Verde centuries ago provides an even deeper appreciation of the cliff palaces that awe thousands of national park visitors every year.

PROFESSIONAL ESSAY

The Plot Against People
Russell Baker

Russell Baker has been a journalist and social commentator for over forty years. His "Observer" columns, written for The New York Times *and syndicated throughout the country, won him both the George Polk Award for Distinguished Commentary and a Pulitzer Prize for journalism. He has written several books, including* Growing Up *(1982), an autobiography that won him a second Pulitzer Prize, and* The Good Times *(1989). This essay originally appeared in* The New York Times *in 1968.*

1   Inanimate objects are classified into three major categories—those that don't work, those that break down and those that get lost.

2   The goal of all inanimate objects is to resist man and ultimately to defeat him, and the three major classifications are based on the method each object uses to achieve its purpose. As a general rule, any object capable of breaking down at the moment when it is most needed will do so. The automobile is typical of the category.

3   With the cunning typical of its breed, the automobile never breaks down while entering a filling station with a large staff of idle mechanics. It waits until it reaches a downtown intersection in the middle of the rush hour, or until it is fully loaded with family and luggage on the Ohio Turnpike.

4   Thus it creates maximum misery, inconvenience, frustration and irritability among its human cargo, thereby reducing its owner's life span.

5   Washing machines, garbage disposals, lawn mowers, light bulbs, automatic laundry dryers, water pipes, furnaces, electrical fuses, television tubes, hose nozzles, tape recorders, slide projectors—all are in league with the automobile to take their turn at breaking down whenever life threatens to flow smoothly for their human enemies.

6   Many inanimate objects, of course, find it extremely difficult to break down. Pliers, for example, and gloves and keys are almost totally

incapable of breaking down. Therefore, they have had to evolve a different technique for resisting man.

7   They get lost. Science has still not solved the mystery of how they do it, and no man has ever caught one of them in the act of getting lost. The most plausible theory is that they have developed a secret method of locomotion which they are able to conceal the instant a human eye falls upon them.

8   It is not uncommon for a pair of pliers to climb all the way from the cellar to the attic in its single-minded determination to raise its owner's blood pressure. Keys have been know to burrow three feet under mattresses. Women's purses, despite their great weight, frequently travel through six or seven rooms to find hiding space under a couch.

9   Scientists have been struck by the fact that things that break down virtually never get lost, while things that get lost hardly ever break down.

10   A furnace, for example, will invariably break down at the depth of the first winter cold wave, but it will never get lost. A woman's purse, which after all does have some inherent capacity for breaking down, hardly ever does; it almost invariably chooses to get lost.

11   Some persons believe this constitutes evidence that inanimate objects are not entirely hostile to man, and that a negotiated peace is possible. After all, they point out, a furnace could infuriate a man even more thoroughly by getting lost than by breaking down, just as a glove could upset him far more by breaking down than by getting lost.

12   Not everyone agrees, however, that this indicates a conciliatory attitude among inanimate objects. Many say it merely proves that furnaces, gloves, and pliers are incredibly stupid.

13   The third class of objects—those that don't work—is the most curious of all. These include such objects as barometers, car clocks, cigarette lighters, flashlights and toy-train locomotives. It is inaccurate, of course, to say that they never work. They work once, usually for the first few hours after being brought home, and then quit. Thereafter, they never work again.

14   In fact, it is widely assumed that they are built for the purpose of not working. Some people have reached advanced ages without ever seeing some of these objects—barometers, for example—in working order.

15   Science is utterly baffled by the entire category. There are many theories about it. The most interesting holds that the things that don't work have attained the highest state possible for an inanimate object, the state to which things that break down and things that get lost can still only aspire.

16   They have truly defeated man by conditioning him never to expect anything of them, and in return they have given man the only peace he receives from inanimate society. He does not expect his barometer to work, his electric locomotive to run, his cigarette lighter to light or his

flashlight to illuminate, and when they don't, it does not raise his blood pressure.

17   He cannot attain that peace with furnaces and keys and cars and women's purses as long as he demands that they work for their keep.

Questions on Content, Structure and Style

1. What is Baker's purpose in writing this classification? What reaction do you think Baker wants to evoke from his reading audience?

2. Where is Baker's thesis statement? Would his essay be more effective if his thesis were preceded by a fully developed lead-in? Why or why not?

3. Identify Baker's categories and principle of classification. What do these categories have in common?

4. Why does Baker give examples of items that belong to each category? Does this strengthen his essay? Why or why not?

5. Of the categories of inanimate objects discussed in the essay, which one is most effectively developed? List some examples of details.

6. Consider Baker's use of personification as he talks about inanimate objects. Give some examples of descriptions that give human qualities to these items. What effect does this have on tone and style?

7. How does Baker's word choice affect his tone? Would it be possible to write an effective essay about this subject from a more serious, informative standpoint? Why or why not?

8. What does Baker's title contribute to his tone and his readers' understanding of his classifying principle?

9. Evaluate Baker's conclusion. Is it effective or too abrupt?

10. What other categories of inanimate objects might you add to this essay? What items could you include under these new classifications?

Vocabulary

inanimate (1)	virtually (9)
cunning (3)	inherent (10)
league (5)	constitutes (11)
evolve (6)	conciliatory (12)
locomotion (7)	barometer (13, 14)

◣ A REVISION WORKSHEET

As you write your rough drafts, consult Chapter 5 for guidance through the revision process. In addition, here are a few questions to ask yourself as you revise your classification essay:

1. Is the purpose of the essay clear to the reader?

2. Is the principle of classification or division maintained consistently throughout the essay?

3. If the essay presents a formal division or classification, has the subject been narrowed so that all the parts of the subject are accounted for?

4. If the essay presents an informal or humorous division or classification, does the paper nevertheless make a significant or entertaining point?

5. Is each category developed with enough specific detail? Where might more details be effectively added?

6. Is each class distinct, with no overlap among categories?

7. Is the essay organized logically and coherently with smooth transitions between the discussions of the categories?

After you've revised your essay extensively, you might exchange rough drafts with a classmate and answer these questions for each other, making specific suggestions for improvement wherever appropriate. (For advice on productive participation in classroom workshops, see pp. 114–117.)

Reviewing Your Progress

After you have completed your essay developed by classification or division, take a moment to measure your progress as a writer by responding to the following questions. Such analysis will help you recognize growth in your writing skills and may enable you to identify areas that are still problematic.

1. What is the best feature of your essay? Why?

2. Which category do you think is the clearest or most persuasive in your essay? Why does that one stand above the others?

3. What part of your essay gave you the most trouble? How did you overcome the problem?

4. If you had more time to work on this essay, what would receive additional attention? Why?

5. What did you learn about your topic from writing this essay? About yourself as a writer?

STRATEGY SIX: DEVELOPMENT BY CAUSAL ANALYSIS

Causal analysis explains the cause-and-effect relationship between two (or more) elements. When you discuss the condition producing something, you are analyzing *cause;* when you discuss the result produced by something, you are analyzing *effect.* To find examples of causal analysis, you need only look around you. If your car stops running on the way to class, for example, you may discover the cause was an empty gas tank. On campus, in your history class, you may study the causes of the Civil War; in your economics class, the effects of teenage spending on the cosmetics market; and in your biology class, both the causes and effects of heart disease. Over dinner you may discuss the effects of some crisis in the Middle East on American foreign policy, and, as you drift to sleep, you may ponder the effects of your studying—or *not* studying—for your math test tomorrow.

To express it most simply, *cause* asks:

why did "X" happen?

or, why does "X" happen?

or, why will "X" happen?

Effect, on the other hand, asks:

what did "Y" produce?

or, what does "Y" produce?

or, what will "Y" produce?

Some essays of causal analysis focus on the cause(s) of something; others analyze only the effect(s); still others discuss both causes and effects. If, for example, you wanted to concentrate on the major causes of the Wall Street crash of 1929, you might begin by briefly describing the effects of the crash on the economy, then devote your thesis and the rest of your essay to analyzing the major causes, perhaps allotting one major section (or one paragraph, depending on the complexity of the reasons) to each cause. Conversely, an effect paper might briefly describe the causes of the crash and then detail the most important effects. An essay covering both the causes and effects of something usually demands a longer paper so that each part will be clear. (Your assignment will frequently indicate which kind of causal analysis to write. However, if the choice is yours, let your interest in the subject be your guide.)

Developing Your Essay

Whether you are writing an essay that primarily discusses either causes or effects, or one that focuses on both, you should follow these rules:

Present a reasonable thesis statement. If your thesis makes dogmatic, unsupportable claims ("Medicare will lead to a complete collapse of quality medical treatment") or overly broad assertions ("Peer pressure causes alcoholism among students"), you won't convince your reader. Limit or qualify your thesis whenever necessary by using such phrases as "may be," "a contributing factor," "one of the main reasons," "two important factors," and so on ("Peer pressure is *one of the major causes* of alcoholism among students").

Limit your essay to a discussion of recent, major causes or effects. In a short paper you generally don't have space to discuss minor or remote causes or effects. If, for example, you analyzed your car wreck, you might decide that the three major causes were defective brakes, a hidden yield sign, and bad weather. A minor, or remote, cause might include being tired because of too little sleep, too little sleep because of staying out late the night before, staying out late because of an out-of-town visitor, and so on—back to the womb. In some cases you may want to mention a few of the indirect causes or effects, but do be reasonable. Concentrate on the most immediate, most important factors. Often, a writer of a 500- to 800-word essay will discuss no more than two, three, or four major causes or effects of something; trying to cover more frequently results in an underdeveloped essay that is not convincing.

Organize your essay clearly. Organization of your causal analysis essay will vary, of course, depending on whether you are focusing on the causes of something or the effects, or both. To avoid becoming tangled in causes and effects, you might try sketching out a drawing of your thesis and essay map before you begin your first draft. Here, for instance, are a couple of sketches for essays you might write on your recent traffic accident:

Thesis Emphasizing the Causes:

Cause (defective brakes)
Cause (hidden yield sign)   produced   Effect (my car wreck)
Cause (bad weather)

Thesis Emphasizing the Effects:

                                        Effect (loss of car)
Cause (my car wreck)   produced   Effect (doctor bills)
                                        Effect (higher insurance rates)

Sometimes you may discover that you can't isolate "the three main causes/effects of 'X'"; some essays do in fact demand a narrative explaining a chain reaction of causes and effects. For example, a paper on the rebellion of the American colonies might show how one unjust British law or restriction after another led to the war for independence. In this kind of causal analysis essay, be careful to limit your subject so that you'll have the space necessary to show your readers how each step in the chain led to the next. Here's a sketch of a slightly different car-wreck paper presented in a narrative or chain-reaction format:

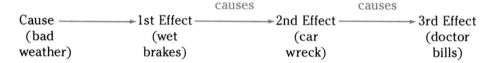

```
                           causes                    causes
Cause ─────────→ 1st Effect ─────────→ 2nd Effect ─────────→ 3rd Effect
 (bad                (wet                  (car               (doctor
weather)            brakes)               wreck)              bills)
```

Sometimes the plan for organizing your causal analysis paper will be suggested by your subject matter; often, however, you'll have to devote some of your prewriting time to deciding, first, whether you want to emphasize causes or effects and, then, in what arrangement you will present your analysis.

Convince your reader that a causal relationship exists by showing how the relationship works. Let's suppose you are writing an essay in which you want to discuss the three major changes you've undergone since coming to college. Don't just state the changes and describe them; your job is to show the reader how college has *brought about* these changes. If, for instance, your study habits have improved, you must show the reader how the academic demands of your college courses caused you to change your habits; a simple description of your new study techniques is not enough. Remember that a causal analysis essay should stress *how* (and sometimes *why*) "X" caused "Y," rather than merely describing "Y" as it now exists.

Problems to Avoid

Don't oversimplify by assigning one all-encompassing cause to some effect. Most complex subjects have more than one cause (or effect), so make your analysis as complete and objective as you can, especially when dealing with your own problems or beliefs. For example, was that car wreck really caused only by the bad weather—or also because of your carelessness? Did your friend do poorly in math only because the instructor didn't like her? Before judging a situation too quickly, investigate your own biases. Then provide a thoughtful, thorough analysis, effectively organized to convince your readers of the validity of your viewpoint.

Avoid the *post hoc* fallacy. This error in logic (from the Latin phrase *post hoc, ergo propter hoc,* meaning "after this, therefore because of this") results when we mistake a temporal connection for a causal relationship—or in other words, when we assume that because one event follows another in time, the first event caused the second. Most of our superstitions are *post hoc* fallacies; we now realize that bad luck after walking under a ladder is a matter of coincidence, not cause and effect. The *post hoc* fallacy provided the basis for a rather popular joke in the 1960s' debates over decriminalizing marijuana. Those against argued that marijuana led to heroin because most users of the hard drug had first smoked grass. The proponents retorted that milk, then, was the real culprit, because both marijuana and heroin users had drunk milk as babies. The point is this: in any causal analysis, you must be able to offer proof or reasoned logic to show that one event *caused* another, not just that it preceded it in time.

Avoid circular logic. Often causal essays seem to chase their own tails when they include such circular statements as "There aren't enough parking spaces for students on campus because there are too many cars." Such a statement merely presents a second half that restates what is already implied in the first half. A revision might say, "There aren't enough parking spaces for students on campus because the parking permits are not distributed fairly." This kind of assertion can be argued specifically and effectively; the other is a dead end.

▶ ESSAY TOPICS

The suggestions below may be developed into essays emphasizing cause or effect, or both.

1. a pet peeve or bad habit

2. a change of mind about some important issue or belief

3. an accident or misadventure

4. a family tradition or ritual

5. the popularity of some sport, hobby, fad, or style

6. ownership of a particular possession

7. a radical change in your appearance

8. a form of pollution or crime

9. academic cheating or dishonesty

10. an important decision or action

11. an act of heroism or sacrifice

12. an important idea or discovery in your field of study

13. a superstition or irrational fear

14. a place that is special to you

15. a disappointment or a success

16. racism or sexism or some other kind of discrimination or prejudice that you've witnessed or experienced

17. a friendship or influential person

18. a political action (campus, local, state, national) or a piece of legislation or a social movement

19. stress or an addiction or an illness

20. an academic or professional controversy

A Topic Proposal for Your Essay

Selecting the right subject matter is important to every writer. To help you clarify your ideas and strengthen your commitment to your topic, here is a proposal sheet that asks you to describe some of your preliminary ideas about your subject before you begin drafting. Although as you draft your ideas may change (they will almost certainly become more refined), thinking through your choice of topic now may help you avoid several false starts.

1. What is the subject of your causal analysis essay? Is this subject appropriately narrowed and focused for a discussion of major causes or effects?

2. Will you develop your essay to show the effects or the causes of your topic? Or a causal chain?

3. Why are you interested in this topic? Do you have a personal or professional connection to the subject? State at least one reason for your choice of topic.

4. Is this a significant topic of interest to others? Why? Who specifically might find it interesting, informative, or entertaining?

5. List at least two major causes or effects that you might develop in the discussion of your topic.

6. What difficulties, if any, might arise during your drafting on this topic? For example, how might you convince a skeptical reader that your causal relationship is not merely a temporal one?

▲ SAMPLE STUDENT ESSAY

In the following essay, a student explains why working in a local motel damaged her self-esteem, despite her attempts to do a good job. Note that the writer uses many vivid examples and specific details to show the reader how she was treated and, consequently, how such treatment made her feel.

It's Simply Not Worth It

Introduction: Her job as a motel maid

It's hard to get a job these days, and with our town's unemployment rate reaching as high as ten percent, most people feel obligated to "take what they can get." But after working as a maid at a local motel for almost a year and a half, I decided no job is worth keeping if it causes a person to doubt his or her worth. My hard work rarely received recognition or appreciation, I was underpaid, and I was required to perform some of the most disgusting cleaning tasks imaginable. These factors caused me to devalue myself as a person and ultimately motivated me to return to school in hope of regaining my self-respect.

Thesis and map: Causes of her poor self-esteem

Cause one: Lack of appreciation

It may be obvious to say, but I believe that when a maid's hours of meticulous cleaning are met only with harsh words and complaints, she begins to lose her sense of self-esteem. I recall the care I took in making the motel's beds, imagining them as globs of clay and molding them into impeccable pieces of art. I would teeter from one side of a bed to the other, over and over again, until I smoothed out every intruding wrinkle or tuck. And the mirrors—I would vigorously massage the glass, erasing any toothpaste splotches or oil smudges that might draw my customer's disapproval. I would scrutinize the mirror first from the left side, then I'd move to the right side, once more to the left until every possible angle ensured an unclouded reflection. And so my efforts went, room after room. But, without fail, each day more than one customer would approach me, not with praise for my tidy beds or spotless mirrors, but with nitpicking complaints that undermined my efforts: "Young lady, I just checked into room 143 and it only has one ashtray. Surely for $59.95 a night you people can afford more ashtrays in the rooms."

If it wasn't a guest complaining about ashtrays, it was an impatient customer demanding extra towels or a fussy stay-over insisting his room be cleaned by the time he returned from breakfast at 8:00 A.M. "Can't you come to work early to do it?" he would urge thoughtlessly. Day after day, my spotless rooms went unnoticed, with no spoken rewards for my efforts from either guests or management. Eventually, the ruthless complaints and thankless work began wearing me down. In my mind, I became a servant undeserving of gratitude.

Cause two: Low pay

The lack of spoken rewards was compounded by the lack of financial rewards. The $3.35 appraisal of my worth was simply not enough to support my financial needs or my self-esteem. The measly $1.12 I earned for cleaning one room took a lot of rooms to add up, and by the end of the month I was barely able to pay my bills and buy some food. (My mainstay became twenty-two cent, generic macaroni and cheese dinners.) Because the flow of travelers kept the motel full for only a few months of the year, during some weeks I could only work half time, making a mere $250.00 a month. As a result, one month I was forced to request an extension on my rent payment. Unsympathetically, my landlord threatened to evict me if I didn't pay. Embarrassed, yet desperate, I went to a friend and borrowed money. I felt uneasy and awkward and regretted having to beg a friend for money. I felt like a mooch and a bum; I felt degraded. And the constant reminder from management that there were hundreds of people standing in lines who would be more than willing to work for $3.35 an hour only aided in demeaning me further.

Cause three: Repulsive duties

In addition to the thankless work and the inadequate salary, I was required to clean some of the most sickening messes. Frequently, conventions for high school clubs booked the motel. Once I opened the door of a conventioneer's room one morning and almost gagged at the odor. I immediately beheld a trail of vomit that began at the bedside and ended just short of the bathroom door. At that moment I cursed the inventor of shag carpet, for I knew it would take hours to comb this mess out of the fibers. On another day I spent thirty minutes dislodging the bed linen from the toilet where it had been stuffed. And I spent what seemed like hours removing from one of my spotless mirrors the lipstick-drawn message that read, "Yorktown Tigers are number one." But these inconsiderate acts were relaying another message, a message I took personally: "Lady, you're not worth the consideration—you're a maid and you're not worth respecting."

Conclusion: Review of
the problem and a brief
explanation of the
solution she chose
I've never been afraid to work hard or do jobs that weren't particularly "fun." But the line must be drawn when a person's view of herself becomes clouded with feelings of worthlessness. The thankless efforts, the inadequate wage, and the disgusting work were just parts of a total message that degraded my character and caused me to question my worth. Therefore, I felt compelled to leave this demeaning job in search of a way to rebuild my self-confidence. Returning to school has done just that for me. As my teachers and fellow students take time to listen to my ideas and compliment my responses, I feel once again like a vital, valued, and worthwhile person. I feel human once more.

PROFESSIONAL ESSAY

Scaring the Public to Death
Frank Trippett

Frank Trippett is a journalist, author, and editor who has written for Newsweek, Look, *and* Time, *where he currently works. His books include* The States: United They Fell *(1967),* The First Horseman *(1974), and* Child Ellen *(1975). This essay appeared in* Time *in 1987.*

> *On city streets and country roads, the war rages against cyclists*
> *—newspaper headline*

> **bicycle**: lightweight, two-wheeled, steerable machine propelled by its rider; the bicycle is said to be the most efficient means yet devised to convert human energy into propulsion.—The New Encyclopaedia Britannica

1   A marvel of efficiency, the bicycle is also cheap, handy, nimble. It can sprint like a cat, then stop on a dime and give you nine cents change. It is easy to ride and speedy enough for any sane short-distance traveler. In the typical bumper-to-bumper city creepathon the bike can outrun a Porsche.

2   Unlike the car, truck, and bus, the bike does not spew stinky fumes and carcinogens. A bike is easy to park in a sliver of space, and of precious oil it needs only a smidgen to keep the wheels squeakless. Riders may turn rowdy, but the vehicle itself is quiet—a blessed virtue amid the squawk-bleat-scream-grind-growl-honk-toot-wail-shriek that is the voice of the big city.

3   Given such merits, the bicycle ought to be universally embraced by human-kind as a sensible way of getting about in the strangling,

traffic-plagued city. Bicycles have long been a major mode of transport in Europe and Asia; there are as many as 230 million of them in China. Now they have taken to U.S. streets with a vengeance. According to Bill Wilkinson, director of the Bicycle Federation of America, roughly 2 million people commute to work on bikes, up from approximately 500,000 a decade ago.

4   Still, though Americans have always liked two-wheelers as a child's plaything, and currently own 111 million of them, they have never truly welcomed the bike as a serious vehicle. In fact, wherever it appears in numbers, the bicycle provokes tension, annoyance, outrage or hostility. This year bikers from Manhattan to Denver, from Oregon to Missouri, have wound up in conflicts: bikers vs. motorists, bikers vs. pedestrians, bikers vs. runners, bikers vs. police.

5   In Washington the overlap of bicyclists and Pentagon-based joggers has turned the Arlington Memorial Bridge over the Potomac River into an anger zone. Last month bikers were banned from hiking trails in California's Santa Monica mountains. In St. Louis, where a motorist has been known to slosh a bucket of water on a cyclist in cold weather, someone sprinkled tacks on the route of a Labor Day cycle tour and flattened the tires of some 40 bikes. Motorist-biker tensions around St. Louis grew high last month after bicyclist John S. Reif, Jr., 22, a nationally ranked triathlete, was fatally injured in a head-on collision with a car. Speaking of the current mood, Deeds Fletcher, 47, a municipal-bond dealer and a cyclist, says it often feels as if "cars are going after people. It's like the Christians and the lions."

6   In Boulder police in July snared and ticketed a flight of 55 cyclists racing past a stop sign, and Steve Clark, the city's bicycle-program coordinator, applauded the crackdown: "When one segment of the group creates bad p.r., it hurts all cyclists." In Eugene, Ore., according to Bicycle Coordinator Diane Bishop of the public-works department, police patrol university areas, especially in their annual autumn bike-safety campaign, in which, she says, "they ticket as many as 100 riders a month." Proliferating cyclists reduced Denver POST Sport Columnist John McGrath to epithet: "Look around: geeks in long black shorts are hunched over a pair of handlebars at every urban intersection, on every country road."

7   Nowhere has the bike provoked such a sustained and official skirmish as in New York City. Mayor Ed Koch, who suffered a pro-bike mood in 1980 and had bike lanes built, had them eliminated a few months later. By this year Koch had become so antibike that he banned the cycles from several major Manhattan avenues. The state supreme court in Manhattan overturned the ban last month, but did not overturn Police Commissioner Benjamin Ward's opinion about the city's pedalers. "They are scaring the public to death," says Ward, "and we've got to do something about it."

8   "It" means the free-form riding habits of 5,000 or so messengers. Inspired by the fact that more deliveries mean more money, many messengers

whiz around the city in pseudokamikaze style, heeding neither red lights nor one-way signs, zagging on and off sidewalks, leaving behind a wake of screeching tires and cursing pedestrians. Many messengers even opt for bikes without brakes, to save on a few pounds of heavy metal.

9   There were 640 reported incidents of bikes colliding with pedestrians in New York City last year, up from 339 in 1981. Three New York City pedestrians were killed by cyclists in 1986, while nine bikers were killed by motorists. "They are like roaches," complains Anita Sockol, who was crossing Lexington Avenue in June when she was floored by a speeding cyclist. She suffered a broken hip and wrist, and now limps. "They come at you from all sides," she adds.

10   Even cyclists admit that some bike riders act like pit bulls on wheels, but enthusiasts attribute most accidents to impatient walkers, many of whom insist on waiting in crosswalks for the light to change. "Most pedestrians don't look before they cross the street," says Eric Williams, a Manhattan messenger. "I've pulled so hard to stop that I've got scars to prove it."

11   The numbers prove that Manhattan's reckless-bike-riding problem is not trivial. Even so, the ire stirred by the bikers is striking. Some argue (not too convincingly) that the antipathy toward messengers, who are mostly black, is racially motivated. But that does not explain the shouts of anger directed at white speed demons by startled white pedestrians.

12   Efforts are being made all over to educate bikers about traffic rules and to train motorists in the ways of bikers. In Los Angeles, state and county planners are even contemplating a $2\frac{1}{2}$-mile-long overhead bikeway that would rise above the congested streets around UCLA. But the real culprit on American roads, as conspicuous among cars, cabs and trucks as among cyclists, is an arrogant, scofflaw spirit that sends vehicles— those with four as well as two wheels—streaking through red lights and stop signs, just as it tempts pedestrians into habitual jaywalking.

Questions on Content, Structure, and Style

1. According to Trippett, the increased number of bicycles on the roads today have produced what effects?

2. Why does Trippett introduce his essay by defining and describing the merits of the bicycle?

3. In paragraph 6, why does Trippett offer a list of groups in conflict with bikers?

4. Cite some examples that Trippett uses to offer support for his thesis. Which examples show the effects of bicycles most persuasively? Why?

5. Why does Trippett quote a number of people throughout this essay? Is some testimony more convincing than others? Why?

6. What does Trippett's use of statistics add to the support of his causal analysis?

7. Where did Trippett find the idea for his title? Is the title effective? Why or why not?

8. Point out two examples of vivid figurative language Trippett uses to create images for his readers. What, for example, is the effect of such phrases as "bike riders act like pit bulls on wheels"?

9. Why does Trippett conclude his essay with a reference to an "arrogant, scofflaw spirit"?

10. Did Trippett's essay offer enough evidence to convince you of his thesis? If you were to write a similar essay today, what sorts of evidence would you offer to support your attitude toward bicyclists?

Vocabulary

efficiency (1)   antipathy (11)
carcinogens (2)   culprit (12)
vengeance (3)   arrogant (12)
skirmish (7)   scofflaw (12)
ire (11)

◣ A REVISION WORKSHEET

As you write your rough drafts, consult Chapter 5 for guidance through the revision process. In addition, here are a few questions to ask yourself as you revise your causal analysis essay:

1. Is the thesis limited to a reasonable claim that can be supported in the essay?

2. Is the organization clear and consistent so that the reader can understand the purpose of the analysis?

3. Does the essay focus on the most important causes and/or effects?

4. If the essay has a narrative form, is each step in the chain reaction clearly connected to the next?

5. Does the essay convincingly show the reader how or why relationships between the causes and effects exist, instead of merely naming and describing them?

6. Does the essay provide enough evidence to show the connections between causes and effects? Where could additional details be added to make the relationships clearer?

7. Has the essay avoided the problems of oversimplification, circular logic, and the *post hoc* fallacy?

After you've revised your essay extensively, you might exchange rough drafts with a classmate and answer these questions for each other, making specific suggestions for improvement wherever appropriate. (For advice on productive participation in classroom workshops, see pp. 114–117.)

Reviewing Your Progress

After you have completed your essay developed by causal analysis, take a moment to measure your progress as a writer by responding to the following questions. Such analysis will help you recognize growth in your writing skills and may enable you to identify areas that are still problematic.

1. What do you like best about your essay? Why?

2. After considering your essay's presentation of the major causes or effects, which part of your analysis do you think readers will find the most convincing? Why?

3. What part of your essay gave you the most trouble? How did you overcome the problem?

4. If you had more time to work on this essay, what would receive additional attention? Why?

5. What did you learn about your topic from writing this essay? About yourself as a writer?

9

ARGUMENTATION

•
•
•

Almost without exception, each of us, every day, argues for or against something with somebody. The discussions may be short and friendly ("Let's go to this restaurant rather than that one") or long and complex ("Mandatory seatbelt laws are an intrusion on civil rights"). Because we do argue our viewpoints so often, most of us realized long ago that shifting into high whine did not always get us what we wanted; on the contrary, we've learned that we usually have a much better chance at winning a dispute or having our plan adopted or changing someone's mind if we present our side of an issue in a calm, logical fashion, giving sound reasons for our position. This approach is just what a good argumentative essay does: it presents logical reasoning and solid evidence that will persuade your readers to accept your point of view.

Some argumentative essays declare the best solution to a problem ("Raising the drinking age will decrease traffic accidents"); others argue a certain way of looking at an issue ("Beauty pageants degrade women"); still others may urge adoption of a specific plan of action ("Voters should pass ordinance 10 to fund the new ice rink"). Whatever your exact purpose, your argument essay should be composed of a clear thesis and body paragraphs that offer enough sensible reasons and persuasive evidence to convince your readers to agree with you.

DEVELOPING YOUR ESSAY

Here are some suggestions for developing and organizing an effective argumentative essay:

Know why you hold your views. We human beings, being opinionated creatures, frequently voice beliefs that we, when pressed, can't always support effectively. Sometimes we hold an opinion simply because on the surface it seems to make good sense to us or because it fits comfortably with our other social, ethical, or political beliefs. Or we may have inherited some of our beliefs from our families or friends, or perhaps we borrowed ideas from people we admired. In some cases, we may have held an opinion for so long that we can't remember why we adopted it in the first place. We may also have a purely sentimental or emotional attachment to some idea or position. Whatever the original causes of our beliefs, we need to examine the real reasons for thinking what we do before we can effectively convince others.

Once you've selected a topic for your argument essay, try writing down a list of the reasons or points that support your opinion on that subject. Then study the list—are your points logical and persuasive? Which aren't, and why not? After this bit of prewriting, you may discover that although you believe something strongly, you really don't have the kinds of factual evidence or reasoned arguments you need to support your opinion. In some cases, depending on your topic, you may wish to talk to others who share your position or to research your subject (for help with research, see Chapter 12); in other cases, you may just need to think longer and harder about your topic and your reasons for maintaining your attitude toward it. With or without formal research, the better you know your subject, the more confident you will be about writing your argumentative essay.

Anticipate opposing views. An argument assumes that there is more than one side to an issue. To be convincing, you must be aware of your opposition's views on the subject and then organize your essay to answer or counter those views. If you don't have a good idea of the opposing arguments, you can't effectively persuade your readers to dismiss their objections and see matters your way. Therefore, before you begin your first rough draft, write down all the opposing views you can think of and an answer to each of them so that you will know your subject thoroughly. (For the sake of clarity throughout this chapter, your act of responding to those arguments against your position will be called *refuting the opposition;* "to refute" means "to prove false or wrong," and that's what you will try to do to some of the arguments of those who disagree with you.)

Know and remember your audience. Although it's important to think about your readers' needs and expectations whenever you write, it is essential to consider carefully the audience of your argumentative essay both before and as you write your rough drafts. Because you are trying to persuade people to adopt some new point of view or perhaps to take some action, you need to decide what kinds of supporting evidence will be most convincing to your particular readers. Try to analyze your audience by asking yourself a series of questions. What do they already know about your topic? What information or terms do they need to know to understand your point of view? What biases might they already have for or against your position? What special concerns might your readers have that influence their receptiveness? To be convincing, you should consider these questions and others by carefully reviewing the discussion of audience on pages 20–24 *before* you begin your prewriting.

Decide which points of argument to include. Once you have a good sense of your audience and of your own position and your opposition's strongest arguments, try making a Pro-and-Con Sheet to help you sort out which points you will discuss in your essay.

Let's suppose you want to write an editorial on the sale-of-class-notes controversy at your school. Should professional note-takers be allowed to sit in on a course and then sell their notes to class members? After reviewing the evidence on both sides, you have decided to argue that your school should prohibit professional note-taking services from attending classes and selling notes. To help yourself begin planning your essay, you list all the pro-and-con arguments you can think of concerning the controversy:

MY SIDE: AGAINST THE SALE OF CLASS NOTES	MY OPPOSITION'S SIDE: FOR THE SALE OF CLASS NOTES
1. unfair advantage for some students in some classes	1. helps students to get better test, course grades
2. note-taking is a skill students need to develop	2. helps students to learn, organize material
3. rich students can afford and poor can't	3. helps if you're sick and can't attend class
4. prevents students from learning to organize for themselves	4. shows students good models for taking notes and outlining them
5. encourages class cutting	5. other study guides are on the market, why not these?
6. missing class means no chance to ask questions, participate in discussions	6. gives starving graduate students jobs
7. notes taken by others are often inaccurate	7. no laws against sale of notes, free country

8. some professors don't like
strangers in classroom

9. students need to think for
themselves

After making your Pro-and-Con Sheet, look over the list and decide which of your strongest points you want to argue in your paper and also which of your opposition's claims you want to refute. At this point you may also see some arguments on your list that might be combined and some that might be deleted because they're irrelevant or unconvincing. (Be careful not to select more arguments or counterarguments to discuss than the length of your writing assignment will allow. It's far better to present a persuasive analysis of a few points than it is to give an underdeveloped, shallow treatment of a host of reasons.)

Let's say you want to cover the following points in your essay:

- professional note-taking services keep students from developing own thinking and organizational skills (combination of 4 and 9)

- professional note-taking services discourage class attendance and participation (5 and 6)

- unfair advantages to some students (1 and 3).

Your assignment calls for an essay of 750 to 1,000 words, so you figure you'll only have space to refute your opposition's strongest claim, and you decide that is

- helps students to learn and organize material (2).

The next step is to formulate a working thesis. At this stage you may find it helpful to put your working thesis in an "although-because" format so you can clearly see both your opposition's arguments and your own. An "although-because" statement for the note-taking essay might look something like this:

> *Although* some students maintain that using professional note-taking services helps them learn more, such services should be banned from our campus *because* they prevent students from developing their own thinking and organizational skills, they discourage class attendance, and they give unfair advantages to some students.

Frequently your "although-because" thesis will be too long and awkward to use in the later drafts of your essay. But for now, it can serve as a guide, allowing you to see your overall position before the writing of the first draft begins.

Organize your essay clearly. Although there is no set model of organization for argumentative essays, here are some common patterns that you might use or that you might combine in some effective way.

Important note: For the sake of simplicity, the first two outlines present two of the writer's points and two opposing ideas. Naturally, your essay may contain any number of points and refuted points, depending on the complexity of your subject and the assigned length of your essay.

In Pattern A you devote the first few body paragraphs to arguing points on your side and then turn to refute or answer the opposition's claims.

Pattern A: Thesis

Body paragraph 1: you present your first point and its supporting evidence

Body paragraph 2: you present your second point and its supporting evidence

Body paragraph 3: you refute your opposition's first point

Body paragraph 4: you refute your opposition's second point

Conclusion

Sometimes you may wish to clear away the opposition's claims before you present the arguments for your side. To do so, you might select Pattern B:

Pattern B: Thesis

Body paragraph 1: you refute your opposition's first point

Body paragraph 2: you refute your opposition's second point

Body paragraph 3: you present your first point and its supporting evidence

Body paragraph 4: you present your second point and its supporting evidence

Conclusion

In some cases you may find that the main arguments you want to present are the very same ones that will refute or answer your opposition's primary claims. If so, try Pattern C, which allows each of your argumentative points to refute one of your opposition's claims in the same paragraph:

Pattern C: Thesis

Body paragraph 1: you present your first point and its supporting evidence, which also refutes one of your opposition's claims

Body paragraph 2: you present a second point and its supporting evidence, which also refutes a second opposition claim

Body paragraph 3: you present a third point and its supporting evidence, which also refutes a third opposition claim

Conclusion

Now you might be thinking, "What if my position on a topic as yet has no opposition?" Remember that almost all issues have more than one side, so try to anticipate objections and then answer them. For example, you might first present a thesis that calls for a new traffic signal at a dangerous intersection in your town and then address hypothetical counter-arguments, such as "The City Council may say that a stop light at Lemay and Columbia will cost too much, but the cost in lives will be much greater" or "Commuters may complain that a traffic light there will slow the continuous flow of north-south traffic, but it is precisely the uninterrupted nature of this road that encourages motorists to speed." By answering hypothetical objections, you impress your readers by showing them you've thought through your position thoroughly before you asked them to consider your point of view.

You might also be thinking, "What if my opposition actually has a valid objection, a legitimate point of criticism? Should I ignore it?" Hoping that an obviously strong opposing point will just go away is like hoping the IRS will cancel income taxes this year—a nice thought but hardly likely. Don't ignore your opposition's good point; instead, acknowledge it, but then go on quickly to show your readers why that reason, though valid, isn't compelling enough by itself to motivate people to adopt your opposition's entire position. Or you might concede that one point while simultaneously showing why your position isn't really in conflict with that criticism, but rather with other, more important, parts of your opponent's viewpoint. By admitting that you see some validity in your opposition's argument, you can again show your readers that you are both fair-minded and informed about all aspects of the controversy.

If you are feeling confident about your ability to organize an argumentative essay, you might try some combination of patterns, if your material allows such a treatment. For example, you might have a strong point to argue, another point that simultaneously answers one of your opposition's strongest claims, and another opposition point you want to refute. Your essay organization might look like this:

Combination: Thesis

Body paragraph 1: A point for your side

Body paragraph 2: One of your points, which also refutes an opposition claim

Body paragraph 3: Your refutation of another opposition claim

In other words, you can organize your essay in a variety of ways as long as your paper is logical and clear. Study your Pro-and-Con Sheet and then decide which organization best presents the arguments and counterarguments you want to include. Try sketching out your essay following each of the patterns; look carefully to see which pattern (or variation on one of the patterns) seems to put forward your particular material most persuasively, with the least repetition or confusion. Sometimes your essay's material will clearly fall into a particular pattern of organization, so your choice will be easy. More often, however, you will have to arrange and rearrange your ideas and counter-arguments until you see the best approach. Don't be discouraged if you decide to change patterns after you've begun a rough draft; what matters is finding the most effective way to persuade the reader to your side.

If no organizational pattern seems to fit at first, ask yourself which of your points or counter-arguments is the strongest or most important. Try putting that point in one of the two most emphatic places: either first or last. Sometimes your most important discussion will lead the way to your other points and consequently should be introduced first; perhaps more often, effective writers and speakers build up to their strongest point, presenting it last as the climax of their argument. Again, the choice depends on your material itself, though it's rare that you would want to bury your strongest point in the middle of your essay.

Now let's return to the essay on note-taking first discussed on page 261. After selecting the most important arguments and counter-arguments (p. 262), let's say that you decide that your main point concerns the development of students' learning skills. Since your opposition claims the contrary, that their service does promote learning, you see that you can make your main point as you refute theirs. But you also wish to include a couple of other points for your side. After trying several patterns, you decide to put the "thinking skills" rebuttal last for emphasis and present your other points first. Consequently, Pattern A best fits your plan. A sketchy outline might look like this:

- *Revised working thesis and essay map:* Professional note-taking services should be banned from our campus. Not only do they give some students unfair advantages and discourage class attendance, they prevent students from developing and practicing good thinking skills.

- *Body paragraph 1 (a first point for the writer's side):* Services penalize some students—those who haven't enough money or take other sections or enroll in classes without notes.

- *Body paragraph 2 (another point for the writer's side):* The service encourages cutting class and so students miss opportunities to ask questions, participate in discussion, talk to instructor, see visual aids, etc.

- *Body paragraph 3 (rebuttal of the opposition's strongest claim):* Services claim they help students learn more, but they don't because they're doing the work students ought to be doing themselves. Students must learn to think and organize for themselves.

Once you have a general notion of where your essay is going, plan to spend some more time thinking about ways to make each of your points clear, logical, and persuasive to your particular audience. (If you wish to see how one student actually developed an essay based on the outline above, turn to the sample student paper on pp. 275–278.)

Argue your ideas logically. To convince your readers, you must provide sufficient reasons for your position. You must give more than mere opinion— you must offer logical arguments to back up your assertions. Some of the possible ways of supporting your ideas should already be familiar to you from writing expository essays; listed below are several methods and illustrations:

1. Give examples (real or hypothetical): "Cutting class because you have access to professional notes can be harmful; for instance, you might miss seeing some slides or graphics essential to your understanding of the lecture."

2. Present a comparison or contrast: "In contrast to reading 'canned' notes, outlining your own notes helps you remember the material."

3. Show a cause-and-effect relationship: "Dependence on professional notes may mean that some students will never learn to organize their own responses to classroom discussions."

4. Argue by definition: "Passively reading through professional notes isn't a learning experience in which one's mind is engaged."

The well-thought-out arguments you choose to support your case may be called *logical appeals* because they appeal to, and depend on, your readers' ability to reason and to recognize good sense when they see it. But there is another kind of appeal often used today: the *emotional appeal*.

Emotional appeals are designed to persuade people by playing on their feelings rather than appealing to their intellect. Rather than using thoughtful, logical reasoning to support their claims, writers and speakers using *only* emotional appeals often try to accomplish their goals by misleading their audiences. Frequently, emotional appeals are characterized by language that plays on people's fears, material desires, prejudices, or sympathies; such language often triggers highly favorable or unfavorable responses to a subject. For instance, emotional appeals are used constantly in advertising, where feel-good images, music, and slogans ("Come to Marlboro Country"; "The Heartbeat of America Is Today's Chevy Truck") are designed to sway potential customers to a product without them thinking about it too much. Some politicians also rely heavily on emotional appeals, often using scare tactics to disguise a situation or to lead people away from questioning the logic of a particular issue.

But in some cases, emotional appeals can be used for legitimate purposes. Good writers should always be aware of their audience's needs, values, and states of mind, and they may be more persuasive in some cases if they can frame their arguments in ways that appeal to both their readers' logic and their emotions. For example, when Martin Luther King, Jr., delivered his famous "I Have A Dream" speech to the crowds gathered in Washington in 1963 and described his vision of little children of different races walking hand-in-hand, being judged not "by the color of their skin but by the content of their character," he certainly spoke with passion that was aimed at the hearts of his listeners. But King was not using an emotional appeal to keep his audience from thinking about his message; on the contrary, he presented powerful emotional images that he hoped would inspire people to act on what they already thought and felt, their deepest convictions about equality and justice.

Appeals to emotions are tricky: you can use them effectively in conjunction with appeals to logic and with solid evidence, but only if you use them ethically. And too many appeals to the emotions are overwhelming; readers tire quickly from too many tugs on the heartstrings. To prevent your readers from suspecting deception, support your assertions with as many logical arguments as you can muster and use emotional appeals only when they legitimately advance your cause.

Offer evidence that effectively supports your claims. In addition to presenting thoughtful, logical reasoning, you may wish to incorporate a variety of convincing evidence to persuade your readers to your side. Your essay might profit from including, where appropriate, some of the following kinds of supporting evidence:

- personal experiences
- the experiences or testimony of others whose opinions are pertinent to the topic
- factual information you've gathered from research
- statistics from current, reliable sources
- charts, graphs, or diagrams
- testimony from authorities and experts

You'll need to spend quite a bit of your prewriting time thinking about the best kinds of evidence to support your case. Remember that not all personal experiences or research materials are persuasive. For instance, the experiences we've had (or that our friends have had) may not be representative of a universal experience and consequently may lead to unconvincing generalizations. Even testimony from an authority may not be convincing if the person is not speaking on a topic from his or her field of expertise; famous football players, for instance, don't necessarily know any more about panty hose or soft drinks than anyone else. Always put yourself in the skeptical reader's place and ask, "Does this point convince me? If not, why not?" (For more information on incorporating research material into your essays, see Chapter 12. For more advice on the selection of evidence, see the section on critical thinking in Chapter 5.)

Find the appropriate tone. Sometimes when we argue, it's easy to get carried away. Remember that your goal is to persuade and perhaps change your readers, not alienate them. Instead of laying on insults or sarcasm, present your ideas in a moderate let-us-reason-together spirit. Such a tone will persuade your readers that you are sincere in your attempts to argue as truthfully and fairly as possible. If your readers do not respect you as a reasonable person, they certainly won't be swayed to your side of an issue. Don't preach or pontificate either; no one likes—or respects—a writer with a superior attitude. Write in your natural "voice"; don't adopt a pseudointellectual tone. In short, to argue effectively you should sound logical, sincere, and informed. (For additional comments on tone, review pp. 156–159.)

Consider using Rogerian techniques, if they are appropriate. In some cases, especially those involving tense situations or highly sensitive issues, you may wish to incorporate some techniques of the noted psychologist Carl Rogers, who developed a procedure for presenting what he calls the nonthreatening argument. Rogers believes that people involved in a debate should strive for clear, honest communication so that the problem under discussion can be resolved. Instead of going on the defensive and trying to "win" the argument, each side should try to recognize common ground and then develop a solution that will address the needs of both parties.

A Rogerian argument uses these techniques:

1. a clear, objective statement of the problem or issue

2. a clear, objective summary of the opposition's position that shows you understand its point of view and goals

3. a clear, objective summary of your point of view, stated in nonthreatening language

4. a discussion that emphasizes the beliefs, values, and goals that you and your opposition have in common

5. a description of any of your points that you are willing to concede or compromise

6. an explanation of a plan or proposed solution that meets the needs of both sides.

By showing your opposition that you thoroughly understand its position and that you are sincerely trying to effect a solution that is in everyone's—not just your—best interests, you may succeed in some situations that might otherwise be hopeless because of their highly emotional nature. Remember, too, that you can use some of these Rogerian techniques in any kind of argument paper you are writing, if you think they would be effective.

Problems to Avoid

Writers of argumentative essays must appear logical or their readers will reject their point of view. Here is a short list of some of the most common *logical fallacies*—that is, errors in reasoning. Check your rough drafts carefully to avoid these problems.

Students sometimes ask, "If a logical fallacy works, why not use it? Isn't all fair in love, war, and argumentative essays?" The honest answer is "maybe." It's quite true that speakers and writers do use faulty logic and irrational emotional appeals to persuade people every day (one needs only to look at television or a newspaper to see example after example). But the cost of the risk is high: if you do try to slide one by your readers and they see through your trick, you will lose your credibility instantly. On the whole, it's far more effective to use logical reasoning and strong evidence to convince your readers to accept your point of view.

COMMON LOGICAL FALLACIES

Hasty generalization: The writer bases the argument on insufficient or unrepresentative evidence. Suppose, for example, you have owned two poodles and they have both attacked you. If you declare that all poodles are vicious dogs, you are making a hasty generalization. There are, of course, thousands of poodles who have not attacked anyone. Similarly, you're in error if you interview only campus athletes and then declare, "University students favor a new stadium." What about the opinions of the students who aren't athletes? In other words, when the generalization is drawn from a sample that is too small or select, your conclusion isn't valid.

Non sequitur ("it doesn't follow"): The writer's conclusion is not necessarily a logical result of the facts. An example of a *non sequitur* occurs when you conclude, "Professor Smith is a famous historian, so he will be a brilliant history teacher." As you may have realized by now, just because someone knows a subject well does not automatically mean that he or she can communicate the information clearly; hence, the conclusion is not necessarily valid.

Begging the question: The writer presents as truth what is supposed to be proven by the argument. For example, in the statement "All useless laws such as Reform Bill 13 should be repealed," the writer has already assumed the bill is useless without assuming responsibility for proving that accusation. Similarly, the statement "Dangerous pornography should be banned" begs the question (that is, tries like a beggar to get something for nothing from the reader) because the writer gives no evidence for what must first be argued, not merely asserted—that pornography is dangerous.

Red herring: The writer introduces an irrelevant point to divert the readers' attention from the main issue. This term originates from the old tactic used by escaped prisoners, of dragging a smoked herring, a strong-smelling fish, across their trail to confuse tracking dogs by making them follow the wrong scent. For example, roommate A might be criticizing roommate B for his repeated failure to do the dishes when it was his turn. To escape facing the charges, roommate B brings up times in the past when the other roommate failed to repay some money he borrowed. Although roommate A may indeed have a problem with remembering his debts, that discussion isn't relevant to the original argument about sharing the responsibility for the dishes. (By the way, you might have run across a particular newspaper photograph of a California ecology group demonstrating for more protection of dolphins, whales, and other marine life; look closely to see, over in the left corner, almost hidden by the host of placards and banners, a fellow slyly holding up a sign that reads "Save the Red Herring!" Now, who says rhetoricians don't have a good sense of humor?)

Post hoc, ergo propter hoc: See page 249.

Argument *ad hominem* ("to the man"): The writer attacks the opponent's character rather than the opponent's argument. The statement "Dr. Bloom can't be a competent marriage counselor because she's been divorced twice" may not be valid. Bloom's advice to her clients may be excellent regardless of her own marital status.

Faulty use of authority: See pages 267–268 and pages 329–330.

Argument *ad populum* ("to the people"): The writer evades the issues by appealing to readers' emotional reactions to certain subjects. For example, instead of arguing the facts of an issue, a writer might play on the readers' negative response to such words as "communism," "fascism," or "radical" and their positive response to words like "God," "country," or "liberty." In the statement "If you are a true American, you will vote against the referendum on busing," the writer avoids any discussion of the merits or weaknesses of the bill and merely substitutes an emotional appeal. (Advertisers, of course, play on consumers' emotions by filling their ads with pictures of babies, animals, status objects, and sexually attractive men and women.)

Circular thinking: See page 249.

Either/or: The writer tries to convince the readers that there are only two sides to an issue—one right, one wrong. The statement "If you don't go to war against Iceland, you don't love your country" is irrational because it doesn't consider the other possibilities, such as patriotic people's right to oppose war as an expression of love for their country. A classic example of this sort of oversimplification was illustrated in the 1960s' bumper sticker that was popular during the debate over the Vietnam War: "America: Love It or Leave It." Obviously, there are other choices ("Change It or Lose It," for instance, to quote another either/or bumper sticker).

Hypostatization: The writer uses an abstract concept as if it were a concrete reality. Always be suspicious of a writer who frequently uses statements beginning "History has taught us . . . " or "Science has proven . . . " or "Research has discovered. . . ." The implication in each case is that history or science (or any other discipline) has only one voice, one opinion. On the contrary, "history" is written by a multitude of historians who hold a variety of opinions; doctors and scientists also frequently disagree. Instead of generalizing about a particular field, quote a respected authority or simply qualify your statement by referring to "many" or "some" scientists, historians, or other professionals.

Bandwagon appeal: The writer tries to validate a point by intimating that "everyone else believes in this." Such a tactic evades discussion of the issue itself. Advertising often uses this technique: "Everyone who demands real taste smokes Phooey cigarettes"; "Discriminating women use Smacky-Mouth lipstick." (The ultimate in "bandwagon" humor may have appeared on a recent Colorado bumper sticker: "Eat lamb—could 1000s of coyotes be wrong?")

Straw man: The writer selects the opposition's weakest or most insignificant point to argue against, to divert the readers' attention from the real issues. Instead of addressing the opposition's best arguments and defeating them, the writer "sets up a straw man"—that is, the writer picks out a trivial (or irrelevant) argument against his or her own position and easily knocks it down, just as one might easily push over a figure made of straw. Perhaps the most famous example of the "straw man" occurred in 1952 when, during his vice-presidential campaign, Richard Nixon was accused of misappropriating campaign funds for his personal use. Addressing the nation on television, Nixon described how his six-year-old daughter, Tricia, had received a little cocker spaniel named Checkers from a Texas supporter. Nixon went on about how much his children loved the dog and how, regardless of what anyone thought, by gosh, he was going to keep that cute dog for little Tricia. Of course, no one was asking Nixon to return the dog; they were asking about the $18,000 in missing campaign funds. But Nixon's canine gift was much easier for him to defend, and the "Checkers'" speech is now famous as one of the most notorious "straw man" diversions.

Faulty analogy: The writer uses an extended comparison as proof of a point. Look closely at all extended comparisons and metaphors to see if the two things being compared are really similar. For example, in a recent editorial a woman protested the new laws requiring parents to use car seats for small children, arguing that if the state could require the seats they could just as easily require mothers to breastfeed instead of using formula. Are the two situations alike? Car accidents are the leading cause of death of children under four; is formula dangerous? Or perhaps you've read that putting teenagers in sex education classes is like taking an alcoholic to a bar. Is it? If the opinion isn't supported by evidence, the analogy may not be persuasive. Moreover, remember that even though a compelling analogy might suggest similarities, it alone cannot *prove* anything.

Quick fix: The writer leans too heavily on catchy phrases or empty slogans. A clever turn-of-phrase may grab one's attention, but it may lose its persuasiveness when scrutinized closely. For instance, a banner at a recent rally to protest a piece of antigun legislation read, "When guns are outlawed, only outlaws will have guns." Although the sentence had nice balance, it over-simplified the issue. The legislation in question was not trying to outlaw all guns, just the sale of the infamous Saturday Night Specials, most often used in crimes and domestic violence; the sale of guns for sport, such as hunting rifles, would remain legal. Other slogans sound good but are simply irrele-vant: a particular soft drink, for example, may be "the real thing," but what drink isn't? Look closely at clever lines substituted for reasoned argument; always demand clear terms and logical explanations.*

▶ PRACTICING WHAT YOU'VE LEARNED

Errors in reasoning can cause your reader to doubt your credibility. In the following mock essay, for example, the writer includes a variety of fallacies that undermine his argument; see if you can identify all his errors.

Ban Those Books!

A serious problem faces America today, a problem of such grave importance that our very existence as a nation is threatened. We must either cleanse our schools of evil-minded books, or we must reconcile ourselves to seeing our children become welfare moochers and homeless bums.

History has shown time and time again that place-ment of immoral books in our schools is part of an insidi-ous plot designed to weaken the moral fiber of our youth from coast to coast. In Wettuckett, Ohio, for example, the year after books by Mark Twain such as *Tom Sawyer* and *Huckleberry Finn* were introduced into the school li-brary by liberal free-thinkers and radicals, the number of

---

* Sometimes advertisers get more for their slogans than they bargained for. According to one news source, a popular soft-drink company had to spend millions to revise its slogan after introducing its product into parts of China. Apparently the slogan "Come alive! Join the Blah-Blah-Cola Generation!" translated into some dialects as "Blah-Blah Cola Brings Your Ancestors Back from the Dead"!

students cutting classes rose by six percent. And in that same year the number of high school seniors going on to college dropped from thirty to twenty-two.

The reason for this could either be a natural decline in intelligence and morals or the influence of those dirty books that teach our beloved children disrespect and irresponsibility. Since there is no evidence to suggest a natural decline, the conclusion is inescapable: once our children read about Twain's characters skipping school and running away from home, they had to do likewise. If they hadn't read about such undesirable characters as Huckleberry Finn, our innocent children would never have behaved in those ways.

Now, I am a simple man, a plain old farm boy—the pseudo-intellectuals call me redneck just like they call you folks. But I can assure you that, redneck or not, I've got the guts to fight moral decay everywhere I find it, and I urge you to do the same. For this reason I want all you good folks to come to the ban-the-books rally this Friday so we can talk it over. I promise you all your right-thinking neighbors will be there.

◢ ASSIGNMENT

Search for the following:

1. Two examples of advertisements that illustrate one or more of the fallacies or appeals discussed on pages 269–272

2. One example of illogical or fallacious reasoning in a piece of writing (you might try looking at the editorial page or letters-to-the-editor section of your local or campus newspaper)

3. One example of a logical, persuasive point in a piece of writing

Be prepared to explain your analyses of your samples, but do not write any sort of identifying label or evaluation on the samples themselves. Bring your ads and pieces of writing to class and exchange them with those of a classmate. After ten minutes, compare notes. Do you and your classmate agree on the evaluation of each sample? Why or why not?

◢ ESSAY TOPICS

Write a convincing argument attacking or defending one of the following statements. Narrow and focus the topic as necessary. (Note that essays on some of the topics presented below would profit from library research material; see Chapter 12 for help.)

1. The music industry should/should not be required to label rock 'n roll lyrics as "X," "R," "PG," and so on, as the movies do.

2. To prepare students for a highly technical world, high schools should/should not extend their academic year.

3. Bilingual education in this country is beneficial/harmful.

4. Mandatory on-the-job drug tests should/should not be allowed.

5. Television advertising does/does not control the election of our presidents.

6. The advertising of alcohol should/should not be limited to the print media, as are cigarette ads.

7. Students who do poorly in their academic courses should/should not be allowed to participate in athletic programs.

8. Throwaway bottles and cans should/should not be outlawed.

9. Televised instant replays should/should not be used to call plays in football and other sports.

10. The foreign language requirement (or some other rule or requirement) at this college should/should not be abolished.

11. Washington, D.C., should/should not gain statehood.

12. Standardized high school/college competency tests in math and English should/should not be adopted across the country.

13. Students should/should not serve in a youth corps for two years following high school.

14. Organ donors should/should not be allowed to receive financial compensation.

15. Student evaluations should/should not be a major consideration in the rehiring or promotion of a teacher.

16. The Ku Klux Klan (or any controversial organization) should/should not be allowed to speak on campus.

17. The media should/should not release the names of rape victims without permission.

18. Vitamin C (or herbal healing or any kind of nontraditional treatment) can/cannot help relieve illness.

19. In the event of a compulsory military draft, men and women should/should not be equally liable.

20. Controversial names or symbols of athletic teams ("Redskins," the Confederate flag) should/should not be changed.

A Topic Proposal for Your Essay

Selecting the right subject matter is important to every writer. To help you clarify your ideas and strengthen your commitment to your topic, here is a proposal sheet that asks you to describe some of your preliminary ideas about your subject before you begin drafting. Although as you draft your ideas may change (they will almost certainly become more refined), thinking through your choice of topic now may help you avoid several false starts.

1. What is the subject of your argumentative essay? Is it controversial? Debatable? Write a rough statement of your opinion about this subject.

2. Why are you interested in this topic? Is it important to your personal, civic, or professional life? State at least one reason for your choice of topic.

3. Is this a significant topic of interest to others? Why? Is there a particular audience you would like to address?

4. At this point can you list at least two reasons that support your opinion of your topic?

5. Who opposes your opinion? Can you state clearly at least one of your opposition's major criticisms of your position?

6. What difficulties, if any, might arise during drafting? For example, might you need to collect any additional evidence through reading, research, or interviewing to support your points or to refute your opposition?

SAMPLE STUDENT ESSAY

The student who wrote the essay below followed the steps for writing an argumentative paper discussed in this chapter. His intended audience were the readers of his school newspaper, primarily fellow students but instructors as well. To argue his case, he chose Pattern A, presenting two of his own points and then concluding with a rebuttal of an important opposing view. Notice that this writer uses a variety of methods to convince his readers, including hypothetical examples, causal analysis, analogy, and testimony. Does the writer persuade you to his point of view? Which are his strongest and weakest arguments? What might you change to make his essay even more persuasive?

Students, Take Note!

Introduction: Presenting the controversy

A walk across campus this week will reveal students, professors, and administrators arguing about class notes like never before. But they're not engaged in intellectual debates over chemical formulas or literary images. No, they're fighting over the taking of the notes themselves, as professional note-taking services in town are applying for permission to sit in on courses and then sell their notes to the students in those classes. Although the prospect of having "canned" notes looks inviting to many students, our administration should nevertheless ban these services from campus. Not only do such businesses give certain students unfair advantages and discourage class attendance, but they also prohibit the development of students' important learning skills, despite the services' claims to the contrary.

Thesis

Essay map

A point for the writer's position: Note-taking services are unfair to some students

What is bothered for many of us about the professional-notes option is our sense of fair play. Let's face it: like it or not, school is, among other things, a place of competition, as students vie for the best academic records to send to prospective employers, graduate and professional schools, and in some cases, paying parents. In today's classes all students have an equal opportunity to come to class, take notes, study, and pass or fail on their own merits. But the expensive professional notes, already organized and outlined, may give those with plenty of money some advantages that poorer students—those on scholarships or with families, for example—just can't afford. In addition, the notes may be available only to those students who take certain sections of a course and not others, thus giving some students an extra option. The same is true for students who satisfy a requirement by taking one course that has notes available rather than another which has not. Knowing that you're doing your own work may make you feel morally superior to a classmate who isn't, but frankly, on some other level, it just plain feels irritating and unfair, sort of like watching your roommate getting away with plagiarizing his paper for a class after you spent weeks researching yours.

Another point for the writer's position: Professional notes discourage students from attending and participating in class

In addition to being a potential source of conflict among students, the professional-note services aren't winning many friends among the faculty either. Several instructors have complained that the availability of notes will encourage many students, especially the weaker ones, to cut classes, assuming that they have all the material necessary for understanding the lecture, discussion, or lab. But anyone who has ever had to use borrowed notes knows something vital is not there. Someone else's interpretations of the information is often hard or impossible to follow, especially if you must understand complex relationships and problems. Moreover, skipping class may mean missed opportunities for students to ask questions or to participate in experiments or in group discussions, all of which often help clarify concepts under study. Not seeing visual aids or diagrams in person can also result in problems understanding the material. And, last, missing class can mean failure to become comfortably acquainted with the teacher, which, in turn, may discourage a student from asking for individual help when it's needed. All these possibilities are real; even Jeff Allridge, owner of the Quotable Notes service, has admitted to a campus reporter, "There *is* an incentive to skip class."

Despite the admission that professional note-taking encourages class-cutting, the services still promote themselves by claiming that students using their notes learn more. They support this claim by arguing that their notes offer students clearly organized information and, according to one advertising brochure, "good models" for students to follow in other classes. But such arguments miss the larger point: students should be learning how to develop their own note-taking, organizing, and thinking skills rather than swallowing the material whole as neatly packaged and delivered. Memorizing class material as outlined can be important, but it's not really as valuable in the long run as learning how to think about the material and use it to solve problems or come up with new ideas later. Taking your own notes teaches you how to listen and how to spot the important concepts; organizing your own notes teaches you how to pull ideas together in a logical way, all skills students will need in other classes, on jobs, and in life in general. Having memorized the outlines but not really mastered the thinking skills won't help the medical student whose patient's symptoms vary from the textbook description or the engineer whose airplane wings suddenly fail the stress test for no apparent reason.

By appealing to students who believe professional notes will help them accomplish their educational goals easier and quicker, a variety of note-taking services now have franchises across the country. But our campus

[margin note:] Presentation and rebuttal of the opposition's claim that students learn more using professional notes

[margin note:] Conclusion: Restatement of thesis, ending on pun to emphasize the main idea

shouldn't allow them to move in. Students need to recognize that the difference between the services' definition of "learning" and the real learning experiences college can provide is of notable importance.

PROFESSIONAL ESSAYS

The following professional essays present conflicting views on laws requiring motorcyclists to wear helmets. As you read these brief essays, notice how these writers try to support their own points and how they address the opposing position. Which essay do you find the more persuasive? Why? What arguments could you add to either side to make the essays stronger?

Motorcycle Helmet Laws Protect Everyone

This essay, written by the editorial board of USA Today, *appeared in that newspaper on January 3, 1992, as part of a debate on helmet laws.*

1   The motorcycle helmet controversy is on the road again in California.

2   It revved up Wednesday when a new law ordered all motorcyclists—youth and adults—to wear helmets. Outraged cyclists scrambled to revive the national debate on this travel-weary topic. But they haven't realized—or won't acknowledge—that the dialogue shifted long ago from personal freedom to public responsibility.

3   Wayne Thomas of the California Motorcyclist Association argues against helmet laws by citing lower accident and death rates in the three states without such laws—Colorado, Illinois and Iowa. He says those rates indicate that helmets reduce cyclists' caution and actually restrict their driving ability.

4   More persuasive arguments appear on the other side of the debate.

5   Of 474 motorcycle-accident victims during almost four years in Orange County, Calif., only six of the 20 who died wore helmets—just one from a head injury. The 238 wearing helmets had no serious neck injuries, had fewer and less-serious head injuries, spent less time on respirators and suffered less permanent physical and mental damage. And their hospital bills averaged $16,000, compared to $30,000 for those who crashed without helmets.

6   When cyclists who don't wear helmets run up hospital bills almost twice as costly as those of riders with helmets, everyone's insurance costs go up. That—not death rates—may have been the most telling consideration for the 22 states that make minors wear helmets and the 24, plus the District of Columbia, that mandate them for all riders.

7   Add other factors—disability and unemployment payments, rehabilitation costs—and states with helmet laws have 43% lower societal costs from motorcycle accidents, says California Assemblyman Richard

Floyd's office. That takes the issue far beyond whether motorcyclists should be protected from themselves.

8   With soaring costs driving even basic health care beyond many families' reach, it's time for cyclists to give this road show rerun a rest.

Motorcycle Helmet Laws Mock Freedom
Paul Lax

Paul Lax practices law in Los Angeles. He is also the state director of Abate of California, a group that works against the passage of motorcycle helmet laws. This essay appeared in the editorial section of USA Today *on January 3, 1992, in opposition to the position argued in the preceding essay.*

1   Last March, I was in Sacramento lobbying against the proposed California helmet law. A large yellow bow was tied around the Capitol dome and Gov. Pete Wilson made a speech about the debt we all owed to those fighting against Iraq for the cause of freedom. Freedom. The word trips effortlessly from the lips of politicians, but lip service is all it got in California.

2   What's wrong with helmet laws? One, they don't work. Two, they destroy individual freedom.

3   In California, we put evidence of the ineffectiveness of helmet laws before the legislature. Fatality rates in states that require everyone to wear helmets are higher, per 100 accidents, than in free states. Helmet laws are a placebo.

4   The second reason should worry everyone, even if you never go near a motorcycle. The helmet law was passed on the claim that freedom was costing the state money. Proponents blamed unhelmeted riders for avoidable medical costs. The numbers used to pass the law were false, it's now been acknowledged.

5   But even if they had been correct, what sort of precedent does this establish? Whether I wear a helmet or not, who is affected? Obviously, only me. To the best of my knowledge, no one is yet claiming that a head injury can result from being near a person who isn't wearing a helmet.

6   If cost is the prime factor, then there is no activity the state cannot regulate. The reasoning used to pass this law could be used to outlaw smoking or require us all to eat a good breakfast.

7   Is liberty still an inalienable right, or can you yell "costs" at our legislators and have them trample freedom like so many frightened sheep? If so, one of your most cherished freedoms may be next.

Questions on Content, Structure, and Style

1. State the problem these two essays address. Does their debate convince you that this problem deserves serious attention?

2. Identify the thesis of each essay. Is each one clearly presented?

3. Describe the general pattern of organization of the essay supporting helmet laws. Is it an effective choice? Why or why not?

4. Describe the general pattern of organization of John Lax's essay. How does it differ from the essay written by the *USA Today* editorial board in favor of helmet laws? Does one pattern of organization seem more effective than the other? Why or why not?

5. Which is the strongest argument in the pro-helmet editorial? How is this point supported? Which is the weakest point in this essay? Why?

6. Which is Lax's strongest point? Weakest? Why?

7. Do these writers address their opposition's arguments? Which essay is more successful in refuting the opposition? Why?

8. Are there valid points in favor of either position that are not presented? How might either position be strengthened?

9. Consider the tone and choice of language in each of these essays. What, for example, is the effect of Lax's references to "freedom" and "liberty"? To "frightened sheep"?

10. Do you find any logical fallacies in either essay? Overall, which essay do you find more persuasive? Why?

Vocabulary

dialogue (*USA TODAY*, 2)	placebo (Lax, 3)
mandate (*USA TODAY*, 6)	precedent (Lax, 5)
rehabilitation (*USA TODAY*, 7)	inalienable (Lax, 7)

PRO/CON ADVERTISING: "I'M THE NRA" AND "A $29 HANDGUN SHATTERED MY FAMILY'S LIFE"

The National Rifle Association has published a series of advertisements to tell people about the organization. According to the NRA, one of their purposes is to protect Second Amendment rights. However, after the attempted assassination of President Ronald Reagan and the shooting of his Press Secretary James Brady, an organization called Handgun Control, Inc., supported by Sarah Brady, countered with ads of its own. Study the two ads on the following pages to determine what appeals they use to persuade readers to their side. Which appeals do you find the more persuasive and why?

REP. ALBERTO GUTMAN: Florida Legislator, Businessman, Husband, Member of the National Rifle Association.

"Being from a country that was once a democracy and turned communist, I really feel I know what the right to bear arms is all about. In Cuba, where I was born, the first thing the communist government did was take away everybody's firearms, leaving them defenseless and intimidated with fear. That's why our constitutional right to bear arms is so important to our country's survival.

"As a legislator I have to deal with reality. And the reality is that gun control does not work. It actually eliminates the rights of the law-abiding citizen, not the criminal. Criminals will always have guns, and they won't follow gun control laws anyway. I would like to see tougher laws on criminals as opposed to tougher laws on legitimate gun owners. We need to attack the problem of crime at its roots, instead of blaming crime on gun ownership and citizens who use them lawfully.

"It's a big responsibility that we face retaining the right to bear arms. That's why I joined the NRA. The NRA is instrumental in protecting these freedoms. It helps train and educate people, supporting legislation that benefits not only those who bear arms but all citizens of the United States. The NRA helps keep America free." **I'm the NRA.**

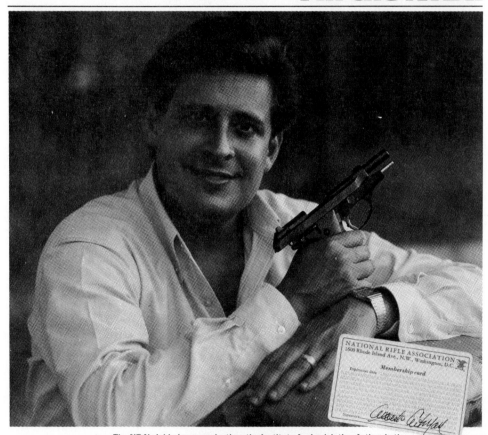

The NRA's lobbying organization, the Institute for Legislative Action, is the nation's largest and most influential protector of the constitutional right to keep and bear arms. At every level of government and through local grassroots efforts, the Institute guards against infringement upon the freedoms of law-abiding gun owners. If you would like to join the NRA or want more information about our programs and benefits, write J. Warren Cassidy, Executive Vice President, P.O. Box 37484, Dept. AG-15, Washington, D.C. 20013.

Paid for by the members of the National Rifle Association of America. Copyright 1986.

Reprinted with permission of the National Rifle Association.

Reprinted with permission of Handgun Control, Inc.

TWO ADVERTISEMENTS IN A SERIES: "NUCLEAR ENERGY MEANS CLEANER AIR"

The advertisements on pages 284 and 285 were part of a series published by the U.S. Council for Energy Awareness to promote nuclear energy and the building of more nuclear energy plants. Study the appeals of both ads. Although the purpose of the ads is the same and some of the text is similar, how do these ads differ in argumentative techniques? Do they appeal to the same or different audiences? Which techniques are the most and least successful? Do you find one ad more persuasive than the other? Why?

If you were hired to draft an advertisement that argues against nuclear energy in our country, what would your ad say? What photograph or drawing would you select to accompany your argument? Why?

◤ A REVISION WORKSHEET

As you write your rough drafts, consult Chapter 5 for guidance through the revision process. In addition, here are a few questions to ask yourself as you revise your argumentative essay:

1. Does this essay present a clear thesis limited to fit the assigned length of this paper?

2. Does this essay contain a number of strong, persuasive points in support of its thesis?

3. Is the essay organized in an easy-to-follow pattern that avoids repetition or confusion?

4. Does the essay present enough supporting evidence to make each of its points convincing? Where could additional examples, factual information, testimony, or other kinds of supporting material be added to make the arguments even more effective?

5. Will all the supporting evidence be clear to the essay's particular audience? Do any terms or examples need additional explanation or special definition?

6. Have the major opposing arguments been refuted?

7. Does the essay avoid any logical fallacies or problems in tone?

After you've revised your essay extensively, you might exchange rough drafts with a classmate and answer these questions for each other, making specific suggestions for improvement wherever appropriate. (For advice on productive participation in classroom workshops, see pp. 114–117.)

SOME ARGUMENTS FOR NUCLEAR ENERGY ARE SMALLER THAN OTHERS.

Around the nuclear electric plant on Florida's Hutchinson Island, endangered wildlife have a safe haven. The baby sea turtles hatching on nearby beaches are more evidence of the truth about nuclear energy: it peacefully coexists with the environment.

America's 110 operating nuclear plants don't pollute the air, because they don't burn anything to generate electricity. Nor do they eat up valuable natural resources such as oil and natural gas.

Still, more plants are needed—to help satisfy the nation's growing need for electricity without sacrificing the quality of our environment. For a free booklet on nuclear energy, write to the U.S. Council for Energy Awareness, P.O. Box 66080, Dept. TR01, Washington, D.C. 20035.

NUCLEAR ENERGY MEANS CLEANER AIR.

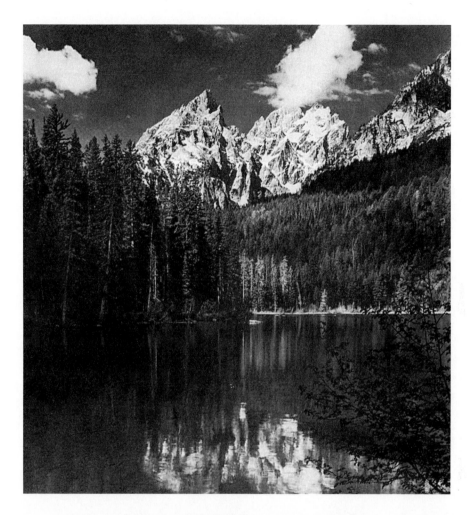

To confirm the benefits of nuclear energy, we got an outside opinion.

In the words of the President's National Energy Strategy, "Nuclear power is a proven electricity-generating technology that emits no sulfur dioxide, nitrogen oxides, or greenhouse gases."

In fact, nuclear energy helps *reduce* air-borne pollutants in the U.S. by over 19,000 tons every day. That's because the 111 nuclear plants now operating in this country don't burn anything to generate electricity.

The air we breathe is cleaner because of nuclear energy. But we need more nuclear plants. Because the more plants we have, the more energy we'll have for the future of our planet.

For more information, write to the U.S. Council for Energy Awareness, P.O. Box 66080, Dept. BE02, Washington, D.C. 20035.

Nuclear energy means cleaner air.

This advertisement is provided courtesy of the United States Council for Energy Awareness, Washington, D.C.

Reviewing Your Progress

After you have completed your argument essay, take a moment to measure your progress as a writer by responding to the following questions. Such analysis will help you recognize growth in your writing skills and may enable you to identify areas that are still problematic.

1. Which part of your essay do you like best? Why?

2. After analyzing your essay's reasoning and evidence, which particular argument or point do you consider the strongest? What makes it so convincing?

3. What part of your essay gave you the most trouble? How did you overcome the problem?

4. If you had more time to work on this essay, what would receive additional attention? Why?

5. What did you learn about your topic from writing this essay? About yourself as a writer?

10

DESCRIPTION

•
•
•

The writer of description creates a word-picture of persons, places, objects, and emotions, using a careful selection of details to make an impression on the reader. If you have already written expository or argumentative essays in your composition course, you almost certainly have written some descriptive prose. Nearly every essay, after all, calls for some kind of description; for example, in the student comparison/contrast essay (pp. 214–217), the writer describes two kinds of stores; in the professional process essay (pp. 201–206), the writer describes the embalming procedure in great detail. To help you write better description in your other essays, however, you may want to practice writing descriptive paragraphs or a short descriptive essay.

HOW TO WRITE EFFECTIVE DESCRIPTION

Regardless of the kind of description you are writing, you should follow the four basic suggestions that follow:

Recognize your purpose. Description is not free-floating; it appears in your writing for a particular reason—to help you explain, persuade, or create a mood. In some essays you will want your description as *objective* as you can make it; for example, you might describe a scientific experiment or a business transaction in straight factual detail. Most of the time, however, you will want to convey a particular attitude toward your subject; this approach to description is called *subjective* or *impressionistic*. Note the differences between the following two descriptions of a tall, thin boy: the objective writer sticks to the facts by saying, "The eighteen-year-old boy was 6′1″ and weighed 125 pounds," whereas the subjective writer gives an impressionistic description, "The young boy was as tall and scrawny as a birch tree in winter." Before you begin describing anything, you must first decide your purpose and then whether it calls for objective or subjective reporting.

Describe clearly, using specific details. To make any description clear to your reader, you must include a sufficient number of details that are specific rather than fuzzy or vague. If, for example, your family dog had become lost, you wouldn't call the animal shelter and ask if they'd seen a "big brown dog with a short tail"—naturally, you'd mention every distinguishing detail about your pet you could think of: size, color, breed, cut of ears, and special markings. Similarly, if your car was stolen, you'd give the police as clear and as complete a description of your vehicle as possible.

Look at the two paragraphs below. Which more fully tells what a vaulting horse is?

> A vaulting horse is a thing usually found in gyms that has four legs and a beam and is used by gymnasts making jumps.

If you didn't already know what a vaulting horse was, you might have trouble picking it out in a gymnasium crowded with equipment. A description with additional details would help you locate it:

> A vaulting horse is a piece of equipment used by gymnasts during competition to help propel them into the air when they perform any of a variety of leaps known as vaults. The gymnasts usually approach the vaulting horse from a running start and then place their hands on the horse for support or for a push off as they perform their vaults. The horse itself resembles a carpenter's sawhorse, but the main beam is made of padded leather rather than wood. The rectangular beam is approximately 5 feet, 3 inches long and 13½ inches wide. Supported by four legs usually made of steel, the padded leather beam is approximately 4 feet, ½ inch above the floor in men's competitions and 3 feet, 7 inches in women's competitions. The padded leather beam has two white lines marking off three sections on top: the croup, the saddle, and the neck. The two end sections—the croup and the neck—are each 15½ inches long. Gymnasts place their hands on the neck or croup, depending on the type of vault they are attempting.

Moreover, the reader cannot imagine your subject clearly if your description is couched in vague generalities. The following sentence, for example, presents only a hazy picture:

Larry is so overweight that his clothes don't fit him right.

Revised, the picture is now sharply in focus:

Larry is so fat that his shirt constantly bulges over his belt, his trousers will not stay snapped, and his countless chins spill over his collar like dough rising out of a too-small pan.

Specific details can turn cloudy prose into crisp, clear images that can be reproduced in the mind like photographs.

Select only appropriate details. In any description the choice of details depends largely on the writer's purpose and audience. However, many descriptions—especially the more subjective ones—will present a *dominant impression;* that is, the writer selects only those details that communicate a particular mood or feeling to the reader. The dominant impression is the controlling focus of a description; for example, if you wrote a description of your grandmother to show her thoughtfulness, you would select only those details that convey an impression of a sweet, kindly old lady. Below are two brief descriptions illustrating the concept of dominant impression. The first writer tries to create a mood of mystery:

Down a black winding road stands the abandoned old mansion, silhouetted against the cloud-shrouded moon, creaking and moaning in the wet chill wind.

The second writer tries to present a feeling of joy and innocence.

A dozen kites filled the spring air, and around the bright picnic tables spread with hot dogs, hamburgers, and slices of watermelon, Tom and Annie played away the warm April day.

In the description of the deserted mansion, the writer would have violated the impression of mystery had the sentence read,

Down the black winding road stands the abandoned old mansion, surrounded by bright, multicolored tulips in early bloom.

Including the cheerful flowers as a detail in the description destroys the dominant mood of bleakness and mystery. Similarly, the second example would be spoiled had the writer ended it this way:

Tom and Annie played away the warm April day until Tom got so sunburned he became ill and had to go home.

Therefore, remember to select only those details that advance your descriptive purpose. Omit any details you consider unimportant or distracting.

See if you can determine the dominant impression of each description below:

The wind had curled up to sleep in the distant mountains. Leaves hung limp and motionless from the silent trees, while birds perched on the branches like little statues. As I sat on the edge of the clearing, holding my breath, I could hear a squirrel scampering through the underbrush. Somewhere far away a dog barked twice, and then the woods were hushed once more.

This poor thing has seen better days, but one should expect the sofa in a fraternity house den to be well worn. The large, plump, brown corduroy pillows strewn lazily on the floor and propped comfortably against the threadbare arms bear the pencil-point scars of frustrated students and foam-bleeding cuts of multiple pillow wars. No less than four pairs of rotting Nikes stand twenty-four-hour guard at the corners of its carefully mended frame. Obviously the relaxed, inviting appearance masks the permanent odors of cheap cigars and Michelob from Thursday night poker parties; at least two or three guests each weekend sift through the popcorn kernels and Doritos crumbs, sprawl face down, and pass out for the duration. However, frequent inhabitants have learned to avoid the dark stains courtesy of the house pup and the red-punch designs of the chapter klutz. Habitually, they strategically lunge over the back of the sofa to an unsoiled area easily identifiable in flight by the large depression left by previous regulars. The quiet *hmmph* of the cushions and harmonious squeal of the exhausted springs signal a perfect landing and utter a warm greeting from an old and faithful friend.

Make your descriptions vivid. By using clear, precise words, you can improve any kind of writing. Chapters 7 (on words) and 6 (on sentences) offer a variety of tips on clarifying your prose style. In addition to the advice given there, here are two other ways to enliven your descriptions, particularly those that call for a subjective approach:

Use sensory details. If it's appropriate, try using images that appeal to your readers' five senses. If, for example, you are describing your broken leg and the ensuing stay in a hospital, tell your readers how the place smelled, how it looked, what your cast felt like, how your pills tasted, and what noises you heard. Below are some specific examples using sensory details:

Sight   The clean white corridors of the hospital resembled the set of a sci-fi movie, with everyone scurrying around in identical starched uniforms.

Hearing   At night, the only sounds I heard were the quiet squeakings of sensible white shoes as the nurses made their rounds.

Smell   The green beans on the hospital cafeteria tray smelled stale and waxy, like crayons.

Touch   The hospital bed sheet felt as rough and heavy as a feed sack.

Taste   Every four hours they gave me an enormous gray pill whose after-taste reminded me of the castor oil my grandmother insisted on giving me when I was a kid.

By appealing to the readers' senses, you better enable them to identify with and imagine the subject you are describing. Joseph Conrad, the famous nineteenth-century novelist, agreed, believing that all art "appeals primarily to the senses, and the artistic aim when expressing itself in written words must also make its appeal through the senses, if its highest desire is to reach the secret spring of responsive emotions." In other words, to make your readers feel, first make them "see."

Use figurative language when appropriate. As you may recall from Chapter 7, figurative language produces images or pictures in the readers' minds, helping them to understand unfamiliar or abstract subjects. Here are some devices you might use to clarify or spice up your prose:

1. Simile: a comparison between two things using the words "like" or "as" (see also pp. 169–171)

Example   Seeing exactly the shirt he wanted, he moved as quickly as a starving teenager finding a piece of favorite pie in a refrigerator full of leftover vegetables.

2. Metaphor: a direct comparison between two things that does not use "like" or "as" (see also pp. 169–171)

Example   After the holidays her body resembled the "before" shots in every diet ad she'd ever seen.

3. Personification: the attribution of human characteristics and emotions to inanimate objects, animals, or abstract ideas

Example   The old stuffed teddy bear sat in a corner, dozing before the fireplace.

4. Hyperbole: intentional exaggeration or overstatement

Example   "Bring me a steak that's still mooing," roared the cowboy.

5. Understatement: intentional representation of a subject as less important than the facts would warrant (see also irony, p. 157)

Example "The reports of my death are greatly exaggerated."—Mark Twain

6. Synecdoche: a part of something used to represent the whole

Example   A hundred tired feet hit the dance floor for one last jitterbug. [Here "feet" stand for the dancing couples themselves.]

Using figures of speech in appropriate places can make your descriptions clear, lively, and memorable.

Problems to Avoid

Keep in mind these three pieces of advice to solve problems that frequently arise in description.

Remember your audience. Sometimes the object of our description is so clear in our minds we forget that our readers haven't seen it too. Consequently, the description we write turns out to be vague, bland, or skimpy. Ask yourself about your audience: what do they need to know to see this sight as clearly as I do? Then fill in your description with ample, precise details that reveal the best picture possible. Don't forget to define or explain any terms you use that may be puzzling to your audience.

Avoid an erratic organization of details. Too often descriptions are a hodgepodge of details, jotted down randomly. When you write a lengthy description, you should select a plan that will arrange your details in an orderly fashion. Depending on your subject matter and your purpose, you might adopt a plan calling for a description of something from top to bottom, left to right, front to back, and so on. For example, a description of a woman might begin at the head and move to the feet; furniture in a room might be described as your eyes move from one side of the room to another. A second plan for arranging details presents the subject's outstanding characteristics first and then fills in the lesser information; a child's red hair, for example, might be his most striking feature and therefore would be described first. A third plan presents details in the order you see them approaching: dust, then a car, then details about the car, its occupants, and so on. Or you might describe a subject as it unfolds chronologically, as in some kind of a process or operation. Regardless of which plan of organization you choose, the reader should feel a sense of order in your description.

Avoid any sudden change in perspective. If, for example, you are describing the White House from the outside, don't suddenly include details that could be seen only from inside. Similarly, if you are describing a car from a distance, you might be able to tell the car's model, year, and color, but you could hardly describe the upholstery or reveal the mileage. It is, of course, possible for you—or your observer—to approach or move around the subject of your description, but the reader must be aware of this movement. Any shift in point of view must be presented clearly and logically, with no sudden, confusing leaps from a front to a back view, from outside to inside, and so on.

ESSAY TOPICS

Here are some suggestions for a descriptive essay or paragraph; narrow your topic to fit your assignment. Don't forget that every description, whether objective or subjective, has a purpose and that every detail should support that purpose.

1. a campus character

2. a childhood photograph of yourself or a picture of an ancestor

3. a piece of equipment important to your major or to a hobby or favorite sport

4. a building or place you're fond of

5. one dish or foodstuff that should be forever banned

6. a family member or family pet

7. your most valuable material possession

8. the ugliest/most beautiful building on your campus or in town

9. a typical family dinner or ritual in your home

10. your first or worst car (or your dream car)

11. a place where you've worked, lived, or visited

12. a strange-but-wonderful friend or relative

13. an act of heroism or personal success

14. a favorite painting, sculpture, photograph, or art object

15. your most unforgettable character

16. an event in nature

17. a doctor's waiting room or some other crowded public place

18. a historical figure or event that holds importance for you

19. a special time in your life (birthday, holiday, graduation, etc.)

20. the inside of your refrigerator or closet or some other equally loathsome place in your home

A Topic Proposal for Your Essay

Selecting the right subject matter is important to every writer. To help you clarify your ideas and strengthen your commitment to your topic, here is a proposal sheet that asks you to describe some of your preliminary ideas about your subject before you begin drafting. Although as you draft your ideas may change (they will almost certainly become more refined), thinking through your choice of topic now may help you avoid several false starts.

1. What subject will your essay describe? Will you describe this subject objectively or subjectively? Why?

2. Why are you interested in this topic? Do you have a personal or professional connection to the subject? State at least one reason for your choice of topic.

3. Is this a significant topic of interest to others? Why? Who specifically might find it interesting, informative, or entertaining?

4. In one or two sentences describe the major effect you'd like your descriptive essay to have on your readers. What would you like for them to understand or "see" about your subject?

5. List at least three details that you think will help clarify your subject for your readers.

6. What difficulties, if any, might arise during drafting? For example, what organizational strategy might you think about now that would allow you to guide your readers through your description in a coherent way?

SAMPLE STUDENT ESSAY

In her descriptive essay, this student writer recalls her childhood days at the home of her grandparents to make a point about growing up. Notice that the writer uses both figurative language and contrasting images to help her readers understand her point of view.

Treeclimbing

Introduction: The conversation that triggers her memory

It was Mike's eighteenth birthday and he was having a little bit of a breakdown. "When was the last time you made cloud pictures?" he asked me absently as he stared up at the ceiling before class started. Before I could answer, he continued, "Did you know that by the time you're an adult, you've lost 85 percent of your imagination?" He paused. "I don't want to grow up." Although I doubted the authenticity of his facts, I understood that Mike—the hopeless romantic with his long ponytail, sullen black clothes, and glinting dark eyes—was caught in a Peter Pan complex. He drew those eyes from the ceiling and focused on me. "There are two types of children. Tree children and dirt children. Kids playing will either climb trees or play in the dirt. Tree children are the dreamers—the hopeful, creative dreamers. Dirt children, they just stay on the ground. Stick to the rules," he trailed off, and then picked up again. "I'm a tree child. I want to make cloud pictures and climb trees. And I don't ever want to come down." Mike's story reminded me of my own days as a tree child, and of the inevitable fall from the tree to the ground.

My childhood was a playground for imagination. Summers were spent surrounded by family at my grandparents' house in Milwaukee, Wisconsin. The rambling Lannonstone bungalow was located on North 46th Street at Burleigh, a block away from center-city Milwaukee, two blocks from Schuster's department store and the Pfister hotel. In the winter, all the houses looked alike, rigid and militant, like white-bearded old generals with icicles hanging from their moustaches. One European-styled house after the other lined the streets in strict parallel formation, block after block.

The grandparents' neighborhood remembered in military images and sensory details

But in the summer it was different . . . softer. No subzero winds blew lonely down the back alley. Instead, kids played stickball in it. I had elegant, grass-stained tea parties with a neighborhood girl named Shelly, while my grandfather worked in his thriving vegetable garden among the honeybees, and watched things grow. An ever-present warming smell of yeast filtered down every street as the nearby breweries pumped a constant flow of fresh beer. Looking up, the summer sky looked like an Easter egg God had dipped in blue dye.

Those summer trips to Milwaukee were greatly anticipated events back then. My brother and I itched with repressed energy throughout the long plane ride from the West Coast. We couldn't wait to see Grandma and Papa. We couldn't wait to see what presents Papa had for us. We couldn't wait to slide down the steep, blue-carpeted staircase on our bottoms, and then on our stomachs. Most of all, we couldn't wait to go down to the basement.

The basement was better than a toy store. Yes, the old-fashioned milk chute in the kitchen wall was enchanting, and the laundry chute was fun because it was big enough to throw down Ernie, my stuffed dog companion, so my brother could catch him below in the laundry room, as our voices echoed up and down the chute. But the basement was better than all of these, better even than sliding down those stairs on rug-burned bottoms.

The basement in
contrast to other
parts of the house

It was always deliciously cool down in the basement. Since the house was built in the '30s, there was no air conditioning. Upstairs, we slept in hot, heavy rooms. My lace-edged nightgown stuck to the sheets, and I would lie awake in the dusky room, listening to crickets, inhaling the beer-sweet smell of the summer night, hoping for a cool breeze. Nights were forgotten, however, as my brother and I spent hours every day in the basement. There were seven rooms in the basement; some darker rooms I had waited years to explore. There was always a jumbled heap of toys in the middle room, most of which were leftovers from my father's own basement days. It was a child's safe haven; it was a sacred place.

Adventures in the
basement

The times spent in the basement were times of a gloriously secure childhood. Empires were created in a day with faded colored building blocks. New territories were annexed when either my brother or I got the courage to venture into one of those Other Rooms—the dark, musty ones without windows—and then scamper back to report of any sightings of monsters or other horrific childhood creatures. In those basement days everything seemed safe and wholesome and secure, with my family surrounding me, protecting me. Like childhood itself, entering the basement was like entering another dimension.

The house and
neighborhood years later

Last summer I returned to Milwaukee to help my grandparents pack to move into an apartment. I went back at 17 to find the house—my kingdom—up for sale. I found another cycle coming to a close, and I found myself separated from what I had once known. I looked at the house. It was old; it was crumbling; it needed paint. I looked down the back alley and saw nothing but trash and bums. I walked to the corner and saw smoke-choked, dirty streets and thick bars in shop windows, nothing more than another worn-out midwestern factory city. I went back to the house and down to the basement, alone.

The basement
years later

It was gray and dark. Dust filtered through a single feeble sunbeam hitting a cracked window pane. It was empty and barren. The toys were gone, either packed or thrown away. The silence was unbearable as I walked in and out of rooms. My footsteps echoed as the quietness filled my ears. There was an undeniable musty smell, and in the back of my head the sounds of childhood laughter and chatter played like an old recording.

The dark rooms were filled not with monsters but with remnants of my grandfather's business. A neon sign was propped against the wall in a corner: Ben Strauss Plumbing. Piles of heavy pipes and metal machine parts lay scattered about on shelves. A dusty purple ribbon was thumbtacked to a door. It said SHOOT THE WORKS in white letters. I gently took it down. The ribbon hangs on my door at home now, and out of context it somehow is not quite so awe-inspiring and mystifying as it once was, amidst the dust and the memories and the aspirations. However, it does serve its purpose.

Conclusion: A return to the introduction's images and some advice

All children are tree children, I believe. The basement used to be my tree, the place I could dream in. That last summer I found myself, much to Mike's disappointment, quite mature, quite adult. Maybe Mike fell from his tree and got bruised. Climbing down from that tree doesn't have to be something to be afraid of. One needn't hide in the tree for fear of touching the ground and forgetting how to climb back up when necessary. I think there is a way to balance the two extremes. Climb down gracefully as you grow up, and if you fall, don't land in quicksand. I like to think I'm more of a shrubbery child: not so low as to get stuck in the mud and just high enough to look at the sky and make cloud pictures.

PROFESSIONAL ESSAY

The Discus Thrower
Richard Selzer

Richard Selzer has taught surgery at Yale Medical School and has contributed both stories and essays to a number of magazines. He has published two collections of short stories and four collections of essays, Mortal Lessons *(1977),* Confessions of a Knife *(1979),* Letters to a Young Doctor *(1982), and* Taking the World in for Repairs *(1986) as well as his recent memoir,* Down from Troy: A Doctor Comes of Age *(1992). This essay was published in* Harper's *in 1977.*

I spy on my patients. Ought not a doctor to observe his patients by any means and from any stance, that he might the more fully assemble evidence? So I stand in the doorways of hospital rooms and gaze. Oh, it is not all that furtive an act. Those in bed need only look up to discover me. But they never do.

2 From the doorway of Room 542 the man in the bed seems deeply tanned. Blue eyes and close-cropped white hair give him the appearance of vigor and good health. But I know that his skin is not brown from the sun. It is rusted, rather, in the last stage of containing the vile repose within. And the blue eyes are frosted, looking inward like the windows of a snowbound cottage. This man is blind. This man is also legless—the right leg missing from midthigh down, the left from just below the knee. It gives him the look of a bonsai, roots and branches pruned into the dwarfed facsimile of a great tree.

3 Propped on pillows, he cups his right thigh in both hands. Now and then he shakes his head as though acknowledging the intensity of his suffering. In all of this he makes no sound. Is he mute as well as blind?

4 The room in which he dwells is empty of all possessions—no get-well cards, small, private caches of food, day-old flowers, slippers, all the usual kickshaws of the sickroom. There is only the bed, a chair, a nightstand, and a tray on wheels that can be swung across his lap for meals.

5 "What time is it?" he asks.

"Three o'clock."

"Morning or afternoon?"

"Afternoon."

He is silent. There is nothing else he wants to know.

10 "How are you?" I say.

"Who is it?" he asks.

"It's the doctor. How do you feel?"

He does not answer right away.

"Feel?" he says.

15 "I hope you feel better," I say.

I press the button at the side of the bed.

"Down you go," I say.

"Yes, down," he says.

He falls back upon the bed awkwardly. His stumps, unweighted by legs and feet, rise in the air, presenting themselves. I unwrap the bandages from the stumps, and begin to cut away the black scabs and the dead, glazed fat with scissors and forceps. A shard of white bone comes loose. I pick it away. I wash the wounds with disinfectant and redress the stumps. All this while, he does not speak. What is he thinking behind those lids that do not blink? Is he remembering a time when he was whole? Does he dream of feet? Of when his body was not a rotting log?

20 He lies solid and inert. In spite of everything, he remains impressive, as though he were a sailor standing athwart a slanting deck.

"Anything more I can do for you?" I ask.

For a long moment he is silent.

"Yes," he says at last and without the least irony. "You can bring me a pair of shoes."

In the corridor, the head nurse is waiting for me.

25 "We have to do something about him," she says. "Every morning he orders scrambled eggs for breakfast, and, instead of eating them, he picks up the plate and throws it against the wall."

"Throws his plate?"

"Nasty. That's what he is. No wonder his family doesn't come to visit. They probably can't stand him any more than we can."

She is waiting for me to do something.

"Well?"

30 "We'll see," I say.

The next morning I am waiting in the corridor when the kitchen delivers his breakfast. I watch the aide place the tray on the stand and swing it across his lap. She presses the button to raise the head of the bed. Then she leaves.

In time the man reaches to find the rim of the tray, then on to find the dome of the covered dish. He lifts off the cover and places it on the stand. He fingers across the plate until he probes the eggs. He lifts the plate in both hands, sets it on the palm of his right hand, centers it, balances it. He hefts it up and down slightly, getting the feel of it. Abruptly, he draws back his right arm as far as he can.

There is the crack of the plate breaking against the wall at the foot of his bed and the small wet sound of the scrambled eggs dropping to the floor.

And then he laughs. It is a sound you have never heard. It is something new under the sun. It could cure cancer.

35 Out in the corridor, the eyes of the head nurse narrow.

"Laughed, did he?"

She writes something down on her clipboard.

A second aide arrives, brings a second breakfast tray, puts it on the nightstand, out of his reach. She looks over at me shaking her head and making her mouth go. I see that we are to be accomplices.

"I've got to feed you," she says to the man.

40 "Oh, no you don't," the man says.

"Oh, yes I do," the aide says, "after the way you just did. Nurse says so."

"Get me my shoes," the man says.

"Here's oatmeal," the aide says. "Open." And she touches the spoon to his lower lip.

"I ordered scrambled eggs," says the man.

45 "That's right," the aide says.

I step forward.

"Is there anything I can do?" I say.

"Who are you?" the man asks.

In the evening I go once more to that ward to make my rounds. The head nurse reports to me that Room 542 is deceased. She has discovered this quite by accident, she says. No, there had been no sound. Nothing. It's a blessing, she says.

50   I go into his room, a spy looking for secrets. He is still there in his bed. His face is relaxed, grave, dignified. After a while, I turn to leave. My gaze sweeps the wall at the foot of the bed, and I see the place where it has been repeatedly washed, where the wall looks very clean and very white.

Questions on Content, Structure, and Style

1. This essay presents several scenes in a hospital. From whose point of view do we see these scenes? How is this point of view introduced?

2. Does this essay contain objective or subjective description or both? Are there enough clear, specific details to make the descriptions vivid to the reader? Cite some details to support your answer.

3. What does Selzer's description of the hospital room itself suggest about the patient?

4. Why does the patient throw his eggs on the wall each day? Why does he laugh? Call for his shoes? What do these details tell you about the patient and his attitude toward his situation?

5. What is Selzer's attitude toward his patient? How do you know? What is the attitude of the head nurse?

6. What is Selzer's purpose in describing this patient and his actions? Why doesn't he "do something" about the patient, as the nurse wants?

7. Point out several examples of metaphor and simile in this essay. What do these add to the effectiveness of Selzer's descriptions?

8. Why does Selzer use dialogue in some occasions instead of describing what is taking place?

9. Why does Selzer end his essay by referring to the clean wall? Is this an effective conclusion? Why or why not?

10. Selzer's subtitle for this essay was "Do Not Go Gentle," a reference to a well-known poem by Dylan Thomas. In the poem Thomas tells his dying father "Do not go gentle into that good night/Rage, rage against the dying of the light." Why is Selzer's subtitle an appropriate complement to this essay?

Vocabulary

furtive (1)	caches (4)	athwart (20)
vile (2)	kickshaws (4)	irony (23)
repose (2)	shard (19)	
facsimile (2)	inert (20)	

◣ A REVISION WORKSHEET

As you write your rough drafts, consult Chapter 5 for guidance through the revision process. In addition, here are a few questions to ask yourself as you revise your description:

1. Is the descriptive essay's purpose clear to the reader?

2. Are there enough specific details in the description to make the subject matter distinct to readers who are unfamiliar with the scene, person, or object? Where might more detail be added?

3. Are the details arranged in an order that's easy to follow?

4. If the assignment called for an objective description, are the details as "neutral" as possible?

5. If the assignment called for a subjective description, does the writer's particular attitude come through clearly with a consistent use of well-chosen details or imagery?

6. Could any sensory details or figurative language be added to help the reader "see" the subject matter?

7. Does this essay end with an appropriate conclusion or does description merely stop?

After you've revised your essay extensively, you might exchange rough drafts with a classmate and answer these questions for each other, making specific suggestions for improvement wherever appropriate. (For advice on productive participation in classroom workshops, see pp. 114–117.)

Reviewing Your Progress

After you have completed your descriptive essay, take a moment to measure your progress as a writer by responding to the following questions. Such analysis will help you recognize growth in your writing skills and may enable you to identify areas that are still problematic.

1. What is the best feature of your essay? Why?

2. Which descriptive detail or image do you think is the clearest or most vivid in your essay? Why does that one stand above the others?

3. What part of your essay gave you the most trouble? How did you overcome the problem?

4. If you had more time to work on this essay, what would receive additional attention? Why?

5. What did you learn about your topic from writing this essay? About yourself as a writer?

NARRATION

When many people hear the word "narrative," they think of a made-up story. But not all stories are fiction. In this chapter we are not concerned with writing literary short stories—that's a skill you may work on in a creative writing class—but rather with nonfiction *narratives,* stories that may be used in your essays to explain or prove a point. We most often use two kinds of these stories:

1. the *extended narrative*—a long episode that by itself illustrates or supports an essay's thesis

2. the *brief narrative*—a shorter incident that is often used in a body paragraph to support or illustrate a particular point in an expository or argumentative essay.

Let's suppose, for example, you wanted to write an essay showing how confusing the registration system is at your school. To illustrate the problems vividly, you might devote your entire essay to the retelling of a friend's seven-hour experience signing up for classes last fall, thus making use of extended narration. Or take another example: in an argumentative essay advocating the nationwide use of automobile air bags, you might use a brief narrative about a car wreck to support a paragraph's point about air bags' ability to save lives. Regardless of which type of narrative best fits your purpose, the telling of a story or incident can be an informative, persuasive means of swaying your readers to your point of view.

HOW TO WRITE EFFECTIVE NARRATION

Know your purpose. Writers frequently use narratives to explain or emphasize a point, to persuade readers to accept an idea, or to share an important experience or point of view. To ensure their readers' understanding of their purpose, some writers of narratives present a thesis statement at the beginning of their stories; others clearly imply their main point through the unfolding action and descriptive details. Whichever way you choose, your readers should not find themselves at the end of your essay wondering, "What was this all about? What was the reason for telling this story?" Once you have a good sense of your purpose, tailor all the events and details in your narrative to communicate your main point or thesis to your readers. (An implied thesis is always riskier than a stated one, of course. If you do choose to imply your thesis, you might avoid the danger of losing your readers if you write a statement of your purpose at the top of your drafts and refer to it often as you develop your narrative.)

Select an appropriate point of view. In an essay-length narrative you should decide whether the story will be told by you in the first person; by a character involved in the action; or by an omniscient ("all-knowing") narrator, who may reveal the thoughts, feelings, and actions of any character. The selection of a narrator is important because it determines the point of view through which the readers hear the story. For example, if a child is narrating the story, the writer must be careful not to slip into sophisticated description that only an adult would be capable of making. Similarly, if you are telling your own story, you might describe someone else's actions or character, but you could not suddenly reveal his or her innermost, unspoken thoughts. Once you have decided which point of view is best for your purpose, be consistent. Unless you have a compelling artistic reason for doing so, don't change your point of view in mid-story.

Follow a logical time sequence. Many narrative essays—and virtually all brief stories used in other kinds of essays—follow a chronological order, presenting events as they naturally occur in the story. Occasionally, however, a writer will use the flashback technique, which takes the readers back in time to reveal an incident that occurred before the present scene of the story. Many novelists and short-story writers use a variety of techniques to alter time sequences in their fiction; Joseph Heller's famous novel *Catch-22,* for example, contains chaotic time shifts to emphasize the absurd nature of war. If you decide to use shifts in time, use transition phrases or other signals to ensure that your readers don't become confused or lost.

Use details to present the setting. Most extended narratives are set in particular times and places. If the setting plays an important role in your story, you must describe it in vivid terms so that your readers can imagine it easily. For example, let's suppose you are pointing out the necessity of life preservers on sailboats by telling the story of how you spent a stormy night in the lake, clinging to your capsized boat. To convince your readers, let them "feel" the stinging rain and the icy current trying to drag you under; let them "see" the black waves and the dark menacing sky; let them "hear" the howling wind and the gradual splitting apart of the boat. Effective narration often depends on effective description, and effective description depends on vivid, specific detail. (For more help on writing description, see Chapter 10.)

Make your characters believable. Again, the use of detail is crucial. Your readers should be able to visualize the people in your narrative clearly; if your important characters are drawn too thinly or if they seem phony or stereotyped, your readers will not fully grasp the intensity of your story, and thus its meaning will be lost. Show your readers a picture of the major characters (as you see them) by commenting unobtrusively on their appearances, speech, and actions. In addition, a successful narrative depends on the reader's understanding of people's motives—why they act the way they do in certain situations. A narrative about your hometown's grouchiest miser who suddenly donated a large sum of money to a poor family isn't very believable unless we know the motive behind the action. In other words, let your readers know what is happening to whom by explaining or showing why.

Use dialogue realistically. Writers often use dialogue, their characters' spoken words, to reveal action or personality traits of the speakers. By presenting conversations, writers show rather than tell, often creating emphasis or a more dramatic effect. If your narrative would profit from dialogue, be certain the word choice and the manner of speaking are in keeping with each character's education, background, age, location, and so forth. Don't, for example, put a sophisticated philosophical treatise into the mouth of a ten-year-old boy or the latest campus slang into the speeches of an auto mechanic from Two Egg, Florida. Also, make sure that your dialogue doesn't sound "wooden" or phony. The right dialogue can help make your characters more realistic and interesting, provided that the conversations are essential to the narrative and are not merely padding the plot. (To see excellent use of dialogue throughout an essay, read "The Discus Thrower," pp. 297–300. For help in punctuating dialogue, see pp. 383–385 in Part Three.)

Problems to Avoid

Weak, boring narratives are often the result of problems with subject matter or poor pacing; therefore, you should keep in mind the following advice:

Choose your subject carefully. Most of the best narrative essays come from personal experience, and the reason is fairly obvious: it's difficult to write convincingly about something you've never seen or done or read about. You probably couldn't, for instance, write a realistic account of a bullfight unless you'd seen one or at least had studied the subject in great detail. The simplest, easiest, most interesting nonfiction narrative you can write is likely to be about an event with which you are personally familiar. This doesn't mean that you can't improvise many details or create a hypothetical story to illustrate a point. Even so, you will probably still have more success basing your narrative—real or hypothetical—on something or someone you know well.

Limit your scope. When you wish to use an extended narrative to illustrate a thesis, don't select an event or series of actions whose retelling will be too long or complex for your assignment. In general, it's better to select one episode and flesh it out with many specific details so that your readers may clearly see your point. For instance, you may have had many rewarding experiences during the summer you worked as a lifeguard, but you can't tell them all. Instead, you might focus on one experience that captures the essence of your attitude toward your job—say, the time you saved a child from drowning—and present the story so vividly that the readers can easily understand your point of view.

Don't let your story lag with insignificant detail. At some time you've probably listened to a storyteller who became stuck on some insignificant detail ("Was it Friday or Saturday the letter came? Let's see now. . . ." "Then Joe said to me—no, it was Sally—no, wait, it was. . . ."). And you've probably also heard bores who insist on making a short story long by including too many unimportant details or digressions. These mistakes ruin the *pacing* of their stories; in other words, the story's tempo or movement becomes bogged down until the readers are bored witless. To avoid putting your readers to sleep, dismiss all unessential information and focus your attention—and use of detail—on the important events, people, and places. Skip uneventful periods of time by using such phrases as "A week went by before Mr. Smith called . . ." or "Later that evening, around nine o'clock. . . ." In short, keep the story moving quickly enough to hold the readers' interest. Moreover, use a variety of transition devices to move the readers from one action to another; don't rely continuously on the "and then . . . and then . . ." method.

▶ ESSAY TOPICS

Use one of the topics below to suggest an essay that is developed by narration. Remember that each essay must have a clear purpose.

1. an experience with an older person or a child

2. the worst mix-up of your life

3. your best holiday or special occasion

4. your worst accident or brush with death

5. an act of courage or cowardice

6. your most frightening or wonderful childhood experience

7. a memorable event governed by nature or one of historical significance

8. a time you gained self-confidence

9. an event that changed your thinking on a particular subject

10. challenging an authority

11. an event that led to an important decision

12. your experience with prejudice or with an act of charity or friendship

13. giving in to or resisting peer pressure

14. a loss of something or someone important

15. a risk that paid off (or a triumph against the odds)

16. a nonacademic lesson learned at school or on a job

17. a trip or special time spent by yourself

18. a bad habit that got you into (or out of) trouble

19. a family story passed down through the generations

20. an episode marking your passage from one stage of your life to another

A Topic Proposal for Your Essay

Selecting the right subject matter is important to every writer. To help you clarify your ideas and strengthen your commitment to your topic, here is a proposal sheet that asks you to describe some of your preliminary ideas about your subject before you begin drafting. Although as you draft your ideas may change (they will almost certainly become more refined), thinking through your choice of topic now may help you avoid several false starts.

1. In a sentence or two, briefly tell the subject of your narrative. Did you or someone you know participate in this story?

2. Why did you select this narrative? Does it have importance for you personally, academically, or professionally? In some other way? Explain your reason for picking this story to tell.

3. Will others be informed or entertained by this story? Who might be especially interested in hearing your narrative?

4. What is the primary effect you would like your narrative to have on your readers? What would you like them to feel or think about after they read your story? Why?

5. What is the critical moment in your story? At what point, in other words, does the action reach its peak? Summarize this moment in a few descriptive words.

6. What difficulties, if any, might this narrative present as you are drafting? For example, if the story you want to tell is long or complex, how might you focus on the main action and pace it appropriately?

SAMPLE STUDENT ESSAY

In this narrative a student uses a story about a sick but fierce dog to show how she learned a valuable lesson in her job as a veterinarian's assistant. Notice the student's good use of vivid details that makes this well-paced story both clear and interesting.

Never Underestimate the Little Things

Introduction: A
misconception

When I went to work as a veterinarian's assistant for Dr. Sam Holt and Dr. Jack Gunn last summer, I was under the false impression that the hardest part of veterinary surgery would be the actual performance of an operation. The small chores demanded before this feat didn't occur to me as being of any importance. As it happened, I had

Thesis

been in the veterinary clinic only a total of four hours before I met a little animal who convinced me that the operation itself was probably the easiest part of treatment. This animal, to whom I owe thanks for so enlightening me, was a chocolate-colored chihuahua of tiny size and immense perversity named Smokey.

Description of the main
character: His
appearance

Now Smokey could have very easily passed for some creature from another planet. It wasn't so much his gaunt little frame and overly large head, or his bony paws with nearly saberlike claws, as it was his grossly infected eyes. Those once-shining eyes were now distorted and swollen into grotesque balls of septic, sightless flesh. The only vague similarity they had to what we'd normally think of as the organs of vision was a slightly upraised dot, all that was left of the pupil, in the center of a pink and purply

His personality

marble. As if that were not enough, Smokey had a temper to match his ugly sight. He also had surprisingly good aim, considering his largely diminished vision, toward any moving object that happened to place itself unwisely before his ever-inquisitive nose, and with sudden and wholly vicious intent he would snap and snarl at whatever blocked the little light that could filter through his swollen and ruptured blood vessels. Truly, in many respects, Smokey was a fearful dog to behold.

The difficulty of moving the dog to the surgery room

Such an appearance and personality did nothing to encourage my already flagging confidence in my capabilities as a vet's assistant. How was I supposed to get that little demon out of his cage? Jack had casually requested that I bring Smokey to the surgery room, but did he really expect me to put my hands into the mouth of the cage of that devil dog? I suppose it must have been my anxious expression that saved me, for as I turned uncertainly toward the kennel, Jack chuckled nonchalantly and accompanied me to demonstrate how professionals in his line of business dealt with professionals in Smokey's. He took a small rope about four feet long with a slipnoose at one end and began to unlatch Smokey's cage. Then cautiously he reached in and dangled the noose before the dog's snarling jaws. Since Smokey could only barely see what he was biting at, his attacks were directed haphazardly in a semicircle around his body. The tiny area of his cage led to his capture, for during one of Smokey's forward lunges, Jack dropped the noose over his head and dragged the struggling creature out onto the floor. The fight had only just begun for Smokey, however, and he braced his feet against the slippery linoleum tiling and forced us to drag him, like a little pull toy on a string, to the surgery.

In the surgery room: The difficulty of moving the dog to the table

Once in the surgery, however, the question that hung before our eyes like a veritable presence was how to get the dog from the floor to table. Simply picking him up and plopping him down was out of the question. One glance at the quivering little figure emitting ominous and throaty warnings was enough to assure us of that. Realizing that the game was over, Jack grimly handed me the rope and reached for a muzzle. It was a doomed attempt from the start; the closer Jack dangled the tiny leather cup to the dog's nose the more violent did Smokey's contortions and rage-filled cries become and the more frantic our efforts became to try to keep our feet and fingers clear of the angry jaws. Deciding that a firmer method had to be used, Jack instructed me to raise the rope up high enough so that Smokey'd have to stand on his hind legs. This greatly reduced his maneuverability but served to increase his tenacity, for at this the little dog nearly went into paroxysms of frustration and rage. In his struggles, however, Smokey caught his forepaw on his swollen eye, and the blood that had been building up pressure behind the fragile cornea burst out and dripped to the floor. In the midst of our surprise and the twinge of panic startling the three of us, Jack saw his chance and swiftly muzzled the animal and lifted him to the operating table.

The difficulty of putting the dog to sleep before the surgery

Even at that point it wasn't easy to put the now terrified dog to sleep. He fought even the local anesthesia and caused Jack to curse as he was forced to give Smokey far more of the drug than should have been necessary for such a small beast. After what seemed an eternity, Smokey lay prone on the table, breathing deeply and emitting soft snores and gentle whines. We also breathed deeply in relief, and I relaxed to watch fascinated, while Jack performed a very delicate operation quite smoothly and without mishap.

Conclusion: The lesson she learned

Such was my harrowing induction into the life of a veterinary surgeon. But Smokey did teach me a valuable lesson that has proven its importance to me many times since: wherever animals are concerned, even the smallest detail should never be taken for granted.

PROFESSIONAL ESSAY

Graduation
Maya Angelou

Maya Angelou is an American author, actress, civil-rights activist, and professor at Wake Forest University. Raised in Stamps, Arkansas, Angelou has traveled and performed in Europe and Africa as well as in the United States. She has written several volumes of poetry and four popular autobiographical works, including her most recent memoir All God's Children Need Traveling Shoes *(1986). This essay is a chapter from her first autobiography,* I Know Why the Caged Bird Sings *(1969).*

1   The children in Stamps[1] trembled visibly with anticipation. Some adults were excited too, but to be certain the whole young population had come down with graduation epidemic. Large classes were graduating from both the grammar school and the high school. Even those who were years removed from their own day of glorious release were anxious to help with preparations as a kind of dry run. The junior students who were moving into the vacating classes' chairs were tradition-bound to show their talents for leadership and management. They strutted through the school

[1] A small town in Arkansas

and around the campus exerting pressure on the lower grades. Their authority was so new that occasionally if they pressed a little too hard it had to be overlooked. After all, next term was coming, and it never hurt a sixth grader to have a play sister in the eighth grade, or a tenth-year student to be able to call a twelfth grader Bubba. So all was endured in a spirit of shared understanding. But the graduating classes themselves were the nobility. Like travelers with exotic destinations on their minds, the graduates were remarkably forgetful. They came to school without their books, or tablets or even pencils. Volunteers fell over themselves to secure replacements for the missing equipment. When accepted, the willing workers might or might not be thanked, and it was of no importance to the pregraduation rites. Even teachers were respectful of the now quiet and aging seniors, and tended to speak to them, if not as equals, as beings only slightly lower than themselves. After tests were returned and grades given, the student body, which acted like an extended family, knew who did well, who excelled, and what piteous ones had failed.

2   Unlike the white high school, Lafayette County Training School distinguished itself by having neither lawn, nor hedges, nor tennis court, nor climbing ivy. Its two buildings (main classrooms, the grade school and home economics) were set on a dirt hill with no fence to limit either its boundaries or those of bordering farms. There was a large expanse to the left of the school which was used alternately as a baseball diamond or a basketball court. Rusty hoops on the swaying poles represented the permanent recreational equipment, although bats and balls could be borrowed from the P.E. teacher if the borrower was qualified and if the diamond wasn't occupied.

3   Over this rocky area relieved by a few shady tall persimmon trees the graduating class walked. The girls often held hands and no longer bothered to speak to the lower students. There was a sadness about them, as if this old world was not their home and they were bound for higher ground. The boys, on the other hand, had become more friendly, more outgoing. A decided change from the closed attitude they projected while studying for finals. Now they seemed not ready to give up the old school, the familiar paths and classrooms. Only a small percentage would be continuing on to college—one of the South's A&M (agricultural and mechanical) schools, which trained Negro youths to be carpenters, farmers, handymen, masons, maids, cooks and baby nurses. Their future rode heavily on their shoulders, and blinded them to the collective joy that had pervaded the lives of the boys and girls in the grammar school graduating class.

4   Parents who could afford it had ordered new shoes and readymade clothes for themselves from Sears and Roebuck or Montgomery Ward. They also engaged the best seamstresses to make the floating graduation dresses and to cut down secondhand pants which would be pressed to a military slickness for the important event.

5   Oh, it was important, all right. Whitefolks would attend the ceremony, and two or three would speak of God and home, and the Southern way of life, and Mrs. Parsons, the principal's wife, would play the graduation march while the lower-grade graduates paraded down the aisles and took their seats below the platform. The high school seniors would wait in empty classrooms to make their dramatic entrance.

6   In the Store I was the person of the moment. The birthday girl. The center. Bailey had graduated the year before, although to do so he had had to forfeit all pleasures to make up for his time lost in Baton Rouge.

7   My class was wearing butter-yellow piqué dresses, and Momma launched out on mine. She smocked the yoke into tiny crisscrossing puckers, then shirred the rest of the bodice. Her dark fingers ducked in and out of the lemony cloth as she embroidered raised daisies around the hem. Before she considered herself finished she had added a crocheted cuff on the puff sleeves, and a pointy crocheted collar.

8   I was going to be lovely. A walking model of all the various styles of fine hand sewing and it didn't worry me that I was only twelve years old and merely graduating from the eighth grade. Besides, many teachers in Arkansas Negro schools had only that diploma and were licensed to impart wisdom.

9   The days had become longer and more noticeable. The faded beige of former times had been replaced with strong and sure colors. I began to see my classmates' clothes, their skin tones, and the dust that waved off pussy willows. Clouds that lazed across the sky were objects of great concern to me. Their shiftier shapes might have held a message that in my new happiness and with a little bit of time I'd soon decipher. During that period I looked at the arch of heaven so religiously my neck kept a steady ache. I had taken to smiling more often, and my jaws hurt from the unaccustomed activity. Between the two physical sore spots, I suppose I could have been uncomfortable, but that was not the case. As a member of the winning team (the graduating class of 1940) I had outdistanced unpleasant sensations by miles. I was headed for the freedom of open fields.

10   Youth and social approval allied themselves with me and we trammeled memories of slights and insults. The wind of our swift passage remodeled my features. Lost tears were pounded to mud and then to dust. Years of withdrawal were brushed aside and left behind, as hanging ropes of parasitic moss.

11   My work alone had awarded me a top place and I was going to be one of the first called in the graduating ceremonies. On the classroom blackboard, as well as on the bulletin board in the auditorium, there were blue stars and white stars and red stars. No absences, no tardiness, and my academic work was among the best of the year. I could say the preamble to the Constitution even faster than Bailey. We timed ourselves often: WethepeopleoftheUnitedStatesinordertoformamoreperfectunion. . . ." I had memorized the Presidents of the United States

from Washington to Roosevelt in chronological as well as alphabetical order.

12   My hair pleased me too. Gradually the black mass had lengthened and thickened, so that it kept at last to its braided pattern, and I didn't have to yank my scalp off when I tried to comb it.

13   Louise and I had rehearsed the exercises until we tired out ourselves. Henry Reed was class valedictorian. He was a small, very black boy with hooded eyes, a long, broad nose and an oddly shaped head. I had admired him for years because each term he and I vied for the best grades in our class. Most often he bested me, but instead of being disappointed I was pleased that we shared top places between us. Like many Southern Black children, he lived with his grandmother, who was as strict as Momma and as kind as she knew how to be. He was courteous, respectful and soft-spoken to elders, but on the playground he chose to play the roughest games. I admired him. Anyone, I reckoned, sufficiently afraid or sufficiently dull could be polite. But to be able to operate at a top level with both adults and children was admirable.

14   His valedictory speech was entitled "To Be or Not to Be." The rigid tenth-grade teacher had helped him to write it. He'd been working on the dramatic stresses for months.

15   The weeks until graduation were filled with heady activities. A group of small children were to be presented in a play about buttercups and daisies and bunny rabbits. They could be heard throughout the building practicing their hops and their little songs that sounded like silver bells. The older girls (non-graduates, of course) were assigned the task of making refreshments for the night's festivities. A tangy scent of ginger, cinnamon, nutmeg and chocolate wafted around the home economics building as the budding cooks made samples for themselves and their teachers.

16   In every corner of the workshop, axes and saws split fresh timber as the woodshop boys made sets and stage scenery. Only the graduates were left out of the general bustle. We were free to sit in the library at the back of the building or look in quite detachedly, naturally, on the measures being taken for our event.

17   Even the minister preached on graduation the Sunday before. His subject was "Let your light so shine that men will see your good works and praise your Father, Who is in Heaven." Although the sermon was purported to be addressed to us, he used the occasion to speak to backsliders, gamblers and general ne'er-do-wells. But since he had called our names at the beginning of the service we were mollified.

18   Among Negroes the tradition was to give presents to children going only from one grade to another. How much more important this was when the person was graduating at the top of the class. Uncle Willie and Momma had sent away for a Mickey Mouse watch like Bailey's. Louise gave me four embroidered handkerchiefs. (I gave her three crocheted doilies.) Mrs. Sneed, the minister's wife, made me an underskirt to wear

for graduation, and nearly every customer gave me a nickel or maybe even a dime with the instruction "Keep on moving to higher ground," or some such encouragement.

19   Amazingly the great day finally dawned and I was out of bed before I knew it. I threw open the back door to see it more clearly, but Momma said, "Sister, come away from that door and put your robe on."

20   I hoped the memory of that morning would never leave me. Sunlight was itself still young, and the day had none of the insistence maturity would bring it in a few hours. In my robe and barefoot in the backyard, under cover of going to see about my new beans, I gave myself up to the gentle warmth and thanked God that no matter what evil I had done in my life He had allowed me to live to see this day. Somewhere in my fatalism I had expected to die, accidentally, and never have the chance to walk up the stairs in the auditorium and gracefully receive my hard-earned diploma. Out of God's merciful bosom I had won reprieve.

21   Bailey came out in his robe and gave me a box wrapped in Christmas paper. He said he had saved his money for months to pay for it. It felt like a box of chocolates, but I knew Bailey wouldn't save money to buy candy when we had all we could want under our noses.

22   He was as proud of the gift as I. It was a soft-leather-bound copy of a collection of poems by Edgar Allan Poe, or, as Bailey and I called him, "Eap." I turned to "Annabel Lee" and we walked up and down the garden rows, the cool dirt between our toes, reciting the beautifully sad lines.

23   Momma made a Sunday breakfast although it was only Friday. After we finished the blessing, I opened my eyes to find the watch on my plate. It was a dream of a day. Everything went smoothly and to my credit. I didn't have to be reminded or scolded for anything. Near evening I was too jittery to attend to chores, so Bailey volunteered to do all before his bath.

24   Days before, we had made a sign for the Store and as we turned out the lights Momma hung the cardboard over the doorknob. It read clearly: CLOSED. GRADUATION.

25   My dress fitted perfectly and everyone said that I looked like a sunbeam in it. On the hill, going toward the school, Bailey walked behind with Uncle Willie, who muttered, "Go on, Ju." He wanted him to walk ahead with us because it embarrassed him to have to walk so slowly. Bailey said he'd let the ladies walk together, and the men would bring up the rear. We all laughed, nicely.

26   Little children dashed by out of the dark like fireflies. Their crepe-paper dresses and butterfly wings were not made for running and we heard more than one rip, dryly, and the regretful "uh uh" that followed.

27   The school blazed without gaiety. The windows seemed cold and unfriendly from the lower hill. A sense of ill-fated timing crept over me, and if Momma hadn't reached for my hand I would have drifted back to Bailey and Uncle Willie, and possibly beyond. She made a few slow jokes about my feet getting cold, and tugged me along to the now-strange building.

28   Around the front steps, assurance came back. There were my fellow "greats," the graduating class. Hair brushed back, legs oiled, new dresses and pressed pleats, fresh pocket handkerchiefs and little handbags, all homesewn. Oh, we were up to snuff, all right. I joined my comrades and didn't even see my family go in to find seats in the crowded auditorium.

29   The school band struck up a march and all classes filed in as had been rehearsed. We stood in front of our seats, as assigned, and on a signal from the choir director, we sat. No sooner had this been accomplished than the band started to play the national anthem. We rose again and sang the song, after which we recited the pledge of allegiance. We remained standing for a brief minute before the choir director and the principal signaled to us, rather desperately I thought, to take our seats. The command was so unusual that our carefully rehearsed and smooth-running machine was thrown off. For a full minute we fumbled for our chairs and bumped into each other awkwardly. Habits change or solidify under pressure, so in our state of nervous tension we had been ready to follow our usual assembly pattern: the American National Anthem, then the pledge of allegiance, then the song every Black person I knew called the Negro National Anthem. All done in the same key, with the same passion and most often standing on the same foot.

30   Finding my seat at last, I was overcome with a presentiment of worse things to come. Something unrehearsed, unplanned, was going to happen, and we were going to be made to look bad. I distinctly remember being explicit in the choice of pronoun. It was "we," the graduating class, the unit, that concerned me then.

31   The principal welcomed "parents and friends" and asked the Baptist minister to lead us in prayer. His invocation was brief and punchy, and for a second I thought we were getting back on the high road to right action. When the principal came back to the dais, however, his voice had changed. Sounds always affected me profoundly and the principal's voice was one of my favorites. During assembly it melted and lowed weakly into the audience. It had not been in my plan to listen to him, but my curiosity was piqued and I straightened up to give him my attention.

32   He was talking about Booker T. Washington, our "late great leader," who said we can be as close as the fingers on the hand, etc. . . . Then he said a few vague things about friendship and the friendship of kindly people to those less fortunate than themselves. With that his voice nearly faded, thin, away. Like a river diminishing to a stream and then to a trickle. But he cleared his throat and said, "Our speaker tonight, who is also our friend, came from Texarkana to deliver the commencement address, but due to the irregularity of the train schedule, he's going to, as they say, 'speak and run.'" He said that we understood and wanted the man to know that we were most grateful for the time he was able to give us and then something about how we were willing always to adjust to another's program, and without more ado—"I give you Mr. Edward Donleavy."

33   Not one but two white men came through the door offstage. The shorter one walked to the speaker's platform, and the tall one moved over to the center seat and sat down. But that was our principal's seat, and already occupied. The dislodged gentleman bounced around for a long breath or two before the Baptist minister gave him his chair, then with more dignity than the situation deserved, the minister walked off the stage.

34   Donleavy looked at the audience once (on reflection, I'm sure that he wanted only to reassure himself that we were really there), adjusted his glasses and began to read form a sheaf of papers.

35   He was glad "to be here and to see the work going on just as it was in the other schools."

36   At the first "Amen" from the audience I willed the offender to immediate death by choking on the word. But Amen's and Yes, sir's began to fall around the room like rain through a ragged umbrella.

37   He told us of the wonderful changes we children in Stamps had in store. The Central School (naturally, the white school was Central) had already been granted improvements that would be in use in the fall. A well-known artist was coming from Little Rock to teach art to them. They were going to have the newest microscopes and chemistry equipment for their laboratory. Mr. Donleavy didn't leave us long in the dark over who made these improvements available to Central High. Nor were we to be ignored in the general betterment scheme he had in mind.

38   He said that he had pointed out to people at a very high level that one of the first-line football tacklers at Arkansas Agricultural and Mechanical College had graduated from good old Lafayette County Training School. Here fewer Amen's were heard. Those few that did break through lay dully in the air with the heaviness of habit.

39   He went on to praise us. He went on to say how he had bragged that "one of the best basketball players at Fisk sank his first ball right here at Lafayette County Training School."

40   The white kids were going to have a chance to become Galileos and Madame Curies and Edisons and Gauguins, and our boys (the girls weren't even in on it) would try to be Jesse Owenses and Joe Louises.

41   Owens and the Brown Bomber were great heroes in our world, but what school official in the white-goddom of Little Rock had the right to decide that those two men must be our only heroes? Who decided that for Henry Reed to become a scientist he had to work like George Washington Carver, as a bootblack, to buy a lousy microscope? Bailey was obviously always going to be too small to be an athlete, so which concrete angel glued to what country seat had decided that if my brother wanted to become a lawyer he had to first pay penance for his skin by picking cotton and hoeing corn and studying correspondence books at night for twenty years?

42   The man's dead words fell like bricks around the auditorium and too many settled in my belly. Constrained by hard-learned manners I couldn't

look behind me, but to my left and right the proud graduating class of 1940 had dropped their heads. Every girl in my row had found something new to do with her handkerchief. Some folded the tiny squares into love knots, some into triangles, but most were wadding them, then pressing them flat on their yellow laps.

43   On the dais, the ancient tragedy was being replayed. Professor Parsons sat, a sculptor's reject, rigid. His large, heavy body seemed devoid of will or willingness, and his eyes said he was no longer with us. The other teachers examined the flag (which was draped stage right) or their notes, or the window which opened on our now-famous playing diamond.

44   Graduation, the hush-hush magic time of frills and gifts and congratulations and diplomas, was finished for me before my name was called. The accomplishment was nothing. The meticulous maps, drawn in three colors of ink, learning and spelling decasyllabic words, memorizing the whole of *The Rape of Lucrece*—it was nothing. Donleavy had exposed us.

45   We were maids and farmers, handymen and washerwomen, and anything higher that we aspired to was farcical and presumptuous. Then I wished that Gabriel Prosser and Nat Turner had killed all whitefolks in their beds and that Abraham Lincoln had been assassinated before the signing of the Emancipation Proclamation, and that Harriet Tubman had been killed by that blow on her head and Christopher Columbus had drowned in the *Santa Maria*.

46   It was awful to be Negro and have no control over my life. It was brutal to be young and already trained to sit quietly and listen to charges brought against my color with no chance of defense. We should all be dead. I thought I should like to see us all dead, one on top of the other. A pyramid of flesh with the whitefolks on the bottom, as the broad base, then the Indians with their silly tomahawks and teepees and wigwams and treaties, the Negroes with their mops and recipes and cotton sacks and spirituals sticking out of their mouths. The Dutch children should all stumble in their wooden shoes and break their necks. The French should choke to death on the Louisiana Purchase (1803) while silkworms ate all the Chinese with their stupid pigtails. As a species, we were an abomination. All of us.

47   Donleavy was running for election, and assured our parents that if he won we could count on having the only colored paved playing field in that part of Arkansas. Also—he never looked up to acknowledge the grunts of acceptance—also, we were bound to get some new equipment for the home economics building and the workshop.

48   He finished, and since there was no need to give any more than the most perfunctory thank-you's, he nodded to the men on the stage, and the tall white man who was never introduced joined him at the door. They left with the attitude that now they were off to something really important. (The graduation ceremonies at Lafayette County Training School had been a mere preliminary.)

49   The ugliness they left was palpable. An uninvited guest who wouldn't leave. The choir was summoned and sang a modern arrangement of "Onward, Christian Soldiers," with new words pertaining to graduates seeking their place in the world. But it didn't work. Elouise, the daughter of the Baptist minister, recited "Invictus," and I could have cried at the impertinence of "I am the master of my fate: I am the captain of my soul."

50   My name had lost its ring of familiarity and I had to be nudged to go and receive my diploma. All my preparations had fled. I neither marched up to the stage like a conquering Amazon, nor did I look in the audience for Bailey's nod of approval. Marguerite Johnson, I heard the name again, my honors were read, there were noises in the audience of appreciation, and I took my place on the stage as rehearsed.

51   I though about colors I hated: ecru, puce, lavender, beige and black.

52   There was shuffling and rustling around me, then Henry Reed was giving his valedictory address, "To Be or Not to Be." Hadn't he heard the whitefolks? We couldn't *be,* so the question was a waste of time. Henry's voice came out clear and strong. I feared to look at him. Hadn't he got the message? There was no "nobler in the mind" for Negroes because the world didn't think we had minds, and they let us know it. "Outrageous fortune"? Now, there was a joke. When the ceremony was over I had to tell Henry Reed some things. That is, if I still cared. Not "rub," Henry, "erase." "Ah, there's the erase." Us.

53   Henry had been a good student in elocution. His voice rose on tides of promise and fell on waves of warnings. The English teacher had helped him to create a sermon winging through Hamlet's soliloquy. To be a man, a doer, a builder, a leader, or to be a tool, an unfunny joke, a crusher of funky toadstools. I marveled that Henry could go through with that speech as if we had a choice.

54   I had been listening and silently rebutting each sentence with my eyes closed; then there was a hush, which in an audience warns that something unplanned is happening. I looked up and saw Henry Reed, the conservative, the proper, the A student, turn his back to the audience and turn to us (the proud graduating class of 1940) and sing, nearly speaking,

> Lift ev'ry voice and sing
> Till earth and heaven ring
> Ring with the harmonies of Liberty . . .[2]

It was the poem written by James Weldon Johnson. It was the music composed by J. Rosamond Johnson. It was the Negro National Anthem. Out of habit we were singing it.

---

[2] "Lift Ev'ry Voice and Sing"—words by James Weldon Johnson and music by J. Rosamond Johnson. © Copyrighted: Edward B. Marks Music Corporation. Used by permission.

55   Our mothers and fathers stood in the dark hall and joined the hymn of encouragement. A kindergarten teacher led the small children onto the stage and the buttercups and daisies and bunny rabbits marked time and tried to follow:

> Stony the road we trod
> Bitter the chastening rod
> Felt in the days when hope, unborn, had died.
> Yet with a steady beat
> Have not our weary feet
> Come to the place for which our fathers sighed?

56   Every child I knew had learned that song with his ABC's and along with "Jesus Loves Me This I Know." But I personally had never heard it before. Never heard the words, despite the thousands of times I had sung them. Never thought they had anything to do with me.

57   On the other hand, the words of Patrick Henry had made such an impression on me that I had been able to stretch myself tall and trembling and say, "I know not what course others may take, but as for me, give me liberty or give me death."

58   And now I heard, really for the first time:

> We have come over a way that with tears has been watered,
> We have come, treading our path through the blood of the slaughtered.

59   While echoes of the song shivered in the air, Henry Reed bowed his head, said "Thank you," and returned to his place in the line. The tears that slipped down many faces were not wiped away in shame.

60   We were on top again. As always, again. We survived. The depths had been icy and dark, but now a bright sun spoke to our souls. I was no longer simply a member of the proud graduating class of 1940; I was a proud member of the wonderful, beautiful Negro race.

61   Oh, Black known and unknown poets, how often have your auctioned pains sustained us? Who will compute the lonely nights made less lonely by your songs, or the empty pots made less tragic by your tales?

62   If we were a people much given to revealing secrets, we might raise monuments and sacrifice to the memories of our poets, but slavery cured us of that weakness. It may be enough, however, to have it said that we survive in exact relationship to the dedication of our poets (include preachers, musicians and blues singers).

Questions on Content, Structure, and Style

1. What is Angelou's purpose in writing this narrative? Is she successful?

2. Does Angelou have a specific audience in mind?

3. In the beginning of her narrative, why does Angelou devote so many paragraphs to the students and preparations for the graduation ceremony? What would be lost if she omitted these descriptions?

4. Select several details that help the readers understand the various characters in the narrative. How do these details help readers to "see" the students? Donleavy? Angelou herself?

5. How does Angelou make clear her reaction to Donleavy's speech? What would be the effect if Angelou had not chosen to tell her story in the first person?

6. Why does Angelou "hear" the words of the Negro National Anthem for the first time? What effect do they have on her?

7. Why does Angelou end her narrative by addressing "Black known and unknown poets"?

8. How does Angelou's "voice" change in the course of this narrative? Contrast, for example, her tone and choice of diction at the beginning of the story to her reaction to Donleavy and then again to her voice in the last several paragraphs. Are these shifts appropriate to the action?

9. What does Angelou's use of figurative language contribute to the vividness of her narrative? Cite some examples to illustrate your answer.

10. Briefly describe the structure of Angelou's narrative. Where does the climax of the story occur? What effect does the structure of this narrative have on the reader's reaction to the story?

Vocabulary

trammeled (10)	farcical (45)	impertinence (49)
explicit (30)	presumptuous (45)	rebutting (54)
penance (41)	perfunctory (48)	
meticulous (44)	palpable (49)	

◤ A REVISION WORKSHEET

As you write your rough drafts, consult Chapter 5 for guidance through the revision process. In addition, here are a few questions to ask yourself as you revise your narrative:

1. Is the narrative essay's purpose clear to the reader?

2. Is the thesis plainly stated or at least clearly implied?

3. Does the narrative convincingly support or illustrate its intended point? If not, how might the story be changed?

4. Does the story maintain a logical point of view and an understandable order of action?

5. Are the characters, actions, and settings presented in enough vivid detail to make them clear and believable? Where could more detail be effectively added?

6. Is the story coherent and well paced or does it wander or bog down in places because of irrelevant or repetitious details? What might be condensed or cut?

7. Does the essay end in a satisfying way or does the action stop too abruptly?

After you've revised your essay extensively, you might exchange rough drafts with a classmate and answer these questions for each other, making specific suggestions for improvement wherever appropriate. (For advice on productive participation in classroom workshops, see pp. 114–117.)

Reviewing Your Progress

After you have completed your narrative essay, take a moment to measure your progress as a writer by responding to the following questions. Such analysis will help you recognize growth in your writing skills and may enable you to identify areas that are still problematic.

1. What do you like best about your narrative essay? Why?

2. After reading through your essay, select the description, detail, or piece of dialogue that you think best characterizes a major figure or most effectively advances the action in your story. Explain the reason for your choice in one or two sentences.

3. What part of your essay gave you the most trouble? How did you overcome the problem?

4. If you had more time to work on this essay, what would receive additional attention? Why?

5. What did you learn about your topic from writing this essay? About yourself as a writer?

12

WRITING A PAPER USING RESEARCH

-
-
-

Although the words "upcoming research paper" have been known to produce anxiety worse than that caused by the sound of a dentist's drill, you should try to relax. A "research paper" is similar to the kinds of expository and argumentative essays described in the earlier parts of this book, the difference being the use of documented source material to support, illustrate, or explain your ideas. Research papers still call for thesis statements, logical sequences of paragraphs, well-developed supporting evidence, smooth conclusions—or in other words, all the skills you've been practicing throughout this book. By citing sources in your essays or reports, you merely show your readers that you have investigated your ideas and found support for them. In addition, using sources affords your readers the opportunity to look into your subject further if they so desire, following your references as a guide to additional readings.

The process described in the next few pages should help you write a paper using research that is carefully and effectively documented. This chapter also contains sample documentation forms and a sample student paper (pp. 348–352).

SEARCHING FOR YOUR TOPIC

In some cases you will be assigned your topic, and you will be able to begin your research right away. In other classes, however, you may be encouraged to select your own subject, or you may be given a general subject ("cults"; "pornography"; "violence on television") that you must narrow and then focus into a specific, manageable topic. If the topic is your choice, you need to do some preliminary thinking about what interests you; as in any assignment, you should make the essay a learning experience from which both you and your readers will profit. Therefore, you may want to brainstorm for a while on your general subject before you go to the library, asking yourself questions about what you already know and don't know. Some of the most interesting papers are problem-solving essays in which writers set about to find an answer to a controversy or to find support for a solution they suspect might work. Other papers, sometimes called "research reports," expose, explain, or summarize a situation or a problem for their audience. Whatever the goal of your particular research, remember that your readers want to finish your paper knowing more about a significant subject than when they started.

BEGINNING YOUR LIBRARY RESEARCH

Let's assume at this point that you have a general topic in mind and that your assignment asks for library research. The next step calls for familiarizing yourself with the school or public library where you will do your research. Most libraries have handouts, maps, or librarians who will help you locate the important parts of the library; do not be shy about asking for such information *before* you start your search.

After you become comfortable in the library, you can begin to compile a *working bibliography,* that is, a list of possible sources for your topic. You may find it useful to start by investigating one or more of the following reference room tools:

The Card Catalog

The card catalog is usually a series of cabinets containing alphabetized index cards; in some libraries the card catalog is divided into three parts so that you may look up information under "subject," "author," and "title." Unless you are already familiar with authorities or their books on your subject, you will most likely begin with the "subject" catalog. If your subject is "acupuncture," you might find a typical subject card that looks like the sample on page 325. You may have to look under several headings in the subject catalog to find the one your library uses for your topic. Once you have a call number, consult a library map to determine the book's location on the shelves.

If your library has become computerized, as most have in the past several years, the information you would ordinarily find in the card catalog will

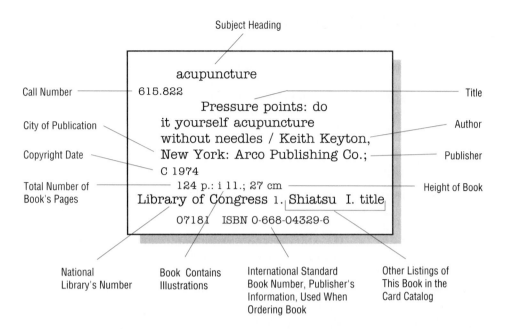

now be found on a computer screen. Because libraries today are often in a state of transition, you may need to consult your librarian about the system in current use at your school or public library.

Periodical Indexes

Periodical indexes list magazines and journals that may contain articles you will wish to consult. There are several kinds of periodical indexes, and your library will carry a number of them to help you with your search. (Some of them may be on computer disks; if you need help, consult your librarian.) If your subject is of interest to a general audience, you might begin by checking *The Readers' Guide to Periodical Literature,* an index that lists magazines of general interest, such as *Time* and *Newsweek.* The *Magazine Index,* a microfilm reader that indexes 400 periodicals, is also available in many libraries today. (*The New York Times* newspaper index may be useful if your subject has been in the national or international news.) If your subject is particular to a field of study, you may wish to try those indexes that list only magazines and journals in specific areas, such as the *Business Periodicals Index,* the *Humanities Index,* the *Applied Science and Technology Index,* or the *Social Sciences Index.* Note too that your topic may be listed under slightly different headings from index to index (for instance, "domestic abuse" in one index might be "battered spouse syndrome" in another). If you can't find your subject under the headings that first come to your mind, ask your librarian for the *Library of Congress Subject Headings,* a common reference book that will suggest other names for your topic.

Data-Base Searches

A data-base search allows people to use a computer to scan electronic indexes that list thousands of bibliographic sources and abstracts. Many libraries today subscribe to information services that will lead you to an appropriate data base for your subject. Ask your librarian for assistance. (You should also know that data-base searching may cost you money and that some services are more expensive than others.)

Special Collections

Your library may also contain special collections that will help you research your subject. Some libraries, for example, have extensive collections of government documents or educational materials or newspapers from certain cities. Other libraries may have invested in manuscripts from famous authors or in a series of works on a particular subject, such as your state's history, a Vietnam War collection, or studies on human rights in post-World War II Latin America. Remember, too, that some libraries contain collections of early films, rare recordings, or unique photographs. Consult your librarian or the handouts describing your library's special holdings.

Preparing a Working Bibliography

Looking through the catalog and various indexes may take time, but seeing what's been published on your subject may help you focus on a specific topic. You may also find it useful at this point to skim a number of articles on your subject, so that eventually you reach the specific idea you want to research and write about. (And don't underestimate the value of browsing—sometimes the most interesting book on your subject is on the shelf next to the book you were looking for.)

Once you have a narrowed focus, prepare a *working bibliography,* a list of the most promising sources for your paper. To compile a working bibliography, you should copy on an index card the following information for each source: author's name, full title of the book, publisher, date and city of publication, page numbers of the material you're interested in, and library call number. If the source is a magazine or journal, the card should contain the author's name, journal's name, article's name, volume number, issue number, date of issue, and page numbers of the article within the journal.

TAKING NOTES

Begin to look up the sources listed in your working bibliography and take notes on *content* cards. Most researchers recommend that you take notes on index cards rather than on notebook paper because the cards can be shuffled around more easily later when you are organizing your paper. In addition, you may find it helpful to use cards of a different color or size from the bibliography cards, just for ease of sorting.

When you find a useful book or magazine, be sure you have a bibliography card for it. Plan to use several content cards for each book or article because you may wish to divide your notes into categories of ideas that will later help you organize your paragraphs. Write on one side of the content cards only, to avoid having some material out of sight and mind while you're organizing your notes for your first rough draft. Always note the page numbers from which you are collecting information.

Your notes will probably be of four kinds:

1. *Direct quotations.* When you lift material word for word,* you must always use quotation marks and note the precise page number of the quotation. If the quoted material runs from one page onto another, use some sort of signal to yourself such as a slash bar (child/abuse) or arrow (→ p. 10) at the break so if you use only part of the quoted material in your paper, you will know on which page it appeared. If the quoted material contains odd, archaic, or incorrect spelling, punctuation marks, or grammar, insert the word [*sic*] in brackets next to the item in question; [sic] means "this is the way I found it in the original text," and such a symbol will remind you later that you did not miscopy the quotation. Otherwise, always double-check to make sure you did copy the material accurately and completely to avoid having to come back to the source as you prepare your essay. If the material you want to quote is lengthy, you will find it easier—though not cheaper—to photocopy the material rather than transcribe it (almost all libraries have one or more photocopy machines, but be prepared to bring your own bag of correct change).

2. *Paraphrase.* You paraphrase when you put into your own words what someone else has written or said. Please note: *Paraphrased ideas are borrowed ideas, not your original thoughts, and consequently they must be attributed to their owner just as direct quotations are.*

To remind yourself that certain information on your note cards is paraphrased, always leave space in the left-hand margin for some sort of notation, such as a circled Ⓟ. Quotation marks will always tell you what you borrowed directly, but sometimes when writers take notes one week and write their first draft a week or two later, they cannot remember if a note was paraphrased or if it was original thinking. Writers occasionally plagiarize unintentionally because they believe only direct quotations and statistics must be attributed to their proper sources, so make your notes as clear as possible (for more information on avoiding plagiarism, see pp. 333–336).

3. *Summary.* You may wish to condense a piece of writing so that you may offer it as support for your own ideas. Using your own words, you should present in shorter form the writer's thesis and supporting ideas. In addition,

---

* Please note that all tables, graphs, and charts that you copy must also be directly attributed to their sources, though you do not enclose graphics in quotation marks.

you may find it helpful to include a few direct quotations in your summary to retain the flavor of the original work. Of course, you will tell your readers what you are summarizing and by whom it was written. Remember to make a note in the margin to indicate summarized, rather than original, material.

4. *Your own ideas.* Your note cards may also contain your personal comments (judgments, flashes of brilliance, notions of how to use something you've just read, notes to yourself about connections between sources, and so forth) that will aid you in the writing of your paper. It might be helpful to jot these down in a different-colored pen or put them in brackets that you've initialed, so that you will recognize them later as your own responses when your note cards are cold.

DISTINGUISHING PARAPHRASE FROM SUMMARY

Because novice writers sometimes have a hard time telling the difference between paraphrase and summary, here is a sample of each. First, here is a paragraph from an article that might be pertinent in a paper you're preparing on the current theories for controlling teenage crime.

> Another successful approach to the prevention of criminality has been to target very young children in a school setting before problems arise. The Perry Preschool Program, started 22 years ago in a low socioeconomic area of Ypsilanti, Michigan, has offered some of the most solid evidence to date that early intervention through a high-quality preschool program can significantly alter a child's life. A study released this fall tells what happened to 123 disadvantaged children from preschool age to present. The detention and arrest rates for the 58 children who had attended the preschool program was 31 percent, compared to 51 percent for the 65 who did not. Similarly, those in the preschool program were more likely to have graduated from high school, have enrolled in postsecondary education programs and be employed, and less likely to have become pregnant as teenagers.
>
> —from "Arresting Delinquency,"
> Dan Hurley, *Psychology Today,*
> March 1985, p. 66

A *paraphrase* puts the information in the researcher's own words, but it does follow the order of the original text, and it does include the important details.

Paraphrase

> Quality preschooling for high-risk children may help stop crime before it starts. A recent study from the twenty-two-year-old Perry Preschool Program located in a poor area of Ypsilanti, Michigan, shows that of 123 socially and economically disadvantaged children the 58 who attended preschool had an arrest rate of 31 percent as compared to 51 percent for those 65 who did not attend. The

adults with preschool experience had also graduated from high school in larger numbers; in addition, more of them had attended postsecondary education programs, were employed, and had avoided teenage pregnancy (Hurley 66).

A *summary* is generally much shorter than the original; the researcher picks out the key ideas but often omits many of the supporting details.

Summary

A recent study from the Perry Preschool Program in Michigan suggests that disadvantaged children who attend preschool are less likely to be arrested as adults. Those in this study with preschool experience also chose more education, had better employment records, and avoided teenage pregnancy more often than those without preschool (Hurley 66).

> **Remember:**
> Both paraphrased and summarized ideas must be attributed to their sources, even if you do not reproduce exact words or figures.

CHOOSING YOUR SOURCES

Once you have collected and reviewed your notes, you may be ready to begin sketching your outline and first draft. In doing so, you must decide which sources to use, where to use them, and in what form: paraphrase, summary, or direct quotation.

To help you choose your sources, here are some questions to consider as you try to decide which facts, figures, and testimonies will best support or illustrate your ideas.

Are your sources reliable? Newspapers are frequently faulted for basing entire stories on unnamed, so-called "reliable sources." Be sure that your sources are dependable and well respected in the particular area under discussion. An expert in organic chemistry, for example, might know an enormous amount about his or her own field but actually very little about genetics.

Are your sources unreasonably biased? Some authorities stand to gain economically or politically from taking a particular point of view. The president of a tobacco company, for instance, might insist that secondary smoke from the cigarettes of others will not harm nonsmokers, but does he or she have an objective opinion? Try to present testimony from those authorities whose views will sway your readers.

Is your research sensibly balanced? Your treatment of your subject—especially if it's a controversial one—should show your readers that you investigated all sides of the issue before reaching a conclusion. If your sources are drawn only from authorities well known for voicing one position, your readers will tend to become skeptical about the quality of your research. For instance, if on a paper on prayer in the schools, you refer only to the opinions of William Buckley, Phyllis Schaefly, Ronald Reagan, and George Will, all well-known conservatives, you may antagonize the reader who wants a thorough analysis of all sides of the question. Do use sources that support your position—but don't overload your argument with only obviously biased sources. (Be careful with certain publications, too; check the origins and publishers of your magazines and pamphlets. Naturally, a brochure on abortion by Planned Parenthood will have a different point of view from one by the local right-to-life organization.)

Are your sources reporting valid research? Is your source the original researcher or is he or she reporting someone else's study?* If the information is being reported secondhand, has your source been accurate and clear? Is the original source named or footnoted in some way so that the information could be checked? Look too at the way the information was obtained in the first place. Did the original researchers themselves draw the logical conclusions from their evidence? Did they run their study or project in a fair, impartial way? For example, a survey of people whose names were obtained from the rolls of the Democratic party will hardly constitute a representative sampling of voters' opinions on an upcoming election.

Moreover, be especially careful with statistics as they can be manipulated quite easily to give a distorted picture. A recent survey, for instance, asked a large sample of people to rate a number of American cities on questions dealing with quality of life. Pittsburgh—a lovely city, to be sure—came out the winner, but only if one agrees that all the questions should be weighted equally; that is, the figures gave Pittsburgh the highest score only if one rates "weather" as equally important as "educational opportunities," "amount of crime," "cultural opportunities," and other factors. In short, always evaluate the quality of your sources' research and the validity of their conclusions before you decide to incorporate their findings into your own paper. (And don't forget Mark Twain's reference to "lies, damned lies, and statistics.")

Are your sources still current? Although it's true that some famous experiments or studies have withstood the years, for many controversial topics you should use research as current as possible. What may have been written ten, or even five, years ago may have been disproved or surpassed since, especially in some of our rapidly expanding fields of technology. If they're appropriate, journals and other periodicals may contain more up-to-date reports than books printed several years ago. Readers usually appreciate hearing the current word on the topic under examination, though you certainly shouldn't ignore a "classic" study on your subject, especially if it is the one against which all the other studies are measured.

---

* Interviews, surveys, studies, and experiments conducted firsthand are referred to as *primary* sources; reports and studies written by someone other than the original researcher are called *secondary* sources.

Are you using your sources in a clear, logical way? First, make certain that you understand your source material well enough to use it in support of your own thoughts. Once you have selected the best references to use, be as convincing as possible. Ask yourself if you're using enough evidence and if the information you're offering really does clearly support your point. As in any essay, you need to avoid oversimplification, hasty generalizations, *non sequiturs,* and other problems in logic (for a review of common logical fallacies, see pp. 269–272). Resist the temptation to add quotations, facts, or statistics that are interesting but not really relevant to your paper.

(For more advice to help you think critically about your sources, see pp. 107–109 in Chapter 5.)

INCORPORATING YOUR SOURCE MATERIAL

Remember that a research paper is not a massive collection of quotations and paraphrased ideas glued together with a few transition phrases. It is, instead, an essay in which you offer *your* thesis and ideas based on and supported by your research. Consequently, you will need to incorporate and blend in your reference material in a variety of smooth, persuasive ways. Here are some suggestions:

Don't overuse direct quotations. It's best to use a direct quotation *only* when it expresses a point in a far more impressive, emphatic, or concise way than you could say it yourself. Suppose, for instance, you were analyzing the films of a particular director and wanted to include a sample of critical reviews.

> As one movie critic wrote, "This film is really terrible, and people should ignore it". (Dennison 14)

The direct quotation above isn't remarkable and could be easily paraphrased.

> As one movie critic wrote, "This film's plot is so inane that the director must have intended it for people who move their lips not only when they read but also when they watch T.V." (Dennison 14).

You might be tempted to quote the line above to show your readers an emphatically negative review of this movie.

When you do decide to use direct quotations, don't merely drop them in next to your prose. Instead, lead into them smoothly so that they obviously support or clarify what you are saying.

Dropped in Scientists have been studying the ill effects of nitrites on test animals since 1961. "Nitrites produced malignant tumors in 62 percent of the test animals within six months" (Smith 109).

Better   Scientists have been studying the ill effects of nitrites on test
                  animals since 1961. According to Dr. William Smith, head of the
                  Farrell Institute of Research, "Nitrites produced malignant tu-
                  mors in 62 percent of the test animals within six months" (109).

   Vary your sentence pattern when you present your quotations. Here
are some sample phrases for quotations:

   In his introduction to *The Great Gatsby,* Professor William Smith points
   out that "Fitzgerald wrote about himself and produced a narcissistic
   masterpiece" (5).

   William Smith, author of *Impact,* summarized the situation this way:
   "Eighty-eight percent of the sales force threaten a walkout" (21).

   "Only the President controls the black box," according to the White
   House Press Secretary (Smith 129).

   As drama critic William Smith observed last year in *The Saturday Review,* the play was "a rousing failure" (212).

   Perhaps the well-known poet William Smith expressed the idea best
   when he wrote, "Love is a spider waiting to entangle its victims" (14).

   Congressman William Smith presented the opposing view when he
   claimed, "Employment figures are down three percent from last year"
   (32).

In other words, don't simply repeat "William Smith said," "John Jones said,"
"Mary Brown said."

   Punctuate your quotations correctly. The proper punctuation will help
your reader understand who said what. For information on the appropriate
uses of quotation marks, see pages 383–385.

   **Make certain your support is in the paper, not still in your head or
back in the original source.** Sometimes when you've read a number of persuasive facts in an article or book, it's easy to forget that your reader doesn't
know them as you do now. For instance, the writer of the paragraph below
isn't as persuasive as she might be because she hides the support for her
point in the reference to the article, forgetting that the reader needs to know
what the article actually said:

   An organ transplant from one human to another is becoming an everyday
   occurrence in America, an operation that is generally applauded by everyone as
   a life-saving effort. But people are overlooking many of the serious problems
   that come with the increase in transplant surgery. One of the biggest problems
   today is the traffic in the buying and selling of organs on the Black Market. Studies show that the cases recorded recently have risen to an alarming number and
   that poor people are the most affected. (Wood 35)

For the reader to be persuaded, he or she needs to know what the writer learned from the article: what studies? how many cases are there? who has recorded these? in what time period? how and why are poor people affected? Instead of offering the necessary support in the essay, the writer merely points to the article as proof. Few readers will take the time to look up the article to find the information they need to understand your point. Therefore, when you use source material, always be sure that you have remembered to put your support on the page, *in the essay itself*, for the reader to see. Don't let the essence of your case remain hidden.

Don't let reference material dominate your essay. Remember that your reader is interested in *your* thesis and *your* conclusions, not just in a string of references. Use your researched material wisely whenever your statements need clarification, support, or amplification. But don't use quotations, paraphrased, or summarized material at every turn, just to show that you've done your homework.

AVOIDING PLAGIARISM

Unfortunately, most discussions of research must include a brief word about plagiarism. Novice writers often unintentionally plagiarize, as noted before, because they fail to recognize the necessity to attribute paraphrased, summarized, and borrowed ideas to their original owners. And indeed it is difficult sometimes after days of research to know exactly what one has borrowed and what one originally thought. Also, there's frequently a thin line between general or common knowledge ("Henry Ford was the father of the automobile industry in America") that does not have to be documented and those ideas and statements that do ("USX reported an operating loss of four million in its last quarter"). As a rule of thumb, ask yourself whether the majority of your readers would recognize the fact or opinion you're expressing or if it's repeatedly found in commonly used sources; if so, you may not need to document it. For example, most people would acknowledge that the Wall Street crash of 1929 ushered in the Great Depression of the 1930s, but the exact number of bank foreclosures in 1933 is not common knowledge and needs documenting. Similarly, a well-known quotation from the Bible or Mother Goose or even the Declaration of Independence might pass without documentation, but a line from the vice-president's latest speech needs a reference to its source. When in doubt, the best choice is to document anything that you feel may be in question.

To help you understand the difference between plagiarism and proper documentation, here is an original passage and both incorrect and correct ways to use it in a paper of your own:

Original   It is a familiar nightmare: a person suffers a heart attack, and as the ambulance fights heavy traffic, the patient dies. In fact, 350,000 American heart-attack victims each year die without ever reaching a hospital. The killer in many cases is ventricular fibrillation, uncoordinated contraction of the heart muscle. Last week a team of Dutch physicians reported in *The New England Journal of Medicine* that these early deaths can often be prevented by administration of a common heart drug called lidocaine, injected into the patient's shoulder muscle by ambulance paramedics as soon as they arrive on the scene.

—from "First Aid for Heart Attacks," *Newsweek,* November 11, 1985, page 88

Plagiarized   It is a common nightmare: a person with a heart attack dies as the ambulance sits in heavy traffic, often a victim of ventricular fibrillation, uncoordinated contraction of the heart muscle. Today, however, these early deaths can often be prevented by an injection into the patient's shoulder of a common heart drug called lidocaine, which may be administered by paramedics on the scene.

This writer has changed some of the words and sentences, but the passage has obviously been borrowed and must be attributed to its source.

Also plagiarized   According to *Newsweek,* 350,000 American heart attack victims die before reaching help in hospitals ("First Aid for Heart Attacks" 88). However, a common heart drug called lidocaine, which may be injected into the patient by paramedics on the scene of the attack, may save many victims who die en route to doctors and sophisticated life-saving equipment.

This writer did attribute the statistic to its source, but the remainder of the paragraph is still borrowed and must be documented.

Properly documented   Ambulance paramedics can, and often do, play a vital life-saving role today. They are frequently the first medical assistance available, especially to those patients or accident victims far away from hospitals. Moreover, according to a *Newsweek* report, paramedics are now being trained to administer powerful drugs to help the sick survive until they reach doctors and medical equipment. For instance, paramedics can inject the common heart drug lidocaine into heart attack victims on the scene, an act that may save many of the 350,000 Americans who die of heart attacks before ever reaching a hospital ("First Aid for Heart Attacks" 88).

This writer used the properly documented information to support her own point about paramedics and has not tried to pass off any of the article as her own.

Although plagiarism is often unintentional, it's your job to be as honest as possible. If you're in doubt about your use of a particular idea, consult your instructor for a second opinion.

Here's a suggestion that might help you avoid plagiarizing by accident. When you are drafting your essay and come to a spot in which you want to incorporate the ideas of someone else, think of the borrowed material as if it were in a window. Always frame the window at the top with some sort of introduction that mentions the author and frame the window on the bottom with a reference to the location of the material:

(According to art critic Jane Doe,)

> Quotation
> *or*
> Paraphrase
> *or*
> Summary

(*Media* 42)

A sample might look like this:

As writer Mike McGrady once said of housekeeping, "Any job that requires six hours to do and can be undone in six minutes by one small child carrying a plate of crackers and a Monopoly set—this is not a job that will long capture my interest" (13).

In a later draft, you'll probably want to vary your style so that all your borrowed material doesn't appear in exactly the same "window" format (see

p. 332 for suggestions). But until you get the habit of *always* documenting your sources, you might try using the "window" technique in your early drafts.*

▶ PRACTICING WHAT YOU'VE LEARNED

To practice some of the skills you've learned so far, read the following passage on Alexander II of Russia (1855–1881) and do the tasks listed below it.

> Alexander's greatest single achievement was his emancipation of some forty million Russian serfs, a deed which won him the title of "Tsar Liberator." To visit a rural Russian community in the earlier nineteenth century was like stepping back into the Middle Ages. Nine-tenths of the land was held by something less than one hundred thousand noble families. The serfs, attached to the soil, could be sold with the estates to new landlords, conscripted into the nobleman's household to work as domestic servants, or even sent to the factories in the towns for their master's profit. Though some nobles exercised their authority in a kindly and paternal fashion, others overworked their serfs, flogged them cruelly for slight faults, and interfered insolently in their private affairs and family relations. A serf could not marry without his master's consent, could not leave the estate without permission, and might be pursued, brought back, and punished if he sought to escape. He lived at the mercy of his master's caprice.

1. The book from which the above passage was taken contains the information listed below. Select the appropriate information and prepare a working bibliography card.

   A Survey of European Civilization Part Two, Since 1660

   Third Edition
   Houghton Mifflin Company, Publishers
   Boston
   First edition, 1936
   853.21
   1012 pages
   Authors:
   Wallace K. Ferguson, The University of Western Ontario
   Geoffrey Brun, Formerly Visiting Professor of History, Cornell University

---

*I am indebted to Professor John Clark Pratt of Colorado State University for this useful suggestion. Professor Pratt is the author of *Writing from Scratch: The Essay* (1987) published by Hamilton Press, and the editor of the *Writing from Scratch* series.

> Indexes: general, list of maps
> Picture Acknowledgments, xxvii
> copyright 1962
> p. 716
> 44 chapters

2. Paraphrase the passage.

3. Summarize the passage, but do not quote from it.

4. Select an important idea from the passage to quote directly and lead into the quotation with a smooth acknowledgment of its source.

5. Select an idea or a quotation from the passage and use it as support for a point of your own, being careful not to plagiarize the borrowed material.

◤ ASSIGNMENT

In your school or local library, look up a newspaper from any city or state and find the issue published on the day of your birth. Prepare a bibliography card for the issue you chose. Then summarize the most important or "lead" article on the front page. (Don't forget to acknowledge the source of your summary.)

CHOOSING THE DOCUMENTATION STYLE FOR YOUR ESSAY

Once you begin to write your paper incorporating your source material, you need to know how to show your readers where your material came from. You may have already learned a system for using footnotes (or endnotes), but since today's researchers and scholars use a number of different documentation styles, it's important that you know which style is appropriate for your essay. In some cases your instructors (or the audience for whom you are writing) will designate a particular style; at other times, the choice will be yours. In this chapter, we will look at three of the most widely used systems:

1. MLA style

2. Traditional footnotes with bibliography

3. APA style

I. MLA Style

Many instructors in the humanities assign the documentation form prescribed by the Modern Language Association of America (MLA). Since 1984, the

MLA has recommended a form of documentation that no longer uses traditional footnotes or endnotes to show references.* The current form calls for *parenthetical documentation,* most often consisting of the author's last name and the appropriate page number(s) in parentheses immediately following the source material in your paper. The information in the parentheses is then keyed to a "Works Cited" page at the end of your discussion, a list of the sources used in your essay (see pp. 339–343 for more explanation and samples).

MLA Citations in Your Essay

Here are some guidelines for using the MLA parenthetical reference form within your paper:

1. If you use a source by one author, place the author's name and page number right after the quoted, paraphrased, or summarized material. Note that the parentheses go *before* the end punctuation, and there is no punctuation between the author's name and the page number.

Example   Although pop art often resembles the comic strip, it owes a debt to such painters as Magritte, Matisse, and de Kooning (Rose 184).

2. If you use a source by one author and give credit to that author by name in your paper, you need only give the page number in the parentheses.

Example   According to art critic Barbara Rose, pop art owes a large debt to such painters as Magritte, Matisse, and de Kooning (184).

3. If you are directly quoting material of five or more typed lines, set off the material by ten spaces on the left margin, double-space, and do not use quotation marks. Note that in this case, the parentheses appears *after* the punctuation that ends the quoted material.

Example   In addition to causing tragedy for others, Crane's characters who are motivated by a desire to appear heroic to their peers may also cause themselves serious trouble. Collins, in "A Mystery of Heroism," for example, almost causes his own death because of his vain desire to act bravely in front of his fellow soldiers.   (Hall 16)

4. If you are citing more than one work by the same author, include a short title in the parentheses.

Example   Within 50 years the Inca and Aztec civilizations were defeated and overthrown by outside invaders (Thomas, Lost Cultures 198).

---

* If you wish a more detailed description of the current MLA form, you should ask your local bookstore for the *MLA Handbook for Writers of Research Papers,* 3rd ed. (New York: MLA, 1988).

5. If you are citing a work by more than one author, use all last names and page number.

Example Prisons today are overcrowded to the point of emergency; conditions could not be worse, and the state budget for prison reform is at an all-time low (Smith and Jones 72).

6. If you cite a work that has no named author, use the work's title and the page number.

Example Each year 350,000 Americans will die of a heart attack before reaching a hospital ("First Aid for Heart Attacks" 88).

7. If the work you are citing appears in a series, include the volume and page number with the author's name.

Example The most common view camera format is 4″ by 5″, though many sizes are available on today's market (Pursell 1:29).

8. If the material you are citing contains a quoted passage from another source, indicate the use of the quotation in the parentheses.

Example According to George Orwell, "Good writing is like a window-pane" (qtd. in Murray 142).

Compiling a Works Cited List

If you are using the MLA format, at the end of your essay you should include a *Works Cited* page—a formal listing of the sources you used in your essay. (If you wish to show all the sources you consulted, whether you used them or not, use a Works Consulted page.) Arrange the entries alphabetically by the authors' last names; if no name is given, arrange your sources by the first important word of the title. Double-space each entry, and double-space after each one. If an entry takes more than one line, indent the subsequent lines five spaces. See the sample entries that follow.

Sample Entries: MLA Style

Here are some sample entries to help you prepare a Works Cited page according to the MLA guidelines. Please note that MLA style recommends shortened forms of publishers' names: Holt for Holt, Rinehart & Winston; Harcourt for Harcourt Brace Jovanovich; UP for University Press; and so forth. Also, omit business descriptions, such as Inc., Co., Press, or House.

Remember, too, when you type your paper, the titles of books and journals should be underlined even though you may see them printed in books or magazines in italics, and the titles of articles, essays, and chapters should be enclosed in quotation marks.

Books

- Book with one author
  Tuchman, Barbara.   A Distant Mirror: The Calamitous Fourteenth Century.   New York: Knopf, 1978.

- Two books by same author
  Tuchman, Barbara.   A Distant Mirror: The Calamitous Fourteenth Century.   New York: Knopf, 1978.

  ———.   Stillwell and the American Experience in China.   New York: Macmillan, 1971.

- Book with two or three authors
  Weider, Ben, and David Hapgood.   The Death of Napoleon.   New York: Congdon, 1982.

- Book with more than three authors
  Guerin, Wilfred L., et al.   A Handbook of Critical Approaches to Literature.   New York: Harper, 1979.

- Book with author and editor
  Chaucer, Geoffrey.   The Tales of Canterbury.   Ed. Robert Pratt.   Boston: Houghton, 1974.

- Book with corporate authorship
  United States Council on Fire Prevention.   Stopping Arson Before It Starts.   Washington: Edmondson, 1982.

- Book with an editor
  Baugh, Albert C., ed.   A Literary History of England.   New York: Appleton, 1974.

- Selection or chapter from an anthology or collection with an editor
  Chopin, Kate.   "La Belle Zoraide."   Classic American Women Writers.   Ed. Cynthia Griffin Wolff.   New York: Harper, 1980.   250–273.

- Work in more than one volume
  Sharp, Harold.   Handbook of Pseudonyms and Personal Nicknames.   2 vols.   New York: Scarecrow, 1972.

- Work in a series
  Berg, Barbara L.   The Remembered Gate: Origins of American Feminism.   Urban Life in America Series.   New York: Oxford UP, 1978.

- Translation
Proust, Marcel. Remembrance of Things Past. Trans. C. K. S. Moncrieff. New York: Random, 1970.

- Reprint
Thaxter, Celia. Among the Isles of Shoals. 1873. Hampton, NH: Heritage, 1978.

Magazines and Periodicals

- Signed article in magazine
Dellinger, Walter. "Another Route to the ERA." Newsweek 2 Aug. 1982: 8.

- Unsigned article in magazine
'Men's and Women's Trenchcoats." Consumer Reports Oct. 1982: 491–97.

- Signed article in periodical
Lockwood, Thomas. "Divided Attention in *Persuasion.*" Nineteenth-Century Fiction 33 (1978): 309–23.

- A review
Musto, Michael. Rev. of Goddess, The Secret Lives of Marilyn Monroe, by Anthony Summers. Saturday Review Dec. 1985: 65–66.

Newspapers

- Signed article in newspaper
Branscombe, Art. "American Students Not Getting 'Basics.'" Denver Post 19 Sept. 1982: A17.

- Unsigned article in newspaper
"Soviet Union Buys 7.6 Million Metric Tons of Grain from Canada." Wall Street Journal 14 Oct. 1982: A18.

- Unsigned editorial
"Give Life after Death." Editorial. Coloradoan [Ft. Collins, CO] 23 Dec. 1985: A4.

(If the newspaper's city of publication is not clear from the title, put the location in brackets following the paper's name, as shown above.)

- A letter to the newspaper
Franklin, Charles. Letter. Denver Post 10 Sept. 1985: B10.

Encyclopedias, Pamphlets, Dissertations

- Signed article in an encyclopedia

  Langlotz, Ernst. "Greek Art." Encyclopedia of World Art. 1963 ed.

- Unsigned article in an encyclopedia

  "Sailfish." The International Wildlife Encyclopedia. 1970.

- A pamphlet

  Young, Leslie. Baby Care Essentials for the New Mother. Austin: Hall, 1985.

- A government document

  Department of Health. National Institute on Drug Abuse. Drug Abuse Prevention. Washington: GPO, 1980.

  Unpublished dissertations and theses

  Harmon, Gail A. "Poor Writing Skills at the College Level: A Program for Correction." Diss. U of Colorado, 1992.

Films, Television, Radio, Performances, Records

- A film

  La Cage aux Folles. Dir. Edouard Molinaro. With Ugo Tognazzi and Michel Serrault. United Artists, 1979.

If you are referring to the contribution of a particular individual, such as the director, writer, actor, or composer, begin with that person's name:

  Molinaro, Edouard, dir. La Cage aux Folles. With Ugo Tognazzi and Michel Serrault. United Artists, 1979.

- A television or radio show

  Innovation. WNET, Newark. 12 Oct. 1985.

If your reference is to a particular episode or person associated with the show, cite that name first, before the show's name:

  "A Tribute to Beethoven." Sounds Alive. CBS. WXYZ, Dallas. 10 May 1983.

  Moyers, Bill, writ. and narr. Bill Moyers' Journal. PBS. WABC, Denver. 30 Sept. 1980.

- Performances (plays, concerts, ballets, operas)

> <u>Julius Caesar</u>. By William Shakespeare. With Royal Shakespeare Company. Booth Theater, New York. 13 Oct. 1982.

If you are referring to the contribution of a particular person associated with the performance, put that person's name first:

> Shostakovich, Maxim, cond. New York Philharmonic Orch. Concert. Avery Fisher Hall, New York. 12 Nov. 1982.

- A record

> Seger, Bob. "Night Moves." Rec. 20 May 1980. <u>Nine Tonight</u> Capitol, 7777-12182-1, 1981.

Letters, Lectures, and Speeches

- A letter

> Moore, Thomas. Letter to Lord Byron. 28 Oct. 1821. Byron Collection. Yale, New Haven.

- A lecture or speech

Give the speaker's name and the title of the talk first, before the sponsoring organization (or occasion) and location. If there is no title, substitute the appropriate label, such as "lecture" or "speech."

> Dippity, Sarah N. "The Importance of Prewriting." CLAS Convention. Colorado Springs, 15 Feb. 1992.

Interviews

- A published interview

Cite the person interviewed first. Use the word "Interview" if the interview has no title:

> Mailer, Norman. <u>Dialogue with Mailer</u>. With Andrew Gordon. Berkeley Times 15 Jan. 1969.

- A personal interview

> Adkins, Camille. Personal interview. 4 Sept. 1992.
>
> Clay, Marilyn. Telephone interview. 13 April 1992.

II. Footnote/Bibliography Form

In case your assignment calls for traditional footnotes with a bibliography page, rather than for the MLA format, here is a brief description of that form.

Each idea you borrow and each quotation you include must be attributed to its author(s) in a footnote that appears at the bottom of the appropriate page.* Number your footnotes consecutively throughout the essay (do not start over with "1" on each new page), and place the number in the text to the right of and slightly above the end of the passage, whether it is a direction quotation, a paraphrase, or a summary. Place the corresponding number, indented (five spaces) and slightly raised, before the footnote at the bottom of the page. Double-space each entry, and double-space after each footnote if more than one appears on the same page. See below for sample footnote entries.

Once you have provided a first full reference, subsequent footnotes for that source may only include the author's last name and page number. However, some authorities still require the use of Latin abbreviations such as *ibid.* ("in the same place") and *op. cit.* ("in the work cited"); if your assignment does require these Latin abbreviations, use *ibid.* immediately after the original footnote to substitute for the author's name, the title, and the publication information; add a page number only if it differs from the one in the original footnote. Use *op. cit.* with the author's name to substitute for the title in later references.

At the end of your essay, list your sources by author in alphabetical order on a page entitled Bibliography.

First footnote reference	[5]Barbara Tuchman, A Distant Mirror: The Calamitous Fourteenth Century (New York: Knopf, 1978), 77.
Next footnote	[6]Tuchman 82.
Later reference	[12]Tuchman 120.
Bibliographical entry	Tuchman, Barbara. A Distant Mirror: The Calamitous Fourteenth Century. New York: Alfred A. Knopf, Inc., 1978.

III. APA Style

The American Psychological Association (APA) recommends a documentation style for research papers in the social sciences.† Your instructors in

---

* Some writing situations permit the use of endnotes, which appear in a list on a page following the essay before the bibliography. Consult your teacher or the person (or publication) for whom you are writing to see if endnotes are permissible or even preferred.

† If you wish a more detailed description of the APA style, you might order a copy of the *Publication Manual of the American Psychological Association,* 3rd ed. (Washington, DC: Psychological Association, 1983).

psychology and sociology classes, for example, may prefer that you use the APA form when you write essays for them.

The APA style is similar to the MLA style in that it calls for parenthetical documentation within the essay itself, although the information cited in the parentheses differs slightly from that presented according to the MLA format. For example, you will note that in the APA style the date of publication follows the author's last name and precedes the page number in the parentheses. Another important difference concerns capitalization of book and article titles: in the MLA style, all important words are capitalized, but in the APA style, only proper names, the first word of titles, and any words appearing after a colon are capitalized. And instead of a "Works Cited" page, the APA style uses a "References" page at the end of the essay to list those sources cited in the text. A "Bibliography" page lists all works that were consulted.

APA Citations in Your Essay

Here are some guidelines for using the APA parenthetical form within your paper:

1. If you use a source by one author, place the author's name, the date of publication, and the page number in parentheses right after the quoted, paraphrased, or summarized material. Note that in APA style, you use commas between the items in the parentheses, and you do include the "p." abbreviation for page (these are omitted in MLA style). The entire parentheses goes before the end punctuation of your sentence.

Example   One crucial step in developing a so-called "deviant" personality may, in fact, be the experience of being caught in some act and consequently being publicly labeled as a deviant (Becker, 1963, p. 31).

2. If you use a source by one author and give credit to that author by name within your paper, you need give only the date and the page number. Note that the publication date follows directly after the name of the author.

Example   According to Green (1988), gang members from upper-class families are rarely convicted for their crimes and almost never labeled as delinquent (p. 101).

3. If you are citing a work with more than two authors, list all last names in the first reference; in subsequent references, use only the first author's last name and "et al." (which means "all the rest").

Example   *First reference:* After divorce, men's standard of living generally rises some 75% whereas women's falls to approximately 25% of what it once was (Bird, Gordon, & Smith, 1989, p. 203).

Subsequent references: Almost half of all the poor households in America today are headed by single women, most of whom are supporting a number of children (Bird et al., 1989, p. 285).

4. If you cite a work that has a corporate author, cite the group responsible for producing the work.

Example In contrast, the State Highway Research Commission (1989) argues, "The return to the sixty-five-mile-an-hour speed limit on some of our state's highways has resulted in an increase in traffic fatalities" (p. 3).

Compiling a List of References

If you are using the APA style, at the end of your essay you should include a page labeled References—a formal listing of the sources you cited in your essay. Arrange the entries alphabetically by the authors' last names; use initials for the authors' first and middle names. If there are two or more works by one author, list them chronologically, beginning with the earliest publication date. If an author published two or more works in the same year, the first reference is designated *a,* the second *b,* and so on (Feinstein 1989a; Feinstein 1989b).

Remember that in APA style, you underline books and journals but you do not put the names of articles in quotation marks. Although you do capitalize the major words in the titles of magazines, newspapers, and periodicals, you do not capitalize any words in the titles of books or articles except the first word in each title, the first word following a colon, and all proper names. Study the form of the samples given below.

Sample Entries: APA Style

Books

- Book with one author
  Baars, B. J. (1986). The cognitive revolution in psychology. New York: Guilford Press.

- Book with two or more authors
  Garrison, K. C., & Force, D. G. (1965). The psychology of exceptional children. New York: Ronald Press.

- Books by one author published in the same year
  Hall, S. L. (1980a). Attention deficit disorder. Denver: Bald Mountain Press.

  Hall, S. L. (1980b). Taming your adolescent. Detroit: Morrison Books.

- Book with an editor

  Bornstein, M. H. (Ed.). (1980). Comparative methods in psychology. Hillsdale, NJ: L. Erlbaum Associates.

- Selection or chapter from collection with an editor

  Newcomb, T. M. (1958). Attitude development as a function of reference groups: The Bennington study. In E. Maccoby, T. M. Newcomb, & E. L. Hartley (Eds.), Readings in social psychology (pp. 10–12). New York: Holt, Rinehart and Winston.

- A book with a corporate author

  Population Reference Bureau. (1985). 1985 world population data. Washington, DC: U. S. Government Printing Office.

Articles

Use *p.* or *pp.* with page numbers in magazines but not in periodicals.

- An article in a magazine

  Langer, E. T. (1989, May). The mindset of health. Psychology Today, pp. 48-41.

- An article in a periodical

  Nyden, P. W. (1985). Democratizing organizations: A case study of a union reform movement. American Journal of Sociology, 90, 1119–1203.

Note that when a volume number appears, it is also underlined.

- An article in a newspaper

  Noble, K. B. (1986, September 1). For ex-Hormel workers, no forgive and forget. New York Times, p. A5.

Interviews

- A published interview

  Backus, R. (1985). [Interview with Lorena Smith.] In Frank Reagon (Ed.). Today's sociology studies (pp. 32–45). Washington: Scientific Library.

- An unpublished interview

  Bear, F. (1989, June 10). [Personal interview].

USING SUPPLEMENTARY NOTES

Sometimes when writers of research papers wish to give their readers additional information about their topic or about a particular piece of source material, they include *supplementary notes*. If you are using the MLA or APA format, these notes should be indicated by using a raised number in your text (The study seemed incomplete at the time of its publication.[2]); the explanations appear on a page called "Notes" (MLA) or "Footnotes" (APA) that immediately follows the end of your essay. If you are using traditional footnote form, simply include the supplementary notes in your list of footnotes at the bottom of the page or in the list of endnotes following your essay's conclusion.

Supplementary notes can offer a wide variety of additional information.

Examples

[1]For a different interpretation of this imagery, see Spiller 1021–1023.

[2]Simon and Brown have also contributed to this area of investigation. For a description of their results, see Report on the Star Wars Project, 98–102.

[3]It is important to note here that Brown's study followed Smith's by at least six months.

[4]Later in his report Carducci himself contradicts his earlier evaluation by saying, "Our experiment was contaminated from the beginning" (319).

Don't, of course, overdo supplementary notes; use them only when you think the additional information would be truly valuable to your readers. Obviously, information critical to your essay's points should go in the appropriate body paragraphs.

SAMPLE STUDENT PAPER USING MLA STYLE

The "problem-solving" assignment that resulted in this paper asked students to select a controversy in a professional or personal area of interest and research possible solutions. They were then to report on their findings: was there a feasible answer to a particular problem? If not, why not?

The writer of this paper was a non-traditional-aged student who had been for many years both fascinated and repelled by boxing. At first, she wanted to write a paper banning boxing entirely, but, after some thought, she decided to research the most-often suggested reforms. Firmly convinced that the thesis of her paper would call *for* the reforms, she was surprised to discover, after some weeks in the library, that her evidence was mounting *against* the reforms. Consequently, she wrote a rather controversial essay to support a position only discovered after her research. As you read her essay, ask yourself how effectively she uses supporting evidence to back up her analysis. Where might she have used other sources to support her claims? Other kinds of evidence? Do you find her essay convincing or not? Why?

The Case Against Boxing Reforms

General note: Your paper should be typed, double-spaced throughout, including notes and works cited.

For years I've been one of the millions of people who a half-dozen times a year witness the brutality and savagery of a sport whose principal purpose is to incapacitate or maim the opponent: boxing. Although every bit of sense I have tells me I shouldn't approve of this demoralizing contest, some instinctive appeal urges me to sit through the fifteen rounds of bashing blows and paralyzing punches. Yes, I was at television's ringside in 1971 when the hammering left hook of defending heavyweight champion Joe Frazier sent the once-champ Muhammad Ali to the canvas in the fourteenth round to clinch a unanimous decision over the no-longer skipping and dancing Ali, in what the whole world referred to as "The Fight." I witnessed the bout between former champion Larry Holmes and his courageous, although inept, challenger Randall "Tex" Cobb, in what proved to be a massacre of the worst sort. And then there was the knock out (and eventual death) of twenty-three-year-old Duk Koo Kim after a thirty-nine blow bombardment from Boom Boom Mancini in the fourteenth round of his challenge for the WBA championship. Indeed, I saw all of these. I cheered. I cringed. I grieved.

Introduction: The writer's involvement with the subject

The controversy

Since the death of Kim many prominent people have called for the banning of professional boxing, including sports authorities such as former announcer Howard Cosell and sports writer George Vecsey of *The New York Times* ("Abolish Boxing?" 1528). Such powerful organizations as the American Medical Association have called for an end to the sport (Leershen and Katz 67).[1] But cooler heads have pointed out the uselessness of demanding the extinction of one of the world's oldest and most popular sports; instead, they have offered a series of proposals to reduce the number of boxing fatalities caused by head injuries (Axthelm 60). Those proposals most often suggested include changing the weight of gloves, using protective headgear, and requiring rigorous medical tests before and after each match. But while such reforms sound beneficial, they will not, unfortunately, significantly reduce the number of boxing deaths; consequently, they would only be an unnecessary and expensive burden on the sport.

Narrowing the focus to three proposals

Thesis

First reform: Weight
of gloves

Perhaps the most widely voiced proposal calls for an increase in the padding of the gloves. Back in the early 1960s when the deaths of Benny Paret and Davey Moore, among others, raised questions about glove reform, boxers were fighting with six-ounce gloves. After many deaths occurred while fighters were using this glove, the New York State Athletic Commission set down a new rule for the use of a more heavily padded, eight-ounce glove ("Ring Safety" 16). At the time, however, many people associated with the sport agreed that the eight-ounce glove was actually more dangerous because the increase in weight made the glove a heavier weapon, and because the boxer's hands would be better protected, the fighters would be apt to strike with

Conflicting testimony

more force ("Ring Safety" 18). Since then, boxers have fought with various glove weights ranging from six-ounces to fourteen-ounces, and the number of ring deaths has con-

Supporting study

tinued with no significant change (Goldman 100). Because fatal head injuries occur as often with light gloves as heavier ones, imposing larger gloves is not the solution for minimizing the number of unfortunate deaths.

Second reform:
Headgear

A second proposal to reduce the number of fatal injuries calls for the use of protective headgear. But because the record shows that deadly head injuries occur despite the use of head protection, this promising solution takes its own fatal blow. To cite a few cases: in the fight that resulted

Supporting examples

in the 1960 death of Charlie Mohr, a middleweight from the University of Wisconsin, and the subsequent banning of collegiate boxing, the fighters were wearing protective headpieces (Boyle and Ames 54). In 1982 twenty-two-year-old Benjamin Davis died after a fight during which he was required to wear headgear; Charles Love died wearing headgear at the hands of Daryl Stitch that same year (Deford 70). The list goes on. There just isn't any significant correlation between the use of protective headgear and the reduction of fatal head injuries.

Third reform: Medical
exams and tests

A third proposal, raised more recently, demands more rigorous medical exams before and after matches. A prefight exam, for instance, would include an EEG and a CAT scan in order to trace changes or abnormalities in the brain that might mean vulnerability to a blow to the head. But do these exams really help identify potential prob-

Supporting examples

lems? Both Benny Peret and Davey Moore had taken and passed a prefight EEG examination (Boyle and Ames 55); similarly, Koo had no diagnosed medical vulnerabilities

Testimony from medical authority

Supporting fact

Writer reassesses the problem

Supporting studies

Testimony

Supporting statistics

Conclusion: Admission of boxing as violent sport but rejection of current reform proposals

("Abolish Boxing?" 1528). Even the Council on Scientific Affairs of the American Medical Association admits that there exists no reliable test that could identify boxers who are at risk of sudden death ("Brain Injury in Boxers" 256). In addition to the tests' lack of accuracy, one must also consider the high costs of CAT scans and full neurological exams in terms of a fighter's time and money. While the top prize-winners might be able to afford the expensive tests, could fighters just starting out afford the CAT scan that carries a $450 price tag for each use (Boyle and Ames 67)? Once again, the proposed extensive exams don't seem the answer to the problem.

Before requiring new equipment or expensive tests, perhaps one needs to take a closer look at the extent of the problem itself. Boxing does occasionally result in death, but the fatality rate is actually not as bad as in other high risk sports. In studies reported in *Sporting News* and substantiated by two other studies described in the *Journal of the American Medical Association,* popular sports such as mountaineering, sky diving, hang gliding, horse racing, and even scuba diving had higher fatality rates for a given period ("Brain Injury" 255).[2] Dr. Bennet Derby of the New York State Boxing Commission has also pointed out that while football and ice hockey also produce head injuries, they have escaped the furor directed at boxing (Leershen and Katz 67). Moreover, according to *Ring Magazine,* 439 deaths occurred between 1918 and 1982 among amateur and professional boxers worldwide (Callahan 84).[3] This is fewer than seven deaths per year for sixty-four years. Even one death from boxing is deplorable, of course—but when one considers the hundreds of thousands of young men, participating in a sport found virtually in every country on the globe, seven deaths per year seems relatively small, especially compared to the number of annual swimming accidents, for instance.

Obviously, no one wants to see a sporting event result in a death. And boxing *is* violent and it *is* dangerous—that's the nature of the sport. Perhaps Sugar Ray Robinson said it best at the 1947 inquest after the death of Jimmy Doyle. When the judge asked Robinson if he knew Doyle was in trouble, Robinson replied softly, "Sir, getting people in trouble is my business" (qtd. in Callahan 84). If the critics believe a sport that demands "getting people in trouble" is immoral, they should work for its abolition on ethical grounds. But the flurry of recently proposed reforms that have followed the latest tragedy in the ring will do nothing to stop the number of fatalities. If the sport of boxing continues, perhaps we must resign ourselves to looking at the tragic deaths as the few, unfortunate accidents they really are.

Notes*

[1]Interestingly, the critics themselves don't always agree on *why* boxing should be banned. Popular columnist George Will, for example, called for an end to the sport to "protect the audience from a brutalizing spectacle," rather than to save the fighters (qtd. in "Abolish Boxing?" 1528).

[2]The sporting fatalities per 1,000 participants were as follows: boxing: 0.13; mountaineering: 5.1; hang gliding: 5.6; sky diving: 12.3; horse racing: 12.8; and scuba diving: 1.1 ("Brain Injury" 255).

[3]Figures vary slightly as authorities disagree on whether some deaths were the result of the boxing matches. Deford, for example, cites 353 deaths since 1945 (70).

Works Cited*

"Abolish Boxing?" National Review 10 Dec. 1982: 1528–29.

Axthelm, Pete. "Don't Count Boxing Out." Newsweek 20 Dec. 1982: 60.

Boyle, Robert and Wilmur Ames. "Too Many Punches, Too Little Concern." Sports Illustrated 11 April 1983: 44–67.

Callahan, Tom. "Boxing Shadows." Time 29 Nov. 1982: 84–86.

Council on Scientific Affairs. "Brain Injury in Boxers." Journal of the American Medical Association 14 Jan. 1983: 254–57.

Deford, Frank. "An Encounter to Last an Eternity." Sports Illustrated 11 April 1983: 70–82.

Goldman, Herbert G., ed. The Ring, 1982 Record Book and Boxing Encyclopedia. New York: Ring, 1982.

Leershen, Charles and Susan Katz. "The AMA Tries to KO Boxing." Newsweek 17 Dec. 1984: 67.

"The Search for Ring Safety." Sports Illustrated 15 April 1963: 16–18.

---

* In your essay, "Notes" and "Works Cited" entries should be on separate pages. Double-space within and between entries.

PART THREE

A CONCISE HANDBOOK

n this section you will learn to recognize and correct the most common errors in grammar, punctuation, and mechanics. Each error will be explained as simply as possible, with a minimum of technical language. Beside each rule you will find the mark most teachers use to indicate that error in your essays.

13

MAJOR ERRORS IN GRAMMAR

•
•
•

ERRORS WITH VERBS

Faulty Agreement   S-V Agr

Make your verb agree in number with its subject; a singular subject takes a singular verb, and a plural subject takes a plural verb.

Incorrect   *Lester Peabody,* principal of the Kung Fu School of Grammar, *don't* agree that gum chewing should be banned in the classroom.

Correct   *Lester Peabody,* principal of the Kung Fu School of Grammar, *doesn't* agree that gum chewing should be banned in the classroom.

Incorrect   The *actions* of the new senator *hasn't* been consistent with his campaign promises.

Correct   The *actions* of the new senator *haven't* been consistent with his campaign promises.

A compound subject takes a plural verb, unless the subject denotes a single person or a single unit.

Examples   *Bean sprouts* and *tofu are* dishes Jim Bob won't consider eating. ["Bean Sprouts" and "tofu" are two elements in a compound subject; therefore, use a plural verb.]

The *winner* and new *champion refuses* to give up the microphone at the news conference. ["Winner" and "champion" denote a single person; therefore, use a singular verb.]

Listed below are some of the most confusing subject-verb agreement problems:

1. With a collective noun: a singular noun referring to a collection of elements as a unit generally takes a singular verb.

Incorrect   During boring parts of the Transcendental Vegetation lecture, the *class* often *chant* dirty mantras.

Correct   During boring parts of the Transcendental Vegetation lecture, the *class* often *chants* dirty mantras.

Incorrect   The *army* of the new nation *want* shoes, bullets, and weekend passes.

Correct   The *army* of the new nation *wants* shoes, bullets, and weekend passes.

2. With a relative pronoun ("that," "which," and "who") used as a subject: the verb agrees with its antecedent, the word being described.

Incorrect   The boss rejected a shipment of *shirts, which was* torn.

Correct   The boss rejected a shipment of *shirts, which were* torn.

3. With "each," "none," "everyone," and "neither" as the subject: use a singular verb even when followed by a plural construction.

Incorrect   *Each* of the children *think* Mom and Dad are automatic teller machines.

Correct   *Each* of the children *thinks* Mom and Dad are automatic teller machines.

Incorrect   All the students saw the teacher pull out his hair, but *none know* why he did it.

Correct   All the students saw the teacher pull out his hair, but *none knows* why he did it.

Incorrect   *Neither have* a dime left by the second of the month.

Correct   *Neither has* a dime left by the second of the month.

4. With "either . . . or" and "neither . . . nor": the verb agrees with the nearer item.

Incorrect   Neither rain nor dogs nor *gloom of night keep* the mail carrier from delivering bills.

Correct   Neither rain nor dogs nor *gloom of night keeps* the mail carrier from delivering bills.

Incorrect   Either Betty or her *neighbors is* hosting a come-as-you-are breakfast.

Correct   Either Betty or her *neighbors are* hosting a come-as-you-are breakfast.

5. With "here is (are)" and "there is (are)": the verb agrees with the number indicated by the subject following the verb.

Incorrect   *There is* only two good *reasons* for missing this law class: death and jury duty.

Correct   *There are* only two good *reasons* for missing this law class: death and jury duty.

Incorrect   To help you do your shopping quickly, Mr. Scrooge, *here are* a *list* of gifts under a dollar.

Correct   To help you do your shopping quickly, Mr. Scrooge, *here is* a *list* of gifts under a dollar.

6. With plural nouns intervening between subject and verb: the verb still agrees with the subject.

Incorrect   The *jungle,* with its poisonous plants, wild animals, and biting insects, *make* Herman long for the sidewalks of Topeka.

Correct   The *jungle,* with its poisonous plants, wild animals, and biting insects, *makes* Herman long for the sidewalks of Topeka.

7. With nouns plural in form but singular in meaning: a singular verb is usually correct.

Examples   *News travels* slowly if it comes through the post office.

Charades is the exhibitionist's game of choice.

Politics is often the rich person's hobby.

Subjunctive   V Sub

When you make a wish or a statement that is contrary to fact, use the subjunctive verb form "were."

Incorrect   I wish I *was* queen so I could levy a tax on men who spit.

Correct   I wish I *were* queen so I could levy a tax on men who spit. [This expresses a wish.]

Incorrect   If "Fightin' Henry" *was* a foot taller and thirty pounds heavier, we would all be in trouble.

Correct If "Fightin' Henry" *were* a foot taller and thirty pounds heavier, we would all be in trouble. [This proposes a statement contrary to fact.]

Tense Shift   T

In most cases the first verb in a sentence establishes the tense of any later verb. Keep your verbs within the same time frame.

Incorrect Big Joe *saw* the police car coming up behind, so he *turns* into the next alley.

Correct Big Joe *saw* the police car coming up behind, so he *turned* into the next alley.

Incorrect Horace *uses* an artificial sweetener in his coffee all day, so he *felt* a pizza and a hot-fudge sundae *were* fine for dinner.

Correct Horace *uses* an artificial sweetener in his coffee all day, so he *feels* a pizza and a hot-fudge sundae *are* fine for dinner.

Incorrect Rex the Wonder Horse *was* obviously very smart because he *taps* out the telephone numbers of the stars with his hoof.

Correct Rex the Wonder Horse *was* obviously very smart because he *tapped* out the telephone numbers of the stars with his hoof.

Split Infinitive   Sp I

Many authorities insist that you never separate *to* from its verb; today, however, some grammarians allow the split infinitive except in the most formal kinds of writing. Nevertheless, because it offends some readers, it is probably best to avoid the construction unless clarity or emphasis is clearly served by its use.

Traditional A swift kick is needed to *start* the machine properly.

Untraditional A swift kick is needed *to* properly *start* the machine.

Traditional The teacher wanted Lori *to communicate* her ideas clearly.

Untraditional The teacher wanted Lori *to* clearly *communicate* her ideas.

Double Negatives   D Neg

Don't use a negative verb and a negative qualifier together.

Incorrect I *can't hardly* wait until Jim Bob gets his jaw out of traction, so I can challenge him to a bubble gum blowing contest again.

Correct   I *can hardly* wait until Jim Bob gets his jaw out of traction, so I can challenge him to a bubble gum blowing contest again.

Incorrect   Even when he flew his helicopter upside-down over her house, she *wouldn't scarcely* look at him.

Correct   Even when he flew his helicopter upside-down over her house, she *would scarcely* look at him.

Passive Voice   Pass

For the most part, your prose style will improve if you choose strong, active voice verbs over wordy or unclear passive constructions.

Wordy passive construction	It was assumed by David that Jean had used his computer because there was correction fluid on the screen.
Active verb	David assumed Jean had used his computer because there was correction fluid on the screen.
Wordy passive construction	After the successful nose-transplant operation, the surgeon and his staff were given a round of applause by the malpractice lawyers in attendance.
Active verb	After the successful nose-transplant operation, the malpractice lawyers in attendance applauded the surgeon and his staff.
Unclear passive construction	Much protest is being voiced over the new Z.A.P. bomb. [Who is protesting?]
Active verb	Members of the Fuse Lighters Association are protesting the new Z.A.P. bomb.

(For more examples of active and passive voice verbs, see p. 134.)

▶ PRACTICING WHAT YOU'VE LEARNED

Errors with Verbs

Correct the sentences below.

1. None of the students know that both mystery writer Agatha Christie and inventor Thomas Edison was dyslexic.

2. For years Johnny Appleseed was considered a mythical figure by many scholars, but now two local historians, the authors of a well-known book, argues he was a real person named John Chapman.

3. Either the cocker spaniel or the poodle hold the honor of being the most popular breed of dog in the United States, say the American Kennel Club.

4. The team from Snooker Hollow High School are considering switching from basketball to volleyball because passing athletics are required for graduation.

5. Observation of Cuban land crabs show they can run faster than horses.

6. The folklore professor's articles on modern horror stories reminds me of the tale often referred to as "The Hook."

7. In the story of the hook, a couple of teenagers are parked on a lonely road, but neither realize that a crazy man with a hook instead of an arm was lurking nearby.

8. Each of us have heard how the couple decides to quickly drive away and later discover that there is a hook hanging on the car door.

9. Neither Clyde nor his brothers can hardly believe that such stories are being collected by university anthropologists, who refers to them as "urban legends."

10. Tammy wishes she was teaching the class on urban legends, so she could tell the story of the model who fell asleep in the tanning booth.

ERRORS WITH NOUNS   N

Possessive with "-ing" Nouns

When the emphasis is on the action, use the possessive pronoun plus the "-ing" noun.

Example   He hated *my* singing around the house, so I made him live in the garage. [The emphasis is on *singing.*]

When the emphasis is not on the action, you may use a noun or pronoun plus the "-ing" noun.

Example   He hated *me* singing around the house, so I made him live in the garage. [The emphasis is on the person singing—me—not the action; he might have liked someone else singing.]

Misuse of Nouns as Adjectives

Some nouns may be used as adjectives modifying other nouns: "horse show," "movie star," or "theater seats." But some nouns used as adjectives sound awkward or like jargon. To avoid such awkwardness, you may need to change the noun to an appropriate adjective or reword the sentence.

Awkward   The group decided to work on local *environment* problems.

Better   The group decided to work on local *environmental* problems.

Jargon   The executive began a *cost estimation comparison study* of the two products.

Better   The executive began to *study a comparison* of the two products' costs.

(For more information on ridding your prose of multiple nouns, see pp. 140–141.)

ERRORS WITH PRONOUNS

Faulty Agreement   Pro Agr

A pronoun should agree in number and gender with its antecedent (that is, the word the pronoun stands for).

Incorrect   To get a temperamental *actress* to sign a contract, the director would lock *them* in their dressing room.

Correct   To get a temperamental *actress* to sign a contract, the director would lock *her* in her dressing room.

Use the singular pronoun with "everyone," "anyone," and "each."

Incorrect   When the belly dancer asked for a volunteer partner from the audience, *everyone* in the YMCA raised *their* hand.

Correct   When the belly dancer asked for a volunteer partner from the audience, *everyone* in the YMCA raised *his* hand.

Incorrect   *Each* of the new wives decided to keep *their* own name.

Correct   *Each* of the new wives decided to keep *her* own name.

In the past, writers have traditionally used the masculine pronoun "he" when the gender of the antecedent is unknown, as in the following: "If a *spy* refuses to answer questions, *he* should be forced to watch James Bond movies until *he* cracks." Today, however, many authorities prefer the nonsexist "she/he" even though the construction can be awkward when maintained over a stretch of prose. Perhaps the best solution is to use the impersonal "one" when possible or simply rewrite the sentence in the plural: "If *spies* refuse to answer questions, *they* should be forced to watch James Bond movies until *they* crack." (For more examples, see pp. 168–169.)

Vague Reference   Ref

Your pronoun references should be clear.

Vague   If the trained seal won't eat its dinner, throw *it* into the lion's cage. [What goes into the lion's cage?]

Clear   If the trained seal won't eat its dinner, throw *the food* into the lion's cage.

Vague   After the dog bit Harry, *he* raised such a fuss at the police station that the sergeant finally had *him* impounded. [Who raised the fuss? Who was impounded?]

Clear   After being bitten, Harry raised such a fuss at the police station that the sergeant finally had the *dog* impounded.

Sometimes you must add a word or rewrite the sentence to make the pronoun reference clear:

Vague   I'm a lab instructor in the biology department and am also taking a composition course. *This* has always been difficult for me. [What is difficult?]

Clear   I'm a lab instructor in the biology department and am also taking composition, a *course* that has always been difficult for me.

Also clear   I'm a lab instructor in the biology department and am also taking a composition course. Being a teacher and a student at the same time is difficult for me.

Shift in Pronouns   P Sh

Be consistent in your use of pronouns; don't shift from one person to another.

Incorrect   *One* shouldn't eat pudding with *your* fingers.

Correct   *One* shouldn't eat pudding with *one's* fingers.

Correct   *You* shouldn't eat pudding with *your* fingers.

Incorrect   *We* left-handed people are at a disadvantage because most of the time *you* can't rent left-handed golf clubs or bowling balls.

Correct   *We* left-handed people are at a disadvantage because most of the time *we* can't rent left-handed golf clubs or bowling balls.

(For additional examples, see p. 141.)

Incorrect Case   Ca

The case of a pronoun is determined by its function. If the pronoun is a subject, use the nominative case: "I," "he," "she," "we," and "they"; if the pronoun is an object, use the objective case: "me," "him," "her," "us," and "them." To check your usage, all you need to do in most cases is isolate the pronoun in the manner shown here and see if it makes sense alone.

Incorrect   Give the treasure map to Frankie and *I.*

Isolated   Give the treasure map to *I.*

Correct   Give the treasure map to Frankie and *me.*

Incorrect   Bertram and *her* suspect that the moon is hollow.

Isolated   *Her* suspects that the moon is hollow.

Correct   Bertram and *she* suspect that the moon is hollow.

In other cases, to determine the correct pronoun, you will need to add implied but unstated sentence elements:

Examples   Mother always liked Dickie more than *me.* [Mother liked Dickie more than *she liked* me.]

She is younger than *I* by three days. [She is younger than I *am* by three days.]

To solve the confusing *who/whom* pronoun problem, first determine the case of the pronoun in its own clause in each sentence.

1. If the pronoun is the subject of a clause, use "who" or "whoever."

Examples   I don't know *who* spread the peanut butter on my English paper. ["Who" is the subject of the verb "spread" in the clause "who spread the peanut butter on my English paper."]

Rachel is a librarian who only likes books with pictures. ["Who" is the subject of the verb "likes" in the clause "who only likes books with pictures."]

He will sell secrets to *whoever* offers the largest sum of money. ["Whoever" is the subject of the verb "offers" in the clause "whoever offers the largest sum of money."]

2. If the pronoun is the object of a verb, use "whom" or "whomever."

Examples   *Whom* am I kicking? ["Whom" is the direct object of the verb "kicking."]

Sid is a man *whom* I distrust. ["Whom" is the direct object of the verb "distrust."]

Whomever he kicked will probably be angry.

["Whomever" is the direct object of the verb "kicked."]

3. If the pronoun occurs as the object of a preposition, use "whom," especially when the preposition immediately precedes the pronoun.

Examples   *With whom* am I speaking?

To whom does the credit belong for spreading peanut butter on my English paper?

Do not ask *for whom* the bell tolls.

PRACTICING WHAT YOU'VE LEARNED

Errors with Nouns and Pronouns

Correct the sentences below. Skip any correct sentences.

1. The executive knew she was in trouble when her salary underwent a modification reduction adjustment of fifty percent.
2. Of whom did Oscar Wilde once say, "He hasn't a single redeeming vice"?
3. It was a surprise to both Mary and I to learn that Switzerland didn't give women the right to vote until 1971.
4. Each of the young women in the Family Life class decided not to marry after they read that couples today have 2.3 children.
5. Jim Bob explained to Frankie that the best way for him to avoid his recurring nosebleeds was to stay out of his cousin's marital arguments.

6. Those of us who'd had the flu agreed that one can always get your doctor to return your call quicker if you get in the shower.

7. The stranger gave the free movie tickets to Louise and I after he saw people standing in line to leave the theater.

8. The personnel director told each of the employees, most of who opposed him, to signify their "no" vote by saying, "I resign."

9. Clarence and me have an uncle who is so mean he writes the name of the murderer on the first page of mystery novels that are passed around the family.

10. The first movie to gross over one million dollars was *Tarzan of the Apes* (1932) starring Johnny Weismuller, a former Olympic star who became an actor. This didn't happen often in the movie industry at that time.

ERRORS WITH ADVERBS AND ADJECTIVES

Incorrect Usage Adv Adj

Incorrect use of adverbs and adjectives often occurs when you confuse the two modifiers. Adverbs qualify the meanings of verbs, adjectives, and other adverbs; they frequently end in "-ly," and they often answer the question "how?"

Incorrect After Kay argued with the mechanic, her car began running *bad.*

Correct After Kay argued with the mechanic, her car began running *badly.*

Adjectives, on the other hand, describe or qualify the meanings of nouns only.

Example The *angry* mechanic neglected to put oil into Kay's car.

One of the most confusing pairs of modifiers is "well" and "good." We often use "good" as an adjective modifying a noun and "well" as an adverb modifying a verb.

Examples *A Sap's Fables* is a *good* book for children, although it is not *well* organized.

Bubba was such a *good* liar his wife had to call in the children at suppertime.

After eating the Rocky Mountain oysters, Susie did not feel *well*.

Did you do *well* on your math test?

If you cannot determine whether a word is an adverb or adjective, consult your dictionary.

Faulty Comparison   Comp

When you compare two elements to a higher or lower degree, you often add "-er" or "-r" to the adjective.

Incorrect   Of the two sisters, Sarah is the *loudest*.

Correct   Of the two sisters, Sarah is the *louder*.

When you compare more than two elements, you often add "-est" to the adjective.

Example   Sarah is the loudest of the four children in the family.

Other adjectives use the words "more," "most," "less," and "least" to indicate comparison.

Examples   Bela Lugosi is *more* handsome than Lon Chaney but *less* handsome than Vincent Price.

Boris Karloff is the *most* handsome, and Christopher Lee is the *least* handsome of all the horror film stars.

ERRORS IN MODIFYING PHRASES

Dangling Modifiers   DM

A modifying—or descriptive—phrase must have a logical relationship to some specific words in the sentence. When those words are omitted, the phrase "dangles" without anything to modify. Dangling modifiers frequently occur at the beginnings of sentences and often may be corrected by adding the proper subjects to the main clauses.

Dangling   Not knowing how to swim, buying scuba gear was foolish.

Correct   Not knowing how to swim, *we* decided that buying scuba gear was foolish.

Dangling   Upset over an embarrassing run-in with a lasso at the round-up, his diet seemed a good idea.

Correct   Upset over an embarrassing run-in with a lasso at the round-up, Jim Bob admitted that his new diet seemed a good idea.

(For additional examples, see p. 129.)

Misplaced Modifiers   MM

When modifying words, phrases, or clauses are not placed near the word they describe, confusion or unintentional humor often results.

Misplaced   Teddy swatted the fly still dressed in his pajamas.

Correct   Still dressed in his pajamas, Teddy swatted the fly.

Misplaced   The cook prepared vegetable tartu for his guests made primarily of spinach.

Correct   The cook prepared vegetable tartu, made primarily of spinach, for his guests.

(For additional examples, see pp. 128–129.)

▶ PRACTICING WHAT YOU'VE LEARNED

Errors with Adverbs, Adjectives, and Modifying Phrases

Correct the errors in the sentences below.

1. Squeezing the can, it was hard to tell if the tomatoes were ripe.

2. Although liver is probably the worse food in the world, buttermilk is hardly more better.

3. After the optometrist pulled her eye tooth, Hortense didn't behave very (good/well) in the waiting room.

4. He didn't think the car would make it over the mountains, being eight years old.

5. The James brothers decided to have their cattle engraved instead of branded, since they were so rich.

6. In the Death Valley Swim Meet, Maria could use the backstroke or sidestroke in the first race, whichever was best for her.

7. I didn't do (good/well) on my nature project because my bonsai sequoia tree grew real bad in its small container.

8. After boarding Hard Luck Airways, the meals we were offered convinced us to return by ship.

9. I've read that a number of modern sailors, like Thor Heyerdahl, have sailed primitive vessels across the ocean in a book from the public library.

10. We are enclosing with this letter the new telephone number for notifying the fire department of any fires that may be attached to your telephone.

ERRORS IN SENTENCES

Fragments   Frag

A complete sentence must contain a subject and a verb. A fragment is an incomplete sentence; it is often a participial phrase or dependent clause that belongs to the preceding sentence. To check for fragments, try reading your prose, one sentence at a time, starting at the *end* of your essay. If you find a "sentence" that makes no sense alone, it's probably a fragment that should either be rewritten or connected to another sentence.

Incorrect   Bubba's parents refuse to send him to a psychiatrist. Although they both know he eats shoelaces and light bulbs.

Correct   Bubba's parents refuse to send him to a psychiatrist although they both know he eats shoelaces and light bulbs.

Incorrect   This tape recording of the symphony's latest concert is so clear you can hear every sound. Including the coughs and whispers of the audience.

Correct   This tape recording of the symphony's latest concert is so clear you can hear every sound, including the coughs and whispers of the audience.

Incorrect   At Liz's most recent wedding, the photographer used an instant camera. Because her marriages break up so fast.

Correct   At Liz's most recent wedding, the photographer used an instant camera because her marriages break up so fast.

You can also try this test to see if a group of words is a fragment: say the phrase "It is true that" in front of the words in question. A complete sentence will still make sense, but a fragment won't.

Example   At Liz's most recent wedding, the photographer used an instant camera. Because her marriages break up so fast.

Which is a fragment?

It is true that *at Liz's most recent wedding the photographer used an instant camera.* [This sentence makes sense, so it's not a fragment.]

It is true that *because her marriages break up so fast.* [Yes, this is a fragment.]

Comma Splice   CS

A comma splice occurs when two sentences are linked with a comma. To correct this error, you can (1) separate the two sentences with a period, (2) separate the two sentences with a semicolon, (3) insert a coordinating conjunction (such as "and," "or," "nor," "so," "yet") after the comma, (4) subordinate one clause.

Incorrect	Grover won a stuffed gila monster at the church raffle, his mother threw it away the next day while he was in school.
Correct	Grover won a stuffed gila monster at the church raffle. His mother threw it away the next day while he was in school.
Correct	Grover won a stuffed gila monster at the church raffle; his mother threw it away the next day while he was in school.
Correct	Grover won a stuffed gila monster at the church raffle, but his mother threw it away the next day while he was in school.
Correct	Although Grover won a stuffed gila monster at the church raffle, his mother threw it away the next day while he was in school.

(For more help on correcting comma splices, see pp. 375–376; coordination and subordination are discussed in detail on pp. 144–147.)

Run-On Sentence   R-O

Don't run two sentences together without any punctuation. Use a period, a semicolon, a comma plus a coordinating conjunction (if appropriate), or subordinate one clause.

Incorrect	The indicted police chief submitted his resignation the mayor accepted it gratefully.
Correct	The indicted police chief submitted his resignation. The mayor accepted it gratefully.
Correct	The indicted police chief submitted his resignation; the mayor accepted it gratefully.

Correct   The indicted police chief submitted his resignation, and the mayor accepted it gratefully.

Correct   When the indicted police chief submitted his resignation, the mayor accepted it gratefully.

Faulty Parallelism   //

Parallel thoughts should be expressed in similar constructions.

Awkward   Boa constrictors like *to lie* in the sun, *to hang* from limbs, and *swallowing* small animals.

Better   Boa constrictors like *to lie* in the sun, *to hang* from limbs, and *to swallow* small animals.

Awkward   Whether *working* on his greasy car, *fistfighting* at the hamburger joint, or in bed, my brother always kept his hair combed.

Better   Whether *working* on his greasy car, *fistfighting* at the hamburger joint, or *lounging* in bed, my brother always kept his hair combed.

False Predication   Pred

This error occurs when the predicate (that part of the sentence that says something about the subject) doesn't fit properly with the subject. Illogical constructions result.

Incorrect   The meaning of the sermon deals with love. [A "meaning" cannot deal with anything; the author, speaker, or work itself can, however.]

Correct   The sermon deals with love.

Incorrect   Energy is one of the world's biggest problems. ["Energy" itself is not a problem.]

Correct   The lack of fuel for energy is one of the world's biggest problems.

Incorrect   True failure is when you make an error and don't learn anything from it. [Avoid all "is when" and "is where" constructions. The subject does not denote a time, so the predicate is faulty.]

Correct   You have truly failed only when you make an error and don't learn anything from it.

Incorrect   Her first comment after winning the lottery was exciting. [Her comment wasn't exciting; her feeling was.]

Correct   Her first comment after winning the lottery expressed her excitement.

(For other examples of faulty predication, see p. 130.)

Mixed Structure   Mix S

"Mixed structure" is a catchall term that applies to a variety of sentence
construction errors. Usually, the term refers to a sentence in which the writer
begins with one kind of structure and then shifts to another in midsentence.
Such a shift often occurs when the writer is in a hurry, and the mind has
already jumped ahead to the next thought.

Confused   By the time one litter of cats is given away seems to bring a new
one.

Clear   Giving away one litter of cats seems to tell the mother cat that
it's time to produce a new batch.

Confused   The bank robber realized that in his crime spree how very little
fun he was having.

Clear   The bank robber realized that he was having very little fun in his
crime spree.

Confused   The novel is too confusing for what the author meant.

Clear   The novel is too confused for me to understand what the author
meant.

Confused   Children with messages from their parents will be stapled to the
bulletin board.

Clear   Children will find messages from their parents stapled to the bulletin board.

(For other examples of mixed structure, see p. 130.)

▶ PRACTICING WHAT YOU'VE LEARNED

Errors in Sentences

Correct the following sentences; skip any that are correct.

1. Mary Lou decided not to eat the alphabet soup the letters spelled
out "botulism."

2. An example of his intelligence is when he brought home a twenty-pound block of ice after ice fishing all day.

3. A friend of mine offers this definition of nasty theater critics on opening night, according to him, they're the people who can't wait to stone the first cast.

4. My father told me never to ask people where they're from because if they're from Texas they'll tell you, however, if they're not, don't embarrass them.

5. The mother of the triplets got rid of her headache by following the advice on the aspirin bottle of taking two pills and keep away from children.

6. Americans forget how large the blue whale is, for example, it has a heart as large as a Volkswagen Beetle and can hold an elephant on its tongue.

7. The new baby kept the textbook author awake all night. Thus causing her to conclude that people who say they sleep like a baby don't have one in the house.

8. Is it true that Superman could leap tall buildings, run faster than a locomotive, and that bullets would bounce off his skin?

9. People always find the time to complain about how busy they are. Despite the fact that they say they are too busy to stop.

10. According to a study by the Fish and Wildlife Service, Americans' favorite animals are dogs, horses, swans, robins, and butterflies. Whereas their least favorites are cockroaches, mosquitos, rats, wasps, and rattlesnakes.

14

A CONCISE GUIDE TO PUNCTUATION

•
•
•

Punctuation marks do not exist, as one student recently complained, to make your life miserable. They are used to clarify your written thoughts so that the reader understands your meaning. Just as traffic signs and signals tell a driver to slow down, stop, or go faster or slower, so punctuation is intended to guide the reader through your prose. Look, for example, at the confusion in the sentences below when the necessary punctuation marks are omitted:

Confusing   Has the tiger been fed Bill? [Bill was the tiger's dinner?]

Clear   Has the tiger been fed, Bill?

Confusing   After we had finished raking the dog jumped into the pile of leaves. [Raking the dog?]

Clear   After we had finished raking, the dog jumped into the pile of leaves.

Confusing   The coach called the swimmers names. [Was the coach fired for verbally abusing the swimmers?]

Clear   The coach called the swimmers' names.

Because punctuation helps you communicate clearly with your reader, you should familiarize yourself with the following rules.

THE PERIOD (.)   P

1. Use a period to end a sentence.

Examples   Ralph quit school to go live with the Pygmies in Africa. He returned shortly thereafter.

2. Use a period after initials and many abbreviations.

Examples   W. B. Yeats, 12 A.M., Dr., etc., M.A.

3. Only one period is necessary if the sentence ends with an abbreviation.

Examples   The elephant was delivered C.O.D.

To find a good job, you should obtain a B.S. or B.A.

THE QUESTION MARK (?)   P

1. Use a question mark after every direct question.

Examples   May I borrow your galoshes?

Is the sandstorm over now?

2. No question mark is necessary after an indirect question.

Examples   Jean asked why no one makes a paper milk carton that opens without tearing.

Dave wondered how the television detective always found a parking place next to the scene of the crime.

THE EXCLAMATION POINT (!)   P

The exclamation point follows words, phrases, or sentences to show strong feelings.

Examples   Fire! Call the rescue squad!

THE COMMA (,)   P

1. Use a comma to separate two independent clauses* joined by a coordinating conjunction. To remember the coordinating conjunctions, think of the

---

* An independent clause looks like a complete sentence; it contains a subject and a verb, and it makes sense by itself.

acronym FANBOYS: "for," "and," "nor," "but," "or," "yet," and "so." Always use one of the FANBOYS and a comma when you join two independent clauses.

Examples   You can bury your savings in the backyard, *but* don't expect Mother Nature to pay interest.

I'm going home tomorrow, *and* I'm never coming back.

After six weeks Louie's diet was making him feel lonely and depressed, *so* he had a bumper sticker printed that said, "Honk if you love groceries."

Do *not* join two sentences with a comma only; such an error is called a comma splice. Use a comma plus one of the coordinating conjunctions listed previously, a period, a semicolon, or subordination.

Comma splice   Beatrice washes and grooms the chickens, Samantha feeds the spiders.

Correct   Beatrice washes and grooms the chickens, and Samantha feeds the spiders.

Correct   Beatrice washes and grooms the chickens. Samantha feeds the spiders.

Correct   Beatrice washes and grooms the chickens; Samantha feeds the spiders.

Correct   When Beatrice washes and grooms the chickens, Samantha feeds the spiders.

Comma splice   Jack doesn't like singing groups, he won't go with us to hear Fed Up with People.

Correct   Jack doesn't like singing groups, so he won't go with us to hear Fed Up with People.

Correct   Jack doesn't like singing groups. He won't go with us to hear Fed Up with People.

Correct   Jack doesn't like singing groups; he won't go with us to hear Fed Up with People.

Correct   Because Jack doesn't like singing groups, he won't go with us to hear Fed Up with People.

(For additional help, see p. 369.)

2. Conjunctive adverbs, such as "however," "moreover," "thus," "consequently," and "therefore," are used to show continuity and are frequently set off by commas when they appear in midsentence.

Examples   She soon discovered, *however,* that he had stolen her mono-
grammed towels in addition to her pet avocado plant.

She felt, *consequently,* that he was not trustworthy.

When a conjunctive adverb occurs at the beginning of a sentence, it may
be followed by a comma, especially if a pause is intended. If no pause is intended, you may omit the comma, but inserting the comma is never wrong.

Examples   *Thus,* she resolved never to speak to him again.
Thus she resolved never to speak to him again.

Therefore, he resolved never to speak to her again.
Therefore he resolved never to speak to her again.

Please note that "however" can never, never be used as a coordinating
conjunction joining two independent clauses. Incorrect use of "however" most
often results in a comma splice.

Comma splice   The police arrested the thief, *however,* they had to release
him because the plant wouldn't talk.

Correct   The police arrested the thief; *however,* they had to release
him because the plant wouldn't talk.

Also correct   The police arrested the thief. *However,* they had to release
him because the plant wouldn't talk.

3. Set off with a comma an introductory phrase or clause.

Examples   After we had finished our laundry, we discovered one sock was
missing.

According to the owner of the laundromat, customers have conflicting theories about missing laundry.

For example, one man claims his socks make a break for freedom
when no one is watching the dryers.

4. Set off nonessential phrases and clauses. If the information can be
omitted without changing the meaning of the main clause, then the phrase or
clause is nonessential. Do *not* set off clauses or phrases that are essential to
the meaning of the main clause.

Essential   He reminds me of my friend *who was always confused by a
discussion of anything more complicated than a Phillips screwdriver.* [The "who" clause is essential to explain which
friend.]

The storm *that destroyed Mr. Peartree's outhouse* left him
speechless with anger. [The "that" clause is essential to explain why the storm angered Mr. Peartree.]

The movie *showing now at the Ritz* is very obscene and very popular. [The participial phrase is essential to identify the movie.]

Nonessential   Joe Medusa, *who won the jalapeno-eating contest last year,* is this year's champion cow-chip tosser. [The 'who" clause is nonessential because it only supplies additional information to the main clause.]

Black widow spiders, *which eat their spouses after mating,* are easily identifiable by the orange hourglass design on their abdomens. [The "which" clause is nonessential because it only supplies additional information.]

The juke box, *now reappearing in local honky-tonks,* first gained popularity during the 1920s. [The participial phrase is nonessential because it only supplies additional information.]

5. Use commas to separate items in a series of words, phrases, or clauses.

Examples   Julio collects coins, stamps, bottle caps, erasers, and pocket lint.

Mrs. Jones chased the burglar out the window, around the ledge, down the fire escape, and into the busy street.

Although journalists and some grammarians permit the omission of the last comma before the "and," many authorities believe the comma is necessary for clarity. For example, how many pints of ice cream are listed in the sentence below?

Please buy the following pints of ice cream: strawberry, peach, coffee, vanilla and chocolate swirl.

Four or five pints? Without a comma before the "and," the reader doesn't know if vanilla and chocolate swirl are (is?) one item or two. By inserting the last comma, you clarify the sentence:

Please buy the following pints of ice cream: strawberry, peach, coffee, vanilla, and chocolate swirl.

6. Use commas to separate adjectives of equal emphasis that modify the same noun. To determine if a comma should be used, see if you can insert the word "and" between the adjectives; if the phrase still makes proper sense with the substituted "and," use a comma.

Examples   She finally moved out of her cold, dark apartment.
She finally moved out of her cold and dark apartment.

I have a sweet, handsome husband.
I have a sweet and handsome husband.

He called from a convenient telephone booth.
But not: He called from a convenient and telephone booth. ["Convenient" modifies the unit "telephone booth," so there is no comma.]

Hand me some of that homemade pecan pie.
But not: Hand me some of that homemade and pecan pie. ["Homemade" modifies the unit "pecan pie," so there is no comma.]

7. Set off a direct address with commas.

Examples   Gentlemen, keep your seats.

Car fifty-four, where are you?

Not now, Eleanor, I'm busy.

8. Use commas to set off items in addresses and dates.

Examples   The sheriff followed me from Austin, Texas, to question me about my uncle.

He found me on February 2, 1978, when I stopped for gas in Fairbanks, Alaska.

9. Use commas to set off a degree or title following a name.

Examples   John Dough, M.D., was audited when he reported only $5.68 in taxable income last year.

The Neanderthal Award went to Samuel Lyle, Ph.D.

10. Use commas to set off dialogue from the speaker.

Examples   Alexander announced, "I don't think I want a second helping of possum."

"Eat hearty," said Marie, "because this is the last of the food."

11. Use commas to set off "yes," "no," "well," and other weak exclamations.

Examples   Yes, I am in the cat condo business.

No, all the units with decks are sold.

Well, perhaps one with a pool will do.

12. Set off interrupters or parenthetical elements appearing in the midst of a sentence. A parenthetical element is additional information placed as explanation or comment within an already complete sentence. This element may be a word (such as "certainly" or "fortunately"), a phrase ("for example" or "in fact"), or a clause ("I believe" or "you know"). The word, phrase, or clause is parenthetical if the sentence parts before and after it fit together and make sense.

Examples   Jack is, *I think,* still a compulsive gambler.

Harvey, *my brother,* sometimes has breakfast with him.

Jack cannot, *for example,* resist shuffling the toast or dealing the pancakes.

► PRACTICING WHAT YOU'VE LEARNED

Errors with Commas, Periods, Question Marks

The sentences below contain errors that may be corrected by changing, adding, or deleting commas, periods, and question marks.

1. The father decided to recapture his youth, he took his son's car keys away.

2. Researchers in Balboa, Panama have discovered that the poisonous, yellow-belly, sea snake which descended from the cobra, is the most deadly serpent in the world.

3. Yes in fact I have often asked myself why it's always the last key on the key ring that fits the lock?

4. Lulu Belle, my cousin, spent the week of Sept 1–7, 1986 in the woods near Dimebox, Texas looking for additions to her extinct, butterfly collection, however she wasn't at all successful in her search.

5. William Faulkner, the famous writer was apparently not such a great father, for example, when his daughter Jill begged him to stop drinking he scornfully asked her who ever heard of Shakespeare's child?

6. "Tom did you realize," said Janie. "That khaki pants first gained popularity during Queen Victoria's Afghan campaigns, unfortunately, the British soldier's traditional white uniform made too good a target"

7. Although ice cream didn't appear in America until the 1700s our country now leads the world in ice-cream consumption, Australia is second I think.

8. Last summer the large friendly family that lives next door flew Discount Airlines and visited three cities on their vacation, however, their suitcases visited five.

9. According to the Georgia-Pacific Corporation which is a wood products company, the phrase "by hook or crook" originated in feudal times when all forests belonged to the local lord of the manor, peasants could gather only those sticks of wood they could cut with a pruning hook, or snare with a shepherd's crook.

10. Arthur thought that most of the movies made in Hollywood California were too silly, therefore he started a letter writing campaign urging the film producers to shoot less film and more writers.

THE SEMICOLON (;)   P

1. Use a semicolon to link two closely related independent clauses.

Examples   Jean has been cooking Cajun-style for years without realizing it; her specialty is blackened eggs.

Kate's mother does not have to begin a jogging program; she gets all the exercise she needs by worrying in place.

2. Use a semicolon to avoid a comma splice when connecting two independent clauses with words like "however," "moreover," "thus," "therefore," and "consequently."

Examples   Vincent Van Gogh sold only one painting in his entire life; however, in 1987 his *Sunflowers* sold for almost $40 million.

All Esmeralda's plants die shortly after she gets them home from the store; consequently, she has the best compost heap in town.

This town is not big enough for both of us; therefore, I suggest we expand the city limits.

3. Use a semicolon in a series between items that already contain internal punctuation.

Examples   Last year the Wildcats suffered enough injuries to keep them from winning the pennant, as Jake Pritchett, third baseman, broke his arm in a fight; Hugh Rosenbloom, starting pitcher, sprained his back on a trampoline; and Boris Baker, star outfielder, ate rotten clams and nearly died.

Her children were born a year apart: Moe, 1936; Curley, 1937; and Larry, 1938.

THE COLON (:)   P

1. Use a colon to introduce a long or formal list, but do not use one after "to be" verbs.

Correct   Please pick up these items at the store: garlic, wolfbane, mirrors, a prayer book, a hammer, and a wooden stake.

Incorrect   Jean is such a bad cook that she thinks the four basic food groups are: canned, frozen, ready-to-mix, and take-out.

Correct Jean is such a bad cook that she thinks the four basic food groups are canned, frozen, ready-to-mix, and take-out.

Avoid needless colons.

Incorrect At the store I couldn't find: wolfbane or a wooden stake.

Correct At the store I couldn't find wolfbane or a wooden stake.

2. A colon may be used to introduce a quotation or definition.

Examples The late statesman Hubert Humphrey once jokingly apologized to reporters about his having been born in a small apartment above a drugstore: "They were short on log cabins that year."

Chicago film critic Roger Ebert once offered this definition of the ever-popular movie "crash scene": "An alternative to dialogue; a substitute for Burt Reynolds' continuing growth as an actor."

In singer Jimmy Buffett's Margaritaville shop and café in Key West, a sign warns: "Shoplifters will be forced to listen to Barry Manilow."

3. Use a colon to introduce a word, phrase, or sentence that emphatically explains, summarizes, or amplifies the preceding sentence.

Examples Harriet knew the one ingredient that would improve any diet dinner: chocolate.

Zsa Zsa Gabor's advice for becoming a marvelous housekeeper is simple: every time you leave a relationship, keep the house.

Horace made a big mistake at the office party: he kissed his boss's wife hello and his job goodbye.

▶ PRACTICING WHAT YOU'VE LEARNED

Errors with Semicolons and Colons

Correct the semicolon and colon errors below by adding, deleting, or substituting an appropriate mark of punctuation. Skip any correct sentences.

1. My doctor failed in his career as a kidnapper, no one could read his ransom notes.

2. Some of the cars manufactured between 1907 and 1912 that didn't achieve the popularity of the Model T were: the Black Crow, the Swallow, the Bugmobile, and the Carnation.

3. The highest point in the United States is Mt. McKinley at 20,320 feet, in contrast, the lowest point is Death Valley at 282 feet below sea level.

4. There's only one thing that can make our yard look as good as our neighbor's; snow.

5. In a Thurmont, Maryland, cemetery can be found this epitaph "Here lies an Atheist, all dressed up, and no place to go."

6. According to an 1863 book of etiquette, the perfect hostess will see to it that the works of male and female authors are properly separated on her bookshelves, however, if the authors happen to be married, their proximity may be tolerated.

7. Some inventors who named weapons after themselves include Samuel Colt, the Colt revolver, Henry Deringer, Jr., the derringer pistol, Dr. Richard J. Gatling, the crank machine gun, Col. John T. Thompson, the submachine or "tommy" gun, and Oliver F. Winchester, the repeating rifle.

8. George Bernard Shaw, the famous playwright, claimed he wanted the following epitaph on his tombstone: "I knew if I stayed around long enough, something like this would happen."

9. As we drove down the highway we saw a sign that said "See the World's Largest Prairie Dog Turn Right at this Exit," therefore we stopped to look.

10. The next billboard read "See Live Rattlesnakes Pet Baby Pigs"; making us want to stop again.

THE APOSTROPHE (')   AP

1. Use an apostrophe to indicate a contraction.

Examples   *It's* too bad your car burned.*

Wouldn't the insurance company believe your story?

2. Add an apostrophe plus "s" to a noun to show possession.

Examples   *Jack's* dog ate the *cat's* dinner.

The *veterinarian's* assistant later doctored the *puppy's* wounds.

---

* Don't confuse the contraction "it's" (for "it is") with the possessive pronoun "its," which never takes an apostrophe. (The car was old, but *its* coat of paint was new.)

3. Add only an apostrophe to a plural noun ending in "s" to show possession.

Examples   Goldilocks invaded the *bears'* house.

She ignored her *parents'* warning about breaking and entering.

4. In some cases you may add an apostrophe plus "s" to a singular word ending in "s," especially when the word is a proper name.

Examples   Bill Jones's car

Doris's chair

the class's project

5. To avoid confusion, you may use an apostrophe plus "s" to form the plurals of letters, figures, and words discussed as words; no apostrophe is also acceptable.

Examples   He made four *"C's"* last fall. [or *"Cs"*]

The right to resist the draft was a major issue in the *1960's*. [or *1960s*]

You use too many *"and's"* in your sentence. [or *"ands"*]

QUOTATION MARKS (" " and ' ')   P

1. Use quotation marks to enclose someone's spoken or written words.

Examples   The daughter wrote, "Remember, Daddy, when you pass on you can't take your money with you."

"But I've already bought a fireproof money belt," answered her father.

2. Use quotation marks around the titles of essays,* articles, chapter headings, short stories, short poems, and songs.

Examples   "How to Paint Ceramic Ashtrays"

"The Fall of the House of Usher"

"Stopping by Woods on a Snowy Evening"

"Yankee Doodle"

---

* Do *not,* however, put quotation marks around your own essay's title on either the title page or the first page of your paper.

3. You may either underline or place quotation marks around a word, phrase, or letter used as the subject of discussion.

Examples   Never use "however" as a coordinating conjunction.

The word "bigwig," to mean an important person, is derived from the large wigs worn by seventeenth-century British judges.

Is your middle initial "X" or "Y"?

Her use of such adjectives as "drab," "bleak," and "musty" gives the poem a somber tone.

4. Place quotation marks around uncommon nicknames and words used ironically. Do not, however, try to apologize for slang or clichés by enclosing them in quotation marks; instead, substitute specific words.

Examples   "Scat-cat" Malone takes candy from babies.
Her "friend" was an old scarecrow in an abandoned barn.

Slang   After work Chuck liked to "simple out" in front of the television.

Specific   After work Chuck liked to relax by watching old movies on television.

5. The period and the comma go inside quotation marks; the semicolon and the colon go outside. If the quoted material is a question, the question mark goes inside; if the quoted material is a part of a whole sentence that is a question, the mark goes outside. The same is true for exclamation points.

Examples   According to cartoonist Matt Groening, "Love is a snowmobile racing across the tundra; suddenly it flips over, pins you underneath, and at night the ice weasels come."

"Love is a snowmobile racing across the tundra; suddenly it flips over, pins you underneath, and at night the ice weasels come," says cartoonist Matt Groening.

According to cartoonist Matt Groening, "Love is a snowmobile . . . suddenly it flips over, pins you underneath, and at night the ice weasels come"; Groening also advises that bored friends are one of the first signs that you're in love.

Did he really say, "At night the ice weasels come"?

Sally asked, "Do you think you're in love or just in a snowmobile?"

6. Use single quotation marks to enclose a quotation (or words requiring quotation marks) within a quotation.

Examples   Professor Hall asked his class, "Do you agree with Samuel Johnson, who once said that a second marriage represents 'the triumph of hope over experience'?"

"One of my favorite songs is 'In My Life' by the Beatles," said Jane.

"I'm so proud of the 'A' on my grammar test," Sue told her parents.

▶ PRACTICING WHAT YOU'VE LEARNED

Errors with Apostrophes and Quotation Marks

Correct the errors below by adding, changing, or deleting apostrophes and quotation marks; skip any correct sentences.

1. Its true that when famous wit Dorothy Parker was told that President Coolidge, also known as Silent Cal, was dead, she exclaimed, How can they tell?

2. When a woman seated next to Coolidge at a dinner party once told him she had made a bet with a friend that she could get more than two words out of him, he replied You lose.

3. Twenty-one of Elvis Presleys albums have sold over a million copies; twenty of the Beatles albums have also done so.

4. Cinderellas stepmother wasn't pleased that her daughter received an F in her creative writing class on her poem Seven Guys and a Gal, which she had plagiarized from her friend's Snow White and Dopey.

5. Wasn't it Mae West who said, When choosing between two evils, I always like to try the one I've never tried before? asked Olivia.

6. Horace said Believe me, its to everybodies' advantage to sing the popular song You Stole My Heart and Stomped That Sucker Flat, if thats what the holdup man wants.

7. A scholars research has revealed that the five most commonly used words in written English are the, of, and, a, and to.

8. The triplets mother said that while its' hard for her to choose, O. Henrys famous short story The Ransom of Red Chief is probably her favorite.

9. Despite both her lawyers advice, she used the words terrifying, hideous, and unforgettable to describe her latest flight on Golden Fleece Airways, piloted by Jack One-Eye Marcus.

10. Its clear that Bubba didnt know if the Christmas' tree thrown in the neighbors yard was ours, theirs', or your's.

PARENTHESES ( )   P

1. Use parentheses to set off statements that give additional information or explain or qualify the main thought.

Examples   To encourage sales, some automobile manufacturers name their cars after fast or sleek animals (Impala, Mustang, and Thunderbird, for example).

The Ford Motor Company once rejected the name Utopian Turtletop for one of its new cars, choosing instead to call it the Edsel (that name obviously didn't help either).

2. The period comes inside the close parenthesis if a complete sentence is enclosed; it occurs after the close parenthesis when the enclosed matter comes at the end of the main sentence and is only a part of the main sentence.

Examples   The Colorado winters of 1978 and 1979 broke records for low temperatures. (See pages 72–73 for temperature charts.)

Jean hates Colorado winters and would prefer a warmer environment (such as Alaska, the North Pole, or a meat locker in Philadelphia).

3. If you are confused trying to distinguish whether information should be set off by commas, parentheses, or dashes, here are three general guidelines:

a. Use commas to set off information closely related to the rest of the sentence.

Example   When Billy Clyde married Maybelle, his brother's young widow, the family was shocked. [The information identifies Maybelle and tells why the family was shocked.]

b. Use parentheses to set off information loosely related to the rest of the sentence or material that would disturb the grammatical structure of the main sentence.

Examples   Billy Clyde married Maybelle (his fourth marriage, her second) in Las Vegas on Friday. [The information is merely additional comment not closely related to the meaning of the sentence.]

Billy Clyde married Maybelle (she was previously married to his brother) in Las Vegas on Friday. [The information is an additional comment that would also disturb the grammatical structure of the main sentence were it not enclosed in parentheses.]

c. Use dashes to set off information dramatically or emphatically.

Example   Billy Clyde eloped with Maybelle—only three days after her husband's funeral—without saying a word to anyone in the family.

BRACKETS [ ]   P

1. Use brackets to set off editorial explanations in quoted material.

Examples   According to the old letter, the treasure map could be found "in the library taped to the back of the portrait [of Gertrude the Great] that faces north."

The country singer ended the interview by saying, "My biggest hit so far is 'You're the Reason Our Kids Are Ugly'" [original version by Lola Jean Dillon].

2. Use brackets to set off editorial corrections in quoted material. By placing the bracketed word "sic" (meaning "thus") next to an error, you indicate that the mistake appeared in the original text and that *you* are not misquoting or misspelling.

Examples   The student wrote, "I think it's unfair for teachers to count off for speling [sic]."

["Sic" in brackets indicates that the student who is quoted misspelled the word "spelling."]

The highway advertisement read as follows: "For great stakes [sic], eat at Joe's, located right behind Daisy's Glue Factory." [Here, "sic" in brackets indicates an error in word choice; the restaurant owner incorrectly advertised "stakes" instead of "steaks."]

THE DASH (—)   P

1. Use a dash to indicate a strong or sudden shift in thought.

Examples   Now, let's be reasonable—wait, put down that ice pick!

"It's not athlete's foot—it's deadly coreopsis!" cried Dr. Mitty.

2. Use dashes to set off parenthetical matter that deserves more emphasis than parentheses denote.

Examples   Wanda's newest guru—the one who practiced catatonic hedonism—taught her to rest and play at the same time.

He was amazed to learn his test score—a pitiful 43.

(To clear up any confusion over the uses of dashes, commas, and parentheses, see the guidelines on pp. 386–387.)

3. Use a dash before a statement that summarizes or amplifies the preceding thought. (Dashes can also be used to introduce a humorous or ironic twist on the first idea in the sentence.)

Examples   Aged wine, delicious food, someone else picking up the check—the dinner was perfect.

Not everyone agrees with football coach Vince Lombardi, who said, "Winning isn't everything—it's the only thing."

According to Hollywood star Cher, "The trouble with some women is that they get all excited about nothing—and then marry him."

THE HYPHEN (-)   P

1. Use a hyphen to join words into a single adjective before a noun.

Examples   a wind-blown wig

the mud-caked sneakers

a made-for-television movie

a well-written essay

a five-year-old boy

Do not use a hyphen when the modifier ends in "ly."

Examples   a highly regarded worker

a beautifully landscaped yard

2. Some compound words use a hyphen; always check your dictionary when you're in doubt.

Examples   mother-in-law

president-elect

runner-up

good-for-nothing

twenty-one

3. Some words with prefixes use a hyphen; again, check your dictionary if necessary.

Examples   all-American

ex-wife

self-esteem

non-English

4. Use a hyphen to mark the separation of syllables when you divide a word at the end of a line. Do not divide one-syllable words; do not leave one or two letters at the end of a line. (In most dictionaries, dots are used to indicate the division of syllables. Example: va • ca • tion.)

Examples   In your essays you should avoid using fragment sentences.

Did your father try to help you with your homework?

ITALICS (UNDERLINING) (_____)   Ital

1. Underline or place quotation marks around a word, phrase, or letter used as the subject of discussion. Whether you underline or use quotation marks, always be consistent. (See also p. 384.)

Examples   No matter how I spell offered, it always looks wrong.

Is your middle initial X or Y?

Her use of such words as drab, bleak, and musty give the poem a somber tone.

2. Underline the title of books, magazines, newspapers, movies, works of art, television programs (but use quotation marks for individual episodes), airplanes, trains, and ships.

Examples   Moby Dick

The Reader's Digest

Texarkana Gazette

Gone with the Wind

Mona Lisa

Sixty Minutes

Spirit of St. Louis

Queen Mary

Exceptions: Do not underline the Bible or the titles of legal documents, including the United States Constitution, or the name of your own essay when it appears on your title page. Do not underline the city in a newspaper title unless the city's name is actually part of the newspaper's title.

3. Underline foreign words that are not commonly regarded as part of the English language.

Examples   He shrugged and said, "C'est la vie."

Under the "For Sale" sign on the old rusty truck, the farmer had written the words "caveat emptor," meaning "let the buyer beware."

4. Use underlining sparingly to show emphasis.

Examples   Everyone was surprised to discover that the butler didn't do it.

"Do you realize that your son just ate a piece of my priceless sculpture?" the artist screamed at the museum director.

THE ELLIPSIS MARK (. . . or . . . .)   P

1. To show an omission in quoted material within a sentence, use three periods, with spaces before and after each one.

Example   Every time my father tells the children about having to trudge barefooted to school in the snow, the walk gets longer and the snow gets deeper.

Every time my father tells the children about having to trudge barefooted to school . . . the snow gets deeper.

2. Three periods with spaces may be used to show an incomplete or interrupted thought.

Example   My wife is an intelligent, beautiful woman who wants me to live a long time. On the other hand, Harry's wife . . .

3. If you omit any words at the end of a quotation and you are also ending your sentence, use three dots plus a fourth to indicate your period. Do not add space before the first dot.

Example   Lincoln wrote, "Four score and seven years ago our fathers brought forth upon this continent, a new nation. . . ."

4. If the omission of one or more sentences occurs at the end of a quoted sentence, use four periods with no space before the first dot.

Example   "The Lord is my shepherd; I shall not want. . . . he leadeth me
in the paths of righteousness for his name's sake."

▶ PRACTICING WHAT YOU'VE LEARNED

Errors with Parentheses, Brackets, Dashes, Hyphens, Italics, and Ellipses

Correct the errors below by adding, changing, or deleting parentheses, brackets,
dashes, hyphens, italics, and ellipses.

1. Many moviegoers know that the ape in King Kong the original 1933
   version, not the re-make was only an eighteen inch tall animated figure, but not everyone realizes that the Red Sea Moses parted in the
   1923 movie of the Ten Commandments was a quivering slab of Jell O
   sliced down-the-middle.

2. Jean has found a way to keep the oven sparkling clean never turn it on.

3. In a person to person telephone call the twenty five year old starlet
   promised the hard working gossip columnist that she would "tell the
   truth . . . and nothing but the truth" about her highly-publicized
   feud with her exhusband, editor in chief of Meat Eaters' Digest.

4. While sailing across the Atlantic on board the celebrity filled yacht
   the Princess Diana, Dottie Mae Haskell she's the author of the popular
   new self help book Finding Wolves to Raise Your Children confided
   that until recently she thought chutzpah was an Italian side dish.

5. During their twenty four hour sit in at the melt down site, the anti
   nuclear protestors began to sing, "Oh, say can you see . . . "

6. Few people know that James Arness later Matt Dillon in the long running television series Gunsmoke got his start by playing the vegetable creature in the postwar monster movie The Thing 1951.

7. Similarly, the well known TV star Michael Landon he died of cancer
   in 1991 played the leading role in the 1957 classic I Was a Teenage
   Werewolf.

8. A French chemist named Georges Claude invented the first neon
   sign in 1910. For additional information on his unsuccessful attempts to use seawater to generate electricity, see pp. 200-205.

9. When Lucille Ball, star of I Love Lucy, became pregnant with her
   first child, the network executives decided that the word expecting
   could be used on the air to refer to her condition, but not the word
   pregnant.

10. In mystery stories the detective often advises the police to cherchez la
    femme. Editor's note: Cherchez la femme means "look for the woman."

15

A CONCISE
GUIDE TO
MECHANICS

•
•
•

CAPITALIZATION   Cap

1. Capitalize the first word of every sentence.

Example   The lazy horse leans against a tree all day.

2. Capitalize the proper names of people, places, and products, and also proper adjectives.

Examples   John Doe

Austin, Texas

First National Bank

Chevrolets

Japanese cameras

Spanish class

3. Always capitalize the days of the week, the names of the months, and holidays.

Examples   Saturday, December 14

Tuesday's meeting

Halloween parties

4. Capitalize titles when they are accompanied by proper names.

Examples   President Jones, Major Smith, Governor Brown, Judge Wheeler, Professor Plum, Queen Elizabeth

5. Capitalize all the principal words in titles of books, articles, stories, plays, movies, and poems. Prepositions, articles, and conjunctions are not capitalized unless they begin the title or contain more than four letters.

Examples   "The Face on the Barroom Floor"

A Short History of the War Between the States

For Whom the Bell Tolls

6. Capitalize the first word of a direct quotation.

Examples   Shocked at actor John Barrymore's use of profanity, the woman said, "Sir, I'll have you know I'm a lady!"

Barrymore replied, "Your secret is safe with me."

7. Capitalize "east," "west," "north," and "south" when they refer to particular sections of the country but not when they merely indicate direction.

Examples   The South has produced many excellent writers, including William Faulkner and Flannery O'Connor. ["South" here refers to a section of the country.]

If you travel south for ten miles, you'll see the papier-mâché replica of the world's largest hamburger. [In this case, "south" is a direction.]

8. Capitalize a title when referring to a particular person;* do not capitalize a title if a pronoun precedes it.

Examples   The President announced a new national holiday honoring Frank H. Fleer, inventor of bubble gum.

The new car Dad bought is guaranteed for 10,000 miles or until something goes wrong.

---

* Some authorities disagree; others consider such capitalization optional.

My mother told us about a Hollywood party during which Zelda and F. Scott Fitzgerald collected and boiled all the women's purses.

ABBREVIATIONS   Ab

1. Abbreviate the titles "Mr.," "Mrs.," "Ms.," "St.," and "Dr." when they precede names.

Examples   Dr. Scott, Ms. Steinham, Mrs. White, St. Jude

2. Abbreviate titles and degrees when they follow names.

Examples   Charles Byrd, Jr.; David Hall, Ph.D.; Dudley Carpenter, D.D.S.

3. You may abbreviate the following in even the most formal writing: A.M. (*ante meridiem,* before noon), P.M. (*post meridiem,* after noon), A.D. (*anno Domini,* in the year of our Lord), B.C. (before Christ), etc. (*et cetera,* and others), i.e. (*id est,* that is), and e.g. (*exempli gratia,* for example).

4. In formal writing do *not* abbreviate the names of days, months, centuries, states, countries, or units of measure. Do *not* use an ampersand ("&") unless it is an official part of a title.

Incorrect in formal writing	Tues., Sept., 18th century, Ark., Mex., lbs.
Correct	Tuesday, September, eighteenth century, Arkansas, Mexico, pounds
Incorrect	Tony & Gus went to the store to buy ginseng root.
Correct	Tony *and* Gus went to the A & P to buy ginseng root. [The "&" in "A & P" is correct because it is part of the store's official name.]

5. Do *not* abbreviate the words for page, chapter, volume, and so forth, except in footnotes and bibliographies, which have prescribed rules of abbreviation. (For additional information on proper abbreviation, consult your dictionary.)

NUMBERS   Num

1. Use figures for dates, street numbers, page numbers, telephone numbers, and hours with A.M. and P.M.*

---

* 8:00 A.M. but eight o'clock.

Examples   April 22, 1946

710 West 14th Street

page 242

476–1423

10:00 A.M.

2. Some authorities say spell out numbers that can be expressed in one or two words; others say spell out numbers under one hundred.

Examples   Ten thousand dollars or $10,000

Twenty-four hours

Thirty-nine years

Five partridges

$12.99 per pair

1,294 essays

3. When several numbers are used in a short passage, use figures.

Examples   On the punctuation test, Jennifer made 82, Juan made 91, Pete made 86, and I made 60.

The hole in the ground was 12 feet long, 10 feet wide, 21 feet deep, and 2 feet from my house.

4. Never begin a sentence with a figure.

Incorrect   50 spectators turned out to watch the surfing exhibition at Niagara Falls.

Correct   Fifty spectators turned out to watch the surfing exhibition at Niagara Falls.

▶ PRACTICING WHAT YOU'VE LEARNED

Errors with Capitalization, Abbreviations, and Numbers

Correct the errors below by adding, deleting, or changing capitals, abbreviations, and numbers. Skip any correct words, letters, or numbers you may find.

1. According to Abigail Van Buren, newspaper columnist, in 1980 handguns killed 4 people in Australia, 8 in Canada, 18 in Sweden, 8 in England, 23 in Israel, and 11,522 in the United States.

2. My sister, who lives in the east, was amazed to read studies by Thomas Radecki, MD, showing that 12-year-olds commit 300 percent more murders than did the same age group 30 years ago.

3. In sixty-seven A.D. the roman emperor Nero entered the chariot race at the olympic games, and although he failed to finish the race, the judges unanimously declared him the Winner.

4. According to John Alcock, a Behavioral Ecologist at Arizona State University, in the U.S.A. the chances of being poisoned by a snake is 20 times less than that of being hit by lightning and 300 times less than the risk of being murdered by a fellow American.

5. The official chinese news agency, located in the city of xinhua, estimates that there are ten million guitar players in their country today, an amazing number considering that the instrument had been banned during the cultural revolution that lasted 10 years, from nineteen sixty-six to nineteen seventy-six.

6. 231 electoral votes were cast for James Monroe but only 1 for John Quincy Adams in the 1820 Presidential race.

7. The british soldier T. E. Lawrence, better known as "lawrence of arabia," stood less than 5 ft. 6 in. tall.

8. Drinking a glass of french wine makes me giddy before my 10 a.m. english class, held in wrigley field every other friday except on New Year's day.

9. When a political opponent once called him "two-faced," president Lincoln retorted, "if I had another face, do you think I would wear this one?"

10. In 1883, when american aviator Orville Wright was in the 6th grade, he was expelled from his Richmond, Ind., school for mischievous behavior.

SPELLING Sp

For some folks, learning to spell correctly is harder than trying to herd cats. Entire books have been written to teach people to become better spellers, and copies of some of these are probably available at your local book store (and, no, not listed under witchcraft, either). Here, however, are a few suggestions that seem to work for a number of students:

1. Keep a list of the little beasties you misspell. After a few weeks you may notice that you tend to misspell the same words again and again or that the words you misspell tend to fit a pattern—that is, you can't remember when the *i* goes before the *e* or when to change the *y* to *i* before *ed*. Try to memorize the words you repeatedly misspell, or at least keep the list somewhere handy so you can refer to it when you're editing your last draft (listing the words on the inside cover of your dictionary makes sense).

2. Become aware of a few rules that govern some of our spelling in English. For example, many people know the rule in the jingle "*I* before *E* except after *C* or when it sounds like *A* as in *neighbor* and *weigh.*" Not everyone, however, knows the follow-up line, which contains most of the exceptions to that jingle: "Neither the weird financier nor the foreigner seizes leisure at its height."

3. Here are some other rules, without jingles, for adding suffixes, a common plague for poor spellers:

- Change final *y* to *i* if the *y* follows a consonant.

    bury = buried
    married = marries

- But if the suffix is *-ing,* keep the *y*.

    marry + ing = marrying
    worry + ing = worrying

- If the word ends in a single consonant after a single vowel and the accent is on the last syllable, double the consonant before adding the suffix.

    occur = occurred
    cut = cutting
    swim = swimmer

- If a word ends in a silent *e,* drop the *e* before adding *-able* or *-ing.*

    love + able = lovable
    believe + able = believable

4. And here's an easy rule governing the doubling of letters with the addition of prefixes: most of the time, you simply add all the letters you've got when you mix the word and the prefix.

mis + spell = misspell

un + natural = unnatural

re + entry = reentry

5. Teach yourself to spell the words that you miss often by making up your own silly rules or jingles. For instance:

dessert (one *s* or two?): I always want two helpings so I double the *s.*

separate (separete?): I'd be a *rat* to sepa*rat*e from you, darling.

recommendation (one or two *m*'s?): *Mm,* let me think of something good to say about her.

a lot (or alot?): A cot (not acot) provides *a lot* of comfort.

And so on.

6. Don't forget to proofread your papers carefully. Anything that looks misspelled probably is, and deserves to be looked up in your dictionary. Reading your paper one sentence at a time from the end helps too, because you tend to start thinking about your ideas when you read from the beginning of your paper. (And if you are writing on a word processor that has a spell program, don't forget to run it!)

Although these few suggestions won't completely cure your spelling problems, they may make a dramatic improvement in the quality of your papers and give you the confidence to continue learning and practicing other rules that govern the spelling of our language. Good luck!

INDEX

Abbreviations:
  exercises, 396–397
  usage, 395
Abstraction, 139–140, 164, 226
Accuracy, 154–155
Adjectives:
  errors with, 365–366
  exercises, 367–368
  faulty comparison, 366
  incorrect usage, 365–366
Adverbs:
  conjunctive, 375–376
  errors with, 365–366
  exercises, 367–368
  faulty comparison, 366
  incorrect usage, 365–366
Advertising:
  argumentation and, 283
  bandwagon appeal technique, 271
  connotations and, 159
  pro/con advertising, 280
Allen, Woody, 164
American Psychological Association (APA), 344
Analysis, 13
"Androgynous Male, The" (Perrin), 230–233
Angelou, Maya, 310–319
Anger, 109, 156
APA documentation style, 344–347
Apology, 91
Apostrophe:
  exercises, 385–386
  usage, 382–383
Argumentation:
  anticipate opposing views, 260
  audience, 260–261, 267
  development, 260–269
  emotional appeal, 266–267, 270

evidence, 267–268
examples, 266
exercises, 272–273
function of, 259
logic, 266–267
logical fallacies, 269–272
organization, 263–267
persuasion, 260, 268
Pro-and-Con sheet, 261–262, 265
problems to avoid, 269
professional essays, 278–279
purpose, 259
revision worksheet, 283
Rogerian techniques, 268–269
sample student essay, 275–278
tone, 268
topic proposals, 275
working thesis, 262
Aristotle, 15
Attitude, 22, 114–115
Audience:
  attraction of, 87–88
  awareness of, 29, 91, 292
  as critic, 107
  details and, 125
  discovering, 20–21, 24
  forgetting, 332
  identifying, 20–24
  insulting, 38
  logic and, 72
  revisions regarding, 105
  role as, 116
  supporting evidence and, 62
  tips regarding, 23–24
  writing for, 4
Awkwardness, 91, 141

Baker, Russell, 242–244
"Ban Those Books!" 272–273

Beginnings:
  development of, 87–92
  exercises, 92, 96
  summary, 97
Bias, 22, 109
Bibliography:
  card entry, 324–325
  note-taking, 326–328
  "References" list, 345
  working, 326
  works cited in, 338–339
"Blind Paces," 228–230
Body:
  defined, 47
  paragraph, see Paragraphs, body
  planning of, 47–50
Boomerang, 11–12
Boredom, 23, 138, 171
Brackets:
  exercises, 391
  usage, 387
Brady, James, 280
Brainstorming, 7
"Breatharianism," 24
"Bringing Back the Joy of Market Day," 214–217
Brown University, 139
Bureaucratic jargon, 165, 174–175
Burke, Kenneth, 17

Calhoun, John C., 3
Capitalization:
  exercises, 396–397
  guidelines for, 393–395
Card catalog, 324–325
"Catching Garage Sale Fever," 198–201
Catch-22, 304
Catchy phrases, 272
Catton, Bruce, 217–220

Causal analysis:
  cause/effect relationship, 246, 248
  circular logic, 249
  defined, 246
  development, 247–248
  limitations, 247
  organization, 247–248
  oversimplification, 248
  post hoc fallacy, 249
  problems to avoid, 248–249
  professional essays, 253–255
  revision worksheet, 256–257
  sample student essay, 251–253
  thesis statement, 247
  topic proposals, 250
Cause and effect, 246, 248
Checklist, for effective essays, 113–114
Choppiness, 75, 84, 140, 146, 212
Christie, Agatha, 122
Chronological order, 194
Circular definitions, 226
Circumstance, 16
Citations, see Bibliography; Documentation
Clarity:
  lack of, 36
  process analysis and, 194–195
  revisions and, 110–111
  revision workshops and, 115–116
  sentences and, 123–130
  significance of, 4, 32, 36, 38, 113, 138, 237
Classification:
  basis of, 236
  categories, 237–238
  clarity and audience, 237
  defined, 136
  development, 236–237
  dividing a subject into its parts, 237
  problems to avoid, 237–238
  professional essays, 242–244
  revision worksheet, 245
  sample student essay, 240–242

topic proposals, 239
types of, 237
Clauses, 132, 140, 145–146
Clichés, 163–164, 384
Clustering, 12
Coherence:
  lack of, 185
  need for, 44, 71–77
College campus, 5
Collette, 99
Colloquial language, 155
Colon:
  exercises, 381–382
  usage, 381
Comma:
  conjunctive adverbs and, 375–376
  exercises, 379–380
  quotation marks and, 384
  splice, 375–376
  usage, 374–379
Comma splice, 375–376
Commitment, 4
Common knowledge, 332–333
Communication:
  goal of, 4
  modes of, 177–178
Comparison and contrast:
  block, 210–211
  choppy essay, 212
  clear and distinct descriptions, 212
  cross-examination and, 16
  cubing and, 13
  development of, 209–211
  point by point, 209–210
  problems to avoid, 211–212
  professional essays, 217–220
  revision worksheet, 221
  sample student essay, 214–216
  "so-what" thesis, 211–212
  thesis statement and, 209
  topic proposals, 214
Complaints, 91
Compound words, 388
Compromise, 270–271
Computers, word processing programs, 103–104
Conciseness, 130
Conclusions:
  avoiding errors in, 94–95
  significance of, 196
  suggestions for, 92–94

tips for, 92–94, 97
topic sentence and, 56
Confucius, 153
Confusion, 23, 33, 95, 128, 154, 170–171
Conjunctions:
  coordinating, 144–145
  subordinating, 145–147
Conjunctive adverbs, 375–376
Connotation, 159–160
Conrad, Joseph, 3, 64, 291
Content, questions regarding, 191–192, 206–207, 220–221, 233–234, 244, 255–256, 279–280, 300, 319–320
Contractions, 382
Coordination:
  equally weighted ideas, 144
  of sentences, 144–145
Creativity, 28, 96
Critical thinking:
  defined, 107
  process of, 107–109
Cross-examination, 15–16
Cubing, 12–13, 15

Dangling modifiers, 129, 366–367
Dash(es):
  exercises, 391
  usage, 387–388
Data-base searches, 326
Day book, see Journal
Deadwood construction, 131–133
Deception, 270
Deductive order, 73
Definition, circular, 226
Definition, Extended:
  clarity and audience, 224–225
  cross-examination and, 15
  development, 223–225
  generalities, 226
  incomplete, 225
  problems to avoid, 225–226
  professional essays, 230–233
  purpose, 223–224
  quotations, 225–226
  reasons for, 223
  revision worksheet, 234–235
  sample student essay, 228–230

Definition, Extended
    (Continued)
    sensory details, 290–291
    topic proposals, 227
    vagueness, 226
Denotation, 159–160
Description:
    approaches, 288
    appropriate details, 289–290
    audience, awareness of,
      292
    dominant impression,
      289–290
    objective, 287–288
    organization, 292
    perspective, change in, 292
    problems to avoid, 292
    professional essays,
      297–300
    purpose, 287–288
    revision worksheet, 301
    sample student essay,
      294–297
    sensory details, 290–291
    specific details, 288–289
    subjective, 288
    topic proposals, 293–294
    vividness, 290–292
Details:
    audience and, 125
    insignificant, 306
    lack of, 184–185
    narration and, 304–306
    sensory, 139, 290–291
    specific, 125–126, 288
Development:
    argumentation, 260–269
    causal analysis, 247–248
    comparison and contrast,
      209–214
    definition, 223–227
    division and classification,
      236–237
    example, 184–185
    paragraphs, 60–64
    process analysis, 193–196
Dialogue, 305, 378
Dictionary, as source, 112,
    154–155, 389
Diminutives, 169
Directional process analysis,
    193
Directions, 193
Direct quotations, *see*
    Quotations

Discovery, 20, 31, 33
"Discus Thrower, The"
    (Selzer), 297–300
Disorder, 23
Division:
    account for all parts of, 237
    basis of, 236
    categories, 237–238
    clarity and audience, 237
    defined, 235–236
    development, 236–237
    dividing a subject into its
      parts, 237
    problems to avoid, 237–238
    professional essays,
      242–244
    revision worksheet, 245
    sample student essay,
      240–242
    topic proposals, 239
Division and classification,
    see Classification;
    Division
Documentation:
    articles, 347
    books, 340–341, 346–347
    dissertations, 342
    encyclopedias, 342
    films, 342
    interviews, 343, 347
    lectures, 343
    letters, 343
    magazines, 341
    newspapers, 341
    performances, 343
    pamphlets, 342
    parenthetical, defined, 338
    periodicals, 341
    radio, 342
    records, 343
    speeches, 343
    styles of, 337–347
    television, 342
Dominant impression,
    289–290
"Dorm Life," 117–119
Double negative, 358–359
Drafts:
    basics of the short essay,
      ten rules, 176
    exercises, 117–120
    first, 90
    format of, 102–103
    preparation for, 102–103
    revisions, 100–111

    saving rough drafts, 103
    summary, 122
Drama, subject and, 17–19

Editing, tips for, 101, 111–112
Effect, questions asked by, 246
Elbow, Peter, 9
Ellipses:
    exercises, 391
    usage, 390–391
Emotions:
    argument *ad populum,* 278
    argumentation, 266–267,
      270
    arousing positive feelings,
      159
    significance of, 22–23, 158
    see also Argumentation,
      emotional appeal
Emphasis:
    significance of, 139–140
    style development, 143–144
Encouragement, significance
    of, 116
Ending:
    exercises, 95–96
    significance of, 92–95
    summary, 97
    See also Conclusion
Endnote form, 343–344
Enthusiasm, 4, 35
Essay:
    basic, ten rules for drafts,
      176
    effective, checklist,
      113–114
    parts, three, 87
Essay map, 41–43
et al. usage, 345
Euphemisms, 166–168
Evidence:
    significance of, 62, 106–107
    supporting, 62, 267–268
    unrepresentative, 269
Examples:
    clarity, 182, 184–185
    coherence, lack of, 185
    development by, 184
    extended, 181
    importance of, 183
    persuasive, 184–185
    problems to avoid, 184–185
    professional essays,
      189–191
    relevant, 184

revision worksheet, 192–193
sample student essay, 187–188
topic proposals, 186–187
weakness, lack of specific detail, 184–185
well chosen, 184
Exclamation point:
exercises, 379–380
usage, 374
Experience, personal, 5
Exposition:
causal analysis, 246–257
comparison and contrast, 209–222
defined, 179
definition essays, 222–235
division and classification, 235–246
example, 180–193
process analysis, 193–208
strategies, 179–257
Extended definition, *see* Definition, Extended

Fallacies, *see* Logical fallacies
Farewell to Arms, A (Hemingway), 99
Fatigue, 104
Faulty predication, 130, 370–371
Fiction, 303
Figurative language, 169–171, 291
Fillers, 131
First impression, 87
First person, 304
Flashback, 304
Flippancy, 115–116, 157–158, 164
Focus:
problems and, 29
significance of, 6–7, 29, 36, 110
works like a camera, 6
Footnote/bibliography documentation style, 343–344
Foreign words, 390
Formal language, 156
Formal writing, 395
Fragments, sentence, 368–369
Free association, 8, 13

Freewriting, 8–9
Freud, Sigmund, 157

Gender, 168–169
Generalities, 62–63, 91, 224, 271, 288
Getting started, 3–4
Gobbledygook, 165
"Graduation" (Angelou), 310–319
Graffiti, 222
Grammar, errors in, 355–372
"Grant and Lee: A Study in Contrasts" (Catton), 217–220

He/she generic pronoun problem, 168–169
Hemingway, Ernest, 99, 126, 222
Hiccup syndrome, 140
Hill, Anita, 223
Hoover, Herbert, 140
However, usage, 374, 376
Humor, effectiveness of, 158, 237
Huxley, Aldous, 168
Hyperbole, 291
Hyphens:
exercises, 391
usage, 388–389

"I," usage, 141
ibid., usage, 344
Idea hook, 84
Ideas:
basic, to writing, 9
confidence in, 4
modifiers, 127
note-taking, 328
related, 144
revisions for, 105–109
saving, 28
Idiomatic phrases, 154–155
"I Have A Dream" (King), 267
Images, 267
Impression:
dominant, 289–290
first, 87
"Indian Era at Mesa Verde, The," 240–242
Inductive order, 74
Infinitive:
phrases, 133
split, 358

Informal language, 155
Informative process, 193–194
"Input to output, 35 minutes," 174–175
Intention, four modes of communication, 177–178
Interrupters, parenthetical elements, 378–379
Interviews, 15, 109
Introduction, *see* Beginnings; Lead-ins; Thesis statements
Introductory phrases, 132, 376
Invective, 156
Inversion, for emphasis, 143–144
Irony, 157
Italics (underlining):
exercises, 391
usage, 389–390
"It's Simply Not Worth It," 251–253

Jargon, avoidance of, 135, 164–166
Journal:
benefits of, 27
uses of, 27–30

Kennedy, John F., 108, 156
Kerr, Jean, 3
Key words, repetition of, 76–77
King, Martin Luther, Jr., 267
King, Rodney, 223
Knowledge, your subject and audience, 21, 91

Language:
levels of, 155–156
sensitivity to, 29
Lax, Paul, 279
Lead-ins:
avoiding errors in, 91–92
benefits of, 97
types of, 87–91
Length of paragraph, 65–66
"Let's make a deal," 121
Levels of language, *see* Language, levels of
Libraries:
card catalog, 324–325
data-base searches, 326
periodical indexes, 325
special collections, 326

Listing, 7–8
Logic, circular, 249
Logical fallacies:
    argument *ad hominem,* 270
    argument *ad populum,* 270
    bandwagon appeal, 271
    begging the question, 269
    circular logic, 226
    common types of, 269–272
    evidence and, 109
    faulty analogy, 271–272
    hasty generalization, 269
    hypostatization, 271
    non sequitur, 269
    one right, one wrong,
        270–271
    post hoc, ergo propter hoc,
        249, 270
    quick fix, 272
    red herring, 270
    straw man, 271
Looping, 9–11

Magazines, 65
Mapping, 12, 16
Marx Brothers, 128
Meaning, connotation and
    denotation, 159–160
Mechanics:
    abbreviations, 395
    capitalization, 393–395
    errors in, 94, 112
    numbers, 395–396
    spelling, 397–399
Metaphor, 170, 291
Miscommunication, 164
Misplaced modifiers, 129,
    367
Mitford, Jessica, 201–206
Mixed construction, 130
MLA documentation style:
    sample student essay,
        348–352
    techniques, 337–343
Modern Language
    Association of America
    (MLA), 337
Modes of communication, *see*
    Communication;
    Strategies
Modifiers:
    dangling, 129, 366–367
    exercises, 367–368
    misplaced, 129, 367
    position of, 127

specific, precise, 139
    vague, 163
Modifying phrases, errors in,
    366–368
Motivation, for writing, 3–4
"Motorcycle Helmet Laws
    Mock Freedom" (Lax),
    279
"Motorcycle Helmet Laws
    Protect Everyone" (*USA
    Today* Editorial Board),
    278–279

Names:
    connotations, 159
    proper, 166–168
Narration:
    brief, 303
    characters, believable, 305
    defined, 303
    details, 304–306
    dialogue, 305
    extended, 303
    insignificant details, 306
    limiting scope, 306
    logical time sequence, 304
    point of view, 304
    problems to avoid, 305–306
    professional essays,
        310–319
    purpose, 304
    revision worksheet,
        320–321
    sample student essay,
        308–310
    subject choice, 305–306
    topic proposals, 307–308
Narrowing a subject, 5–6,
    35–36
National Rifle Association,
    280
"Never Underestimate the
    Little Things" 308–310
Newspapers, 65
Nixon, Richard, 271
Nominalizations, 166
Non sequitur, 269
Nouns:
    misuse as adjectives, 361
    possessive case, 360
    vague, 162–163
Numbers:
    exercises, 396–397
    usage of, 395–396

Obscenity, 156
Observation, 28
"Of" phrases, 133
Omissions, 390
Opinions:
    commitment to, 4
    distinguished from fact,
        107–108
    support of, 108
Order:
    deductive, 73
    inductive, 74
    of information, 72
    logical, chronological, 194
    process analysis, 194
    space, 73
    time, 72
    of words, *see* Word order
Organization:
    argumentation and,
        263–267
    causal analysis, 247–248
    description, 292
    paragraphs and, 50
    process analysis, 195
    revisions regarding,
        109–110
    significance of, 195
Orwell, George, 134
Outlines, 48–50
Oversimplification, 237
Overuse:
    lead-ins, 92
    of similar constructions,
        140–141

Paragraph:
    coherence, 71–77
    composition of, 50–51
    concluding, 92–95
    development, 60–65
    exercises, 56–60, 65–67,
        69–71, 78–83, 95
    first sentence, 83, 97
    length of, 65
    organization, 50
    planning, 47–50
    sequence of, 93
    summary, 85
    topic sentence and, 51–56,
        64, 67, 69
    transitions, 83–84
    unity, 67–70
Parallelism, 77
Paraphrase, use of, 238–239

Parentheses:
  exercises, 391
  usage, 386–387
Parenthetical elements,
    interrupters, 378–379
Passive voice, verbs, 134, 359
Period:
  exercises, 379–380
  quotation marks and, 384
  usage, 374
Perrin, Noel, 230–233
Periodical indexes, 325
Personification, 291
Persuasion:
  techniques of, 156, 333
  tone and, 268
Phrases:
  catchy, 272
  idiomatic, 154–155
  infinitive, 133
  introductory, 132, 376
  modifying, 366–368
  prepositional, 141
Plagiarism, 333–336
Platitudes, 163
"Plot Against People, The"
    (Baker), 242–244
Point of view, 141, 304
Politicians:
  connotation and, 159
  emotional appeal and,
    266–267
Pomposity, avoidance of, 134,
    158–159, 164–165
Possessive case, 360
Preachiness, 158
Predication, faulty, 130,
    370–371
Prepositional phrases, 141
Pretentiousness, avoidance
    of, 24, 134–135, 164–165
Prewriting:
  exercises, 19–20
  summary of, 30
  techniques, 3–30
Pro-and-Con sheet, 261–262,
    265
Process analysis:
  accuracy, 194–195
  clarity, 194–195
  conclusion, 196
  defined, 193
  development of, 194–195
  directional, 193
  equipment description, 194

informative, 193–194
linking words, 195
order, 194
organization, 195
problems to avoid, 196
professional essays,
    201–206
revision worksheet, 208
sample student essay,
    198–201
special terms defined, 194
subject of, 195
thesis, 196
topic proposals, 197–198
Profanity, 38, 156
Professional essays (texts):
  argumentation, 278–279
  causal analysis, 253–255
  classification, 242–244
  comparison and contrast,
    217–220
  definition, 230–233
  description, 297–300
  division and classification,
    242–244
  example, 189–191
  narration, 310–319
  process analysis, 201–206
Progress report, benefits
    of, 29
Pronouns:
  errors with, 361–364
  exercises, 364–365
  faulty agreement, 361–362
  generic problem, 168
  incorrect case, 363–364
  shift in, 362–363
  substituted for nouns, 76–77
  vague reference, 362
Proofreading, 101, 113
Propaganda, 159
Prose, four basic types of,
    177–178
Punctuation:
  apostrophe, 382–383
  brackets, 387
  colon, 380–381
  comma, 374–379, 384
  dash(es), 387–388
  ellipsis mark, 390–391
  exclamation point, 374
  guide to, 373–387
  hyphen, 388–389
  italics (underlining),
    389–390

parentheses, 386–387
period, 374, 384
purpose of, 373
question mark, 374
quotation marks, 383–385
semicolon, 380
Purpose:
  audience and, 237
  drafts and, 150
  finding, 4, 6–7
  recognition of, 287
  revisions regarding,
    105–106
  significance of, 304
  word choice, 155, 159

Question mark:
  exercises, 379–380
  usage, 374
Quick fix, 272
Quotation marks:
  exercises, 385–386
  usage, 332, 383–385
Quotations:
  dropped in, 331–332
  material longer than five
    typed lines, 338
  overuse of, 331
  punctuation, see Quotation
    marks
  varied sentence pattern, 332

Reader, see Audience
Reagan, Ronald, 127, 223, 280
Red herring, 270
Redundancy, 133
Relaxation, 104
Repetition:
  key words and, 76
  result of, 171
Research paper:
  balanced treatment,
    329–330
  biased sources, 329
  borrowed material as
    "window," 335
  choosing sources, 329–331
  current sources, 330
  domination of reference
    material, 333
  incorporating source
    material, 331–333
  library research, 324–326
  logical use of sources, 331
  note-taking, 326–328

Research paper *(Continued)*
  paraphrase vs. summary,
    328–329
  persuasive writing, 333
  reliability of sources, 329
  search for topic, 324
  supplementary notes,
    348
  support, 332–333
  validity of sources, 330
  See also Documentation;
    Plagiarism
Revision:
  defined, 100
  misconceptions regarding,
    100–102
  necessity, 100
  occurrence of, 100
  preparation for, 102–103
  process of, 104–113
  skill improvement, 102
  thinking process, 100
  word choice and, 171
  workshops for, 114–117
Rhetorical question, 91
"River Rafting Teaches
    Worthwhile Lessons,"
    187–188
Rogers, Carl, 268
Roosevelt, Franklin, 135
Rough drafts, *see* Drafts
Run-on sentences, 369–370

Sarcasm, 157, 268
"Scaring the Public to Death"
    (Trippett), 253–255
Selzer, Richard, 297–300
Semicolon:
  exercises, 381–382
  usage, 380
Sensitivity, 29
Sensory details, 139,
    290–291
Sentence:
  average number of words
    in, 111
  beginning with transition
    word, 76
  center-of-gravity, 9–11
  choppiness, 146
  clarity problems, 124
  comma splice, 369
  concise style, 130–135
  content, 124–125

coordination, 144–145
  exercises, 135–137,
    142–143, 147–150,
    371–372
  faulty construction,
    368–370
  faulty parallelism, 370
  faulty predication, 130,
    370–371
  fragments, 368–369
  identically constructed, 140
  mixed construction, 130,
    371
  repeating patterns, 140
  run-on, 369–370
  simple, 126–127
  specific, 125–126
  subordination, 145–147
  summary, 151
  word selection, 134
Sentimentality, 158
Sexist language, 168–169
She/he generic pronoun
    problem, 168–169
sic, usage, 327
Simile, 169–170, 291
Simplicity, 126–127
Sketching, 17, 265
Slang, 164, 384
Slogans, empty, 272
Sources, *see* Documentation;
    Research papers
"So What's So Bad About
    Being So-so?," 189–191
Space, order of, 73
Special terms, defined, 194
Specialized language, 165
Specificity, 115–116
Spelling:
  checking, 112
  improvement, 30
  tips for, 397–399
Split infinitive, 358
Split-page entry, 28
Statistics, 330
Stereotyping, 168
Strategies, of exposition, *see*
    Exposition
Straw man diversions, 271
Strick, Lisa Wilson, 189–191
Structure, questions
    regarding, 191–192,
    206–207, 220–221,
    233–234, 244, 255–256,
    279–280, 300, 319–320

Student essays (text):
  argumentation, 276–278
  causal analysis, 251–253
  comparison and contrast,
    214–217
  cubing, 13
  definition, 228–230
  description, 294–297
  division and classification,
    240–242
  essays developed by
    example, 187–188
  looping, 10–11
  narration, 308–310
  process analysis, 198–201
  sample of MLA style,
    348–352
"Students, Take Note!"
    276–278
Style:
  clear, 124–130
  concise, 130–135
  emphatic, 143–150
  lively, 138–143
  questions regarding,
    191–192, 206–207,
    220–221, 233–234, 244,
    255–256, 279–280, 300,
    319–320
  revisions regarding, 111
  varying sentences, 140
Subject:
  audience knowledge, 21
  caring about, 4
  dramatizing, 17–19
  selection,
    enthusiasm, 4
    narrowing a large
      subject, 5–6
    reader and, 194
    starting early, 4–5
    strong interest, 5
  thesis statement and,
    34–35
Subjunctive, verb, 357–358
Subordination, of sentences,
    145–147
Summarizing, 329
Supplementary notes, 348
Swift, Jonathan, 157
Synecdoche, 291

Tack-on words, 166
Tense shift, 358
Testimony, 16

Textbook, write your own, 29–30
Thesis:
  implied, 37
  significance of, 196
Thesis statement:
  defined, 32
  errors in, 37–39
  essay map, 41–43
  exercises, 39–41, 43–45
  express in one sentence, 32
  formulation of,
    changes in, 32–33
    common errors in, 37–39
    defined, 32
    guidelines for, 33–37
    introduction of, 91
  function of, 32, 46
  lead-in introduction, 91
  limited to fit assignment, 35–36
  location, 37
  one main idea, 34
  opinion, clearly defined, 33
  qualities of good thesis, 33–37
  revisions regarding, 105
  specific terms, 36–37
  summary, 46
  time of discovering, 37, 46
  universalizing, 35
  working, 19, 32, 46
"Thing," use of, 162
Thomas, Clarence, 223
Thurber, James, 101
Time:
  avoiding pressure, 102, 120
  order of, 72
Title:
  function of, 95–97
  rules for, 96–97
"To be," 132, 138
"To Bid the World Farewell" (Mitford), 201–206

Tone, significance of, 22, 88, 156–159, 268
Topic, see Subject
Topic sentence:
  exercises, 56–60
  focus, 54
  function of, 51–54, 65, 67
  placing, 54–56
  recasting, 53
  samples, 51
  specific language, 51
  support for your essay, 51
Transition:
  devices, 75
  key words, 76–77
  paragraphs, 83–84
  parallelism, 77
  pronouns, 76–77
  words and phrases, 74–76
"Treeclimbing" 294–297
Trendy expressions, 164
Trippett, Frank, 253–255
Triteness, 163–164
Twain, Mark, 24, 126, 154, 330
Typed papers, 103

Ultimate in Diet Cults: Don't Eat Anything At All, The, 24–26
Underlining, 389–391
Understatement, 291
Unity, 67–70
USA Today, Editorial Board, 278–279

Vagueness, 115–116
Verbs:
  double negatives, 358–359
  exercises, 359–360
  faulty agreement, 355–357
  passive voice, 134, 359
  specific, descriptive, 138
  split infinitive, 358
  subjunctive, 357–358

tense shift, 358
  vague, 162
Voice, 20

Williams, Robin, 222
Wittig, Susan, 41
Wolfe, Thomas, 31
Wordiness, 130, 138, 165, 171
Word logic, exercises, 160–161, 172–175
Word order:
  emphasis and, 143–144
  significance of, 127–129, 143–144
Word processor, 103–104
Words:
  choice of, 22, 163–164
  confused, 154
  connotation, 159–160
  denotation, 159–160
  exercises, 172–176
  logic, 153–171
  order of, see Word order
  per sentence, 111
  precise, 162
  revision and, 171
  selection of,
    best, 161–171
    correct, 154–161
    simple and direct, 164–166
  unfamiliar, 24
  see also Transition
Working bibliography, see Bibliography
Working thesis:
  changes in, 32–33
  function of, 32
  see also Thesis statement
Works cited list, 338–339
Writer's block, minimizing, 120–122
Writing, only for yourself, 4

COPYRIGHT •••••••••••••••••• ACKNOWLEDGMENTS